KU-153-410

THE RECORD SOCIETY OF LANCASHIRE AND CHESHIRE

FOUNDED TO TRANSCRIBE AND PUBLISH
ORIGINAL DOCUMENTS RELATING TO THE TWO COUNTIES

VOLUME CLI

ISBN 978 0 902593 86 2

Dedicated to the memory of Phyllis M. Hill, *ob.* 2004

Typeset by Carnegie Book Production, Lancaster
Printed in Great Britain by CPI Group (UK) Ltd, Croydon CR0 4YY

CHESHIRE FOREST EYRE ROLL 1357

Edited by the late Phyllis M. Hill, J. Heery
and members of the Ranulf Higden Society

PART ONE:
THE FOREST OF WIRRAL

PRINTED FOR THE SOCIETY
2015

FOR THE SUBSCRIPTION YEAR 2014

COUNCIL AND OFFICERS FOR THE YEAR 2014

President

C. B. Phillips, B.A., Ph.D.

Hon. Council Secretary

Dorothy J. Clayton, M.A., Ph.D., M.C.L.I.P., F.R.Hist.S., F.S.A.,
c/o The University of Manchester Library, Oxford Road, Manchester, M13 9PP

Hon. Membership Secretary

J. C. Sutton, M.A., F.R.I.C.S.,
5 Beechwood Drive, Alsager, Cheshire, ST7 2HG

Hon. Treasurer and Publications Secretary

Fiona Pogson, B.A., Ph.D., c/o Department of History and Politics,
Liverpool Hope University, Hope Park, Liverpool L16 9JD

Hon. General Editor

Martin Heale, M.Phil., Ph.D., F.R.Hist.S., c/o Department of History,
University of Liverpool, 9 Abercromby Square, Liverpool, L69 7WZ

Other Members of the Council

P. H. W. Booth, M.A., Litt.D., F.R.Hist.S.
P. Cotgreave, B.Sc., D.Phil.
A. G. Crosby, M.A., D.Phil., F.R.Hist.S.
Diana E. S. Dunn, B.A., D.Ar.Studies
J. R. H. Pepler, M.A., D.A.A.
B. W. Quintrell, M.A., Ph.D., F.R.Hist.S.
D. Szechi, B.A., D.Phil., F.R.Hist.S., R.S.E.
T. J. Thornton, M.A., D.Phil., F.R.Hist.S.
J. L. Wallwork, M.Phil.

For further information about the Council and the Society, see www.rslc.org.uk

TABLE OF CONTENTS

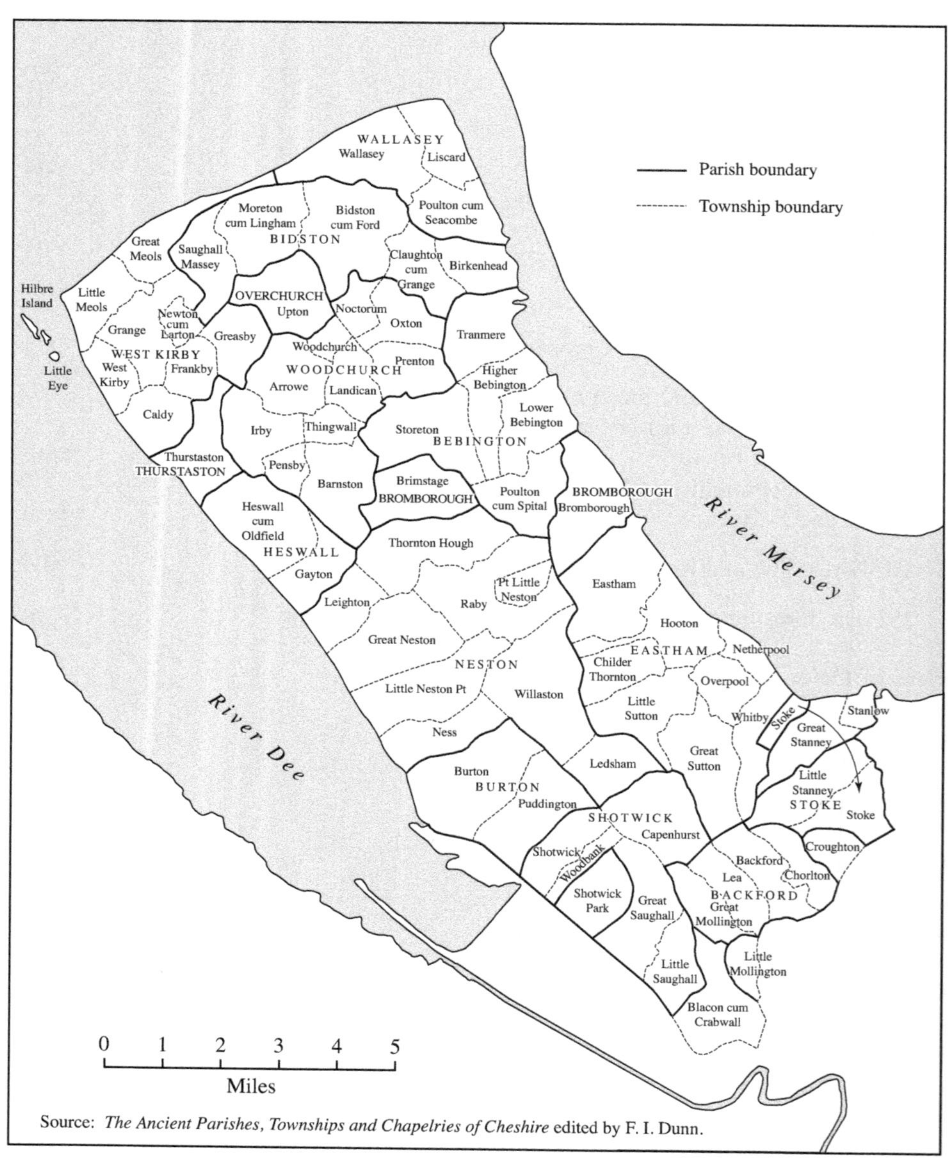

Map of Wirral Townships

FOREWORD

The records of forest eyres are full of interest for the historian and it is good to see another example in print. The record of the Wirral Forest Eyre of 1357 – to be followed by the eyres for the other Cheshire forests of Macclesfield and Delamere – is particularly welcome given the 'peculiar' status of this forest, part of the Black Prince's earldom and county of Chester, and thus, strictly speaking, not a royal forest at all, though generally administered as such. The eyre is here presented both in the original Latin and in a fluent English translation, and one can only be grateful to the editors and the Ranulf Higden Society for adopting this enlightened policy. The ample Introduction places the record in its local social, economic and political context and usefully points the reader to much of what the record contains, from the light thrown on the flora and fauna of the 'forest' to the uses made of forest resources by local people, legally or illegally, and not forgetting a mass of information about many persons of greater or lesser political importance, often local, who held office in the forest or make an appearance in the record for other reasons.

Jean Birrell

EDITOR'S PREFACE

The Cheshire Forest Eyre Roll, 1357 (TNA CHES 33/6) contains abundant, detailed information about the topography, the rural economy, the forest law and the finance and administration of Cheshire in the first half of the fourteenth century. It is a source that has not been used by historians as much as it might be.

The first session of the eyre was held in Chester on 22 September 1357 when the Wirral pleas were tried; most of those charged pleaded guilty and were fined. The Delamere-Mondrum forest pleas were tried at Chester on 27 September and the Macclesfield pleas at Macclesfield on 9 October 1357. The claims of Wirral landowners to special rights in the forest were tried on 25 September and those pleas that had not been resolved by then, because they were based on the claims that had not been fully examined, were further considered at adjournments of the eyre to 26 February 1358 and 20 August 1358. Even then, some cases were still unresolved and so there were ten more adjournments, the final one for Wirral cases being held on 26 February 1361. Further adjournments were held at the Macclesfield sessions of the eyre on 3 March and 12 April 1361.

In the text the pleas of the forest are transcribed and translated in full. The claims are calendared, except for John Domville's which is set out in full as an example. Thirteen of the 34 enrolled charters are given in full text and translation; the reader is referred to other published calendars or transcriptions for the rest. The rolls of attorneys and replevins of lands are calendared.

The Wirral forest eyre is presented as the first of two volumes. The second volume, the Delamere and Mondrum and the Macclesfield eyres, will follow.

GENERAL EDITOR'S NOTE

The Society is pleased to be able to publish this edition, which adds a good deal to our knowledge of fourteenth-century Wirral. The bulk of the general editorial work on the volume was carried out by Dr Paul Booth, to whom I am very grateful.

Martin Heale
University of Liverpool

ACKNOWLEDGEMENTS

This volume is the third to be published by members of the Ranulf Higden Society. The society was formed in 1992 by a group of students who had been attending a 'Latin for Local History' class run at Liverpool University by Paul Booth and John Harrop. Their teachers' enthusiasm and the outstanding quality of tuition encouraged the students to a deeper and more scholarly study of medieval Latin. When this led inevitably to the need to consider publication, the society was formed. Its members are professional and amateur historians whose objective is to make medieval documents more accessible to themselves and others interested in the history mainly (but not exclusively) of Lancashire and Cheshire.

Two decades on, the Ranulf Higden Society is in good heart with a very active membership with two publications so far, and more publications in preparation. Its work is a monument to the foresight and professionalism of John Harrop and Paul Booth to whom its members are extremely grateful.

The document has taken many years to come to fruition and those years have taken a toll of some of those who helped in the difficult work of transcription and translation, when members were first learning the skills of palaeography. Foremost among them is Phyllis Hill, whose leadership of the Cheshire Forest Eyre group until her death in 2004 laid very firm foundations. Others who worked on the eyre and who have since died include Bill Smears, Veronica Slack, Frankla Corris, Barbara Fothergill and Peter Gaskins. Many present and past society members also gave invaluable help in the earlier stages; they are Dilys Firn, Audrey Coney, John Fothergill, Emmeline Garnett, Nigel Coulton, Brian Rankin, Simon Harris, Diana Winterbotham, Astrid Anderson-Bjune, Claire Moorhead, Margaret Lynch, Jim Sutton, Eric Foster and Brooke Westcott. Those who have continued the work during the last few years and have now brought it to completion are Tony Bland, Frank Byrne, Prue Vipond and Graham Walker, under the guidance of Paul Booth and the leadership of Jack Heery.

Sandra Mather has provided the maps for chapter IV. The Hon. Vivian Baring, present owner of the 900-year-old Wirral master forester's horn, has supported the publication and has made the horn available for examination. Cyril J. Cook has kindly allowed us to use his photo of the horn on the dust wrapper.

Amongst others who have given invaluable assistance in many professional aspects of the work, David Crook, formerly Head of Medieval Records at the National Archives, claims a special mention. The society is also most grateful for the help and encouragement in the final stages of the publication from the Record Society's general editor, Martin Heale. This help has been invaluable and is very much appreciated.

Finally, we must thank the Right Hon. the Earl of Derby, the Burton and Neston History Society, The Wirral Society, the Barnston Conservation Society, the Ranulf Higden Society and Pat Heery for their generous contributions towards the cost of publishing the volume.

LIST OF ABBREVIATIONS AND WORKS CITED BY SHORT TITLE

1347	The plea roll of the forest eyre held in Cheshire in 1347
Barraclough, *Charters*	Geoffrey Barraclough, *Charters of the Anglo-Norman Earls of Chester c.1071–1237*, RSLC, vol. cxxvi (1988)
BP	Black Prince
Birrell, *Feckenham*	J. Birrell, ed., *Records of Feckenham Forest, Worcestershire, c. 1236–1377*, Worcestershire Historical Society, NS, 21 (2006)
Birrell, *Cannock*	J. Birrell, ed., *The Forests of Cannock and Kinver: Select Documents 1235–1372*, Staffordshire Record Society, 4th Series, 18 (1999)
Booth, *Financial Administration*	P.H.W. Booth, *The Financial Administration of the Lordship and County of Chester, 1272–1377*, Chetham Society, Third Series, 28 (1981)
Booth, Taxation	P.H.W. Booth, 'Taxation and Public Order: Cheshire in 1353', *Northern History*, 12 (1976)
Booth, 'Last Week'	P.H.W. Booth, 'The Last Week of the Life of Edward the Black Prince', in *Contact and Exchange in Later Medieval Europe: Essays in Honour of Malcolm Vale*, ed. Hannah Skoda, Patrick Lantschner and R.L.J. Shaw (The Boydell Press, Woodbridge, 2012)
B.P.R.	*Register(s) of Edward the Black Prince* (1920–33)
C.C.R.	*Calendar of Charter Rolls*
CH	*Cheshire History*
ChAcc1	*Accounts of the Chamberlain and other Officers of the County of Chester, 1301–1360*, ed. R. Stewart-Brown, RSLC, vol. lix (1910)
ChAcc2	*Account of Master John de Burnham the younger, Chamberlain of Chester, 1361–62*, ed. P.H.W. Booth and A.D. Carr, RSLC, 125 (1991)
Ch.R.R.	*Calendar of Palatinate of Chester Enrolments* in *36th Annual Report of the Deputy Keeper of the Public Records* (1875) – previously referred to as the Chester Recognizance Rolls
C.P.R.	*Calendar of Patent Rolls*
CRO	Cheshire Archives and Local Studies: Cheshire Record Office
CS	*The Cheshire Sheaf*
Dodgson, *Place Names*	J. McN. Dodgson, *The Place Names of Cheshire, Part IV*, Cambridge University Press (1972)
Harding, *Viking*	S. Harding, *Viking Merseyside*, Countyvise Ltd (2002)

Hill, thesis	'Chester County Court Indictment Roll, 1354–77' (Univ. of Liverpool, unpub. M.Phil. thesis, Phyllis Hill, 1996)
Mills, *English Place-Names*	A.D. Mills, *A Dictionary of English Place-Names*, Oxford University Press (1998)
MS	manuscript
Ormerod, *Cheshire*	G. Ormerod, *The History of the County Palatine and City of Chester*, ed. T. Helsby (1882), London
Phillips and Phillips	A.D.M. Phillips and C.B. Phillips, *A New Historical Atlas of Cheshire* Cheshire County Council (2002)
recog.	recognizance
RSLC	Record Society of Lancashire and Cheshire
Shakespeare	Shakespeare Centre Library and Archive Ref: DR/10/1406/c (pp. 8–9)
Smith, *Place-Name Elements*	A.H. Smith, *English Place-Name Elements*, ii (1956)
Stewart-Brown	R. Stewart-Brown, 'Further Notes on the Deafforestation of Wirral', *Transactions of the Historic Society of Lancashire and Cheshire*, 89 (1937)
Stubbs, *Select Charters*	William Stubbs, *Select Charters,* 9th ed. (1870)
Sylvester & Nulty, *Atlas*	Dorothy Sylvester and Geoffrey Nulty, *The Historical Atlas of Cheshire,* Cheshire Community Council (1958)
Talbot Deeds	*Talbot Deeds, 1200–1682,* ed. E.E. Barker, RSLC, vol. ciii, (1948)
TNA	The National Archives/Public Record Office
TNA references:	
C53	Charter Rolls
C66	Patent Rolls
CHES 2	Palatinate of Chester: Enrolments (Recognizance Rolls)
CHES 31/2	Final Concords
CHES 33/2	Wirral Forest Plea Roll 1286
CHES 33/4	Cheshire Forest Eyre Roll, 1347
CHES 33/6	Cheshire Forest Eyre Roll, 1357
DL 39/1/19	Cheshire Forest Eyre Roll 1347, duchy of Lancaster copy
E 36/279	*Black Prince's Register*
Turner, *Select Pleas*	*Select Pleas of the Forest*, ed. G.J. Turner, Selden Society, 13 (1901)
VCH	*Victoria History of Cheshire*

EDITORIAL CONVENTIONS

For transcription and translation, editorial practice has generally followed R.F. Hunniset in *Editing Records for Publication,* British Record Association: Archives and the User No 4, (1977).

1. *Names* Place-names and surnames are not generally extended in the text, and have an apostrophe only if they are abbreviated. Christian names are extended. Place-names that are not surnames are modernised in the translation. Modern forms of Christian names are used in the translation, but surnames are left as in the text.

2. *Letters and numbers* Letters of the alphabet 'c' and 't'; 'u' and 'v'; 'i' and 'j' are transcribed in accordance with modern spelling. Numerals are transcribed using 'i', but 'j' is used for a single or a final digit.

3. *Punctuation* In the text punctuation and indentation, where they are helpful, are used very occasionally. Capital letters are used parsimoniously both in the Latin and in the translation, regardless of the usage in the manuscript. This means using them for proper names only and not for titles. Square brackets enclose everything that is supplied, mainly because of damage to the manuscript, including supplied text, (except for membrane, page and paragraph numbers). Round brackets are used where there is some uncertainty about what the word should be. Marginal notes are inserted in angle brackets except that if they are repeated in the text the words/numbers of the marginal notes are italicised there.

4. *Italics* Italics, in addition to their use to refer to marginal notes (see 3. above), are used for cited works and for Latin words in footnotes and in the introduction.

5. *Corrections* Where the manuscript is corrected because of an assumed error by the scribe, the text is in the corrected form in square brackets with the manuscript form shown in a footnote, as – *quam* MS.

6. *References* For reference and indexing purposes, numbers have been supplied for entries in the text and translation, thus: **1.43; 2.167.**

INTRODUCTION

I. THE RECORD AND THE EYRE'S PROCEDURE

The original record (CHES 33/6 in The National Archives/Public Record Office) consists of 55 membranes; the dorses of membranes 52 and 55 are blank and several membranes have schedules stitched to them. Membranes 1 to 46d contain six separate headed sections, for (i) the pleas and (ii) the claims of landowners in each of the three forests in order. Membranes 47 to 52 contain the 34 enrolled charters, licences, agreements and letters, which were presented to support the claims in all three forests. Membranes 53 to 53d give a list of attorneys for the defendants and claimants, and membranes 54 to 55 are the replevin rolls for Wirral and Delamere. The bulk of the roll and 'other memoranda touching the forest eyre' were written by William Langar, the clerk of Richard Willoughby, the principal justice, and two other unnamed clerks, between the 22 and 25 June, 1359, although some parts were added later.[1]

The heading and the commission (**1.1–1.2** m. 1)
The first paragraph gives the names of the justices appointed by the earl of Chester and the date on which the eyre was to begin, 22 September 1357. Paragraph two, in the earl's own name, appoints the three justices and gives them their remit.

The writ of summons (**1.3–1.11** m. 1)
The writ, issued by the justiciar of Chester on 4 August 1357, sets out in full detail all those who were to be present at the eyre, their duties and the procedures which had to be followed, including the presentation of documents and the publication of the arrangements.

The sheriff's return (**1.12–1.26** mm. 1–1d)
The sheriff's return responds to the writ of summons, gives the names of the forest officials, lists the 66 townships of Wirral and reports that he has summoned all those whose presence is demanded by the earl. The usual practice of a royal forest eyre was to begin the proceedings with 'essoins', that is a list of those not responding to the summons, for example because of sickness or death.[2] This does not seem to have been the normal practice in the palatinate courts and there are none in this eyre.

1 *ChAccl*, p. 252. William was from Langar, in Nottinghamshire, and travelled from there to Chester on 18 October, 1359, for an adjourned session of the eyre (*ChAccl*, p. 272).

2 J. Birrell, ed., *Records of Feckenham Forest, Worcestershire, c. 1236–1377,* Worcestershire Historical Society, NS, 21 (2006), p. xvii.

The records of the forest officials

The summons required the officials and regarders to bring all their records of attachments and regards.

There are sixteen references to the written records which were submitted as proof of the charges made in the eyre (**1.27–1.88**). The record of the regard of Wirral, which was held in 1357, was introduced (in **1.88**) as 'made and presented before the justices...on the oaths of...' William Stanley, forester, and the twelve regarders (one of whom was John Lassels, the riding forester). The preliminary survey work for the regard of 1357 had been done by the chamberlain of Chester and other local officials between 24 April and 26 May 1357, which implies that the 'verdicts' of the foresters and regarders were just a formality, and certainly could not have been made until the date of the order to give William Stanley the master-forestership back on 17 August.[3]

In five cases the court's judgement is said to be made 'by the rolls of William de Stanlegh, forester' (**1.27, 1.38, 1.45, 1.74, 1.75**); in three 'by the rolls of Henry de Hoton, rider' (**1.69, 1.83, 1.84**); in three 'by the presentments of the foresters, (**1.46, 1.47, 1.48**); and twice 'by the rolls of John Doune, late (chief) forester' (**1.64, 1.73**).

There is one response by jurors 'to the article concerning boats plying for passage within the forest' (**1.85**) and one presentment by twelve jurors 'to the articles' (**1.49**). This is a reference to the 'articles' or 'chapters' (*capitula regardi*) of the regard, a set of questions to be answered there, which are often listed in royal documents, most conveniently and fully in the *Close Rolls* of Henry III.[4]

The pleas of Wirral forest (**1.27–1.272** mm. 1d to 9d)

For Wirral forest there are nine membranes, written on both sides, containing the pleas or *placita*; that is, the record of the charges brought by the earl of Chester's officials against those who were alleged to have committed offences against the forest laws. In most of the several hundred cases the records demonstrate that the offence was committed, the court accepted the record and the offender was summarily punished or else was required to appear in person or through his or her attorney. The presentment of these charges was the responsibility of the foresters in the case of the pleas of vert and venison, and of the foresters and regarders jointly in the case of assarts and purprestures.

In the case of fourteen of the principal landowners, while they did not dispute the facts of the charges, they generally claimed that they had a right to do whatever they were accused of doing. The court heard those and other claims on 25 February, 1358. Some cases were resolved on that day, but others were adjourned, first until the following day and then to 20 August, 1358. The records of the claims and the verdicts upon them appear in the calendar of claims (mm. 10 to 21d; **2.1–2.60**). Seventeen

3 Burnham and the others were paid their expenses for measuring *terrarum frussarum* in Wirral forest, including the costs of cords for measuring, in his account for 1356–57 (*ChAcc1*, p. 242, date amended in *ChAcc2*, p. 205). The reinstatement of Stanley proved problematic, as there were three orders to return the bailiwick to him, on 27 August, 13 September and 30 November (*B.P.R.*, iii, pp. 275, 279, 283).

4 *CCR 1258–1259*, pp. 140–41.

other people used the opportunity to bring their claims before the court in order to establish the validity of rights which had not been challenged in the plea hearings, but about which there must have been some uncertainty.

In one case only, that of the abbot of St Werburgh's, Chester, the record in the pleas (**1.45**) contains his claim to ancient rights and is followed by the outcome of the adjourned hearing which was held on 26 February, 1358. The abbot presented the earl of Chester's writ, dated 3 December 1357, and made a fine of £100.

Entries **1.27–1.73** in the pleas list those who had committed offences against the vert, mainly by cutting down oak trees, taking wood and digging peat. Most of them were found guilty and 'made fine'. (NB *finem facere* means 'to agree a fine', rather than to pay it, since no payment was made at this stage, although there was always a pledge given for future payment.)

Entry **1.74** lists the penalties imposed upon eighteen townships and four men for keeping their pigs in the woods, and entries **1.75–1.84** record offences involving the deaths of venison. In the royal forests, the death of deer usually led to a summons for the four nearest townships to appear 'fully', with fines for any failures to attend. **1.82** refers to this practice, but with no reference to any consequential fines.[5]

Entries **1.85–1.87** contain judgements about ferry rights and entries **1.88–1.271** are the record of the regard of the forest, that is assarts and purprestures. These accusations were made by the foresters, together with twelve local landowners called 'regarders'.

Entry **1.271** is simply the marginal reference to Willaston. The pleas of 20 other, unnamed, townships were presumably presented as part of the Wirral regard of 1357, but the record concludes here (in **1.272**) following the agreement made by the community of Wirral to pay a common fine of £1,000, which discharged all other penalties.

The claims of Wirral forest (**2.1–2.60**, mm. 10 to 21d)

One claim to rights in the forest is given in the edition in full text and translation (that of John Domville, the elder, **2.14**) while the remainder are calendared, because of the highly repetitive nature of this material.

There are 60 separate records of Wirral claims *(placita clameorum)*. They consist of submissions by 34 different people, six of whom submitted two claims, so there are 40 claims altogether. 27 of the claims concern rights which would release the claimants from forest obligations that were standard elsewhere in England. They based their rights on Ranulf III's Great Charter to Cheshire (**7.9**), which was issued about 1215 and was probably 'a direct reaction to the granting of the Magna Carta' to quieten the Cheshire barons.[6]

5 For an account of a typical royal court proceeding in Staffordshire, see J. Birrell, ed., *The Forests of Cannock and Kinver: Select Documents 1235–1372,* Staffordshire Record Society, 4th Series, 18 (1999), p. 9.

6 Geoffrey Barraclough, *Charters of the Anglo-Norman Earls of Chester c.1071–1237,* RSLC vol. cxxvi (1988) number 394. See also *The Magna Carta of Cheshire*, Graeme J. White, Cheshire Local History Association (2015).

Although the decision to commute all the Wirral penalties into a single payment of £1,000 meant that the remainder of the regard was not included in the record of the eyre, this did not mean the discontinuation of the legal process of examining the claims. It was normal practice to secure confirmation of ancient rights whenever the opportunity presented itself. Consequently there were twelve adjournments of the eyre, the final one for Wirral taking place on 26 February 1361. Two of these (held on Thursdays) were special hearings for witnesses to testify to the validity of William Stanley's and the duke of Lancaster's claims to rights by inheritance. The first adjournments were held on Mondays, but from 18 October 1359 the hearings were on Fridays.[7]

The enrolment of charters (**7.1–7.34** mm. 47 to 52)
34 charters and other documents were submitted in justification of the claims. Some of them had also been presented in the 1347 eyre, for example **7.16** is the '[Charter] of Will[iam, son of] W[..] Trussel', but in 1347 it was the 'Charter of Warin Trussel.'

The Black Prince's charter to the community of Cheshire (**7.14**) is dated in the twentieth year of Edward III's reign as king of England, and his fourteenth as king of France. These two regnal years do not congrue. Edward's twentieth year as king of England, 25 January 1346–24 January 1347, was not his fourteenth year as king of France, which was 1353, when he was in his twenty-seventh year as king of England. The correct date is 1353. The document repeats the error in all the claims which quote the charter. Until the error was noted, it led to confusion in the writings of some historians of the period.[8]

The attorney rolls (**8.1–8.60** mm. 53 and 53d)
These rolls list all the attorneys who were admitted before the justices to represent individual claimants in the three forests. 41 were approved at the commencement of the eyre in September 1357 and 19 for the beginning of the second adjourned hearing on 20 August 1358.

The replevin rolls (**9.1–9.86** mm. 54, 54d and 55)
These rolls list those who 'repledged' their properties after they had been 'seized into the hands of the lord earl' at the regard of the forests in 1353 (Delamere-Mondrum) or 1357 (Wirral). Replevin was a legal process by which the property in dispute was released back into the hands of the ostensible owners after they had given a surety (on the pledge of a third party) to hand over the land and all its revenues to the earl if the judgement were eventually to be made against them. The roll includes 51 repledges for Delamere forest, (not including that of '[…] […] de Cronton' which is struck from the manuscript,) and 34 for Wirral forest. Macclesfield's regard was held on 27 August 1353, but the replevin roll contains no references to it.

7 The pleas and claims for the forests of Delamere – Mondrum (mm. 22 to 35d) and Macclesfield (mm. 36 to 46d) will be published in volume II, bearing the references **3.1–4.34** and **5.1–6.20**.

8 *ChAcc2*, pp. 214–24.

II. THE FOREST EYRE AND THE COMMUNITY OF WIRRAL

1. *The political, military and financial background to the eyre.*

In 1346, when he was sixteen years old, Edward the Black Prince assumed adult responsibilities for the governance of his estates in England and Wales, and took part in his first major military campaign, that of Crécy-Calais (1346–47). Those estates – the five counties of the principality of Wales, the lands of the duchy of Cornwall and the two counties of the earldom of Chester (Cheshire and Flintshire) – were to be both the training ground for his future role of king of England and sources of men and money for his military campaigns. In both the principality and the earldom (but not the duchy), the prince exercised royal powers of government, which all but excluded his father, King Edward III. In all his estates the prince's council had to work very hard to maintain let alone increase the ordinary sources of revenue, from land, commercial income, and judicial fines. In addition, they had to raise 'extraordinary revenue' in the principality and the earldom for particular campaigns – the equivalent of parliamentary taxation. That was particularly difficult in Cheshire, in that no national parliamentary taxes appear to have been levied in the county since 1292. Consequently a new system of levies had to be devised by the prince's government, based on a mixture of 'subsidies' or 'gifts' granted by the community of the county, of feudal levies that did not require consent, of common fines imposed in law-courts and of grants by the community in return for favours received.[9] A similar system developed at the same time in both the principality and the lordships of the Welsh march.[10] After the Black Death of 1348/49 both ordinary and extraordinary revenue, as well as soldiers, had to be raised from a substantially smaller population.

Right at the beginning of this period the prince's government saw the introduction of the forest eyre as an important way of raising taxation-type revenue in Cheshire. In 1346 Cheshire had granted an 'aid' of £1,000 to help the prince with the expenses of the Crécy expedition. This was negotiated with the community of the county by Peter Gildesburgh, the head of his financial administration, and Sir William Shareshull, his chief legal adviser. There is no evidence for the mechanism used for gaining the county's consent to the aid, and the meagre evidence for its collection suggests that it was paid very reluctantly, if at all. Consequently, new approaches to getting the Cheshire people to support their earl financially had to be devised. The resultant ploy, the forest eyre of 1347, was the first such eyre to be held in Cheshire. Sir Richard Stafford, Peter Gildesburgh and Sir William Sharesull were appointed justices to hold the eyre in December. It was a financial disaster, largely because the bitterness of

9 *ChAcc2*, pp. liv–lv for the extraordinary levies raised in Cheshire between 1340 and 1374.

10 P.H.W. Booth, *The Financial Administration of the Lordship and County of Chester, 1272–1377*, Chetham Society, Third Series, 28 (1981), pp. 116–26.

opposition from the forest communities was not anticipated by the administration. The total fines imposed were £184 in Wirral forest and £178 in Delamere-Mondrum.[11] Little of this money was ever collected. The ground for the community's objection to the eyre, apart from its novelty, was that it entailed the imposition of English forest law upon Cheshire, namely the 1184 Assize of the Forest, and subsequent forest legislation. Before the next such eyre, the actual operation of the new forest law in Cheshire had to be tightened up, which was achieved by sessions held in 1351. By then the administration was headed by Sir John Wingfield, one of the most distinguished and original managers in later medieval England. This turned out to be something of a trial of strength between lord and communities, as the comprehensive complaints laid before the prince's council by the inhabitants of Wirral forest witness.[12]

A second forest eyre was planned to be held during the prince's state visit to Cheshire in 1353, but was postponed until 1357 as part of a general agreement made with the community of the county at that time.[13] Wingfield was clearly not going to be satisfied with the meagre yields of the 1347 eyre, and warned his subordinates that there was a risk that the forest communities would come together in a series of conspiracies to ensure that the 1357 eyre would not work either.[14] The justices were to be Sir Richard Willoughby, Sir Richard Stafford, John Delves (the lieutenant-justiciar of Chester) and Master John Burnham (the chamberlain of Chester). Willoughby was a justice of the common bench,[15] Stafford was a long-serving member of the prince's council, an administrator, and a military retainer.[16] The sessions were to be held in Chester (for Wirral and Delamere-Mondrum forests) and in Macclesfield. Resistance in two of the communities was largely broken, and Wirral forest offered a common fine of £1,000 and Delamere-Mondrum £2,000, both to be payable over five years. These enormous grants replaced the individual fines and financial penalties imposed in the eyres of those two forests and were apportioned between individuals by the forest communities themselves.

Macclesfield forest proved to be more resistant to pressure, probably because it had a strong tradition of communal independence. An attempt was made early in 1358 to persuade all the Macclesfield forest inhabitants to agree to a common fine, but it was unsuccessful. The only agreement was that concluded with the tenants of the seven demesne townships of Macclesfield manor who agreed to pay a common fine of £87.[17] The people of the greater part of this forest clearly benefited from their resistance to pressures from the administration, since their individual fines appear to have amounted to just over £60.[18]

11 Booth, *Financial Administration*, p. 120.
12 *Black Prince's Register*, iii, pp. 14–15, 23–27.
13 P.H.W. Booth, 'Taxation and Public Order: Cheshire in 1353', *Northern History*, 12 (1976), pp. 20–24.
14 Booth, *Financial Administration*, pp. 122–23.
15 D. Crook *Nottingham Medieval Studies* 48 (2004).
16 *B.P.R.*, i, pp. 80, 144; *B.P.R.*, iii, pp. 32–34, 53, 58, 117.
17 *ChAcc2*, p. xliii.
18 Booth, *Financial Administration*, p. 123.

The 5,000-mark common fine of 1353, which resulted in the cancellation of the general eyre and its replacement with a court of trailbaston, could at least be justified as part of a campaign to restore order to a turbulent county. The introduction of the forest eyre to Cheshire in 1347 was just about raising money. The eyre fulfilled no real governmental or policing function. It was a procedure for raising money through fines, and not for modifying human behaviour. It met with very limited success, and even the large Wirral and Delamere common fines of 1357 proved discouragingly difficult to collect.[19] As a result, the use of the forest eyre was abandoned for the rest of the Middle Ages, to see a short-lived resurrection in Henry VII's reign and, later, in the seventeenth century as part of Charles I's ill-advised attempt to raise money without resorting to parliament.

The effects of the policy towards Wirral typified by the 1357 forest eyre were little short of disastrous.[20] The financial success of the eyre had depended on a number of factors. First, the local community had to be prevented from conspiring to conceal evidence of forest offences from the justices, as had most likely happened in the forest eyre of 1347. When Shareshull, Wingfield and Stafford had held trailbaston sessions at Exeter in the king's name in 1354, they were told that fourteen men had conspired two years before the court was to be held to defeat its objects. They had agreed, it was said, to ensure that, if they were chosen to be members of the indictment juries they or their friends would not be indicted, but that their enemies would be.[21] The prince's council suspected that the same would happen in Cheshire in 1357, and so Wingfield sent letters to the justices two weeks before the eyre was due to start stating that he had received information that a widespread conspiracy was planned in the county to defeat the objectives of the eyre, and that they were to postpone the eyre if they found that to be the case.[22] Secondly, there had to be a balance between intimidation and conciliation, in order to persuade the community leaders that there were advantages for them in collaborating with the procedure. This was achieved in part through a campaign of rigorous enforcement of the forest law in the series of inquiries held in 1351, coupled with the introduction of the full extent of English forest law. The other side of that coin were the negotiations that ensued in the face of general indignation among the principal landowners in Wirral, such as Henry Hooton,[23] resulting in a substantial lowering of the initially imposed fines. Combined with that was the third stratagem, namely the recruitment of Wirral landowners of high status and influence to give information, in return for favourable treatment, about the ability of the rest to pay. Philip Raby was one of these, as was Robert Poole, who had been one of the sheriff's two summoners for the eyre.

19 *ChAcc2*, p. xlii.

20 See Paul Booth, 'The Last Week of the Life of Edward the Black Prince', in *Contact and Exchange in Later Medieval Europe: Essays in Honour of Malcolm Vale*, ed. Hannah Skoda, Patrick Lantschner and R.L.J. Shaw (The Boydell Press, Woodbridge, 2012) for the background to what is being written here.

21 TNA JUST 1/191 m. 3. The fourteen were tried, and found not guilty.

22 *B.P.R.*, iii, p. 278.

23 See biographical note, p. xxxv.

(**1.13**). This was such a sensitive issue that Poole was ordered to agree publicly to the amount of the fine assessed on him, on the secret understanding that it would never be collected. The reason given for this was that 'Robert has behaved well and loyally informing members of [the prince's] council of matters concerning his right and lordship [in Wirral forest], [and so the prince] wishes to do him a favour without letting such favour be openly apparent'.[24] Clearly Poole's collaboration went quite a lot further than simply advising the administration on his fellow landowners' ability to pay their fines. Richard Hough had performed a similar service to the prince, and as a result complained that his enemies were maliciously prosecuting him 'because of his loyal service'. Again, he was to be treated favourably, but in strict secrecy, and does not appear in the list of those convicted of forest offences.[25]

It was, though, the master-forester, William Stanley the elder, and his colleague, the deputy riding forester, John Lasselles, who played the crucial role in the events leading up to the eyre and the disasters that followed it. In July 1351 they were awarded twenty shillings each, plus expenses, for their journey to London to discuss forest matters with the prince and his advisers. The previous April, Stanley had been sent the comprehensive set of forest ordinances that were intended to tighten up forest law administration in Cheshire, and compel the imposition of the full rigour of English forest law into the county.[26] This resulted in a major inquiry in Wirral forest, probably at the time of the regard (inquiry into assarts and purprestures) that was held by the justiciar, Sir Thomas Ferrers, Sir John Wingfield and Sir Richard Stafford. More general forest offences were also dealt with in their sessions, but because records of the proceedings do not survive, it is not possible to know how wide the net was cast.[27] The fines arising out of this were imposed on 9th August 1351, and presumably the regard and forest pleas were held then, or shortly before. This led to a fierce campaign of resistance, in which some of the most prominent Wirral landowners were involved, by which it was claimed that Wirral was governed by the forest clauses of earl Ranulf III's common charter of 1215 rather than English legislation. For example, they claimed that the lawing of dogs had never been obligatory in Wirral. After protracted negotiations, the individual fines were lowered, and accepted. In addition, the community agreed to pay a communal fine of 100 marks for the offences of illicit keeping of hunting dogs, digging peat and taking heather tried in the forest of eyre of 1347, as well as another similar fine of £20 for having unlawed dogs, in the same eyre.[28] Stanley and Lasselles, together with the under-foresters, were responsible for searching out, recording and presenting the offences against the vert and the venison, but in addition they formed a team together with

24 *B.P.R.*, iii, pp. 11–12.

25 loc. cit.

26 loc. cit. The ordinances were also sent to Richard Done, master forester of Delamere-Mondrum, as well as to the nine foresters of Macclesfield (where there was no master forester).

27 There is no surviving record of this regard, but for evidence of regards being held for each of the three forests in the financial year 1350–51, see *ChAccl*, pp. 161, 200. See also *B.P.R.*, iii, p. 37.

28 *ChAccl*, p. 164.

the twelve regarders to record the assarts and purprestures, which were potentially a more lucrative source of income to the prince. The campaign of 1351 could not have succeeded without their efforts, as the prince and his council well recognised.

When the trailbaston sessions were held in 1353, the prince and his council must have been made aware of the massive hostility towards Stanley, Lasselles and their subordinates expressed by the majority of Wirral landowners in the accusations of crimes of oppression and extortion made against the foresters before the justices. On the one the hand, the prince was clearly determined to deal with the public order problems in the county, as he stated in the speech he made to the 'whole community' and this seems to have been genuinely meant. For example, the joint master serjeants of the peace of the county, together with their under-serjeants in six of the seven hundreds of the county, were deprived of their income without compensation, and their offices, in effect, were abolished. On the other hand, if such drastic action were in any way to hinder the prince's war effort, or his government's ability to raise extraordinary revenue in the county, then it was a different matter.[29] Stanley, Lasselles and the under-foresters were left in post until 1355. On 23 November in that year, Stanley was imprisoned, but not for anything in connection with his activities as master forester, or as leader of a criminal gang. He held one third of the manor of Storeton, and Richard Bechington, lord of one of the other thirds had been murdered the previous month; both Stanley and Lasselles were accused of being accessories. The result was that Stanley lost his office, and it was likely that Lasselles did also, and they did not receive them back until the month before the 1357 forest eyre was due to be held. Another indication of the prince's favour at this juncture is given by the fact that half the issues of the forest bailiwick during the period of forfeiture were returned to Stanley on 20 August.[30] He continued to be rewarded for the role he played in the eyre, and in the financial year 1360–61, when Willoughby was recalled to Chester for yet another session of the long drawn out affair, Stanley received a gift of 43s. 7d. from the prince.[31]

The forfeiture, which may have ruined any other family, proved to be only a temporary setback and did not hinder the family's struggle for dominance in the community of Wirral, which continued under the forestership of William Stanley the younger from 1361 onwards. Over a period of twenty years, the ruthless and criminal exploitation of their forest office enabled the Stanley family to rise spectacularly in the social hierarchy, from being a very minor landed family in the early fourteenth century to one that spawned three branches: the Stanleys of Hooton, the Stanleys of Alderley and the Stanleys of Knowsley – ultimately lords of the Isle of Man and earls of Derby. Wirral, on the other hand, had become divided into warring factions and was a byword for serious disorder, with the result that Edward the Black Prince on his deathbed ordered its disafforestation (the abolition of forest law in the hundred) both for his soul's salvation and the comfort of his people.

29 Booth, 'Taxation and Public Order', pp. 26, 30.

30 *ChAccl*, p. 255.

31 *B.P.R.*, iii, p. 275; SC 6 772/1 mm. 1, 2, 12d.

2. *The community of Wirral and its leaders*

A great deal is known about tensions and factions within Wirral in the second half of the fourteenth century, because of the survival of Cheshire's exceptionally rich legal and administrative records. There is another aspect to community relations, though, and that is the need for co-operation, particularly between the heads of the most powerful families, in defence of their own and their common interests. The two relatively small common fines imposed in the 1351 forest sessions imply that there was a meeting of at least some of the landowners of Wirral in order to agree the fines, as well as their co-operation to decide upon how to apportion the fines between the forest tenants in general. They would also have had to collect them. This must also have been true of the much larger common fine of £1,000 offered by the community and accepted by the justices in the 1357 eyre, and again there must have been some sort of assembly of at least the most powerful people within the hundred to negotiate this, work out the apportionment and arrange for the collection. No evidence at all survives for these processes, as the prince's administration was only concerned with the actual payment of the various instalments to the chamberlain of Chester, whose accounts do not even record the names of those men who paid the money into the Chester exchequer on the community's behalf.

It is of interest, therefore, to examine the social positions and activities of at least some of the magnates of the area, as it is they who would have made the crucial decisions in these matters. Their full biographical details, plus references, are given at the end of this section. The most important lay landowners in Wirral were the duke of Lancaster, who had inherited the Cheshire barony of Halton and acquired the barony of Dunham in 1347, and the earl of Salisbury to whom the king had granted the Montalt inheritance in 1337, but there was no resident nobility there in the later fourteenth century.[32] The biggest landowner by far was the abbot of Chester, who was represented in Wirral's affairs by the steward of the abbey lands, Ranulf Roter. He served as the abbot's attorney in the the 1357 eyre. He appears, though, to have been largely acting in his own interests in Wirral rather than those of his employer, and was murdered in 1362, as was his son not long afterwards.[33] None of the principal resident landowners was in a position of clear dominance in local society; all were below the status of a knight. The best way, therefore, to investigate the distribution of power is through biography; the biographies of six of them are presented below, to indicate the complexities of a society that had to struggle at times to act as with a common purpose.

John Domville was probably the wealthiest and most influential of the lay landlords of Wirral, and it is likely that he built the stone tower-house that still survives in part at Brimstage. He had probably done military service in his younger days, most likely with his neighbour and close associate, Richard Hough of Thornton Hough. His leadership of the resistance to the Wirral forest sessions of 1351 was very likely what forced the prince's government, very reluctantly to compromise. The refusal by

32 Lancaster's steward was Sir John Legh, who was dead by 1356, and there is no evidence for interests by him in Wirral *ChAcc2*, pp. 143, 154–55, 169–70.

33 *ChAcc2*, p. 168.

the local community at that time to pay William Stanley his puture money, in effect a 'strike' against his oppressive behaviour and collaboration with the prince's officials, was settled by a compromise agreed in Domville's home at Brimstage. In addition not only was he one of the regarders in the 1357 eyre, but he served an unusually large number of times on the increasingly important indictment jury of the county court. His actions on behalf of his family's interests teetered on the verge of legality, and sometimes seem to have crossed over it, in association with his neighbour, Hough. Chance favoured him with a long life, and it appears that his son intended to move the family's main residence to Mobberley, in mid Cheshire. Robert, the elder John's younger son, founded a cadet branch of the family at Lymm. Fate intervened yet again, however, and the younger John, although he also had a long life, died without a male heir, and his estates had to be divided between daughters.

Henry Hooton had much in common with Domville. He was both an important landowner in south Wirral, and an active developer of his property as the records of the 1357 eyre revealed, on which he served as a regarder. During the period when Stanley had forfeited his bailiwick, Hooton served as deputy riding forest together with John Done as acting master forester. This could have led to a life-long feud with Stanley and Lasselles, who received their offices back just weeks before the 1357 eyre was due to begin. However, Henry avoided that and maintained important links with Stanley subsequently, and was one of the jury adjudicating on Stanley's claim to liberties within Wirral forest in 1361. He was not one of Stanley's faction, though. In 1351 he had complained directly to the prince's council about the fines imposed in the Wirral forest sessions of the year, and cited Ranulf III's charter as the foundation of the community's claims. As with the others, his fine was reduced substantially, but there is no evidence that he was one of the 'collaborators' with the prince's administration. He served on the Wirral indictment jury a modest number of times between 1355 and 1368. His tactics seem to have been to tread cautiously in what was a very volatile and dangerous situation. He left no son to succeed him, however, and so agreed in 1376 to the marriage of his daughter and heiress to William Stanley, the eight year old son of William Stanley the younger, and ultimately cemented the Stanley dominance in Wirral.

John Lasselles, however, was unique in the roster of Wirral magnates. His family name is not recorded in the area before 1340 and it disappears from the record after 1377. The acquisition of land by fair means or foul was a temptation for a man in his position. He first appears as deputy rider of the forest when he accompanied William Stanley to London to receive instructions from the prince and his council in 1351. He was the subject of accusations of oppression and criminal conspiracy made against all the Wirral foresters in the 1353 trailbaston sessions, with some indictments reserved for himself which suggest that he was accustomed to using threats of force to get his own way. His and Stanley's importance to the prince's revenue-raising campaign allowed his advance to continue and his wealth to increase, and in 1354 he tried, but failed, in an attempt to purchase the marriage of the heir of Poulton Lancelyn. He was serving regularly on the Wirral indictment jury of the county court at that time. All seemed to be going swimmingly until 1355 when Stanley was arrested and imprisoned as a result of his implication in the murder of Richard Bechington, in which Lasselles was accused of being involved. Lasselles lost his deputy ridership, so it seems, as a result. However, the administration could not manage without the talents, such as they were, of Stanley and Lasselles, and they bounced back and were in post again by the eve of the 1357 forest eyre, in which Lasselles also served as one of the regarders. This recovery enabled Lasselles to buy a significant and lucrative marriage. Lasselles' power was, however, less firmly based than that of Stanley, who held an hereditary office. He died some time before December 1361 – perhaps as early as 1358. Both his sons, John and Thomas, struggled to maintain the gains and position of power that their father had achieved, but they failed, and both of them were dead by 1377, Wirral had been disafforested, and the Lasselles name was heard no more in the area.

John Blount was the most powerful man in our list. His father had been mayor of Chester, and he himself served as mayor for fourteen of the years between 1334 and 1360. As mayor, he was not just chief citizen of Chester, but also the senior judge, and since the grant of the city's new charter in 1354 escheator of the city as well. In addition he had inherited the serjeanty of the North Gate, with its policing role, and the custody of the city gaol. By the time of the 1357 eyre he was presumably ready to retire to the country and establish a dynasty at the Little Neston estate that his father had bought before his death in 1317. He had been fined for forest offences in the 1351 Wirral session, although the fine was reduced substantially. Because of his duties in the city as mayor and judge he held no offices in Wirral, nor did he serve on the county court indictment jury. He had powerful connections outside the county; the grant to him of the right to hunt the hare and fox at Little Neston was made at the urging of Sir Bartholomew Burghersh, the sinecure justiciar of Chester and one of the prince's most important military commanders. We cannot assume, though, that a man of his standing played no role in the Wirral community's decision-making about how to proceed in negotiating with the prince's government, or agreeing on the grant and mechanism of collection of the various common fines. As he was planning to spend much of his retirement on his Wirral manor, he can hardly have been completely detached, but any involvement by him would of necessity have been discreet.

Hamo Massey came from possibly the oldest landed family in Wirral, had done military service for the prince and fought at the battle of Poitiers in 1356, and was to fight in the Rheims campaign of 1359/60. As serjeant of the peace for Wirral hundred in 1352 he clashed with Henry Charlton and Ranulf Racket, the two local officials that were in the pocket of the master forester, William Stanley. This is the first sign of Massey opposition to the Stanley hegemony in Wirral. The convoluted account of the rape of Lucy Meols in a barn at Puddington in 1355 of which Hamo was accused, possibly maliciously, was said to have been organised by two men, one of whom was Richard Bechington of Storeton. Stanley and John Lasselles were later accused of implication in Bechington's murder. Hamo did not serve on the Wirral indictment jury, on account of the pardon that he had been granted for his service in France, but this proved to be a mixed blessing as the jury became the public arena in which much of the faction fighting worked itself out. In 1367 he tried to make good his claim to exact a toll from those using the 'Low Road' on the sands of Dee and passing through his manor of Puddington. Violence ensued, and he was bound over to keep the peace in a large sum of money at the county court where William Stanley was one of his accusers on the Wirral indictment jury. By the late 1360s Hamo was clearly the only Wirral landowner capable of confronting the Stanley rise to dominance in the hundred, and he used the levers of power available to him to achieve a measure of success before his death in 1377/78. His son, John, was knighted, held the offices of lieutenant-justiciar of Chester and county sheriff, had a distinguished military career, and died at the battle of Shrewsbury fighting for Henry IV in 1403.

Philip Raby, the last of the six, had much in common with his fellow Chester citizen, John Blount. Indeed, he acted as Blount's attorney in the 1357 forest eyre. His power base was also in the city where he owned a substantial amount of property, both inside and outside the walls, but he also had land in Wirral. His hereditary office in the castle and his serjeanty of the Bridge Gate made him a man of considerable importance in city affairs. He had not expected to succeed to either office or land, which had only came about as the result of the death of his brother in 1349, followed by that of his brother's young son shortly afterwards. Philip did serve on the Wirral indictment jury of the county court, but only once, in 1355. His pledging in the eyre showed a wide range of connections, including Stanley and Lasselles, as well as the abbot of Basingwerk in Flintshire who had a grange at Caldy. Unlike Blount, though, he did not stand aloof from Wirral affairs, and acted, with Robert Poole, as a government informer to help undermine resistance to the enforcement of forest law in Wirral. He was another who did not manage to leave a male heir, and at his death in early 1362 his properties were divided between his two daughters.

These six men, together with perhaps another six, formed the social and political leadership of Wirral forest and hundred in the two decades after the Black Death. Their power and authority was based on the ownership of land and holding of office, with the mix varying from case to case. They all had a sense of their own importance and a desire to better themselves and their families in the difficult circumstances of the second half of the fourteenth century. Those who had most, like Domville and Hooton, were determined to hold on to what they had, to protect their positions from possible attack, to increase their standing if they could, and pass on their heritage to a son and heir. This last, of course, was not under their control. It was, though, the peculiar position of the Stanleys in this society, a family with little land in Wirral but a very powerful and potentially lucrative office, added to which was the ruthlessness of William Stanley the elder and his two sons, William and John, that threw the whole of community relations out of kilter. The prince's desperate need for money in the late fifties and early sixties, which led to his administration's use and manipulation of forest jurisdiction to extract large sums, the equivalent to heavy taxation, as common fines from the community, helped to poison relationships even further. Some prospered, the Stanley family spectacularly so, others failed, largely it has to be said through the vagaries of chance. But when a great poet in the later fourteenth century wrote that when Sir Gawain crossed the Dee into Wirral it was a place 'where there lived only a few who either God or men of good heart loved' then his hearers would have had no difficulty at all in knowing exactly what he meant.

1. John Domville (Dunfoul, Donvyle), the elder, lord of Oxton and Brimstage, regarder
c. 1295 to 1365
1.22, 1.53, 1.67, 2.5, 2.14, 2.36

He was born c. 1295, and died in November 1365, or shortly afterwards. He married twice: (i) Maud, daughter of William Brereton of Brereton, by whom he had four children and then, c. 1345 (ii) Maud, widow of Sir William Mobberley. His son, John Domville the younger, was born in the mid 1320s. They were the scions of a family that could trace its line back to Hugh Domville, lord of Oxton, in the later twelfth century. As well as his two substantial manors of Brimstage and Oxton in central Wirral, Domville had property nearby in Thingwall, Woodchurch, Barnston and Upton. In addition he had land elsewhere in the county, in Congleton, Kinderton, Bretton and Newton-by-Middlewich, as well as the advowson of Woodchurch.

He occupied a position of considerable power and influence in Cheshire, therefore. In 1331 he was a member of a syndicate that leased Northwich from the prince for two years at annual rent of £52. On 13 January 1340, he was appointed guardian of Vale Royal abbey, which had been going through an exceedingly turbulent period, culminating in the murder of the abbot, Peter, the previous year. In March 1351, both father and son were fined (£200 and ten marks, respectively) for forest offences in Wirral, as were the elder John's brother (Matthew, £5) and son in law (William Bradburn, five marks). It is likely that the Domville family led the resistance by the local community to the imposition of these fines, leading to an offer on 3rd June 1351 to compound for all the offences by those accused in Wirral for a sum of 100 marks. The prince and Wingfield replied indignantly, stating that this must have been made as a joke, and ordered all those involved to be imprisoned in Chester castle until they should come to their senses. Nevertheless, agreement was made on 18th July, 1351, for fines at substantially reduced rates. In parallel to this, on 14th July 1351, an inquiry was ordered into Domville's refusal to pay puture to William Stanley in respect of his two manors in Wirral. The dispute was settled on 8th June, 1352 at a meeting held and recorded at his manor-house in Brimstage. The witnesses to the document were three other Wirral magnates: Robert Poole, Richard Hough and Henry Hooton. He and his neighbour, Richard Hough, were close associates, and may have done military service together in the late 1330s, as both had been given general pardons which they pleaded at the 1353 trailbaston sessions.

Domville was accused in the 1353 sessions, together with Hough, of three assaults in 1336, and of kidnapping men to cross the Mersey with them in 1337 and forcing them to commit 'many crimes' in Lancashire, for which the men forfeited their goods as a result. Domville and Hough were acting as serjeants of the peace for Wirral in the latter year, and were also accused of concealing a treasure trove in Gayton which had been found by one of Domville's tenants, and which Domville appropriated to himself. The pair were also accused of having hunted regularly with greyhounds in Wirral forest, together with thirty others, and of extorting food and drink from the abbot of Basingwerk's lay-brother at Caldy Grange. Serious damage had been done to the abbot's property by their violent behaviour, and that of their horses and dogs. Domville claimed in the eyre the right to hunt in the forest with greyhounds (**2.7**). At the 1353 trailbaston sessions, he pleaded a general pardon, dated 21 January 1340, and was acquitted therefore.

It was alleged that in June 1352 he had ordered his son, John Domville the younger, to abduct Richard, the heir of Thomas Rode, at Rode, from the keeping of his guardian. In 1356, he was accused of taking, and imprisoning Hugh Hullessone, Richard Brownsward's lad.

Domville had a wide circle of connections in Wirral, but seems not to have been part of any particular faction. He pledged a number of people who were fined in the 1357 eyre (**1.28, 1.29, 1.33, 1.34**) and acted as attorney in the eyre for John Brereton, rector of Wallasey. As well as being a regarder in 1357, he served on the jury of presentment of the Chester county court on twelve occasions between 1355 and 1365, on two of which he was accompanied by his son. In 1360, a dispute between John Leycester and Hugh Chadderton about the rightful ownership of the manor of Mobberley was referred to the prince's council in London. In 1362, father and son were accused of backing Hugh to enter and take the manor of Mobberley by force from John Leycester. In return for this help, Hugh granted one third of the manor to the younger Domville and his wife.

The Domvilles were a success story of a sort in the difficult period of later fourteenth century Cheshire. The father was long lived, and was over seventy years old at his death in 1365. His younger son, Robert, founded the family of Domvilles of Lymm. The elder son, John, was also long lived, and gave evidence at the Scrope-Grosvenor trial of 1386, when he claimed to be 'sixty years old and more'. He first arranged, in 1379, for his daughter and heiress, Margery, to be married to Henry, the young son of Henry Tarbock. That did not happen, and in 1386 an agreement was made with Hugh Hulse of Chester. By this time he was described as 'John Domville of Mobberley'. As he left no son to succeed him at his death, the property had to be divided between a number of daughters. The eldest daughter, Margery, received the Wirral estates, and took them to her husband, a 'newcomer on the scene', by then Sir Hugh Hulse.

1295 et seq., for the Domville pedigree and family lands see *Talbot Deeds* (inserted pedigree) and pp. 4, 5 (This has superseded *Ormerod*, ii pp. 431–34.) William de Mobberley. **1333**, recog. for 53s. 4d. to Gervase de Wilford and William de Neuton, chaplain, executors of Robert de Nottingham (*Ch.R.R.*, p. 149). **1340**, 13 Jan., guardian of Vale Royal abbey, *Talbot Deeds*, p. 4; *VCH* iii, p. 160. **1340/46**, he conveyed property and rights, including the manors of Brimstage and Oxton, plus land in Upton, Barnston, Willaston, Buglawton and Congleton to Richard Pigot and Richard del Cros, chaplains, in order to create various entails and reversions. In addition he granted lands in Oxton held on lease and ten acres of waste to his son John and his wife Cecilia (*Talbot Deeds*, pp. 4–6, 23, 25). **1341**, recog. for £100, with Philip and David de Eggerton, Richard Hough and 15 others, to the earl of Chester (*Ch.R.R.*, p. 167). **1342**, recog. for £20, with Henry de Beeston to Ralph de Morton, (ibid., p. 149). **1343** John appears in dispute over the advowson of Woodchurch following the death of Adam Wettenhall (*CS* iii, 2479). **1351**, March, fines for Wirral forest offences, *B.P.R.*, iii, p. 12. **1351**, 3 June, he offered to pay a fine of 100 marks, which was rejected with fury by the administration, *B.P.R.*, iii, 29–31. **1351**, 15 June, recog. for ten marks with John Wettenhall of Dorfold and Peter Wilbraham to the earl of Chester, *Ch.R.R.*, p. 149. **1351**, 14 July, refusal to pay puture to Stanley, *B.P.R.*, iii, p. 34. **1351**, 18 July, settlement of forest fines, *B.P.R.*, iii, pp. 37–8. **1352**, settlement of puture dispute with Stanley, *Talbot Deeds,* pp. 26–7. **1352**, abduction at Rode, Hill, thesis, p. 4. **1353**, trailbaston indictments, *Cheshire History*, 11 (1983) pp. 45–6, 13 (1984) pp. 26–7. **1355/65**, served on county court jury of presentment, Hill, thesis, pp. 27, 33, 47, 57, 77, 103, 255, 279, 285, 301, 323, 331. **1356**, imprisonment of Hullessone, ibid. **1360**, Dec., Mobberley dispute referred to the prince's council, *B.P.R.*, iii, pp. 403–4, 407–8; Hill, thesis, p. 259. **1362**, 15 Dec., recog. for 10 marks, with William Bulkeley of Alpraham, Roger de Hulfeld, John Domville, the younger, William Norbury and William Stanley to Ranulf Roter (*Ch.R.R.*, p. 149). **1365**, recog. for 39s. 8d. to Sir John Delves (ibid., p. 149). **1379**, 18 Sept., marriage agreement with Henry Lostcok, *Talbot Deeds*, p. 34. **1386**, 8 April, marriage agreement with Hugh Hulse, ibid., p. 37.

2. Henry Hooton (de Hoton), lord of Hooton, deputy riding forester, regarder. *fl. 1340/1376*
1.22, 1.23, 1.44, 1.62–63, 1.67, 1.69–71, 1.83–4, 1.88, 1.195, 1.235, 1.239, 1.253–59; 2.30

A landowner of considerable and growing influence in Wirral, based on his important manor of Hooton in the south-east of the hundred. He had acquired two-thirds of the manor of Tranmere in the north-east by 1351, and also had property in Woodbank (Rough Shotwick) in the south-west, and in Chester. The record of the regard shows him to have been an active developer of his landed property, particularly in Hooton, but also elsewhere in Wirral (**1.253 –259**). As rider, he was probably the colleague of John Done, who took over William Stanley the elder's bailiwick during the two-year period (1355/57) it was under forfeiture. (See John Lasselles). He was also close to Stanley, serving as pledge for his claims in respect of his master-forestership in the eyre, and as rider also made a few presentments to the justices from his own roll (**1.69–71, 1.83–84**). Henry Coly served as his deputy (**1.62**). With his experience and social standing, he was well-placed to serve on the jury to inquire into Stanley's claim for liberties within the forest in 1361, and was one of the assembly of Wirral landowners summoned to inquire into Stanley's puture rights the previous year. Despite his connection with Stanley, Henry does not seem to have associated himself, at least overtly, with the armed factions that were becoming a problem in Wirral from before 1353 and after. It was in 1376 that William Stanley the younger agreed with Sir William Hooton to marry his eight-year-old son, another William Stanley, to Sir William's daughter and heiress, Margery. So it was that the Stanleys succeeded to the Hooton estates in 1396, abandoned their newly-built manor-house at Storeton, and the senior branch of the family rose yet another significant notch in the ranks of power and wealth in the community of Wirral Hundred.

The *Black Prince's Register* records a number of protests in 1351 which Henry made direct to the prince's council concerning what he claimed were infringements of his rights by (i) William de Tranemore; (ii) the 'malice of some persons' and (iii) 'the forester, the verderer and the other twelve' for which he and others had been imprisoned without 'mainprise or deliverance' unless they paid a fine admitting guilt. The latter, part of a complaint submitted on behalf of all the men of Wirral and Delamere forests, was claimed to be a general assault on the rights of the men of Wirral, contrary to their entitlements set out in Ranulf III's charter. In 1361 Henry was included in a group of Cheshire landowners who were reminded by the prince that they had already had a letter 'ordering them to arrange among themselves for Sir William of Walsingham to have without dispute .... the £60 granted to him for the repair' (of the church of Bunbury).

He served on the important criminal indictment juries of the Chester county court on five occasions in 1355, 1357 *(bis)*, 1365 and 1368.

On July 18 1351, three entries in the *Black Prince's Register* give an insight into the machinations of the prince's officials in their dealings with the Cheshire gentry. All the fines for the 'trespasses and outrages' were reduced, as were the bonds. Henry's fine was reduced to £10 with a bond for good behaviour of £40. The next record is for the expenses incurred by the forester, William Stanley, and his riding-forester, John de Lasselles, on their visit to London to report to the prince. This is followed by an instruction to the chamberlain to deal favourably with Robert de Pulle, but secretly so that no-one else will find out about it and ask for the same concession. A few months later the prince, having regard to the 'dearness' of the time, agreed that Henry and others could defer payment of a proportion of their fines. He ended up by being treated with considerable leniency, therefore, and without damage to his family's wealth or social standing.

Refs: **1340**, he witnesses grant by John of Pensby of land in Oxton (*Talbot Deeds* no. 43). **1341**, 17 Sept., recog. for 16 marks, with Richard de Hoton and Richard son of Ralph de Hoton, to the abbot of Chester (*Ch.R.R.,* p. 244). **1343**, 20 Dec., he witnesses grant by John Domville, snr, to Richard del Crosse, chaplain, of lands in Upton, Barnston, Willaston, Buglawton and Congleton (*Talbot Deeds* no. 49). **1344**, 9 Sept., recog. for £20, with William de Salopia to the abbot of Chester, (*Ch.R.R.,* p. 244). In **1345**, 13 July, same recog. for £20 (*Ch.R.R.,* p. 244). **1345**, 7 Sept., recog. for £26 13s. 4d., with William Wasteneys, Thomas de Ideshale, Richard de Fitton and Stephen del Greves, to the earl of Chester, (*Ch.R.R.,* p. 244). Fined £40 for forest offences in **1351**, reduced to 40 marks (*B.P.R.,* iii, p. 12). **1351**, 18 May, he set out grievances relating to land within the forest which were being challenged by malicious people which threatened the closure of his mill, and damage of his rights in his other lands, although they had been allowed by the justiciar's and regarders' perambulation (*B.P.R.,* iii, p. 24). **1351**, 18 May, Henry and others were indicted by the forester et al. for hunting hares and other vermin, were imprisoned and not allowed bail without paying fine to the lord. He claimed the accusation was malicious and should have been confirmed by an inquisition (ibid., pp. 24–25). July 18 **1351**, his fine for forest trespasses reduced further, to £10, with a bond for good behaviour of £40 (ibid., p. 37–8). **1351**, 28 Oct., he complained that William de Tranemore had conveyed to him two thirds of Tranmere, a manor held in socage. The escheator had seized the two thirds into the prince's hands, supposing it to be held by knight service. Order to inquire into the matter. The justiciar and chamberlain were to examine three petitions of Henry and take action according to the council's endorsements (ibid., pp. 44–5).

1351, 8 Nov., agreement that Henry and others need only pay between now and August next a proportion of their fines for trespass (ibid., pp. 51–52). **1355, 1357, 1365, 1368** service on county court presentment juries (Hill, thesis, mm. 2d, 6, 7, 16d and 20d). **1357**, 24 July, grant to Thomas del Russhes of property in Chester which bordered property belonging to Henry de Hoton (*B.P.R.*, p. 269). **1361**, Bunbury church dispute (ibid., p. 406). **1361**, 1 Dec., he was a member of the inquisition to consider the profits and franchises claimed by William Stanley (ibid. p. 431). **1360**, 1 Dec., summoned to appear at the county court to consider claims by William Stanley for puture (ibid., p. 434). Sept 9 **1366**, recog. for 20 marks with Henry de Litherlond to John de Whytemore, senior (*Ch.R.R.*, p. 244). **1376**, marriage of Wm Stanley and Margery Hooton (W. Fergusson Irvine, 'The Early Stanleys' *Transactions of the Historic Society of Lancashire and Cheshire*, 105, 1953, p. 59, *Ormerod* ii, p. 410.)

3. John Lasselles, deputy riding forester of Wirral, regarder
fl. 1340/1361
1.23, 1.85, 1.88, 1.138, 2.29, 2.44

Lasselles was a landowner in the north-east corner of Wirral, with property in Poulton-cum-Seacombe, Liscard and elsewhere. He was not just a close associate of the master-forester, William Stanley the elder, but his right-hand man in the armed, criminal faction (the notorious 'covin') made up of the foresters and hundred officials, the coroner and beadle, that Stanley led from the early 1350s onwards. In the 1353 trailbaston sessions he is included in the general accusation by the presentment juries against all the Wirral foresters of oppression and extortion of the most severe kind. In addition, he is accused on his own, as 'under-rider' of Wirral forest, of oppressive conduct against people in the Wallasey area, where the bulk of his land lay. Also, it was alleged that he had been involved with two others in the abduction of a ward, William Meols, in 1350, and using this as a weapon to blackmail his guardians to come to an agreement with them. It was reported to the prince's great council, meeting at Chester in 1353, that David Calveley had challenged Lasselles' membership of a jury of the county court in a property suit because of his kinship with Ellen Calveley and his wife's kinship with another party in the case.

In addition to his forest office, he leased the keeping of the avowries of Cheshire for two years from 1352–54. On 13 May, 1354, he claimed that he had purchased the marriage of the heir of Poulton Lancelyn from the prince, but that the heir's father-in-law, Randolph Bruen, had deprived him of it. He also claimed at that time to have recently lost goods worth ten marks, a clear sign (if true) of his growing prosperity. He served on the presentment jury of the Chester county court three times in 1354/55. In 1357 it was reported that Lasselles had bought the marriage of Alice Laken, heiress to a third of the manor of Storeton, from Roger Saham to whom the marriage had been granted by the prince. Alice had inherited one-third of the manor, worth 67s. 8d. a year, at her father, William's, death in 1349. The first man to whom Lasselles married the girl died, leaving her a widow at the age of eighteen, after which he sold her marriage to Thomas Clotton, for 50 marks, receiving £20 in advance. This was followed by a dispute, unresolved, as to whether Lasselles had any right to sell Alice's remarriage. In 1376 John Stanley was accused of arranging the murder of Clotton, and then fleeing the county. The following year, he was accused of carrying out the murder himself, with the agreement of his brother, William Stanley the younger.

Like William Stanley, Lasselles used his forest office without scruple to intimidate the local community to his own advantage. This made him vulnerable to attacks from others, as in November 1354 when he alleged that 'some of his ill-wishers' were trying to damage his wealth and standing by implicating him wrongfully in a law-suit. In December, 1355, he and Stanley were accused of involvement in the plot to murder Richard Bechinton. Richard, when he was fifteen years old, had inherited another third of the manor of Storeton at his father, Simon's, death in 1349. The family continued their involvement with the Stanley faction after William Stanley the elder's death in April 1360. In 1377, the younger William Stanley and Thomas Lasselles, John's second son, led a small-scale armed rebellion in the Wallasey area, that included lighting warning beacons, to attack the tax-collectors who were coming to the area under the leadership of the main rival faction, led by Hamo Massey of Puddington.

Together with the elder Stanley, Lasselles was key in implementing the prince's government's policy to tighten up the forest law in Cheshire, through the imposition of English law and custom. In July 1351 they were awarded twenty shillings each, plus expenses, for coming to London to discuss forest matters with the prince and his advisers. In April 1353, when Robert Poole handed a petition to the prince asking for the former rights with regard to lawing of dogs in Wirral to be preserved, he claimed to be acting 'with the assent of the whole hundred of Wirral' except for William Stanley and John Lasselles. The accusations made against the pair four months later in the trailbaston sessions were doubtless exacerbated by the extreme resentment felt by many in the community of Wirral at the activities of these two 'collaborators'.

Lasselles's period of office as riding forester is a little uncertain, although in the list of officials at the beginning of the eyre he is clearly in post, and described as *nunc equitator* (**1.23**). His name is followed by that of Henry Hooton, and then by six others, two of whom were called a *serviens* of Lasselles and Hooton, respectively, while two others, Richard le Ryder and Nicholas Hody, are named 'former riders'. Hooton certainly acted as rider in the first part of 1357. The rider was an employee of the earl of Chester, and was paid wages of sixpence a day as can be seen from the appointment of Walter Mundham in 1301 'to live in the forest of Wirral as rider of the same'. In 1312 Nicholas Ody (see 'Hody' above) was appointed to the post, which he still held in 1315–16. By 1320 Richard Weford (possibly the 'Richard le Ryder' referred to above) held the office as a life-appointment, retaining it until September 1327, when he was replaced by John Swynnemour, described as 'chief rider'. Weford was reinstated in 1328 and was still in post in 1331–32. As was so often the case in the fourteenth century, an official post was coming to be awarded as an act of patronage to clients who took the income but left it to deputies to carry out the actual work. In the financial year 1347–48 William Stafford was 'rider of Wirral forest' for life at the usual wages, as he was in 1349–50, 1350–51 and part of 1359–60 (he was succeeded by John Pembridge, another life appointment in December 1359). Both Stafford and Pembridge were yeomen in the prince's household, and so the 'riders' in post between 1347 and 1360, including Hooton and Lasselles, must have acted as their deputies, even if not necessarily called so.

Stanley had been imprisoned by 23 November 1355 for implication in the Bechinton murder, lost his master-forestership, and was not reinstated until August, 1357. It is likely, therefore, that Lasselles, who was also accused of involvement, was deprived of his deputy-ridership at that time and replaced by Henry Hooton under John Done, the acting master-forester, and then reinstated with Stanley shortly before the forest eyre began.

Lasselles was either dead or incapacitated by 1 December 1361, as it was his 'son and heir', John, who was summoned to the assembly of Wirral landlords at the county court to discuss the payment of puture to William Stanley the younger. The younger John had been in the wardship in or before 1358. He in turn was dead by 1377, and the family property passed to his younger brother, Thomas, who died not long afterwards. In the snake pit that was Wirral of the second half of the fourteenth century, John Lasselles had taken all the opportunities open to him, both lawful and unlawful, to thrive, and had achieved a great measure of success. Unlike Stanley, though, he did not manage that leap into the higher echelons of Cheshire society, and by the end of the fourteenth century the family name seems to have disappeared from the scene.

Refs. Strangely, there are no references at all to Lasselles in *Ormerod*, ii, pp. 478–82. **1301**, appointment of Walter Mundham to the ridership, Green, 'Forests: Wirral' Chapter in *VCH*, ii, p. 185; *ChAccl*, p. 6. **1312, 1315–16**, Nicholas Ody acts as rider, ibid., pp. 78, 86. Richard Weford, rider, ibid., pp. 92, 103, 108, *ChAcc2*, p. 200. **c. 1340**, John Lasselles witness (5 out of 5) to an Oxton deed, *Talbot Deeds*, p. 23. **1349**, inquisitions post mortem of Wm Laken and Simon Becheton, *Cheshire History*, 29 (1992), pp. 4–5. **1351**, July, reward to Lasselles after trip to London, *B.P.R.*, iii, p. 38; *ChAccl*, p. 167. (In the *Register* he is called *chivachour*, but in the account 'deputy rider'). **1351**, Oct., complains to the prince about a wrongful distraint, *B.P.R.*, iii, p. 45. **1353**, April, Robt Poole's petition, *B.P.R.*, iii, p. 102. **1353**, August, trailbaston sessions, see Booth, 'Taxation and Public Order'; *ChAcc2* pp. 176–77; *Cheshire History*, 11 (1983), pp. 48–9. **1353–54**, lease of the avowries, for £7 6s. 8d. (the rent used to be £16 a year), TNA SC 6/784/3 m. 3. **1354**, May, report of David Calveley's petition of the previous summer, *B.P.R.*, iii, pp. 157–58; complaint of the loss of the Poulton Lancelyn marriage, ibid., p. 163; complaint that John Done had wrongfully seized ten marks worth of his goods, ibid., **1355**, Nov., he petitioned the prince against the activities of 'his ill-wishers', ibid., p. 216; Stanley imprisoned, *B.P.R.*, iii, p. 217. **1355**, Dec. alleged involvement in the murder of Richard Bechinton, Booth 'Last Week', p. 227. **1357**, Aug., Dec., the Alice Laken remarriage affair, *B.P.R.*, iii, pp. 273, 284. **1357**, Dec., John Lasselles the younger in wardship, Hill, thesis, p. 117. **1358**, 'John Lascelles' fined for non-appearance at the Wirral hundred eyre for his holding at Newton and Poulton in Wallasey, CHES 25/3 m. 47. **1359**, appointment of John Pembridge as rider for life, in succession to Wm Stafford, *B.P.R.*, iii, p. 379. **1361**, Dec., John, heir of John Lasselles summoned to Chester to discuss Stanley's puture rights, ibid., p. 434. **1376, 1377**, murder of Thos Clotton, Booth, 'Last Week', p. 229. **1377**, Feb. ref. to 'Agnes, widow of John Lasselles'; ref. to 'John Lasselles, father of Thomas'; Thos Lasselles dead by April 1377, Hill, thesis, pp. 897, 901, 911.

4. John Blount (Blound, Blund), the younger, mayor of Chester, lord of Little Neston.
fl. 1334/1366
1.208, 2.10, 2.17, 2.48, 8.52, 9.71

Blount was unusual among the grandees of fourteenth-century Wirral in that his main source of wealth and status was from trade, not land. He served as mayor of Chester fourteen times between 1334 and 1360, including the periods 1350–53 and 1355–60. This led to him appearing as a witness to deeds and other documents. For example, in October 1350 he witnessed Stephen Merton's five-year lease from the prince of property near the Dee Mills, Chester. He also accounted as escheator of the city in this final period, in accordance with the charter to Chester of 1354. John Blount the elder, who had also served as mayor, in 1316–17, and died in office, was presumably his father, and had acquired the manor of Little Neston-cum-Hargrave in Wirral shortly before his death. John the younger inherited the manor in 1317 as well as the office of serjeanty of the North Gate of Chester, including the city gaol. This had been acquired by the elder Blount early in the fourteenth century. The Blounts also owned property in Marlston-cum-Lache, near to the city on the south-west. This was in the hands of Roger Blount at his death in 1349.

John Blount the younger was fined 'according to his estate and circumstances' for forest offences in Wirral in March 1351, and the fine was confirmed as 10s. 0d. the following month, when he was bound over for 40 marks. Presumably because of his duties as mayor of Chester, he held no offices in Wirral forest or hundred nor did he serve as a Wirral member of the Chester county court presentment jury. There is no evidence of any links with the factions that were plaguing Wirral at this time. In July 1359, the prince granted him the very rare right to keep greyhounds at Little Neston, and hunt the hare and the fox there. This concession was made at the urging of Sir Bartholomew Burgersh, the non-resident justiciar of Chester and one of the prince's companions in arms. Clearly Blount had powerful connections at the heart of the prince's centre of power. In 1361 he was summoned, along with all the other Wirral landowners, to attend the assembly at Chester to discuss the question of the payment of puture to William Stanley. He would have been in a good position to act as an 'honest broker' in the Wirral community's deliberations about agreeing a common fine for forest eyre offences with the prince's central administration.

He died in 1366, and his inquisition post mortem showed that he was succeeded by his five daughters as co-heiresses, and his properties had been vested in the hands of three feoffees-to-uses. In 1367 his widow, Agnes, was granted a licence for an oratory in the Chester house which had belonged to her husband. It appears, therefore, that John Blount is a good example of a rich city merchant who 'retired to the country' while retaining his house and social position in Chester, although he failed to leave a son to carry on his name or inheritance.

Refs: 1316/17, 1334/60, Blounts as mayors of Chester, *VCH* v:2, pp. 307–8; *CS* iii, no. 7,722. **1317** acquisition of manor of Little Neston, *VCH* v:1, p. 55; inheritance of Northgate serjeanty, *VCH* v:2, p. 221; ownership of Marlston-cum-Lache, ibid., p. 330. **1338/1347**, made seven recognizances to the abbot of Chester, *Ch.R.R.*, p. 41. **1349**, inquisition post mortem of Roger Blount of Chester, *CH* 18, p. 8. **1350**, Dec. recog. for £106 13s. 4d. with Philip Egerton and seven others to the earl of Chester, *Ch.R.R.,* p. 167. **1350–51**, in a payment of a recog. of £6 13s. 4d. to the chamberlain of Chester, he is described as 'John Blount, citizen of Chester', *ChAccl*, p. 163. **1351**, fine for forest offences, *B.P.R.,* iii, pp. 13, 38. **1353**, August, Wm Joliffe, a Chester goldsmith, accused Blount of stealing a seal, an axe, two swords and £20 in small change from him at Marlston on 16 March, 1349, *Cheshire History*, 11, p. 42. **1354–55**, Blount's account as mayor and escheator of the city of Chester, TNA SC 6/784/7 m. 4. **1359**, July permission to hunt in Wirral, ibid., p. 351. **1361**, Dec. summoned to Chester to discuss Stanley's puture rights, ibid., p. 434. **1366**, death and inquisition post mortem, Ormerod, *Cheshire* ii, p. 539. For Blount's 'retirement' see *VCH* v:1, p. 55. **1367**, Agnes Blount's oratory in her late husband's house in Chester, *CS* iii, 10,617.

5. Hamo (Hamonet) Massey (Mascy), lord of Puddington

fl. 1332 to 1377/78

1.44, 1.49, 1.201, 1.216, 2.8, 2.15

His ancestor, another Hamo, who was baron of Dunham Massey, had also held the manor of Puddington in Domesday Book, so his descendant could probably claim to be the longest-established landed family in Wirral. Hamo succeeded to his estates at Puddington, Shotwick and elsewhere in Wirral on the death of his father, Thomas Massey, in 1331/32. In 1351 he was accused of a number of offences in the forest inquiries of that year. As was the case with his fellow substantial landowners, his heavy fine of £40 imposed on 24th March was reduced, in his case to twenty marks on 18th July, and on 26 February 1353 it was further reduced by £10. In April 1353 was pardoned a fine for keeping an unlawed dog.

He stood out from the other resident magnates of Wirral, in that he had a significant military career in the prince's service. His pleading of a charter of pardon at the county court in July 1354 in response to an accusation of seriously damaging a neighbour's property suggests that he might have already taken part in campaigns by that time. He led a substantial contingent of archers from Broxton and Wirral hundreds on the 1355–56 campaign in Aquitaine, jointly with with Hugh Golborne, as Wirral itself was not a particularly fertile recruiting ground for archers at this period compared with central and eastern Cheshire. In May 1355 he was paid £5 as half his war-fee and received letters of protection in advance of setting out on campaign. In September 1355 he was paid £15 9s. 0d. for the archers serving under him in Gascony, and in January 1356 payment was made for the 63 archers led by him and the 28 by his colleague, Robert Brown. He fought in the battle of Poitiers, and in September 1357 was awarded a general pardon for offences committed in Cheshire as a reward for this service. He was exempted from serving on juries and similar bodies, as a further reward from the prince for the same reason in 1358. In August 1359 he was paid, as an esquire of the prince, five marks war-fee for six months, as well as 12d. a day for his wages on the journey to Kent to embark with his troops for the Rheims campaign, and despite the lack of any further evidence there seems to be no reason to doubt that he actually served on this disastrous expedition. His son, Sir John Massey, also served abroad, held the offices of lieutenant-justiciar of Chester and sheriff of the county, constable of Conwy castle, and was killed fighting for Henry IV at the battle of Shrewsbury in 1403.

Wirral claimed the right to choose two serjeants of the peace itself, and not on the nomination of the joint master-serjeants of the county. In 1352, Massey was acting as one of them, it was said wrongfully, and distrained on the goods of two brothers at Rough Shotwick. In doing so, he and unnamed associates forcibly prevented Henry Charlton and Ranulf Racket, the hundred bailiffs, from doing their office, took the distrained goods, and kept them unlawfully. He and the others were found guilty of this at the trailbaston sessions of 1353, and fined £2. Charlton and Racket were close associates of the master forester, William Stanley the elder, in his criminal 'covin'. Two years later, Massey was accused at the county court of having Thomas Chapman and Richard Bechington abduct Lucy, the daughter of Henry Meols, to a barn in Puddington in February 1355, where he raped her. Bechington, lord of one third of the manor of Storeton, had been a ward of Hamo, and was murdered, allegedly at the command of William Stanley, the master-forester, and John Lasselles, his deputy, in October of the same year. After being lured on to a boat in the Mersey, and wounded, Richard was taken to Puddington, where he died. This was, perhaps, the beginning of the struggle for mastery in Wirral that shadowed the local communities for the following thirty years.

Some of this was played out on the Wirral indictment jury of the Chester county court, part of the new system for dealing with serious crime that was set up in the wake of the prince's state visit to his county in 1353. Massey's status meant, of course, that he was ultimately going to play an important role in both the struggle and the legal proceedings. He served on what appears to have been a special inquiry in the county court session for 19th December, 1357, to consider the achievement of his majority by William Wilbraham, together with Sir John Danyers, Sir John Griffin, Sir William Golborne and others. After the grant to him of exemption from serving on juries in September 1357, he did not serve on the county court's indictment jury for twenty years; as it became clear that membership of the jury was an excellent way of damaging one's rivals, this may have been a disadvantage to him. He is also recorded as having served only once on the indictment jury of the annual eyre of the justiciar of Chester, held for Wirral hundred at Backford in December 1354, a court which dealt with less serious crimes.

In the late 1360s, the struggle for power in Wirral reached a new phase, when after the murder of Ranulf Roter in 1361 Massey was the only person left able and willing to confront the hegemony of the Stanley family. Between 1368 and 1378 the conflict between the two factions can be followed in the county court indictment rolls. In July 1368 Hamo was accused by a county court jury of which William Stanley the younger was a member of threatening to commit murder, of horse-stealing and extorting tolls from passers-by for which he was bound over in the large sum of 100 marks. Three years later, in July 1371, Stanley the younger used his authority as master forester to accuse Massey and his associates of serious forest offences in the same court.

Massey then went on the offensive. In January 1377 he and several other Wirral landowners were commissioned to collect a common fine of 660 marks from the people of Wirral. Stanley had war-beacons lit to gather armed men to repel them by force and there was a violent confrontation. This was followed by Stanley's third attempt to neutralise his rival and Massey was accused in February 1377, again by a county court jury of which Stanley was a member, of harbouring a felon at Puddington, the forgery of a title deed, and house-breaking. He elected trial by jury and was acquitted, perhaps demonstrating that the Stanley family, their forest jurisdiction now ended, were no longer the threat that they had once been. Massey responded in kind in March 1377, and served on the indictment jury for Wirral, when Stanley and his brother, John, were accused of serious crimes of oppression and extortion in Wirral, including the murder of Thomas Clotton by John, over the previous eleven years. The Stanleys and their followers had counter-attacked with an armed band in Wirral, presumably to intimidate jurors and witnesses. The two brothers were acquitted, therefore. To resolve the issue, a special court of inquiry was held on the day after the county court meeting at the commissioners' request, which found the allegations against Stanley and his associates to be true.

It all seems to have ended in a draw: Wirral was disafforested by the Black Prince on his death bed, and the bulwark of Stanley power in Wirral was no more. On the other hand, William Stanley's campaign to win compensation from both the community and the administration for lost rights was successful. Hamo Massey had managed to hold on to his property and position in the hundred, while two fortunate marriages brought the Hooton estates to the senior branch of the Stanley family and the Lathom property in Lancashire to the junior branch (later earls of Derby).

Refs. For pedigree see Ormerod, *Cheshire,* ii, pp. 558–61. For the career of Hamo's son, Sir John Massey of Puddington, *oc.* 1403, see Philip Morgan, *War and Society in Medieval Cheshire, 1277–1403*, Chetham Society, third series, 34 (1987) pp. 164, 187, 194–95, 205–8, 216–17. **1086**, Domesday Book, *VCH* i, p. 359. **1130/40**, the manors of Storeton and Puddington were granted by Ranulf II earl of Chester to his official, Alan Sylvester, for the service of half a knight's fee. It has been assumed that the master-forestership of Wirral was associated with this grant, but it is not mentioned in either the earl's charter, or in the subsequent grant of property in Storeton by Alan's son, Robert, to Chester abbey in 1162/66, or the grant of the two manors by Hugh II earl of Chester to Alexander, his son's tutor, together with the marriage of Annabel, Robert's daughter and heiress. See Barraclough, *Charters*, no. 35, 188. **1177/81**, grant to Alexander the tutor, ibid., no. 188. It seems, therefore, that either the Masseys lost Puddington for a period, and then received it back again, or that Sylvester was granted the feudal superiority of the manor, and that the Masseys would hold it from him. **1307**, for Wirral's claim for exemption from the authority of the master-serjeant of the peace for the county, see TNA CHES 29/17 m. 7. **1342**, recog. for £11 with Robt Poole, Henry Sampson, Wm Lakene and Wm, son of Bernard of Tranmere to Thomas de Capenhurst, rector of Bebington, *Ch.R.R.,* p. 385. **1351**, 24 Mar., fined £40 for Wirral forest offences, 40 marks to be paid; fine reduced to 20 marks, 18 July 1351; pardoned £10 of his fine, 26 Feb. 1353. *B.P.R.,* iii, pp. 12, 37, 51–2, 94. **1352**, 1 April, wrongful distraint at Rough Shotwick, *CH* 14, pp. 38–9, Booth, 'Taxation and Public Order', p. 30. **1353**, pardoned his fine for keeping an unlawed dog, *B.P.R.*, iii, p. 98. **1354**, 22 July, accused of damaging property of Gilbert de Podyngton, but pleaded a charter of pardon at Chester county court, Hill, thesis, p. 7. **1354**, Dec., served on the eyre indictment jury at Backford, TNA CHES 25/3 m. 10. **1355**, 8 Feb., accused of rape of Lucy Meols, Hill, thesis, pp. 23–5. **1355**, 21 May, Sir John Danyers, Sir Ralph Mobberley and other captains were in London discussing with the prince the recruitment of soldiers from Cheshire; it was stated that 'There are few archers in Wirral forest' *B.P.R.*, iii, pp. 199–200. **1355**, 26 June, appointed leader of archers with Hugh Golborne from Wirral and Broxton hundreds, *B.P.R.*, iii, p. 204. **1355**, 7 Sept., £15 9s. 0d. paid for his archers, Duchy of Cornwall Office, *Jornale* of John Henxteworth, fo. 2. **1355**, 21 Oct., murder of Richard Bechington, Hill, thesis, pp. 32–5. **1355**, payment [illegible] for archers, *Henxteworth*, fo. 2v. **1357**, 1 July, recog. with Philip Egerton, Robert Poole, David Egerton, Ranulf le Bruen, Robt son of Roger Bruen, David Weaver, Hugh Malpas (rector of Barthomley), Wm Spurstowe, Robt Wardle, Roger Malpas, David Bryd of Broxton, and Philip son of Ranulf Egerton for £366 13s. 4d. for a ten-year lease of half Fulwich and Bickley wood (late of Sir John St Pierre), *Ch.R.R.*, p. 167. **1357**, 10 April (warrant) 26 Sept. (letters) granted a pardon for Cheshire offences, excluding the murders of Bartholomew Northenden (mayor of Chester) and Richard Bechington. (These exclusions were standard form in pardons of this period), *Ch.R.R.*, p. 328. **1358**, 9 April (warrant) 23 July (letters), exemption from serving on juries, etc., for his service in Gascony and at the battle of Poitiers, *Ch.R.R.*, p. 328. **1359**, 16 Aug. order to pay his war-fee and wages, *B.P.R.*, iii, p. 357. **1368**, 18 July, he was bound over in the county court to keep the peace in the large sum of 100 marks for threatening to kill Wm Newton on the sands at Puddington, and at the same time was found guilty of stealing a horse from a chaplain and blocking a road between Puddington and Shotwick in 1367. He was acquitted, though, of the crime of extorting a toll from carters passing on the sands of Dee within Puddington manor. His enemy, Wm Stanley the younger, was on the indictment jury, Hill, thesis, pp. 478–81. **1371**, 15 July, a series of indictments concerning forest offences were made against Massey in the county court by Wm Stanley the younger (master forester), Henry Litherland (verderer and rider) and 'jurors of various hundreds', accusing him of unlawfully hunting deer in Wirral in the company of Sir John Norris, Sir John Danyers and others in 1367 and 1371. He was also accused of building a water-mill in 1371 for which he had felled forty oaks, of enclosing woods and selling timber, Hill, thesis, pp. 554–57. **1377**, 24 Feb., indicted in the county court (Wm Stanley the younger was on the jury) of several serious offences (1) of harbouring a suspected felon at Puddington on 3 Oct. 1367; (2) of having a forged deed made in Aug. 1375 concerning land in Tranmere; (3) of breaking into a house in Jan. 1377 with many others in Wallasey and taking a horse, and at the same time of breaking into several properties belonging to Thos Lasselles and his mother at Seacombe and taking horses from them. He elected trial by jury, and was acquitted, ibid., pp. 888–89. **1377**, 10 March, the county court indictment jury for Wirral made a series of serious allegations of oppression and extortion against Wm Stanley the younger and his brother, John, between 1366 and 1377 for all of which William was acquitted. Unusually, only one member of the jury is mentioned, namely 'Hamo de Mascy', who, as 'Hamo de Mascy de Podynton' also claimed to be the victim of extortion at Stanley's hands in 1376, ibid., pp. 932–47. At the same court session, but with a different indictment jury (probably not from Wirral), Hamo himself was accused of selling the wardship and remarriage of one Cecily (surname illegible) to a Chester citizen, Wm Engineer, for him to marry her to his son, Janyn, for 100 marks. Cecily held property in Caldy, Calveley, Wimboldsley and elsewhere. It was alleged that her land had been held from the prince as earl of Chester in chief by knight service, and so Hamo had no right to do this. He was also accused of selling the wardship and marriage of Amice Prenton, a tenant by knight service of Cecily, for 100 marks. He elected trial by jury in both cases, was acquitted of the first and there is no verdict for the second, ibid., pp. 922–23. For what ensued, see Booth, *'Last week'*, pp. 229–31. **1377/78**, received a quitclaim for puture from Wm Stanley the younger, Stewart-Brown, 'Further Notes on the Deafforestation', pp. 23–27.

6. Philip Raby, hereditary gardener of Chester castle and serjeant of the Bridgegate (Chester), lord of Raby (Wirral).

c. 1319–c. 1362

1.33, 1.61, 1.240, 1.241, 2.9, 2.27, 2.37, 2.60

Philip Raby, who had succeeded his young nephew to his estates and offices somewhat unexpectedly, probably as a result of the Black Death, was a man who had property in both Chester and Wirral. His office as gardener of the castle was not meant to be carried out in person, but as he accounted for the apple crop there he must have appointed a deputy. As serjeant of the Bridge Gate he was paid the customary wages of 3d. a day, had to provide men to look after this gate, and the Shipgate and the Horsegate which were close by, as well, was entitled to take tolls from those passing through, and in return had to organise watches on a section of the wall.

Philip's commitment was mainly to the city, and it is significant that he acted as mayor John Blount's attorney in the forest eyre (**8.50**). Although he served only once on the Wirral indictment jury of the county court, he did have important connections in the area, and acted as a pledge in the eyre for his neighbour, the master forester, William Stanley the elder, for his land in Storeton (**9.72**), as well as pledging (together with John Lasselles, the riding forester) the abbot of Basingwerk's under-bailiff, who had been convicted of a venison trespass (**1.61**). John in return acted as Philip's pledge in respect of his claim (**2.27**). Raby also stood as pledge for the abbot, in respect of his land at Caldy Grange (**2.9**). Despite his connection with Stanley and Lasselles, he appears not to have formed part of any of the criminal or self-defence associations of Wirral in the years after 1350. It was, therefore, his role as informer for the government of Cheshire that was most important. Following the major inquiry into forest offences in Wirral, he and Robert Poole were members of a group in March 1351 that advised Wingfield of the wealth of those accused and of their ability to pay penalties imposed on them. Poole was fined the large sum of £40, but Raby was one of the few Wirral landowners who escaped punishment.

Philip died probably not long after 23 February 1362 (when he executed a deed to feoffees) leaving two daughters, Catherine and Joan. Their father's properties, including the serjeanty, were divided between them.

Refs.: For his pedigree, see Ormerod, *Cheshire,* ii, p. 547. See also *VCH*, viii, p. 223. **1349**, Inquisition Post Mortem of Robt Raby the elder shows that he had at least three houses in the city, plus property outside the walls that was rented out. He had also acquired another piece of land between the walls and the Roodee in 1340, *Talbot Deeds*, pp. xxx. **1349–50**, Philip accounted for 9s. 0d. for the apple crop of the castle garden, *ChAcc*, p. 141. **1350–51**, he accounted in payment to the chamberlain of Chester for 10s. 0d. from the issues of the garden as 'the lord shall have all the fruits except the principal tree called "Restingtree" whose fruit, together with the fruit remaining in the trees after the shaking off of the fruits thereof, the gardener shall have, by ancient custom, and also the same gardener finds the lord's vegetables for his entertainment in the castle.' ibid., pp. 160, 181. **1351**, 24 March, Raby's role as an informer on the ability to pay fines of his fellow forest tenants, *B.P.R.*, iii, p. 12. **1355**, 22 Sept., member of Wirral indictment jury of Chester county court, Hill, thesis, pp. 26–9. **1359**, 19 March, on the Chester castle indictment jury of the county court, held at St Mary on the Hill church, concerning the escape of Master Bennett ap Iorwerth ap Meilor from the castle, ibid., pp. 158–61. **1362**, 23 Feb., he gave power of attorney for the delivery of seisin of his lands in Raby, Chester and Claverton to feoffees, *Talbot Deeds*, pp. 30, 33. **1363**, March, at the audit of the chamberlain's account for 1361–62, the entry relating to the fee to be paid to the heirs of Philip Raby is cancelled, with a note stating that the reason for this is that the heirs are under age and should be in the prince's wardship because the office of gardener is held by grand serjeanty, *ChAcc2*, p. 74. **1363**, 18 July, at the county court Robt Carrington and Richard Golborne were indicted and fined for abducting Catherine, Philip Raby's daughter, the ward of the earl of Chester from Chester nunnery, where she was in the care of the prioress, on 2 June 1363. ibid., pp. 298–301, 304–5. **1365**, 6 Feb., Robert Carrington pardoned the outstanding portion of his fine of £50 for the abduction, for past and future good service, *B.P.R.*, iii, pp. 473–74.

III. FOREST LAW AND ITS ADMINISTRATION

Forest law was introduced into England by William the Conqueror. It was to apply to certain defined areas of land, most of which was in the hands of private landowners, in order to preserve the wild animals, particularly deer, and their habitat, which were under threat from encroachment by the plough on waste and woodland.[34] In Domesday Book, the earl of Chester is reported to have had two forests. At this time, Wirral, which was not placed under forest law until the twelfth century, was sparsely wooded and more closely settled than the more eastern parts of Cheshire, such as the two older forests of Delamere and Macclesfield.[35] A forest was the supreme status symbol of the king, as well as of a small number of members of the nobility, such as the earl of Chester. The forests were places for hunting and for supplying meat, but increasingly came to be used as a very unpopular means of raising revenue through financial penalties.

The charters of Henry I and Stephen issued at their coronations and the 1184 assize of the forest of Henry II state that each of them was retaining the forest area as a previous monarch had had it.[36] The work of Langton and Jones, which is still in progress, has demonstrated that the area of the royal and private forests in England at its maximum extent covered over half the kingdom. The private landowners who lived within the forest areas were, in theory, prevented from doing things with their own property that people took for granted elsewhere. Not only could they not hunt deer or some other beasts, but they could not cut down trees, plough up land, dig ditches, erect buildings on their own landholdings or, indeed, do anything that hindered the free movement of the beasts of the forest over the landscape.

Revenues from fines for offences against the 'vert' (trees) and 'venison' (deer) were relatively small. As the population grew in England between 1086 and the early fourteenth century, though, the pressure to take more and more land into cultivation became ever stronger. This meant that significant amounts of money could be raised as fines for 'purprestures' in the forest – that is the alterations to the landscape that have been referred to above. Licences could also be sold to private landlords to build parks on their land in the forest.

The assize of the forest was the first record to specify the details of forest law.

34 For the background to the nature of forest law in England, and the administration of the forest courts, see Turner, *Select Pleas*, Nellie Neilson 'The Forests' in J.F. Willard and W.A. Morris, *The English Government at Work, 1327–1336*, 1 (1940), Jean Birrell, *Feckenham* and *Cannock*, Charles R. Young, *The Royal Forests of Medieval England* (1979), Raymond Grant, *The Royal Forests of England* (1991), John Langton and Graham Jones, eds, *Forests and Chases of Medieval England & Wales*, (2010). See also the 'Forests and Chases of England and Wales *c.* 1000 to *c.* 1850 website' at http://info.sjc.ox.ac.uk/forests/

35 See the chapter by Judith A. Green entitled 'Forests' in *VCH*, ii, pp. 167–87.

36 Stubbs, *Select Charters*, p. 119 (Henry I), p. 143 (Stephen), p. 186 (Henry II).

No complete official text survives, so William Stubbs combined the various clauses mentioned by different copyists.[37] It included restrictions on the use of bows and arrows, dogs and greyhounds as well as on the giving or selling of anything from the forest which could cause destruction or wasting of the woodland. Where the forest area included a landowner's own woodland, then a forester or warden was to be appointed to protect the hunting area. The assize refers to a 'visitation', the procedure later known as the 'regard', whereby the county sheriff would appoint twelve knights in the forests within his county to hold regular inspections, and report on offences. Assarts – which means the grubbing up and ploughing of woodland, purprestures and wastes (the destruction of trees) – were to be registered. All men over twelve years of age were to swear an oath to protect the forest for hunting. Dogs were to be 'lawed', that is partially disabled. Tanners and bleachers of leather were not allowed to live within the forest. Hunting at night was prohibited on pain of imprisonment for a year. There were to be no living or dead obstructions to the king's beasts. It was this legislation that the Black Prince's officials were to impose in the Cheshire forests in 1347, 1351 and 1357.

Magna Carta of 1215[38] and the subsequent Forest Charter of 1217,[39] issued by Henry III, became part of the law of the land cited in courts of law and appealed to in disputes over rights. The first part of the Forest Charter set out the extent of the forest, and returned it to the area it had occupied at the time of Henry II's coronation (1154). It also made a clean slate by exempting people from fines for purprestures, wastes and assarts during the period from 1154 to 1217. Regards were to be held every three years, were to include an inquiry into dogs that had not been lawed, and a 3s. 0d. fine was to be imposed on those guilty of this. The twelve regarders were to decide on the number of foresters. In addition, attachment courts were to be held every 42 days to consider those cases of 'trespasses' (offences) against the venison and the vert, which the foresters and verderers had recorded on their rolls. Another meeting, called a 'swanimote' was to be held three times a year to consider agistments (the pasturing of animals) and pannage (the same for pigs). Early in the fourteenth century the attachment court was expanded by including regarders, agisters and a jury of principal freeholders and given the name 'swanmote' (spelt without the'i'). In 1351 the Black Prince ordered pleas of swanmote to be held every three weeks in the Cheshire forests, and thereafter the trespasses committed in the forests were to be referred to the justiciar at the next county court, something that had not happened previously.[40]

The Forest Charter also reduced in severity the punishments imposed by the 1184 assize. For example venison offences were to be commuted from loss of life or limb to imprisonment or fines, but non-payment of a fine would result in imprisonment for a year and a day. Some restrictions were to be relaxed. All free men were now able agist their own woods at will and have pannage. Also they were allowed to have a

37 Stubbs, *Select Charters*, p. 186.

38 Stubbs, *Select Charters*, p. 291–300.

39 Stubbs, *Select Charters*, p. 344–348.

40 *B.P.R.*, iii, 25.

mill, fishpond, dam or marlpit on their own land without fear of prosecution as long as it did not harm a neighbour. Free men could keep any hawk's eyrie or honey found in their woods. Archbishops, bishops, earls or barons travelling through the forest might take one or two beasts 'in the view' (under the supervision) of a forester, or in his absence blow a horn to inform people of their presence.

The Cheshire forests were always forests of the earls of Chester, and even when the earldom was in the king's hands they were administered separately from the royal forests of England. The full force and extent of the forest law, including both the assize of 1184 and the forest charter of 1217, were probably never imposed in the county before the mid fourteenth century. After all, Cheshire had its own forest legislation. Shortly after the grant of Magna Carta, Ranulf III, earl of Chester, issued his own 'Great Charter'(**7.9**) – contemporaries called it 'the common charter of Cheshire' – to the people of the county, which permitted them the freedom to assart and cultivate without penalty those lands which had previously been cultivated, as long as no new buildings were put up. Also men were allowed to take housebote and haybote (wood for building and making hedges) without the view of a forester, as well as to give and sell their dead wood to whomever they wished.[41]

The events leading up to 1215 had made it clear that the exercise of forest jurisdiction by the king was a matter of strong resentment, and could become an important political issue. In 1301, after some pressure from the nobility, Edward I was forced to confirm both Magna Carta and the 1217 Charter of the Forest.[42] It should not be surprising, therefore, that when the Black Prince's government decided to tighten up the forest administration in Cheshire with a comprehensive ordinance in March 1351, and impose the full rigour of English forest legislation, considerable opposition was encountered. No longer were the forest tenants in Wirral or Delamere-Mondrum to be allowed to keep unlawed dogs, or to hunt hare, fox and other vermin. In fact, the Wirral claim to be allowed to do at least some of these things this appears to have been specious, since a court to try those who kept unlawed dogs in that forest was held in 1311.[43] The new rules specified that they could dig peat and cut heath and gorse, but only alongside fields and then under the supervision of a forester. The taking of estovers (mostly timber and other types of wood from their own woods) was to be limited to the period between 2 February and 31 May. The carrying of bows was to be restricted to the highway and then only with the cord removed.[44] Pigs were to go into the forests at the time of pannage, and not at all between 1 June and 31 July. These measures caused unrest and many people refused to pay the fines imposed on unlawed dogs and for digging peat and taking gorse on their own soil. Eventually the community of Wirral offered the prince 100 marks in lieu of the amercements (small fines), excluding the non-lawing of dogs. This was rejected and they had to pay a £300 fine over 5 years or remain in prison.[45] Also some Wirral

41 For the claims of the inhabitants of the three forests in 1351, see *B.P.R.*, iii, pp. 24–25.
42 Stubbs, *Select Charters*, p. 490.
43 TNA CHES 29/24 mm. 5, 5d.
44 *B.P.R.*, iii, 15–16.
45 *B.P.R.*, iii, 27–30.

men objected to the making of certain customary payments, known as 'puture' to the master forester, William Stanley.

The administration of forest law in England was carried out by various officials and courts, although not all were applicable to the three Cheshire forests.[46] The officials ordered to attend the 1357 Cheshire forest eyre included foresters, riding foresters, verderers, regarders, and agisters. (**1.5, 3.5, 5.5**) All these were recorded as being present in the Macclesfield forest, but there is no evidence that there had been either verderers or agisters in the Wirral forest in the past.

Some foresters held their office 'in fee' that is by inheritance. In 1361 William Stanley the younger, master forester of Wirral, claimed that he had inherited the bailiwick of the forestership of Wirral forest from his ancestor Alan Silvester, who had been granted it by Ranulf II, earl of Chester.[47] The office had one third of the manor of Storeton attached to it, and had significant franchises and profits pertaining to it. They included 'puture' (**2.11**) , or payment in lieu of hospitality, food and drink for his six underforesters, as well as a reasonable payment for 'escapes' (straying of an animal), certain parts of deer found dead or wounded as well as 'pelf' (confiscation of animals, corn and cloth, when venison had been found in a house). Also as the sign of his office he held a horn, which still survives in the ownership of the Baring family. (See the picture on dust wrapper.) The under foresters were appointed by Stanley, the riding forester by the earl of Chester.

Twelve regarders, who were supposed in theory to be of knightly rank, were to hold a regard and inspect the forest every three years. They were to answer a list of questions (the 'chapters of the regard'), which included: when had assarts been made, how large were they and how often had they produced a crop? Also they had to declare whether any woodland been destroyed or obstacles been made or built to the harm of the beasts. Inquiry was also to be made into whether anyone kept weapons or dogs which could do harm to the king's deer. Details of the regard were to be submitted at the next forest court. In the Wirral forest eyre in membranes 4d to 9d, the regard of 1357 was 'made and presented to (the justices) on 22 September 1357'. **1.88.)**[48]

Part of the plan envisaged by the 1351 forest ordinance would have entailed the appointment of agisters in Wirral forest for the first time. Their job was to collect money to allow tenants in the forest to pasture their cattle and pigs at certain times. They were to attend the swanmote meetings which met three times a year, and again these were new to Wirral. One was supposed to be held a fortnight before Michaelmas (29 September) to arrange the pasturing of pigs. The next was about a fortnight before midsummer (21 June) to collect pannage and the third at the time of fawning of the beasts, when the forest was closed.[49] The other new office to be imposed on the Cheshire forests was that of verderer. They were either knights or important landed gentry. Their main task was to attend forest courts.[50]

46 Turner, *Select Pleas*, pp. xvi–xxvi.
47 *B.P.R.*, iii, 430.
48 See above, p. xx.
49 Turner, *Select Pleas*, pp. xxvii–xxx.
50 Turner, *Select Pleas*, pp. xix–xx; *B.P.R.*, iii, p. 26.

Although a common fine of £1,000 for the Wirral forest was agreed to be paid over a five year term, the 1357 forest eyre does provide an insight into the penalties normally inflicted for forest transgressions. In the eleventh and twelfth centuries the killing or wounding of a beast of the forest, especially a deer, could in theory result in the offender losing life or limb. By the thirteenth century this had been commuted to a fine or possibly imprisonment. Even at the time of the 1357 forest eyre, there was a reluctance to report a dead or wounded deer, the corpse of which had to be taken to Chester Castle and an inquest held. A person or even a township could be convicted and fined. Some people were released from prison after negotiating a fine (10s. or 20s.) for the offence. Fines were also levied for damage to the woodland, particularly the removal of oak trees. The stump of any tree taken at the request of the prince had to be marked to show this fact. In the Wirral eyre the fines imposed were for taking green twigs or branches (4d. to 8d.), an oak tree (1s.), or wasting of woodland (100s.). Animals pasturing at the wrong time or place were impounded and released on payment of a fine, for example 3d. for each pig. The fines for assarts in Wirral were calculated on the cumulative value of the crops over the years since the land had been taken into cultivation, that is 12d. per acre per year for crops such as corn and rye or for grass mown; and 6d. per acre per year where oats, barley, peas were grown or which was used for pasture. Fines for purprestures were 40d. for a cottage or messuage (a house), half a mark (6s. 8d.) for a building with a value of 1s. a year, 40s. for a windmill with half a mark a year value and 40d. for a sheep-fold and 6d. a year value. Unless replevied (bailed out) all the constructions were, in theory, to be removed and the marl pits to be filled in at the expense of the offender. Despite the consistent wording throughout the document, it seems most unlikely that any offending purprestures were actually removed.

Despite complaints, the £1,000 common fine for Wirral forest was nearly paid at the expiration of the 5-year term and the remaining debt pardoned.[51] The main transgressor was Henry, duke of Lancaster, whose fines from assarts, obstacles etc. amounted to about twenty per cent of approximately £1,700 assessed for Wirral forest at the regard. He was pardoned from paying any of it, presumably because of his close connections with the Black Prince and that sum redistributed among the rest of the community.[52] The duke was not only the cousin of the Black Prince but also a commander of the king's forces in Gascony.

51 *B.P.R.*, iii, 458.
52 *B.P.R.*, iii, 389.

IV. THE FOREST AND THE LANDSCAPE OF WIRRAL

In the medieval period the term forest did not necessarily denote a tree-covered area, as it does today. Then a forest was an area set aside as a sanctuary for deer to range freely and where they could be hunted for the royal table, or for the tables of those, such as the earls of Chester, who were privileged to have forests of their own. It was also an area in which people lived and continued with day to day life, notably feeding and housing themselves. It is probable that the king himself hunted in only a small number of the royal forests but that he ordered deer to be sent from the forests for special occasions. The need to nurture game for the benefit of the hunters, by preserving the natural habitat, and the need of the inhabitants to continue with their day to day lives created an inevitable tension. The removal of woodland and the assarting of land to increase agricultural production, as well as the construction of buildings and the digging of marl pits, all contributed to the destruction of the natural environment. Forest officials monitored developments within the forest and at the time of an eyre were able to present all the offences that had taken place within the forest. Any development in the forest which damaged the natural habitat was subject to a fine.

The Wirral section of the Cheshire Forest Eyre Roll of 1357 gives much information concerning the landscape and agriculture of the medieval period in an area of the country for which there is relatively little documentary evidence of land use, and for which existing methods for investigating the landscape, such as aerial photography and field walking, are difficult to use because of the nature of the soil and the current land use.

Wirral hundred is situated on a peninsula lying between the rivers Dee and Mersey. The topography is dominated by north-south ridges formed by outcrops of Permo-Triassic sandstone. Elsewhere the solid geology is concealed by glacial till (boulder clay) (maps 1a and b). The map does not represent Wirral in the medieval period in detail as there have been subsequent alterations to the coastline. Canalization and reclamation of marsh at the south west of Wirral from the early eighteenth century onwards have increased the area of land in that region, and the River Dee has silted up along its banks near Neston and Parkgate. The coastline on the north of the peninsula has been protected by the construction of the Wallasey Embankment. Drainage ditches have been extended in the low-lying areas of Bidston Moss and Wallasey Pool, and on the east, the Manchester Ship Canal has been built. Most of the Wirral soil is glacial tills with outcrops of sandstone bedrock. The exception to this is on the northern coastal region where there is alluvium and recent blown sand.

The eyre roll lists the offences against the vert and those against the venison. The offences against the vert were concerned with the protection of the trees within the forest and those of the venison were for the protection of the game. The pleas for

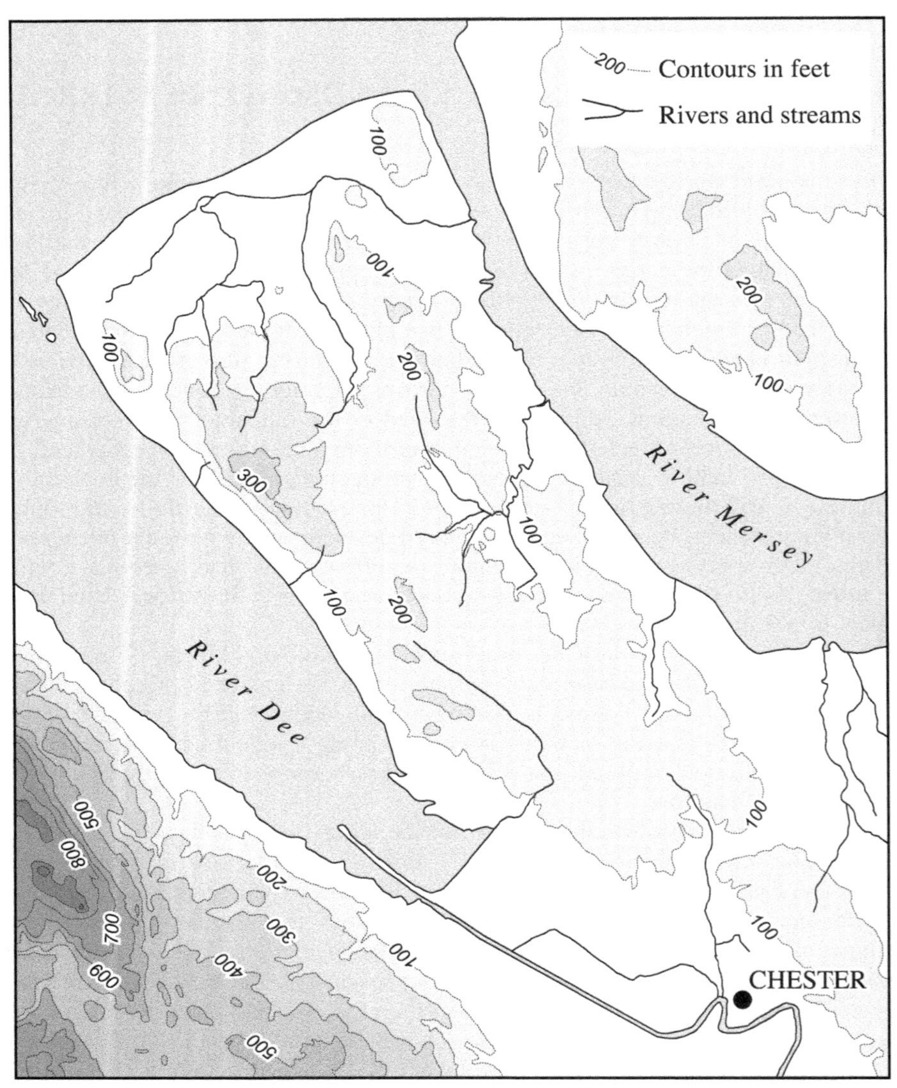

Map 1a *Relief and drainage*

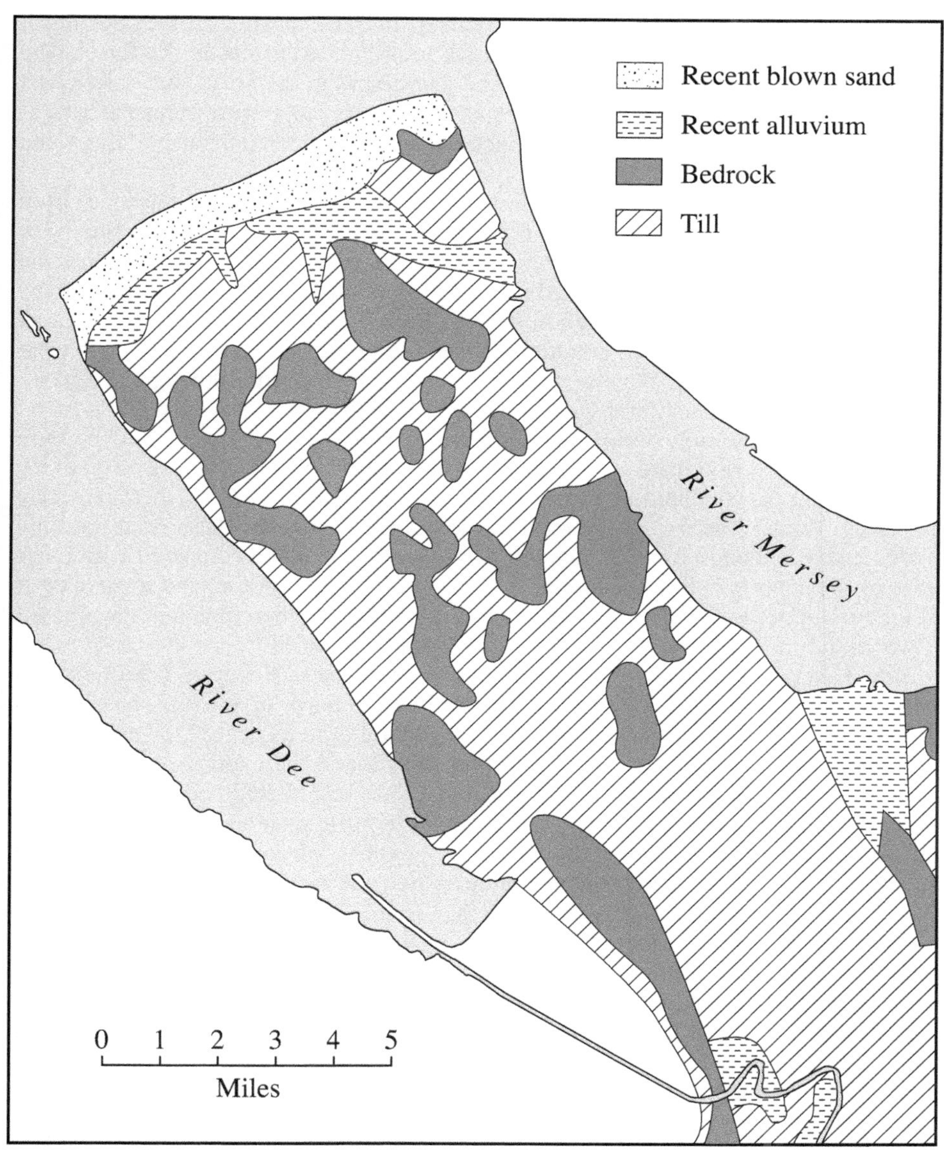

Map 1b *Drift geology*

offences against the vert therefore list any damage to trees, to whoever they belonged, throughout the period and seizure of livestock in prohibited places in the forest. The offences against the venison list all the dead deer found in the area. This is followed by the regard of the forest which itemises all the assarts and purprestures (encroachments) within the forest and includes such things as the erection of buildings and digging of marl pits.

The offences against the vert recorded in the eyre roll cover a period from December 1346 to June 1357. Earlier offences were recorded in the 1347 eyre.[53] For many offences the specific date on which they occurred is given, indicating that the forest officers must have kept detailed records of these offences. Most of the locations were described as 'woods' although in Pensby the reference was to a 'grove'. Some of the woods were called 'greve', an alternate spelling to grove,[54] and three woods were named in places now lost, Wooton, Grescowe and Greves woods, although Dodgson[55] places Wooton in Bidston, and Greves wood in Puddington.

In Domesday the only wood mentioned in Wirral was in Prenton, but the eyre indicates that the woodland was more widespread in 1357 and so it is very likely that the extent of woodland in Wirral was under-recorded in 1086 by the Domesday surveyors. Wirral was one of the most densely settled areas in Cheshire at the time of Domesday, although it was comparatively sparsely populated compared with other areas of the country.[56] It is unlikely that there was pressure on the land to develop it all for agriculture in the eleventh century and it is probable, therefore, that the amount of woodland in Wirral 1086 was greater than that mentioned.

Map 2 shows the townships with woodland mentioned in the eyre. They lie along the estuaries of the rivers Mersey and Dee and on the north of Wirral. There are no references to woodland in the extreme north of Wirral or in its central townships. The difference in soil type on the northern tip of Wirral and the exposure to wind may account for the lack of woodland in that area. The lack of references to woodland in the central belt of Wirral cannot be explained by difference in soil type, although the land in this area is poorly drained. It is possible, of course, that no offences against the vert were committed (or at least detected) in these townships. There was obviously a significant population in this area because a substantial amount of assarting is recorded as having taken place in these townships. Therefore it would seem probable that, if there had been woodland, offences against the vert would have occurred. Either there was no woodland in these townships because the natural vegetation was lowland heath or because it had been destroyed prior to the eyre. It is not likely that the recording of offences against the vert was curtailed, as happened later in the document with the regard when the common fine was agreed, since this section of the eyre roll continues without interruption in the manuscript.

53 TNA CHES 33/4.

54 A.H. Smith, *Place-Name Elements*, pp. 207–8.

55 J.McN. Dodgson, *The Place Names of Cheshire, Part IV*, Cambridge University Press (1972), pp. 310, 215.

56 Phillips, A.D.M. and Phillips, C.B., *A New Historical Atlas, of Cheshire* (2002) Cheshire County Council, p. 28.

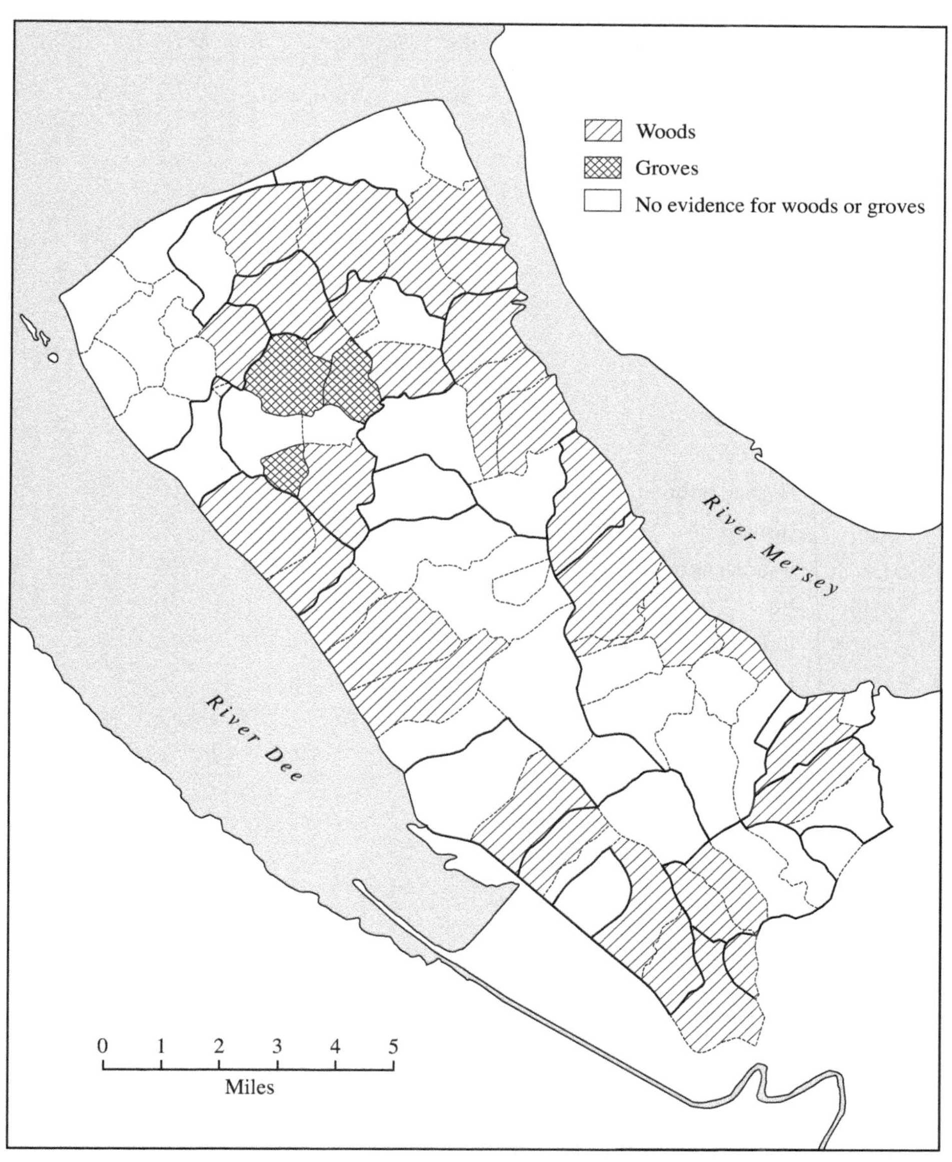

Map 2 *Townships with woods*

	Green oaks	*Saplings*	*Branches*
Arrowegreve	2		
Barnston	2		
Bebington	6		
Bidston	17		+
Birkenhead	4	10	
Bromborough	3		
Eastham	118		+
Gayton	5		
Greasby	4		
Grestowe	7		
Greves	3		
Higher Bebington	3		
Hooton	3		
Landicangreve	2		
Lea	3		
Leighton	9		+
Little Neston	2		
Lower Bebington	15		1
Mollington	2		1
Netherpool	3		
Pensby grove		3	
Puddington	3		
Saughall	12		10+
Saughall and Lea	6		
Stanney	1		
Tranmere	24		2
Woodchurch	2	3	8+
Wootton	4		

+ Indicates branches taken, but the number is not given.

Table 1 *Types of wood removed from each township*

Table 1 shows the amount of the different sorts of timber mentioned in the pleas, and the woods from which they were taken. Most offences involved the felling of green (living) oaks. There are fewer references to branches and saplings.

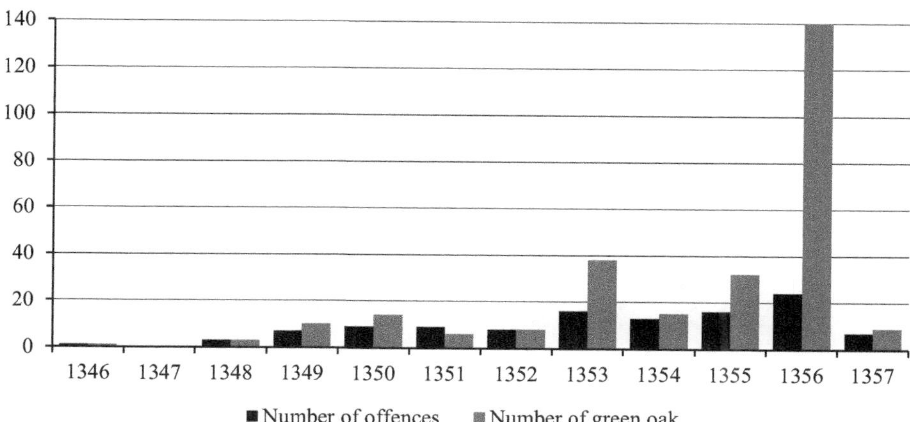

Graph 1 *Number offences against the vert and number of green oak felled each year*

Some of the entries mention the use to which the trees were put. On 21st April 1355, for example, six oaks and branches were taken from Eastham wood in Bromborough by the abbot of Chester to build a mill at Ince (**1.45**). William Stanley's servants took timber and withies from Prenton wood for their plough-teams (**1.58**). In 1352/3 bailiffs of the duke of Lancaster took a total of ten oaks from woods in Bidston and Birkenhead to build a mill in Bidston, and the timber from the old mill was sold (**1.41**). There also are references to oaks being given away (**1.45, 1.49, 1.50, 1.55**) so although the old wood was valued the fact that some oaks were given away suggests that there was still a reasonable amount of timber available. There is no mention of the use to which the branches were put. The saplings could have been used to transplant in other townships. One plea states that three oak saplings were taken from Pensby grove to Thurstaston, but no reason is given for this (**1.34**).

Graph 1 shows the number of offences for each year and the number of green oaks felled each year. There were very few between 1346 and 1348 but thereafter there was a slow increase. (The figures for 1357 are not for a full year and are not strictly comparable). The Black Death arrived in Cheshire in early summer 1349 but it appears that this did not greatly affect the number of offences against the vert. After 1349 there was only a small increase, which might well indicate a slow down in economic activity in the years leading up to the arrival of the Black Death.

Some offences involved the felling of more than one tree and therefore the number of trees felled is usually greater than the number of offences. Those offences involving branches were not included since the number of trees involved is not known. The very large number of trees cut down in 1356 included 103 green oaks felled in Eastham, Bromborough, Welondrys, Fysswhilhull and Lea (by Backford) in the woods by the abbot of Chester's men (**1.45**). This is by far the largest number of

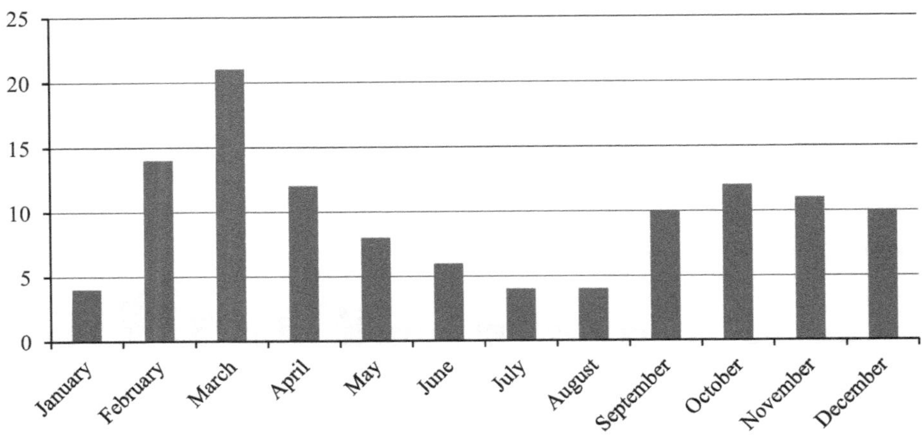

Graph 2 *Number of offences against the vert each month, 1346/47*

trees felled at any one time. The names Welondrys and Fysswhilhull woods are now lost but must have been on the abbot of Chester's land. These numbers suggest that there were large woods in some parts of Wirral. The use to which the timber was put is not recorded, but the scale of the felling suggests that the timber was either for a major building project associated with the abbey, or for sale. The most trees felled in any other offence was sixteen, but usually only one or two oaks were involved, probably for more modest building projects.

Graph 2 shows the months in which the offences against the vert took place. The autumn and the spring were the times of year when most tree work was done. These would have been the periods when there was sufficient time to attend to the woods and when building projects were most likely to have been carried out. In summer there would have been a lot of work in the fields. In January, another low point, the weather probably hindered work felling trees.

Map 3 shows those townships where woods were wasted, damaged or destroyed. There are two entries each for Leighton (**1.52, 1.126**), Tranmere (**1.54, 1.218**) and Lower Bebington woods (**1.56, 1.225**). Leighton wood was destroyed and damaged between 1346 and 1355, and further wasted of oaks and loss of underwood to the value of 40s. Tranmere wood was said to have been wasted and damaged between 1346 and 1355, and Lower Bebington wood was destroyed (undated). Further pleas state that a wood was wasted in Tranmere (undated) and that a waste was made in the wood in Lower Bebington to the value of 40s. Three acres of Prenton wood were wasted and destroyed (**1.121**) and a wood in Leighton wasted of oaks (**1.126**); Blacon wood was pruned of high branches and enclosed (**1.190**).

There is some difficulty in interpreting the meaning of the word 'destroyed'. It does not seem to indicate the complete destruction of the wood. In 1356, a year after Leighton wood was said to have been damaged and destroyed, John Leighton gave

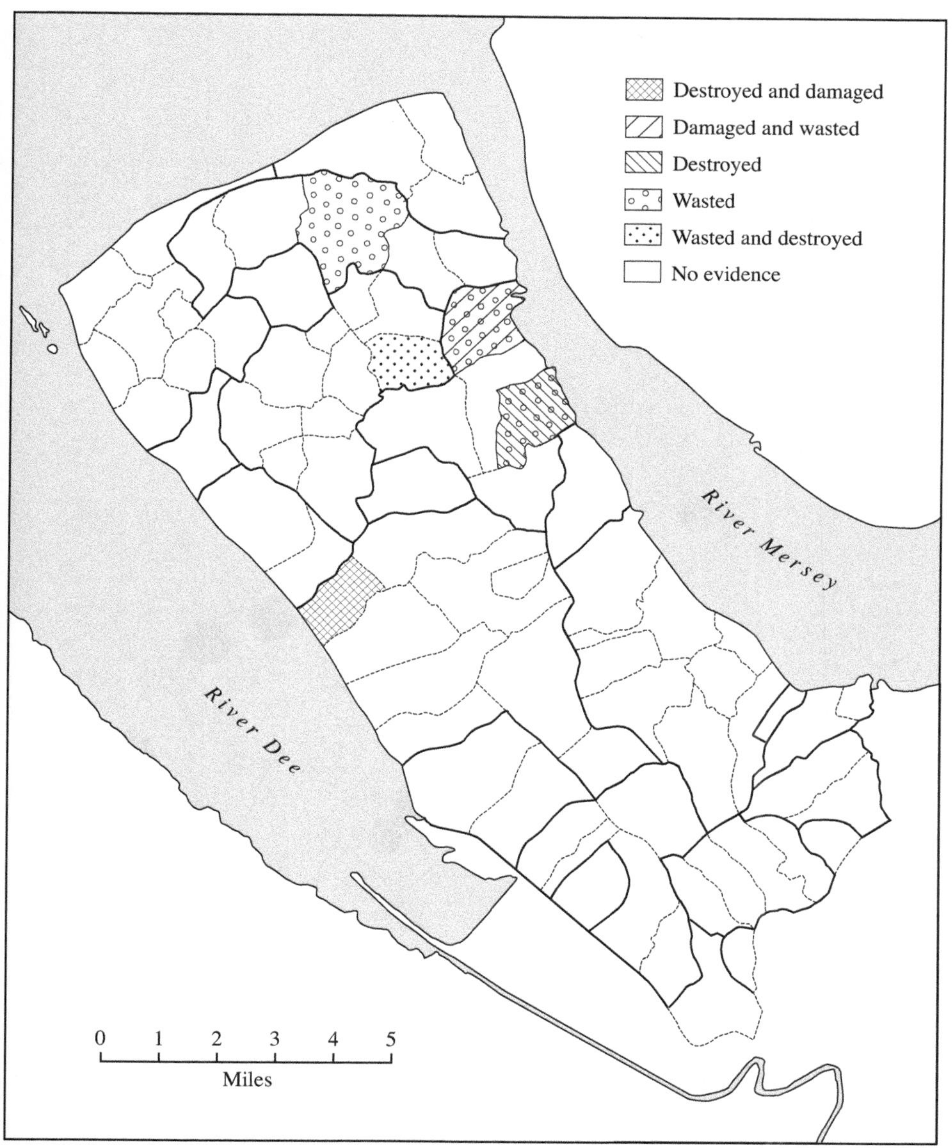

Map 3 *Townships where woodland was damaged*

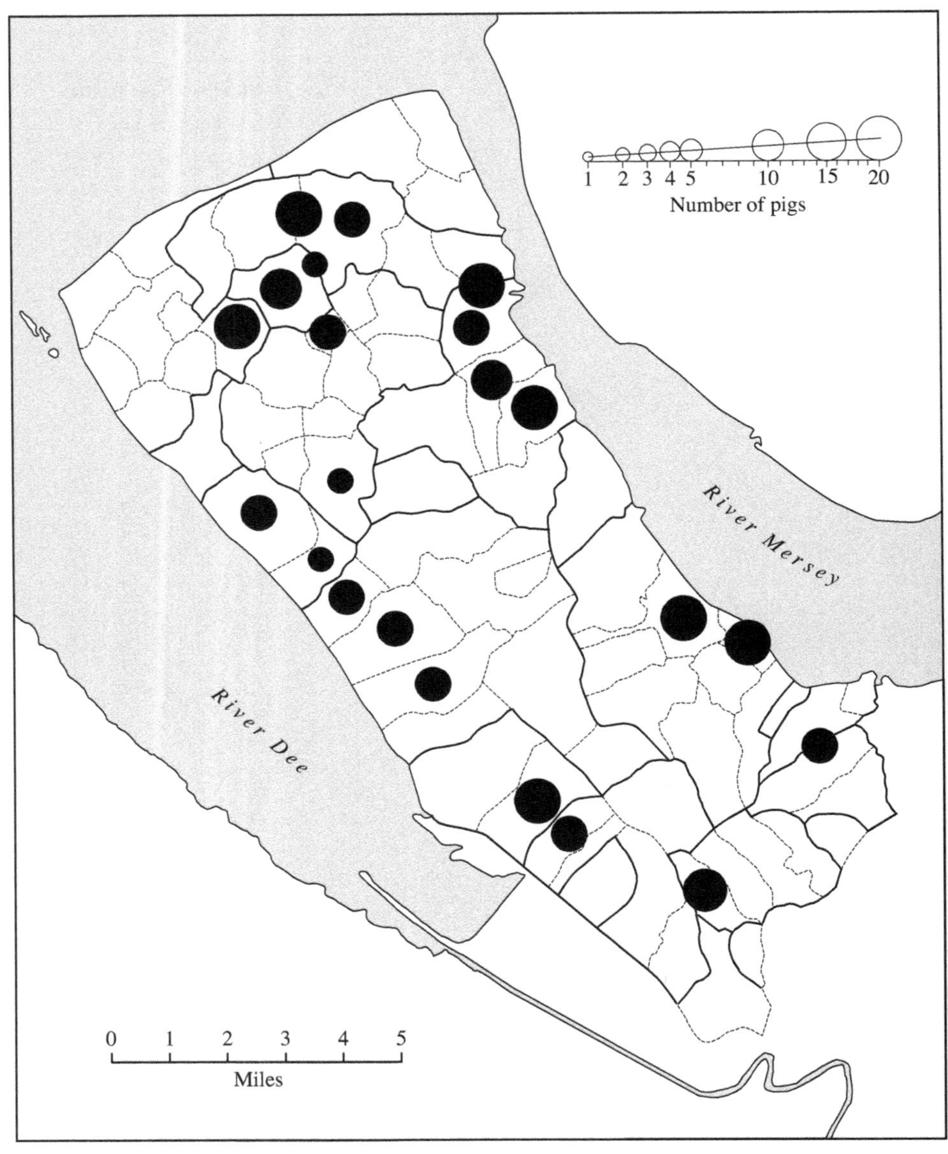

Map 4 *Number of pigs seized in woods*

oaks from the wood to two people and also sold an oak to Neston parish (**1.50**). Therefore there must have been a reasonable number trees remaining in the wood for the trees to be given away. There must be a difference, therefore, between the 'damage and destruction' of wood and the felling of oaks. The destruction and damage of woods may refer to the unjustifiable felling of trees but not the actual assarting of land because this would then be included in the regard.

The pleas of vert also include a list of livestock seized in prohibited places. The only livestock recorded was pigs and map 4 shows the number of pigs in each wood mentioned. Figures on the boundaries of two townships indicate that the pigs were found in the woods of both townships. It has been suggested that the number of pigs in a wood does not reflect the size of the wood in Domesday and this may also have been true for the time of the eyre. It does demonstrate, though, that pannage was still in operation in Wirral into the fourteenth century, although it is not an area where pannage was thought to be important. There are two other references to livestock in the eyre. One, an indirect reference, stated that the abbot of Basingwerk built a sheepfold in Thurstaston (**1.145**). The other concerned the goats of the duke of Lancaster which were not allowed pasture in his woods in Saughall Massie (**2.45**). Obviously livestock itself was not an important factor in the Wirral eyre.

The overall impression gained from the pleas of the vert is that oak trees and branches were felled and the saplings dug up mostly on a relatively small scale to provide for the needs of the local population. However, a large landowner, such as the abbot of Chester, harvested the trees in his woods on a larger scale to be used in places outside the immediate township. Some of the woods must have been of a considerable size to enable large numbers of trees to be felled and it appears that trees cannot have been in very short supply, since some were given away.

The pleas of venison (**1.75–1.84**) start with those concerning the game animals found dead in Wirral. There were seven bucks, five hinds (one with calves), and two does and four stags in the period between 1352 and 1357. Thus, in spite of the relatively high population in Wirral, there was sufficient cover for a reasonable number of deer. Two of the animals were drowned in the river Dee and one was drowned in Bidston moss. A stag was found in Wallasey Pool and a hind was found dead in a wide and deep turbary pit in Bidston. Deer commonly seek escape in water, and those animals may have drowned when fleeing hunters. Some of the other animals were wounded and others just found dead. One of the does was found suffocated by dogs and at first the people said they saw nothing, but later admitted seeing four people with dogs, who were responsible for the death.

A significant section of the eyre concerned the assarts made on the waste. They entailed the removal of trees and the ploughing up of land, and cover a period from 1297 to 1350. The record of the 1347 eyre does not appear to have influenced the 1357 regard. The assarts are all said to have taken place a number of years ago unlike the pleas for vert when the exact date the tree was felled is given. This reflects the nature of assarting since it obviously takes some time to clear land and bring it into cultivation. The number of assarts in each year is shown in Graph 3. The regularity with which the assarts are said to have taken place between 1297 and 1327, that is 60,

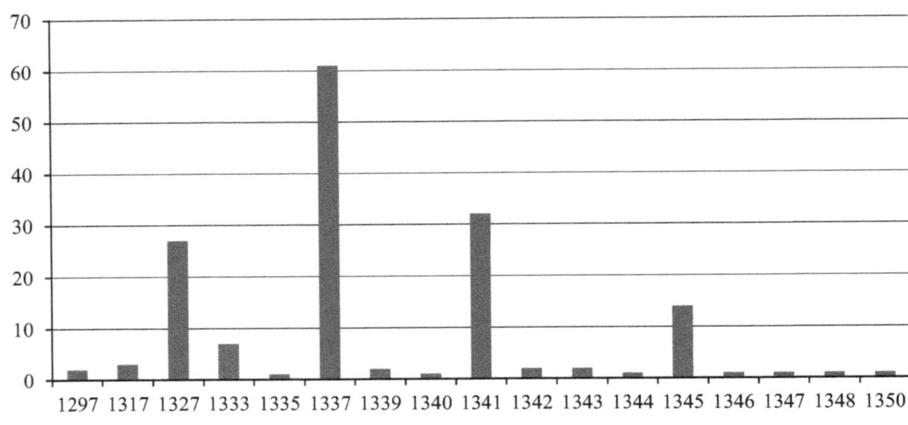

Graph 3 *Number of assarts in each year*

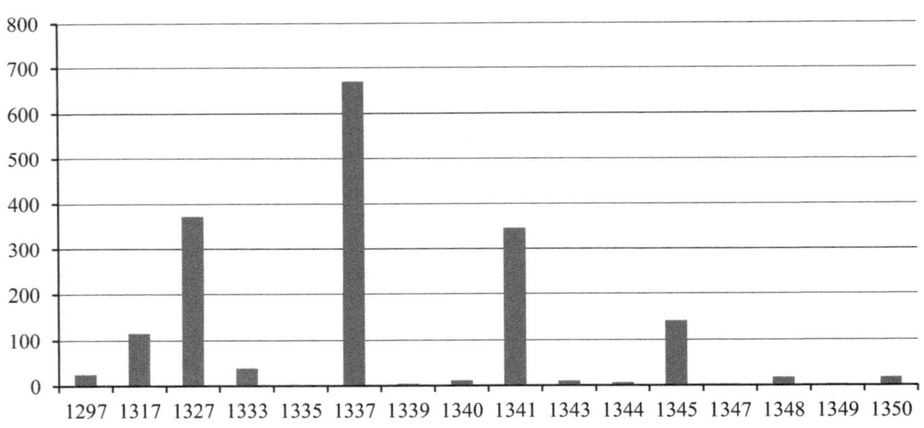

Graph 4 *Area of assarts each year*

40 and 30 years before, suggests that the years are only approximate. The intervals between assarts then become more frequent, namely 24, 22 (one instance) and 20 years before. After that the assarts occur yet more frequently.

Graph 4 shows the area assarted in various years. The area of land assarted correlates approximately to the number of assarts in any one year. Thus in years when there was a relatively small number of assarts the amount of land actually assarted was not great. 1337 was the year in which most assarting occurred but there was a reasonable amount of land assarted in the years 1317, 1327, 1341 and 1345, with relatively small areas assarted in other years. Some assarting even took place in 1350

Arrowe	14a 0r 28½p	Lower Bebington	38a 2r 37¼p
Backford	32a 1r 9p	Mollington	5a 3r 6p
Barnston	37a 2r 9½p	Mollington Torald	91a 2r 26½p
Bidston	318a 0r 22¾p	Moreton	4a 2r 2½p
Blacon	114a 2r 9p	Netherpool	10a 1r 22½p
Brimstage	60a 0r 0p	Newton	1a 0r 0p
Burton	5a 1r 16p	Oxton	23a 2r 38¾p
Caldy Grange	12a 3r 1¼p	Poulton cum Spital	72a 12½p
Capenhurst	149a 0r 0p	Prenton	40a 0r 0p
Church Shotwick	28a 1r 13p	Puddington including Greve	53a 3r 38½p
Claughton	84a 3r 6½p		
Frankby	5a 2r 8p	Raby	4a 3r 30p
Gayton	3a 3r 10½p	Saughall Massie	1a 0r 4p
Great Meols	42a 0r 0p	Stanney	33a 2r 37¼p
Great Neston	40a 0r 0p	Stoke	15a 1r 8p
Heswall	17a 0r 33¼p	Storeton	48a 1r 4p
Higher Bebington	32a 1r 24¼p	Thingwall	5a 2r 14p
Hooton	40a 2r 11 ½p	Thornton Maheu	98a 3r 0p
Landican	29a 0r 33¾p	Thurstaston	6a 3r 1 ¼p
Ledsham	120a 0r 1¾p	Tranmere	38a 1r 26¼p
Leighton	26a 0r 0p	Upton	42a 2r 35p
Little Meols	21a 1r 35p	Wallasey	56a 3r 11⅜p
Little Neston	9a 0r 35p	Woodbank	1a 0r 0p

Table 2 *Area of land assarted in each township*

the year after the Black Death arrived in Cheshire. Therefore the effect of the Black Death cannot have been universally devastating.

The land from which land was assarted was usually described as 'waste'. There were a few exceptions. In Bidston, 105 acres of moss were assarted and approved and enclosed by a hedge with a hey in a separate moss (**1.169**).

The townships where assarts took place are shown in map 5. The eyre concluded before the results of the regard had been fully entered in the eyre roll because the people of Wirral agreed to a common fine. Therefore in some of the townships where no assarts are recorded these are shown in the relevant maps as 'Townships not included in the regard because of agreement of common fine'. Table 2 shows the exact area assarted in each township. Most townships had some assarts

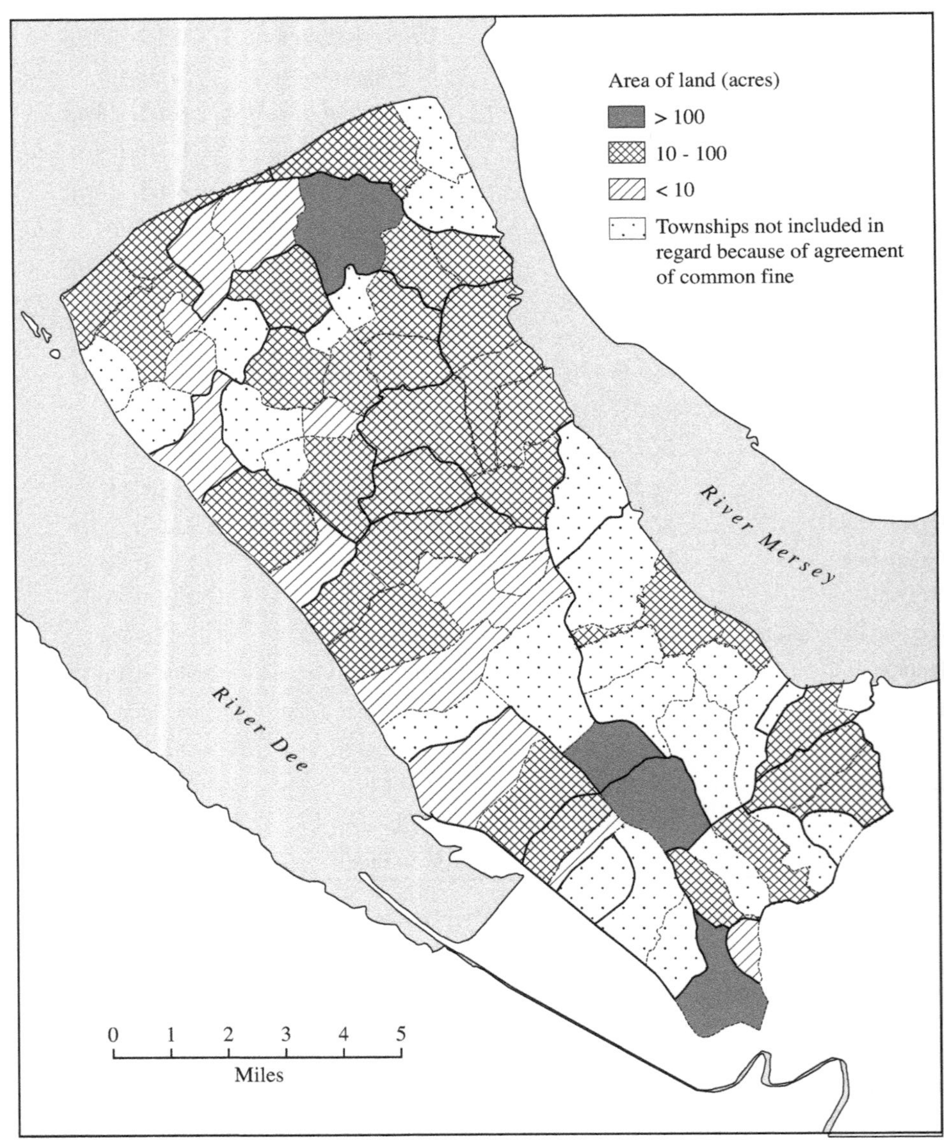

Map 5 *Area of land assarted*

although in some the area was small. The largest area of any one assart was 120 acres 13¾ perches in Ledsham in 1341 (**1.251**). In townships where fewer than ten acres were assarted it may be that there was little room left to increase the area under the plough. The distribution of the townships where small areas of land were assarted is spread throughout Wirral, and cannot be related to a particular soil type. Similarly those townships where there was a large area of land assarted are not related by soil type. A large area of Bidston, where over 300 acres was assarted, (**1.161–1.164**) is in a low-lying and damp region, and as a result was poor agricultural land, but the other townships where large assarts occurred were all on relatively good land.

As we have seen, the assarts in Wirral had been measured and recorded by Master John Burnham, the chamberlain of Chester, together with John de Assewell, chaplain, Robert de Houghton, Richard Stawer and William Bateman between 24th April and 26th May, 1357.[57] These were significant local officials, and the fact that they used measuring equipment indicates that an attempt was made to make accurate measurements of the land that had been ploughed up. There is some suggestion, though, that there may have been some compromise when reaching the figures. An example is the areas given for the assarts in Heswall. 8 acres 36⅝ perches is recorded as having been assarted there in 1327, and exactly same area in 1337 (**1.128, 1.129**). These are unusual figures which suggests that there was only an approximate idea of when the assarts took place and that agreement between the parties was reached to explain the facts. Similarly in Stanney 2½ acres 28 perches of land were assarted in both 1341 and 1343, which again suggests that there was some collaboration between the parties to reach an agreement (**1.247, 1.248**). This may have been the case in other townships but without such unusual figures it is not possible to identify them.

The land assarted was mainly for arable use. The fines were calculated on the basis of the number of years that each acre had borne crops, and there seems to have been some sort of rotation in operation because the fields did not yield crops every year. For example, those fields assarted 60 years before were said to have yielded crops only 40 times and those assarted 20 years ago yielded crops fourteen times. Therefore every third year the fields must have lain fallow. There is reference to crops sown in winter and in summer, but no direct evidence for the nature of the crops.

Most of the assarted arable land was valued at 12d. an acre but in Bidston, Little Meols, Church Shotwick and Poulton cum Spital some land was valued at only 6d an acre. The land in Bidston is valued at '6d. and not more because it is poor' (**1.168**). There is no reason given for the 6d. value in the other townships, but in the same plea concerning Poulton it mentions land near the moss so it may be that the land was in the same area and tended to be wet. Little Meols (now part of Hoylake) is situated on the northern edge of Wirral and it is probable that the sandy soil there was unfavourable for arable cultivation.

Some of the land was assarted for meadow and some for pasture. (In this eyre the term 'assart' is used to include land cleared or enclosed for any purpose, not only for

57 *ChAccl*, p. 242.

land cleared for arable cultivation). Meadow was a very important resource providing hay for the overwintering stock. It was mown each year and the land was valued at 12d. an acre. Map 6 shows the townships in which land for meadow and pasture was assarted. Most of the townships were in the north of Wirral. Generally the area of land assarted for meadow was less than ten acres, but a total of 44 acres 2 roods and 24 perches was assarted in Bidston in various parcels in 1337. It is probable that most townships were already using all available land for meadow by the time of the eyre because of its importance. The land assarted for use as pasture was in Little Meols (**1.144**), Great Meols (**1.146**) and Wallasey (**1.148–1.153**). These three townships are on the north coast of Wirral where there is light sandy soil and therefore the land use may have been different from the rest of the hundred. The pasture was valued at only 6d. an acre.

In Bidston 105 acres 24 perches of moss was assarted and approved in 1317 and ‘enclosed with a hay in a separate moss’ (**1.169**). The land was valued at 12d. an acre. Some, but not all, of the land was mown, and so presumably used as meadow. There is no suggestion that any of the land was used for arable cultivation and therefore the reason why it was all valued at 12d. an acre remains unclear. The ground seemed to be typical of mossland since there is reference to ditches in which many of the lord’s beasts drowned and so it would not seem to be ideal for arable use.

Associated with the arable farming were the marl pits. Marl is a form of calcareous clay which was used as a fertiliser and it occurs widely in Wirral. Pits were dug to extract the marl which was spread over the soil from time to time to improve fertility. They were of importance in the forest eyre because, as well as destroying the natural environment, they were a hazard to animals (and occasionally people) who drowned in them. They were usually ordered to be filled in, although it is unlikely that that actually happened. The marl pit in Calday Grange was surrounded by a stone wall (**1.140**) by the abbot of Basingwerk, which was against the assize of the forest.

Map 7 shows the number of marl pits in the townships in which they are mentioned. The places where they occur are spread throughout Wirral, on the central area as well as along the estuaries. The largest number of pits dug in any one township was the 20 in Poulton cum Spital. These were made in association with new assarts (**1.239**), and must have been dug to improve the newly cultivated soil. When compared with the map showing the area of assarts there is no close correlation between the number of marl pits dug and the area of land assarted. In Blacon over 100 acres of land was assarted and twelve marl pits were dug. Similarly in Ledsham over 100 acres was assarted but only six marl pits dug. In these townships it seems the people were intent on improving the soil. In Leighton and Capenhurst, however, other townships where over 100 acres of land was assarted, no marl pits were reported as having been dug. It seems that digging marl pits depended on the local conditions. Factors would be the fertility of the soil and the inclination of the landholder. Spreading marl involved a number of people and it was heavy and expensive work. If yields in the fields had been low then there would have been an incentive to apply marl. Landholders wishing to improve their land could then have organised the digging of marl pits. Where crop yields were adequate or where

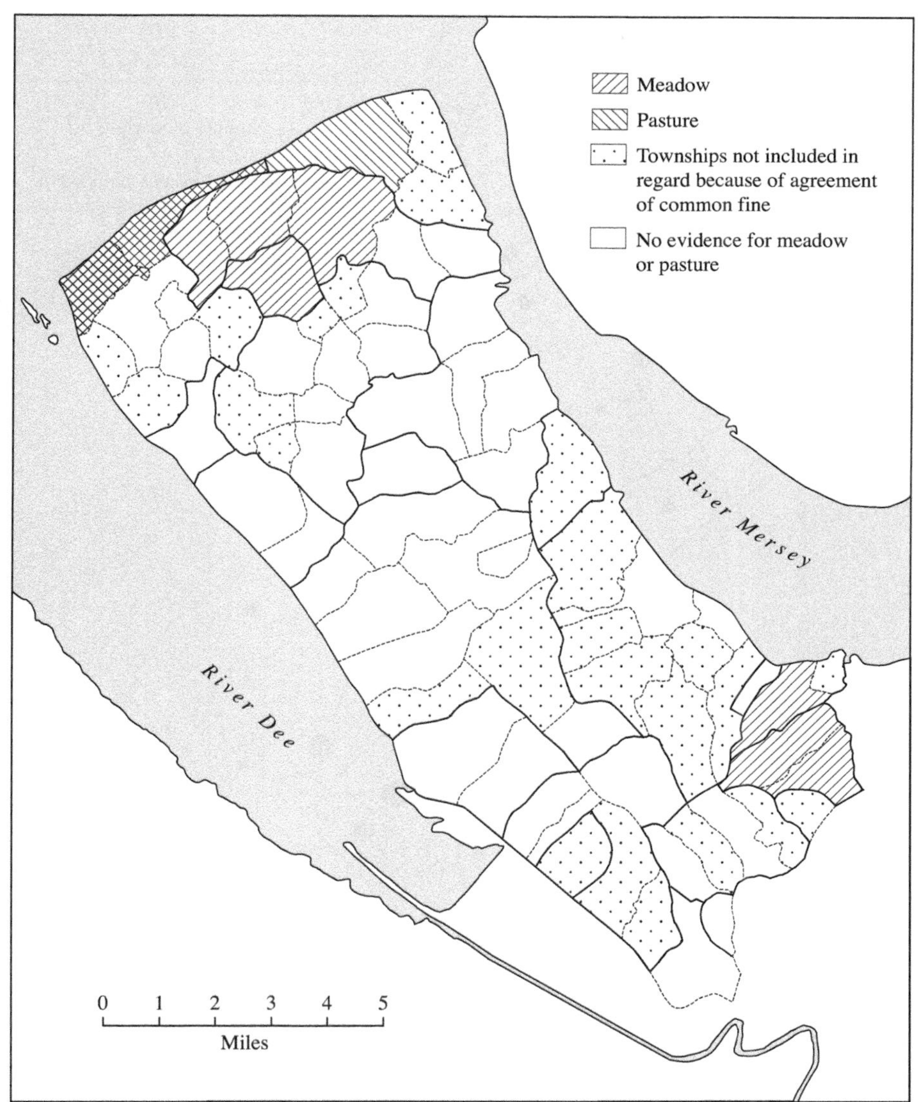

Map 6 *Townships where land was assarted for meadow and pasture*

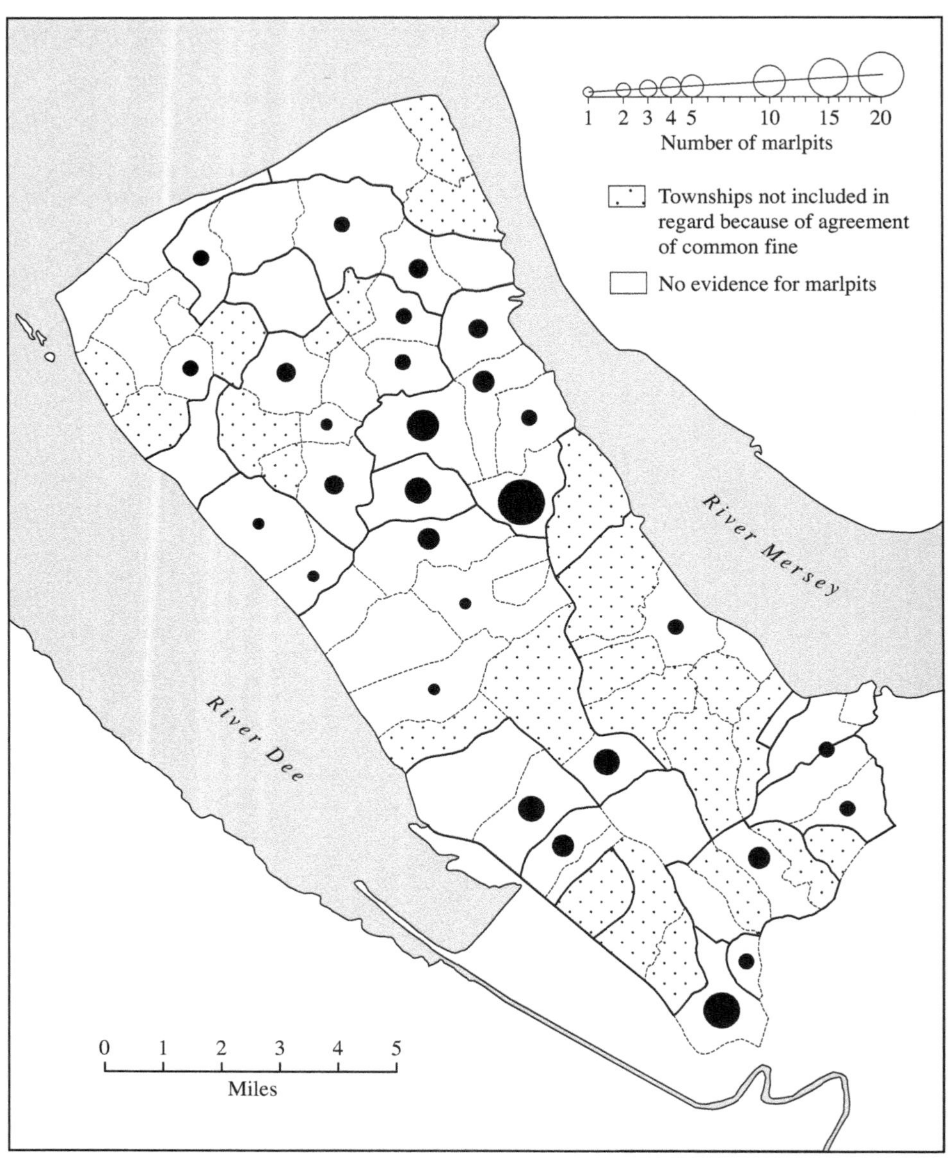

Map 7 *Number of marlpits in each township*

the landowners were not inclined to improve the soil then marl pits would not have been dug.

There is some information about newly-constructed buildings from the regard of the forest, since buildings also reduced the amount of land for the game and obstructed its movement. Map 8 shows the distribution of buildings mentioned. Thirteen windmills mentioned were built within the period of the eyre. Another four, one of two windmills mentioned in both Blacon and Hooton, one in Puddington and another in Poulton, were not recorded as newly-built but used as reference points in the roll for locating an area of assart. Only those windmills built during the period covered by the eyre were subject to a fine. In Bidston an old windmill was replaced in 1352–3. The mills were scattered throughout Wirral. One was in Newton-cum-Larton, which, at less than 500 statute acres, was one of the smallest townships in the Wirral. This implies that most places would have had at least one mill.

The dwellings built were usually described as houses, messuages or cottages. An exception was the newly-built manor-house of Blacon which contained a number of buildings (**1.189**). Two messuages were also built there, a large area of land was asserted, and twelve marl pits dug. This indicates that a significant amount of development was taking place in here. The landholder in Blacon was William Trussell, who was apparently putting a great deal of work into enlarging and improving his holding. Capenhurst was another township where there was a large amount of assarting and where sixteen buildings and a windmill were erected. There were two landholders in this township, Thomas de Capenhurst and Robert de Pulle, both involved in the development.

The claims section of the eyre roll refers, inter alia, to heath and moss in many townships (Map 9). These claims related to the right to dig peat, to cut turves and to take gorse, fern and heather. From the map it can be seen that many of the townships in Wirral had areas suitable for providing these requirements.

Using the field names given in some of the pleas it is interesting to look in detail at the areas where the assarts were taking place. For many townships this is not possible because there is insufficient information. For others, although a lot of names are given, unfortunately the fields cannot be identified from the nineenth-century tithe maps because there have been too many alterations in names over the period in question. One place where it has been possible to identify the areas where assarts were occurring is Bidston. As well as the tithe map dating from 1842[58] there is also a map of some parts of Bidston which is dated 1665.[59] This enables the continuity in field names, from 1357 until the tithe map, to be checked.

58 CRO EDT 47/2.
59 CRO D 4938/1.

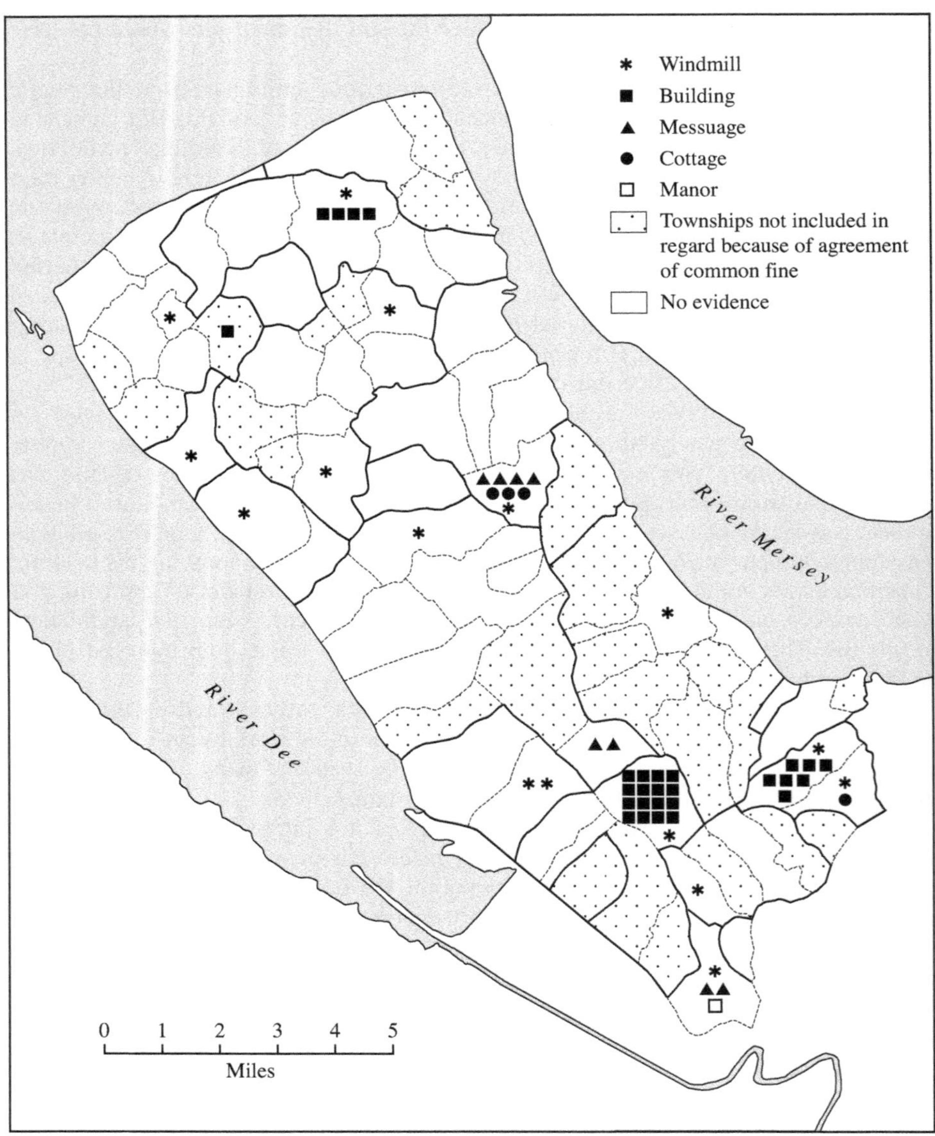

Map 8 *Townships where buildings of all types were recorded*

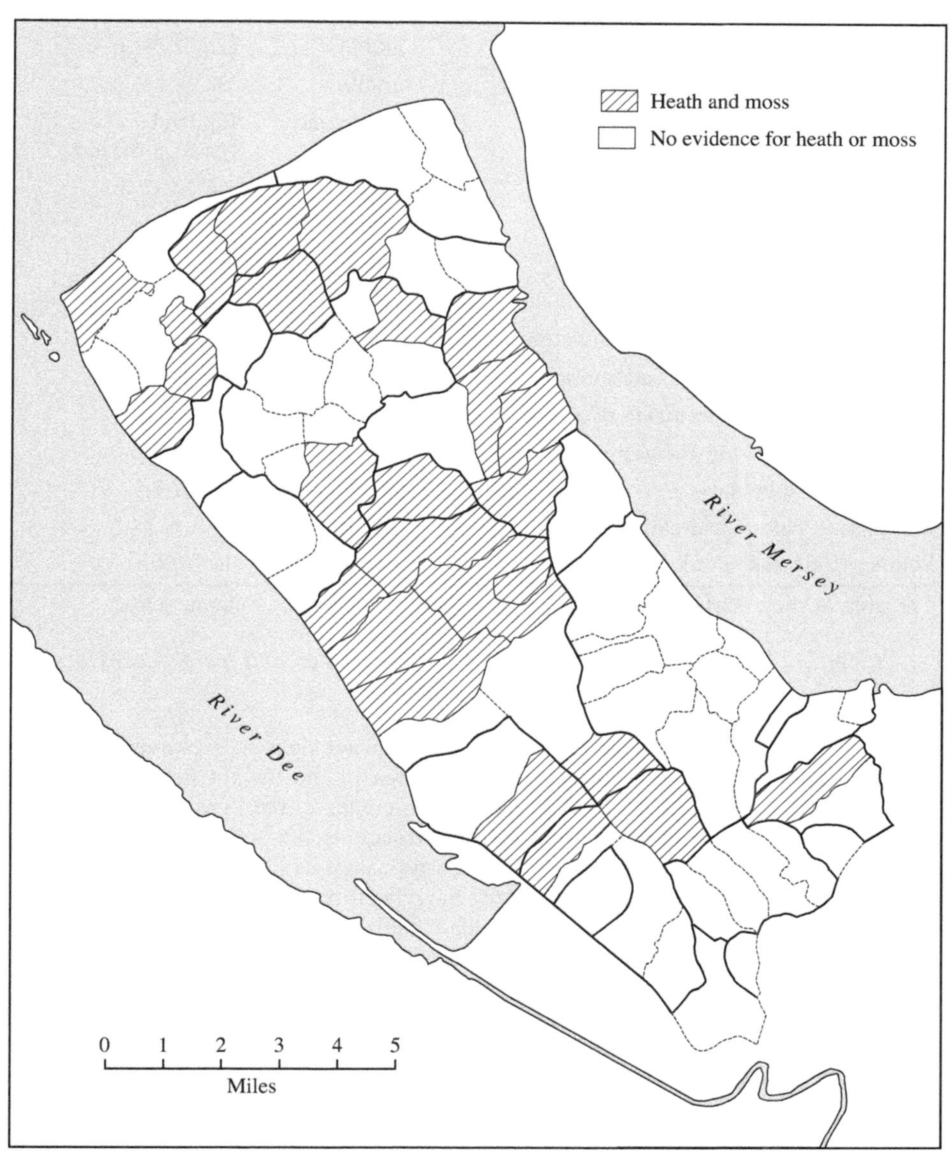

Map 9 *Townships with heath and moss*

Thwayt next to Newemedowe	arable	22a 3r 21½p
Newemedowe from the waste	arable	33a 1r 34¼p
Oldetwayt and Pykemedewe	arable and meadow	16a land 16a 8½p meadow
Parcel of land from waste [...]	arable	51a 3r 32¼p
Meadow next to bridge	meadow	3a 20p
Meadow next to moss towards Kirby	meadow	2r 10p
Northern side of above meadow	arable	7a 25 ½p
Holdefeld and a parcel below Wolleton wood	arable	11a 2r 19¾p
A moss and a hey in separate moss		105a 24p
Another moss on eastern side of a road		12a
Between le Forde and Bidston old wood	arable	12a 3r 8p
Between these bounds	arable	12a 3r 8p
Plot of land below field called Eskeby	arable	6a 21p
Southern side at le Forde	arable	4a 1r 30p

The area of the assarted land is in Cheshire acres, which is 2.12 statute acres.

Table 3 *The land assarted by the duke of Lancaster and his predecessors from 1337*

In 1337 one parcel of land, described as a thwayt next to Newemwdowe, and another, called Oldtwayt, were assarted. The area of the thwayt fields next to the new meadow is given as 22 acres 3 roods 21½ perches in the eyre and 34 a 2 r 1 p on the 1665 map. Therefore it is not possible to equate the actual fields on the two maps but the approximate location of the thwayt assart can be deduced. The thwayt land lying next to the Newemedowe must have been on the west side of the thwayt fields where the tithe map shows four fields called New Meadow.

The Oldetwayt fields measured sixteen acres in 1357. They are associated with the Pyke medewe in the eyre. On the 1665 map there is a field called Great Thwaite to the east of the Pyke medewe measuring 12 a 3 r 5 p. Two Great Thwaite fields in the same position on the tithe map measured 31a 1r 7p (statute). This is approximately fifteen Cheshire acres. Therefore it is possible that the Great Thwaite field is the location of the old Thwaite field. The name thwayt is of interest because it is derives from the old Scandinavian meaning 'clearing',[60] and it is well-known that there were Viking settlements in Wirral from AD 902.[61] This could be the site of one of their settlements. It is curious that one of the thwaite fields was called 'old' since both the thwaite fields were assarted in 1337. It may be that the Old Thwaite was the area

60 Smith, *Place-Name Elements*, pp. 218–20.
61 Harding, *Viking*, p. 33.

of an actual Viking clearing and that it gave its name to the area of Bidston which included the Thwaite fields mentioned earlier.

The Newmeadow, called 'Wallasey New Meadow' on the 1665 map, lies on the west of the township. The area asserted in 1337 was 33 a 1 r 34¼ p. Wallasey New Meadow contained 29 a 14 p. The area of the four fields called New Meadow on the tithe map contained 65 a 2 r 27 p, which is approximately 30 Cheshire acres. This would seem to be a good representation of the Newmeadow assarted in 1357. The Pyke medewe assarted in 1357 contained 16 a 8½ p. On the tithe map the two fields called Pike meadow have a total of 18 a 2 r 27 p (statute measure). This is approximately 9 a (Cheshire measure). On the 1665 map the Pike meadow fields contain 8 a 3 r 18 p (Cheshire). It is possible that the two fields called Black meadow on the tithe map were also part of the area assarted in 1357 and called Pyke meadow since they are adjacent to the Pike meadow fields on the tithe map. The area of the Pike and Black meadow fields is approximately 16 acres (Cheshire) which is close to the area assarted.

The area of the moss assarted in Bidston was large. Some of the assarted moss was used for arable, some as meadow, and the use to which the remainder was put is not stated. Bidston moss is on the north east of the township and there are a number of fields with the 'moss' name which suggest the part of the township where the arable land was assarted. Again it is not possible to correlate the areas said to have been assarted in the eyre with the fields named moss on the tithe map, but an approximate area for the assarting activity can be suggested.

There is also a reference to Bidston Car (**1.48**). A number of people claimed in the eyre to have the right to dig peat in Bidston waste outside the covert (the wooded area), that is in Bidston Car. A carr is a boggy place and Bidston moss is the most likely place where such ground was to be found. It may have been a separate part of the moss or an alternate name for the moss. The moss was a large area, in the fourteenth century most probably larger than the area shown on the tithe map, and there could have been areas set aside for different activities.

Another parcel of land was assarted below Wolleton (Wooton) wood. The area of Wooton Hay is shown on the east of the township at the edge of Bidston Hill on both the 1665 and the tithe map. The land below Wooton Hay would have been on Bidston Moss. The assarted land was valued at only 6d. an acre a year rather than the usual 12d. because the land was 'poor'. This is further indication that the land was on the low-lying Bidston moss.

Entry **1.169** suggests that the assarting of the moss involved digging ditches as well as clearing trees and scrub because it is stated that many of the lord's beasts had drowned in the ditches. Drainage in the moss was obviously a problem. The tithe map shows that a large area remained unenclosed as late as the 1840s, much of which has now been used for landfill.

Many of the other assarts in Bidston are in the Ford area, that is the south of the township. It is more difficult to place the assarts in this area. The reasons are that field names are not given and features used to describe the location of the assarts in the eyre cannot easily be located. One parcel of land is described as lying between le Forde and Bidston old wood, between a hunting station and the bounds. There is an area on the 1665 map tithe map called 'Old Wood' to the north of Ford, so the land may lie between these places. The hunting station cannot be located but it may lie in an area which was emparked following a grant to Matthew Litherland and John Leyland in 1408.[62] The area emparked was 80 acres. The 1665 map shows a deer park in the centre of the township with an area of 74 a 3 r 21 p, which may be the area emparked in 1408. The field called Eskeby is identified by Dodgson as the Hesby fields.[63] Those fields are located in the township on the tithe map. In the 1665 map this area is part of the township which was enclosed as the Deer Park. If the Eskeby fields are the same as the 'Hesby' fields this assumes that the name of the area was retained throughout the time the area was a deer park. Another parcel of land on the southern side of Ford was assarted. There is very little land to the south of Ford so it is fairly easy to identify this area.

The pleas of the vert identify two woods in Bidston, namely 'Bidston Wood' and 'Wooton Wood'. There is also a reference to a wood in the regard of the forest **(1.176)** which was wasted of oaks, which was said to be 'in the same place'. From the context it appears that this wood was in the Ford area since the previous pleas all concern that part of the township. The location of Wooton wood can be deduced from the fields called 'Wooton Hey' on the tithe map. Bidston wood may have been located in the area of the old wood on the tithe map but this is not certain. It also seems probable that there was another wood in the Ford area.

Seventeen oaks as well as branches and twigs were taken from Bidston wood between 1350 and 1356. Wooton wood had four oaks taken between 1350 and 1353. Six of the oaks from Bidston wood and three of the same from Wooton wood, together with another oak from Birkenhead wood, were used for building a mill in the Thwaite in 1352/3. This was 16 years after the Thwayt fields had been assarted, but it replaced an existing mill, the timber from which was sold to Richard Hough **(1.41)**. Although Bidston wood seems to have been of a reasonable size, and trees were available in Wooton wood, it was necessary to get another oak from Birkenhead to build the mill, so the supply of suitable sized oaks must have been becoming restricted.

There are a number of other buildings in Bidston, besides the windmill, mentioned in the eyre. Three were erected on 'the waste outside the covert' and another built elsewhere in an unidentified location. All of these, in theory, had to be pulled down. The buildings on the waste had a ditch made there which formed an enclosure **(1.173)** possibly around them. It is interesting to note that, where appropriate, ditches were used to make enclosures. It suggests the north-west buildings were erected near to the moss on relatively wet ground.

From the information in the eyre roll and the use of the relevant maps it is possible to gain an impression of the area of Bidston where land was being brought into cultivation (Map 10). Most of the work was taking place in the region to the north west of Bidston village, which is sited in the centre of the township. There was some development in the south of the township in the Ford area. The Wooton wood was

62 Ormerod, *Cheshire*, p. 467.
63 Dodgson, *Place Names*, p. 311.

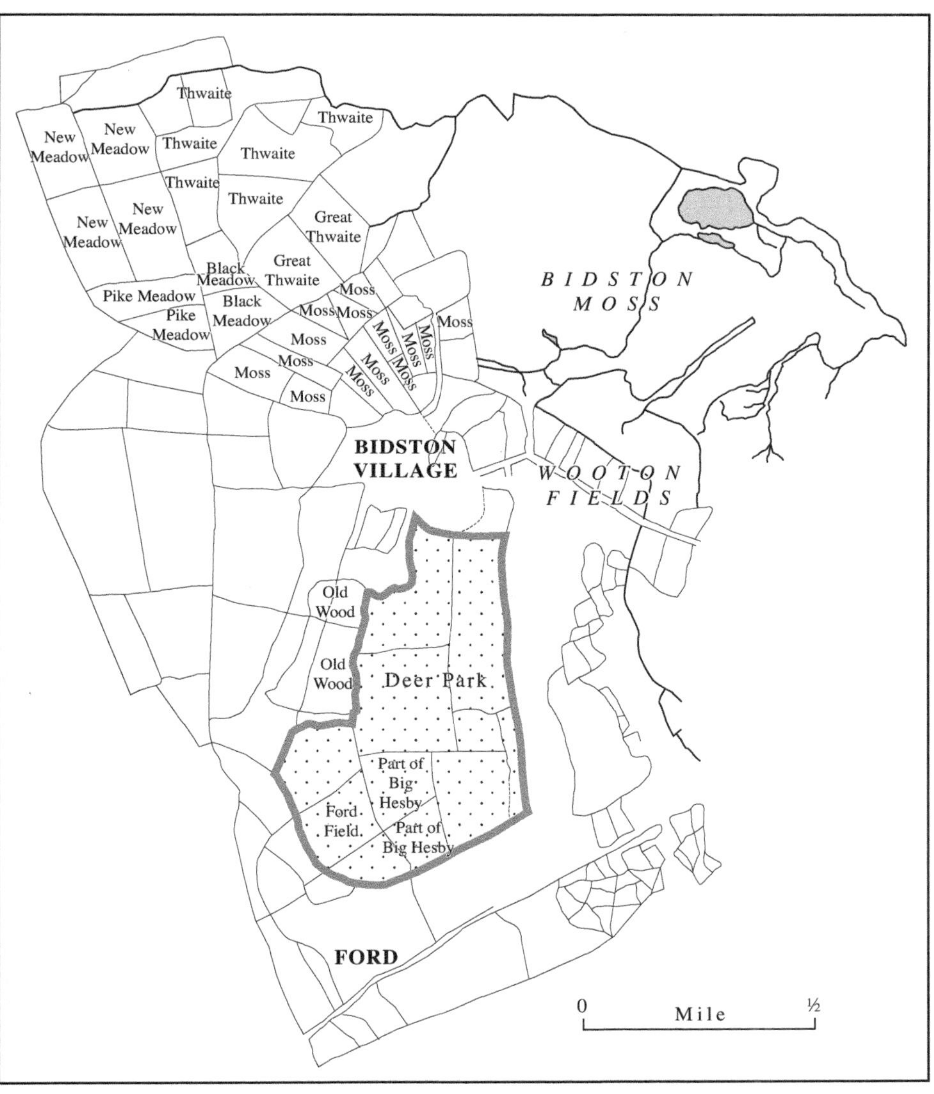

Map 10 *Bidston township (based on tithe map 1842)*

on the east of the township and Bidston wood was probably located south of Bidston village in an area later enclosed as a deer park.

Information about Wirral in the thirteenth and fourteenth centuries is also available from the plea roll of the court of Wirral forest held in 1286[64] and from the eyre of the Cheshire forests held in 1347. Neither of these documents is as comprehensive as the 1357 eyre. The location and date of offences is not as detailed in many instances as they are in the 1357 eyre. Many offences were only said to have taken place 'within the forest of Wirral' and frequently no date is given for the offence.

In 1286 a total of eighteen stags, one hind, two fawns and four does are recorded in the pleas of venison for the whole forest. Few dates are given but the earliest one mentioned is 1270/1. This figure for the number of deer killed is comparable with the eighteen deer recorded in the 1357 eyre. The 1347 eyre has very limited number of pleas of venison, possibly because there was a conspiracy by the local communities to under-record offences. Only five bucks and one stag are mentioned. There is no indication of the period covered. Based on the information from 1286 and 1357 it would seem that the numbers of deer over this period had not declined significantly.

The pleas of the vert are difficult to compare directly between the three documents. The 1357 eyre gives a location and date (day and year) for the trees felled. The 1286 document names the townships in which the offences took place but the year of the offence is not mentioned in every case. The townships in which woodland is recorded are Great Mollington, Mollington, Woodchurch and Bebington. Woodland is also mentioned in the lands of Birkenhead Priory, possibly in Claughton. In Mollington a wood was destroyed and in Great Mollington in a grove called Edenvetisgreve 60 oaks were cut down to clear land for cultivation. Some of Bebington wood is described as containing heath and alders. The need to increase the amount of arable land seems to have been a major factor in the felling of oaks in the 1286 document.

In the 1347 eyre there are over 100 entries for the felling of oaks. This is comparable with the number of offences in the 1357 eyre. No dates are mentioned and only a few township names are given. Mostly the site of the offence is omitted entirely or 'the forest of Wirral' is given as the location. A major difference is that the number of oaks felled in each offence in the 1347 eyre is substantially more than those reported felled in the 1357 eyre. In 1357 the largest number of oaks felled was 118 in Eastham but mostly the numbers were in single figures. In the 1347 eyre there were instances of 525, 240 and 124 oaks being felled and many cases of felling between 10 and 100 oaks. This suggests there was no shortage of wood in 1347 but by 1357 the demand for timber had declined or its supply was more limited than in 1347. There was a fall in population between the two periods because of the Black Death and this may account for the decline in the number of trees felled. In 1357 there is an example of the timber being re-used which also suggests there could have been a decline in the number of suitable trees.

64 TNA Palatinate of Chester, Cheshire Forest Proceedings, CHES 33/2 mm. 2–4d. A calendar of this document was kindly made available by Paul Booth.

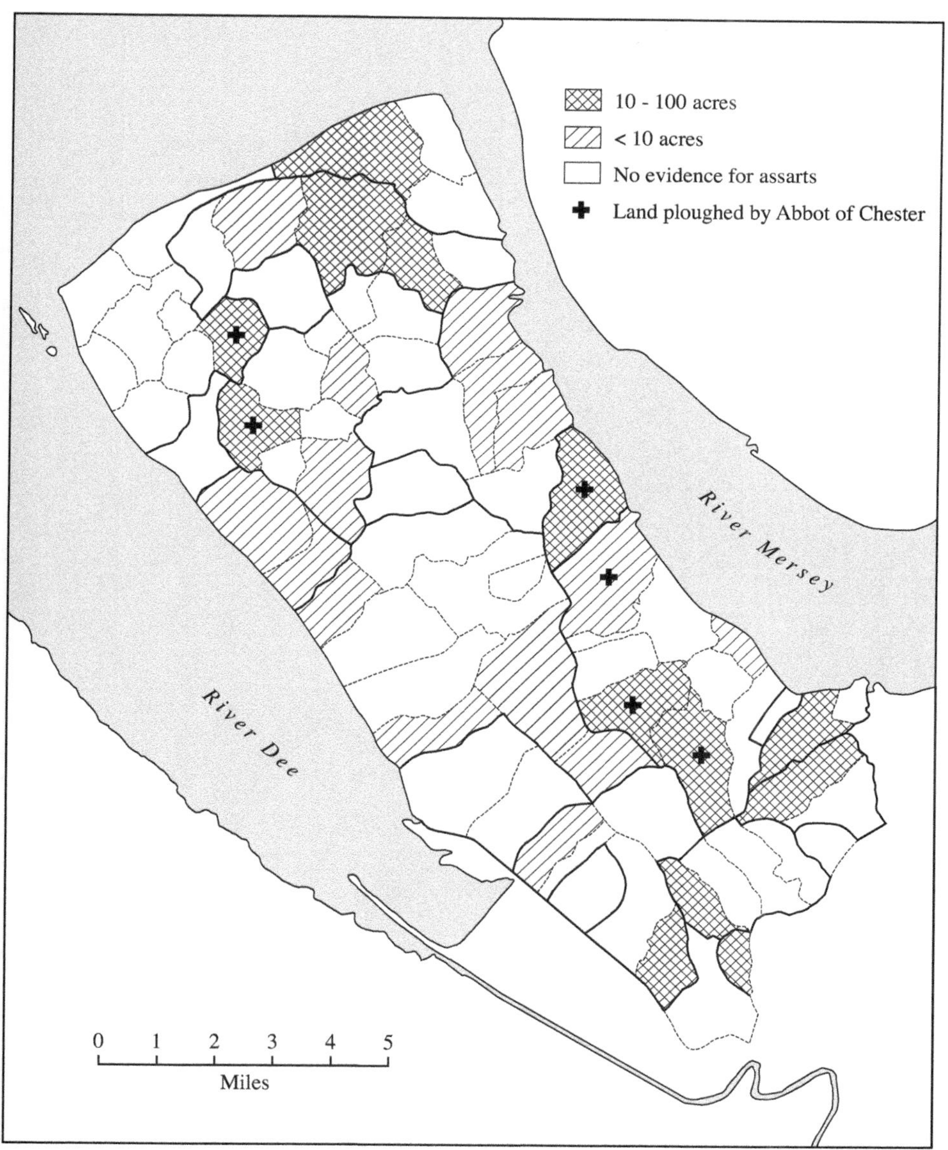

Map 11 *Area of land asserted, 1286*

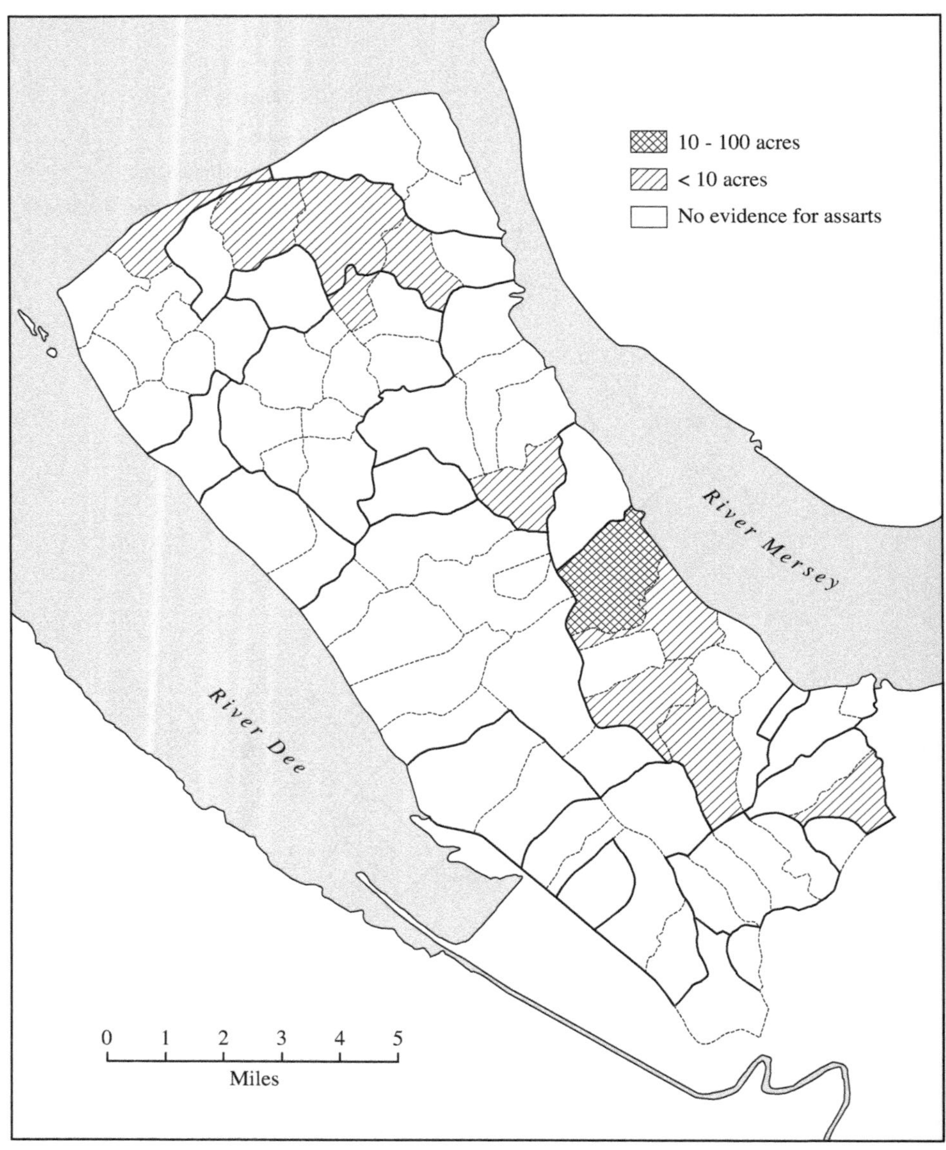

Map 12 *Areas of land assarted in 1347 eyre*

It is also possible to look at the amount of assarting recorded in both the 1286 and 1347 documents and compare it with the assarting recorded in the 1357 eyre. Map 11 shows the townships where assarting is recorded in the 1286 court proceedings. The incidence of assarting was not as widespread as that recorded in the 1357 eyre and it frequently involved quite small areas of land. The abbot of Chester was responsible for a significant amount of it.

Map 12 shows the townships where assarting was recorded in the 1347 eyre. The incidence of assarting was less than in 1286 and confined to the north and the east of Wirral. The total area asserted in the 1347 eyre is just 146 acres 1 rood. There must be some overlap between the assarts in the two eyres since the earliest assarts mentioned in the 1357 eyre occurred in 1297. In the 1347 eyre the earliest assart was 1315. The assarts in the two eyres do not seem to involve the same pieces of land. Those mentioned in 1347 do not recur in 1357. This calls into question the information on which the two eyres were based. The 1357 eyre contains information about assarts which could have been available in 1347 but for some reason was not included in the 1347 eyre, and again suggests that there was significant concealment in the previous court.

Most of the entries concerning purprestures in the 1347 eyre concern the digging of peat, which is of only peripheral importance in the 1357 eyre. In the 1347 eyre the area in which peat was dug is often mentioned, as is the time over which it was dug. In the 1357 eyre references to digging peat occur mainly in the claims to the eyre where the right to dig peat is claimed. The relative importance of the offence of digging peat was much greater in 1347 than in 1357 when assarting land for cultivation was a more important offence.

The records of the 1357 eyre provide invaluable information about the landscape of Wirral in the mid fourteenth century. At that time there remained woodland in many townships although comparison with the 1347 eyre suggests the extent of the woods may have been limited. Deer roamed throughout the area. A significant amount of assarting took place in the first half of the century indicating that, until that time, there was open land which could be taken in for cultivation. In some townships marl was used to improve the soil.

PLEAS OF THE EYRE OF THE FOREST OF WIRRAL

m. 1

1.1

Placita itineris foreste de Wyrhale tenta apud Cestr' coram Ricardo de Wilughby Ricardo de Stafford militibus Johanne de Delves et Johanne de Brunham juniore justiciariis domini Edwardi principis Wallie ducis Cornubie et comitis Cestr' ad itinerandum in omnibus placitis foreste predicte in comitatu Cestr' assignatis die Veneris proxima post festum Sancti Mathei apostoli anno regni Edwardi regis nostri tricesimo primo.

1.2

Edwardus illustris regis Anglie filius princeps Wallie dux Cornubie et comes Cestr' omnibus ballivis ministris et fidelibus suis ad quos presentes littere pervenerint salutem. Sciatis quod constituimus et assignavimus dilectos nobis Ricardum de Wilughby et Ricardum de Stafford milites Johannem de Delves et Johannem de Brunham juniorem justiciarios nostros tres [aut][a] duos ad itinerandum in omnibus placitis foreste nostre de Wyrhale in comitatu nostro Cestr' et ad facienda et excercenda omnia que ad huius placita tam de tempore nostro quam progenitorum nostrorum post ultima placita foreste predicte pertinere dinoscuntur. Et ideo vobis mandamus quod eisdem Ricardo Ricardo Johanni et Johanni tribus aut duobus eorum sitis intendentes et respondentes in premissis. In cuius rei testimonium has litteras nostras fieri fecimus patentes. Dat' apud Cestr' primo die Augusti anno regni domini Edwardi regis patris nostri tricesimo primo.

1.3

Breve quod vicecomiti Cestris' emanavit de predicto itinere summonendo sequitur in hec verba:

1.4

Edwardus illustris regis Anglie filius princeps Wallie dux Cornubie et comes Cestr' vicecomiti Cestris' salutem: Summone per bonos summonitores archiepiscopos episcopos abbates priores duces comites barones milites et omnes libere tenentes qui terras vel tenementa habent infra metas foreste nostre de Wyrhale in balliva tua; et de quolibet burgo xij liberos et legales homines; et de qualibet villa infra metas foreste nostre predicte exsistente quatuor homines et prepositum; et omnes alios qui coram justiciariis nostris ad placita foreste nostre predicte venire debent et solent quod sint apud Cestr' die Veneris in crastino Sancti Mathei apostoli proximo futuro coram dilectis et fidelibus nostris Ricardo de Wilughby Ricardo de Stafford militibus Johanne de Delves et Johanne de Brunham juniore quatuor tribus vel duobus eorum justiciariis nostris ad itinerandum hac vice ad placita foreste nostre predicte audituris et facturis preceptum nostrum de hiis que ad placita predicta pertinent.

a *ad* MS

m. 1

1.1

The pleas of the eyre of Wirral forest held before Richard de Wilughby, Richard de Stafford, knights, John de Delves and John de Brunham, the younger, assigned justices of the lord Edward, prince of Wales, duke of Cornwall and earl of Chester, to hold an eyre in all the pleas of the forest in the county of Chester, on Friday after the feast of St. Matthew, apostle, in the 31st year of the reign of Edward, the king our father. (22 September 1357)

1.2

Edward, son of the illustrious king of England, prince of Wales, duke of Cornwall and earl of Chester, to all his bailiffs, ministers and faithful to whom the present letters will come, greeting. Know that we have appointed and assigned our beloved Richard de Wilughby and Richard de Stafford, knights, John de Delves and John de Brunham, the younger, our justices, three or two, to hold an eyre in all the pleas of our forest of Wirral within our county of Chester and to do and carry out all things which are recognised to pertain to pleas of this kind, both from our own time and from the time of our forefathers since the last pleas of the said forest. And therefore we command that you be intendant to Richard, Richard, John and John, three or two of them, and respond to the premises. In witness whereof we have caused these our letters to be made patent. Given at Chester on the first day of August in the 31st year of the reign of the lord Edward, the king our father. (1 August 1357)

1.3

The writ which was issued to the sheriff of Cheshire concerning the summoning of the said eyre follows in these words:

1.4

Edward, son of the illustrious king of England, prince of Wales, duke of Cornwall and earl of Chester, to the sheriff of Cheshire greeting: Summon by good summoners the archbishops, bishops, abbots, priors, dukes, earls, barons, knights and all free tenants who have lands or tenements within the metes of our forest of Wirral in your bailiwick; and from each borough twelve free and lawful men; and from each township which is within the metes of our forest, four men and a reeve; and all others who are obliged and are accustomed to come before our justices for the pleas of our forest, that they should be at Chester on Friday the day after the next feast of St Matthew, apostle, (22 September 1357) before our beloved and faithful Richard de Wilughby, Richard de Stafford, knights, John de Delves and John de Brunham, the younger, four, three or two of them, our justices in eyre on this occasion to hear the pleas of our forest, and to carry out our command concerning those things which pertain to the aforesaid pleas.

1.5

Facias etiam venire coram eisdem justiciariis nostris omnes forestarios equitatores et viridarios nostros et omnes illos qui fuerunt forestarii equitatores et viridarii foreste nostre predicte post ultima placita eiusdem foreste cum omnibus attachiamentis suis tam de viride quam de venatione que post ultima placita foreste nostre predicte sunt emersa et nondum terminata ad respondendum nobis quemlibet de tempore suo singillatim prout debet et solet.

1.6

Facias etiam venire coram eisdem justiciariis nostris ad predictos diem et locum omnes regardatores et agistatores foreste nostre predicte et omnes illos qui fuerunt[a] regardatores vel agistatores eiusdem foreste nostre post ultima placita eiusdem foreste nostre ita quod habeant ibi tunc omnia regarda et attachiamenta sua forestam nostram predictam tangentia.

1.7

Facias etiam clamari et sciri per totam ballivam tuam quod omnia placita que fuerunt attaminata et non dum terminata seu que fuerunt summonita coram justiciariis de foresta ultimo in partibus predictis itinerantibus sint ibi in eodem statu in quo remanserunt.

1.8

Precipimus etiam tibi quod publice [proclamari][b] facias quod omnes illi qui libertates aliquas in predicta foresta nostra aliquo modo habere clamant, quod sint ibi ad ostendendum cuiusmodi libertates et quo waranto libertates illas habere clamant.

1.9

Et tu ipse tunc sis ibi personaliter una cum ministris et ballivis tuis quibuscumque ad certiorandos predictos justiciarios nostros super hiis et aliis negotium illud tangentibus.

1.10

Precipimus etiam tibi quod per totam ballivam tuam puplice proclamari facias quod omnes conquerentes seu conqueri volentes tam de forestariis equitatoribus viridariis agistatoribus et regardatoribus quam de aliis ballivis et ministris nostris quibuscumque foreste nostre predicte tangentibus veniant coram prefatis justiciariis nostris ibi ad faciendum et recipiendum secundum ordinacionem et tenorem statutorum foreste et juxta articulos prefatis justiciariis nostris inde traditos et prout idem justiciarii nostri tibi [sciri][c] faciant ex parte nostra.

a *illos qui fuerunt* interlined
b *proclamari* omitted in MS
c *scire* MS

1.5
Also cause to come before the same our justices all our foresters, riders and verderers and all those who have been foresters, riders and verderers of our forest since the last pleas of the same forest, with all their attachments both of the vert and of the venison which have been commenced since the last pleas of our said forest and have not yet been decided, to answer to us, each for his time and one by one, just as they are obliged and accustomed to do.

1.6
Also cause to come before our same justices our at the aforesaid day and place all the regarders and agisters of our forest and all those who were regarders or agisters of our same forest since the last pleas of our forest, so that they then have there all their regards and attachments concerning our forest.

1.7
Also cause it to be announced and known throughout your whole bailiwick that all pleas which were commenced and not yet decided, or which were summoned before the justices of the forest the last time they were in eyre in the aforesaid parts, are to be there in the same status in which they remained.

1.8
We also order that you cause it to be publicly proclaimed that all those who in any way claim to have any liberties in our forest should be there to show what kind of liberties they claim and by what right they claim to have those liberties.

1.9
And you yourself are to be there and then in person, together with any of your officials and bailiffs, to inform our justices on these and other matters concerning that business.

1.10
We also order you that you cause it to be publicly proclaimed throughout your whole bailiwick that all those complaining, or wishing to complain, about both foresters, riders, verderers, agisters and regarders, or about any other of our bailiffs and officials who are concerned with our forest, are to come before our aforesaid justices there to act and to receive, in accordance with the ordinance and tenor of the statutes of the forest, and according to the articles then handed over to our justices, and as our same justices are to make known to you on our behalf.

1.11

Et habeas ibi summonitores et hoc breve. Teste Bartholomeo de Burgherssch justiciario nostro Cestr' apud Cestr' quarto die Augusti anno regni domini Edwardi regis patris nostri tricesimo primo.

1.12

Ad quod breve Thomas de Dutton vicecomes Cestris' sic respondet:

Nulli sunt archiepiscopi qui habent terras seu tenementa infra metas foreste de Wyrhale nec aliqui sunt burgi infra metas dicte foreste. Ideo de summonendo archiepiscopos seu xij liberos et legales homines de quolibet burgo infra metas dicte foreste nihil actum est.

1.13

Et omnes episcopi abbates priores duces comites barones milites et omnes liberi tenentes qui habent terras seu tenementa infra metas dicte foreste in balliva mea et de qualibet villa infra metas dicte foreste existente quatuor homines et [prepositus][a] et omnes [alii][b] qui coram justiciariis ad placita foreste predicte venire debent et solent summoniti sunt quod sint ad dictos diem et locum in isto breve contenta coram justiciariis in isto breve nominatis ad facienda ea que istud breve requirit videlicet per Robertum de Pulle et Nicholaum Dod.

1.14

Et nulli sunt viridarii neque agistatores in foresta predicta nec fuerunt post ultima placita foreste. Ideo de executione istius brevis facienda versus viridarios seu agistatores nihil actum est.

1.15

Et quo ad omnes forestarios equitatores et regardatores qui nunc sunt in foresta predicta et qui pro tempore fuerunt post ultima placita dicte foreste in dicta foresta manucapti sunt quod sint ad dictum diem et locum in isto brevi contenta coram justiciariis in isto brevi nominatis cum omnibus attachiamentis et regardis suis ad facienda ea que istud breve requirit ut patet in diversis cedulis huic brevi consutis continentibus nomina eorundem forestariorum equitatorum et regardatorum.

1.16

Et ulterius proclamari clamari et sciri feci per totam ballivam meam omnia et singula precepta articula et mandata in isto brevi nominata et contenta in forma quam istud breve requirit.

a *prepositum* MS

b *alios* MS

1.11
And you are to have there the summoners and this writ. Witness Bartholomew de Burgerssch, our justice of Chester, at Chester on the fourth day of August in the 31st year of the reign of lord Edward, the king our father. (4 August 1357)

1.12
To which writ Thomas de Dutton, sheriff of Cheshire, responds thus:

There are no archbishops who have lands or tenements within the metes of the forest of Wirral, nor are there any boroughs within the metes of the forest. Therefore regarding summoning archbishops or twelve free and lawful men from any borough within the metes of the forest nothing has been done.

1.13
And all bishops, abbots, priors, dukes, earls, barons, knights and all free tenants who have lands or tenements within the metes of the forest in my bailiwick, and four men and a reeve from each township which is within the metes of the said forest, and all others who are obliged and accustomed to come before the justices for the pleas of the forest have been summoned to be present on the day and at the place named in this writ before the justices named in this writ to do those things which this writ requires, that is by Robert de Pulle and Nicholas Dod.

1.14
And there are no verderers nor agisters in the aforesaid forest, nor have there been since the last pleas of the forest. Therefore, for executing this writ against verderers or agisters, nothing has been done.

1.15
And as for all foresters, riders and regarders who are now in the aforesaid forest, and who were for a time in the forest since the last pleas of the forest, they have been mainperned to be present on the day and at the place contained in this writ before the justices named in this writ, with all their attachments and regards, to do those things that this writ requires, as appears in the various schedules sewn to this writ, containing the names of the same foresters, riders and regarders.

1.16
And furthermore I have had proclaimed, announced and made known throughout my whole bailiwick each and every order, article and command named and contained in this writ in the form which this writ requires.

1.17

Et ego vicecomes cum ministris et ballivis meis personaliter ero ad diem et locum per istud breve michi prefixa ad facienda ea que istud breve requirit.

1.18

Et pro villa de Burton que est infra metas foreste predicte mandavi Roberto Horn ballivo episcopi Lich' et Conventr' libertatis sue de Tervyn, [cui executio][a] istius brevis in predicta villa que est infra ballivam suam pertinet facienda etc. qui michi sic respondet:

1.19

Nulli sunt archiepiscopi abbates priores duces comites barones seu milites qui habent terras seu tenementa infra dictam villam neque habuerunt post ultima placita foreste. Ideo de summonendis eis nihil actum est.

1.20

Et omnes liberi tenentes qui habent terras seu [tenementa] infra predictam villam et quatuor homines et prepositus de eadem villa et omnes illi de eadem villa qui coram [justiciariis] ad placita foreste venire solent et debent summoniti sunt quod sint ad dictos diem et locum in isto brevi contenta coram justiciariis in isto brevi nominatis ad facienda ea que istud breve requirit videlicet per Johannem Batyn et Robertum Huss[...].

1.21

Et ulterius predictus ballivus respondet quod nulli sunt forestarii viridarii equitatores regardatores seu agistatores dicte foreste infra dictam villam neque aliquo tempore fuerunt post ultima [placita][b] foreste. Ideo de executione istius brevis facienda nihil actum est.

1.22

Regardatores foreste de Wyrhale qui nunc sunt sequuntur:

Johannes Dounvyll	Robertus de Berneston	Henricus de Chorleton
Adam del Lee	Ricardus del Hough	Johannes de Lasceles
Willelmus Waleys	Johannes Launcelyn	Henricus de Hoton
Thomas de Hokenhull	Robertus Baumvyll	Willelmus Gregory

a *cum executione* MS
b *placita* omitted in MS

1.17
And I the sheriff with my ministers and bailiffs shall be present in person on the day and at the place appointed to me by this writ to do those things which this writ requires.

1.18
And for the township of Burton, which is within the metes of the aforesaid forest, I have given instructions to Robert Horn, bailiff of the bishop of Lichfield and Coventry for his liberty of Tarvin, who is responsible for the execution of this writ in the said township which is within his bailiwick etc., who replies to me thus:

1.19
There are no archbishops, abbots, priors, dukes, earls, barons or knights, who have lands or tenements within the township, or have had since the last pleas of the forest. Therefore regarding summoning them, nothing has been done.

1.20
And all free tenants, who have lands or tenements within the township, and four men and a reeve from the same township and all those from the same township who are accustomed and obliged to come before the justices for the pleas of the forest have been summoned to be present on the day and at the place named in this writ before the justices named in this writ to do those things which this writ requires, that is by John Batyn and Robert Huss[...]

1.21
And furthermore the said bailiff replies that there are no foresters, verderers, riders, regarders or agisters of the forest within the said township, nor have there been at any time since the last pleas of the forest. Therefore regarding executing this writ nothing has been done.

1.22
The present regarders of Wirral forest are as follows:

John Dounvyll	Robert de Berneston	Henry de Chorleton
Adam del Lee	Richard del Hough	John de Lasceles
William Waleys	John Launcelyn	Henry de Hoton
Thomas de Hokenhull	Robert Baumvyll	William Gregory

1.23
Equitatores foreste de Wyrhale qui nuper pro tempore fuerunt nunc sequuntur:

Johannes Lassels nunc equitator dicte foreste	Henricus de Hoton [equitator dicte foreste]
Robertus de Knouselegh serviens dicti Johannis	Henricus Coly serviens dicti Henrici

Et Ricardus le Ryder et Nicholaus Hody nuper equitatores dicte foreste mortui sunt. Non habe[nt] [...] [...] terras seu tenementa bona seu catalla infra ballivam meam. Ideo de executione istius breve versus eos facienda nihil actum est.

Et plures equitatores non sunt in dicta foresta neque fuerunt post ultima placita foreste inventi infra ballivam meam.

1.24
Forestarii de Wyrhale qui nunc sunt sequuntur:

Willelmus de Stanlegh	Radulphus filius Patricii	Rogerus de Hokenhull
Ricardus de Kyngesfeld	Rogerus de Bechynton	Henricus de Clynage
Ranulphus Raket.		

Forestarii foreste de Wyrhale qui pro tempore fuerunt sequuntur:

Johannes Doune	Robertus Starky	Johannes Denys
Ricardus de Pulton	Ricardus de Weverham	Ricardus le Clerk
Robertus Hobkynsone	Robert Benet	Johannes Launcelyn
Johannes filius Ken de Pulford	Henricus de Chorleton	Alanus de la Lyd[e]y[ate].

1.25
Villate infra forestam de Wyrhale nunc sequuntur:

Blaken	Podynton	Leghton	Calday	Kirkeby en Waley
Budston	Salghale	Burton	Gayton	WestKyrkeby
Pulton in Waley		Morton	Salghale Ma[gna]	
Parva Salghale	Nesse	Haselwall	Lytelmeles	Lysecark
Newton	Schotewyk	Parva Neston	Thurstanston	Mukelmeles
Claghton	Upton.			

Respice in tergo residuum villatarum

1.23

Riders of Wirral forest who were formerly appointed for a time are as follows:

John Lassels now rider of the said forest	Henry de Hoton rider of the said forest
Robert de Knouselegh, servant of the said John,	Henry Coly servant of the said Henry.

And Richard le Ryder and Nicholas Hody, former riders of the forest, have died. They do not have [...], [...], lands or tenements, goods or chattels within my bailiwick. Therefore regarding executing this writ against them nothing has been done.

And there are no more riders in the forest nor have any been found within my bailiwick since the last pleas of the forest.

1.24

The present foresters of Wirral are as follows:

William de Stanlegh	Ralph son of Patrick	Roger de Hokenhull
Richard de Kyngesfeld	Roger de Bechynton	Henry de Clynage
Ranulf Raket.		

Foresters of Wirral forest who acted for a time are as follows:

John Doune	Robert Starky	John Denys
Richard de Pulton	Richard de Weverham	Richard le Clerk
Robert Hobkynsone	Robert Benet	John Launcelyn
John, son of Ken de Pulford	Henry de Chorleton	Alan de la Lyd[e]y[ate].

1.25

The townships within the forest of Wirral are as follows:

Blacon	Puddington	Leighton	Caldy	Wallasey
Bidston	Saughall	Burton	Gayton	West Kirby
Poulton cum Seacombe		Moreton	Great Saughall	
Little Saughall	Ness	Heswall	Little Meols	Liscard
Newton	Shotwick	Little Neston	Thurstaston	Great Meols
Claughton	Upton.			

See overleaf for the rest of the townships.

Rotulus primus Wyrhale

m. 1d

Adhuc de villatis infra f[orestam] de Wyrhale

1.26

Franckby	Oxton	Brumburgh	Netherpool	Chorlton
Molynton Banastre		Grevesby	Overbebynton	
Eastham	Wyteby	Bacford	Molynton Torauld	
Wodechurch	Netherbebynton	Hoton	Stanay	Lee
Crabwall	Tranemoll	Poulton Lancelyn		Overpulle
Stoke	Croghton	Capenhurst	Ledesham	Wylaston
Raby	Thornton Maheu	Thyngwal	Brunstath	Barnston
Neston	Landecan	Irreby	Knogburton	Prenton
Mickel Sutton	Chylderthornton	Hallesutton	Pennesby	Arwe

Sequuntur presentationes de viridi

1.27

Compertum est per rotulos Willelmi de Stanlegh forestarii de feodo foreste de Wyrhale quod Ricardus Starky die Martis proxima ante festum Sancti Cedde anno regni domini regis nunc vicesimo quarto cepit et habuit unum quercum viridem in bosco de Tranemol sine visu forestariorum et quod idem Ricardus die Veneris proxima post festum Purificationis Beate Marie anno regni domini regis nunc vicesimo quinto cepit unum quercum viridem in eodem bosco sine visu forestariorum;

et quod idem Ricardus die Sabbati proxima post festum Annunciationis Beate Marie anno regni domini regis nunc vicesimo sexto cepit unum quercum viridem in bosco predicto sine visu forestariorum. Ideo preceptum est vicecomiti quod venire faciat [eum]. Postea venit predictus Ricardus et super hoc convictus liberatus prisone. Postea eductus fecit finem pro *iij s.* per plegium [...] Starky et Willelmi de Neuton.

First roll Wirral

m. 1d

Continuation of the townships within the forest of Wirral

1.26

Frankby	Oxton	Bromborough	Netherpool	Chorlton
Mollington Banastre		Greasby	Higher Bebington	
Eastham	Whitby	Backford	Mollington Torauld	
Woodchurch	Lower Bebington	Hooton	Stanney	Lea
Crabwall	Tranmere	Poulton Lancelyn		Overpool
Stoke	Croughton	Capenhurst	Ledsham	Willaston
Raby	Thornton Hough	Thingwall	Brimstage	Barnston
Neston	Landican	Irby	Noctorum	Prenton
Great Sutton	Childer Thornton	Little Sutton	Pensby	Arrowe

Presentments of the vert follow

1.27

It is found by the rolls of William de Stanlegh, forester in fee of the forest of Wirral, that Richard Starky[1] on Tuesday before the feast of St Chad in the 24th year of the reign of the present lord king (23 February 1350) took and kept a green oak in Tranmere wood without the view of the foresters; and that Richard on Friday after the feast of the Purification of Blessed Mary in the 25th year of the reign of the present lord king (4 February 1351) took a green oak in the same wood without the view of the foresters; and that Richard on Saturday after the feast of the Annunciation of Blessed Mary in the 26th year of the reign of the present lord king (31 March 1352) took a green oak in the wood without the view of the foresters. Therefore the sheriff is ordered to make him come. Afterwards Richard comes and thereupon convicted he is handed over to prison. Afterwards having been brought out he made fine of *3s. 0d.* by the pledge of [...] Starky and William de Neuton.

1 1347 m. 3 Robert Starkey took 20 oaks in Tranmere wood; fined 40d.; pledge William of Tranmere.

1.28

Compertum est etiam quod Willelmus Waleys de Tranemol die Mercurii proxima ante festum Annunciationis Beate Marie anno regni domini regis nunc vicesimo quarto prostravit unam ramam viridem in bosco de Tranemol et idem Willelmus die Lune proxima ante festum Inventionis Sancte Crucis anno regni domini regis nunc vicesimo quinto prostravit unum quercum viridem in bosco de Tranemoll et idem Willelmus die Jovis proxima post festum Purificationis Beate Marie anno regni domini regis nunc vicesimo sexto cepit unum quercum viridem in bosco de Tranemoll;

et quod idem Willelmus die Veneris proxima ante festum Sancti Marci evangeliste anno regni domini regis nunc vicesimo septimo cepit unum quercum viridem in bosco de Tranemoll sine visu forestariorum contra assisam foreste. Ideo preceptum est vicecomiti quod venire faciat eum. Postea venit et super hoc convictus liberatus prisone. Postea eductus fecit finem pro *iij s. vj d.* per plegium Johannis Domville.

1.29

Compertum est etiam quod Robertus de Pulle die Martis proxima post festum Sancti Marci anno regni domini regis nunc vicesimo quarto cepit unum quercum viridem in bosco de Leghton et quod idem Robertus [...] [...] proxima ante festum Sancti Andree apostoli anno regni domini regis nunc vicesimo septimo [cepit][a] unum quercum viridem in bosco de Leghton et quod idem Robertus die Lune proxima post festum Sancti Gregorii pape anno regni domini regis nunc vicesimo nono cepit unum quercum viridem in bosco de Leghton sine visu forestariorum contra assisam foreste. Ideo preceptum est vicecomiti quod venire faciat eum. Postea venit et super hoc convictus liberatus prisone. Postea eductus fecit finem pro *iij s.* per plegium Johannis Domville.

1.30

Convictum est etiam quod Johannes presbiter die Martis proxima post festum Sancti Luce evangeliste anno regni domini regis nunc vicesimo quarto cepit unum ramum viridem in bosco de Netherbebynton;

<iij s.>

et Alicia que fuit[b] uxor Willelmi Torold die Martis proxima post festum Sancti Cedde

a *cepit* omitted in MS
b *que fuit* interlined

1.28

It is also found that William Waleys[1] of Tranmere on Wednesday before the feast of the Annunciation of Blessed Mary in the 24th year of the reign of the present lord king (24 March 1350) cut down a green branch in Tranmere wood; and the same William on Monday before the feast of the Finding of the Holy Cross in the 25th year of the reign of the present lord king (2 May 1351) felled a green oak in Tranmere wood; and that William on Thursday after the feast of the Purification of Blessed Mary in the 26th year of the reign of the present lord king (9 February 1352) took a green oak in Tranmere wood;

and that William on Friday before the feast of St Mark, evangelist, in the 27th year of the reign of the present lord king (19 April 1353) took a green oak in Tranmere wood without the view of the foresters against the assize of the forest. Therefore the sheriff is ordered to make him come. Afterwards he comes and thereupon convicted he is handed over to prison. Afterwards having been brought out he made fine of *3s. 6d.* by the pledge of John Domville.

1.29

It is also found that Robert de Pulle[2] on Tuesday after the feast of St Mark in the 24th year of the present lord king (27 April 1350) took a green oak in Leighton wood; and that Robert on [...] before the feast of St Andrew, apostle, in the 27th year of the reign of the present lord king (1353/54) took a green oak in Leighton wood; and that Robert on Monday after the feast of Gregory, pope, in the 29th year of the reign of the present lord king (16 March 1355) took a green oak in Leighton wood without the view of the foresters against the assize of the forest. Therefore the sheriff is ordered to make him come. Afterwards he comes and thereupon convicted he is handed over to prison. Afterwards having been brought out he made fine of *3s. 0d.* by the pledge of John Domvill.

1.30

It is also established that John the priest on Tuesday after the feast of St Luke, evangelist, in the 24th year of the reign of the present lord king (19 October 1350) took a green branch in Lower Bebington wood;

<3s. 0d.>

and Alice, who was the widow of William Torold, on Tuesday after the feast of

1 1347 m. 1 Richard Waley, 4 oaks; 10s. 0d.; Roger Brown of Wimbolds Trafford.
m. 1 William Waley, 17 oaks and 12 *robora* in Tranmere wood; 40d.; Henry Barnard.
m. 3 William Waleys, 24 oaks in Tranmere wood; 6s. 4d; Richard Starkey.

2 1347 m. 2d Hugh de Pulle took 12 oaks; pauper, no fine.
m. 5d Robert de Pulle 6 oaks in Leighton; fine 40d.; pledge Richard de Haydock and John de Mollington.

episcopi anno regni domini regis nunc vicesimo quinto cepit duos quercos virides in bosco de Molynton;

<ij s.>

et quod eadem Alicia die Jovis proxima post festum Pasche anno regni domini regis nunc supradicto cepit unum ramum viridem in bosco predicto sine visu forestariorum contra assisam foreste. Ideo preceptum est vicecomiti quod venire faciat [eos][a].

Postea veniunt et super hoc convicti liberati prisone. Postea educti idem Johannes fecit finem per plegium Johannis de W[ete]feld videlicet pro *vj d.* et predicta Alicia fecit finem pro duobus solidis per plegium Thome de Warrewyk et Johannis de Scolhalgh.

1.31
Compertum est etiam quod Henricus Bernard de Tranemol die Sabbati proxima post festum Sancti Cedde episcopi anno regni domini regis nunc vicesimo quarto cepit unum ramum viridem in bosco de Tranemoll et quod idem Henricus die Sabbati proxima post festum Annunciationis Beate Marie anno regni regis nunc vicesimo septimo cepit unum quercum viridem in bosco de Tranemoll. Ideo preceptum est vicecomiti quod venire faciat eum. Postea venit et super hoc convictus liberatus prisone. Postea fecit finem pro *xviij d.* per plegium Roberti de Pulle.

1.32
Compertum est etiam quod Willelmus Boydel die Jovis proxima ante festum Sancti Cedde episcopi anno regni regis nunc vicesimo [...] cepit unum quercum viridem in bosco de Tranemoll et quod Ranulphus de Bechynton die Martis proxima post festum Sancti Philippi anno regni regis nunc xxv[to] cepit unum quercum viridem in bosco de Wodechirch et quod Henricus filius Roberti die Lune proxima post festum Sancti Oswaldi anno supradicto cepit ramos et virgas virides in bosco de Wodechirch;

<xij d.>

et quod Robertus Bouthe de Kugghoyrn cepit unum ramum viridem die Jovis proxima post festum Sancti Michelis anno supradicto in eadem bosco.

1.33 <[ij s.]>
et quod Henricus Sampson die Jovis proxima post festum Sancti Andree anno supradicto cepit in bosco de Budeston duos frondes ramos virides et virgas virides;

<vj d.>

a *eum* MS

St Chad, bishop, in the 25th year of the reign of the present lord king (7 March 1351), took two green oaks in Mollington wood;

<2s. 0d.>

and that Alice on Thursday after Easter in the reign of the present lord king in the said year (21 April 1351) took a green branch in the said wood without the view of the foresters against the assize of the forest. Therefore the sheriff is ordered to make them come.

Afterwards they come and thereupon convicted they are handed over to prison. Afterwards having been brought out John made fine by the pledge of John de Wetefeld, that is of *6d.*; and Alice made fine of two shillings by the pledges of Thomas de Warrewyk and John de Scolhalgh.

1.31
It is also found that Henry Bernard[1] of Tranmere on Saturday after the feast of St Chad, bishop, in the 24th year of the reign of the present lord king (6 March 1350) took a green branch in Tranmere wood; and that Henry on Saturday after the feast of the Annunciation of Blessed Mary in the 27th year of the reign of the present king (30 March 1353) took a green oak in Tranmere wood. Therefore the sheriff is ordered to make him come. Afterwards he comes and thereupon convicted he is handed over to prison. Afterwards he made fine of *18d.* by the pledge of Robert de Pulle.

1.32
It is also found that William Boydel[2] on Thursday before the feast of St Chad, bishop, in the twenty[...] year of the reign of the present king took a green oak in Tranmere wood; and that Ranulf de Becheton[3] on Tuesday after the feast of St Philip in the 25th year of the reign of the present king (3 May 1351) took a green oak in Woodchurch wood; and that Henry, son of Robert, on Monday after the feast of St Oswald in the above year (8 August 1351) took green branches and twigs in Woodchurch wood;

<12d.>

and that Robert Bouthe of Noctorum took a green branch on Thursday after the feast of St Michael in the above year (6 October 1351) and in the same wood;

1.33 <2s. 0d.>
and that Henry Sampson on Thursday after the feast of St Andrew in the above year (6 December 1351) took in Bidston wood two leafy boughs and green branches and green twigs;

<6d.>

1 1347 m. 1 Henry Bernard 14 oaks and 3 *robora*; 40d.; William Waleys.
2 1347 m. 6 Adam Boydell 1 oak.
3 1347 m. 4 Simon de Becheton 12 oaks in Greves wood; 10s. 0d.; Roger de Coghull.

et quod Ricardus de Kecwyk die Sabbati proxima ante festum Sancte Katerine anno supradicto cepit unum ramum viridem in bosco de Wodechirch;

<vj d.>

et quod Henricus le Carter de Upton die Veneris proxima post festum Omnium Sanctorum anno supradicto cepit duos ramos virides in bosco de Wodechirch sine visu forestariorum contra assisam foreste. Ideo preceptum est vicecomiti quod venire faciat eos etc. Postea veniunt et super hoc convicti liberati prisone.

Postea predictus Willelmus Boydel fecit finem pro xij d. per plegium Johannis Domvill. Ranulphus de Bechynton fecit finem pro vj d. per plegium Henrici filii Roberti et Henricus filius Roberti pro vj d. per plegium Ranulphi de Bechynton et Robertus Bouth pro vj d. per plegium Henrici Sampson et Henricus Sampson pro *xij d.* per plegium Willelmi Waleys et Henrici Bernard; et Ricardus Kecwyk pro *viij d.* per plegium Philippi de Raby et Henricus le Carter pro *viij d.* per plegium Johannis Launcelyn.

1.34

Compertum est etiam quod Johannes Doune anno supradicto cepit in grova de Pennesby tres querculos et abduxit ad domum suam de Thurstanston et quod idem Johannes cepit tres quercus virides in bosco de Budeston die Martis proxima post festum Sancte Katerine anno regis nunc vicesimo octavo sine visu forestariorum contra assisam foreste. Ideo preceptum est vicecomiti quod venire faciat eum. Postea venit et super hoc convictus liberatus prisone. Postea fecit finem pro duobus solidis per plegium Johannis Donville.

1.35

Compertum est etiam quod Ricardus filius Willelmi die Lune proxima post festum Purificationis Beate Marie anno regis nunc xxvj[to] [cepit][a] unum ramum viridem in bosco de Tranemoll et Johannes de Brereton rector ecclesie de Waley die Martis proxima post festum Sancti Martini anno regis nunc vicesimo septimo cepit unum quercum viridem in bosco de Tranemoll et quod Adam Tynker de Upton die Mercurii proxima ante festum Sancti Michelis anno predicto cepit tres frondes virides in bosco de Wodechirch et quod Henricus le Lytle senior die Veneris proxima ante festum Sancti Marci evangeliste anno supradicto cepit subboscum ramayl[b] et virgas [virides][c] in bosco de Budeston sine visu forestariorum contra assisam foreste.

Ideo preceptum est vicecomiti quod venire faciat eos. Postea veniunt et super hoc convicti liberati prisone. Postea predictus [Ricardus] filius Willelmi fecit finem pro

a *cepit* omitted in MS
b *ramayl* interlined
c *viridas* MS

and that Richard de Kecwyk on Saturday before the feast of St Catherine in the above year (19 November 1351) took a green branch in Woodchurch wood;

<6d.>

and that Henry le Carter of Upton on Friday after the feast of All Saints in the above year (4 November 1351) took two green branches in Woodchurch wood without the view of the foresters against the assize of the forest.

Therefore the sheriff is ordered to make them come etc. Afterwards they come and thereupon convicted they are handed over to prison.

Afterwards William Boydel made fine of 12d. by the pledge of John Domvill.

Ranulf de Bechynton made fine of 6d. by the pledge of Henry son of Robert; and Henry son of Robert of 6d. by the pledge of Ranulf de Bechynton; and Robert Bouth of 6d. by the pledge of Henry Sampson; and Henry Sampson of *12d.* by the pledge of William Waleys and Henry Bernard; and Richard Kecwyk of *8d.* by the pledge of Philip de Raby; and Henry le Carter of *8d.* by the pledge of John Launcelyn.

1.34

It is also found that John Doune in the above year took three oak saplings in the grove of Pensby and removed them to his home in Thurstaston; and that John took three green oaks in Bidston wood on Tuesday after the feast of St Catherine in the 28th year of the reign of the present king (2 December 1354) without the view of the foresters against the assize of the forest.

Therefore the sheriff is ordered to make him come. Afterwards he comes and thereupon convicted he is handed over to prison. Afterwards he made fine of 2s. 0d. by the pledge of John Domville.

1.35

It is also found that Richard son of William on Monday after the feast of the Purification of Blessed Mary in the 26th year of the king (5 February 1352) took a green branch in Tranmere wood; and John de Brereton, rector of the church of Wallasey, on Tuesday after the feast of St Martin in the 27th year of the present king (12 November 1353), took a green oak in Tranmere wood; and that Adam Tynker of Upton on Wednesday before the feast of St Michael in the above year (25 September 1353) took three green leafy branches in Woodchurch wood; and that Henry le Lytle the elder on Friday before the feast of St Mark, evangelist, in the above year (19 April 1353) took branches in the underwood and green twigs in Bidston wood without the view of the foresters against the assize of the forest.

Therefore the sheriff is ordered to make them come. Afterwards they come and thereupon convicted they are handed over to prison. Afterwards the said Richard son of William made fine of 8d. by the pledge of Henry Bernard and William Waleys;

viij d. per plegium Henrici Bernard et Willelmi Waleys et Johannes de Brereton pro xij d. per plegium Johannis Domville et Adam le Tynker pro xij d. per plegium Johannis de Launcelyn et Henricus Lytle pro vj d. per plegium Johannis Launcelyn.

1.36

Compertum est etiam quod Robertus Broun die Martis proxima post festum Sancti Cedde episcopi anno regis nunc vicesimo septimo [cepit] in bosco de Tranemol unum quercum viridem et quod Henricus Broun die Lune proxima post festum Sancti Gregorii pape anno predicto cepit unum quercum viridem in bosco de Tranemoll et quod Rogerus Pekok die Jovis proxima post festum Inventionis Sancte Crucis anno supradicto cepit unum quercum viridem in bosco de Netherbebynton et Willelmus de Neuton die Sabbati proxima post festum Sancti Martini anno supradicto cepit unum quercum viridem in Netherbebynton sine visu forestariorum contra assisam foreste. Ideo preceptum est vicecomiti quod venire faciat eos. Postea veniunt et super hoc convicti liberati prisone.

Postea predictus Robertus Broun fecit finem pro xij d. per plegium Henrici de Hoton et Henricus Broun pro xij d. per plegium Roberti Broun et Willelmi Waleys et Rogerus Pekok pro xij d. per plegium Henrici Bernard et Willelmus de Neuton pro xij d. per plegium Rogeri Pekok et Willelmi [Waleys].

1.37

Convictum est etiam quod Alanus de Waley die Lune proxima post festum Sancti Cedde anno vicesimo octavo cepit unum quercum viridem in bosco de Budeston et quod Johannes Launcelyn die Martis proxima post festum [...] anno predicto cepit unum quercum viridem in bosco de Budeston et quod Henricus de Wylaston die Jovis proxima post festum Sancti Nicholai anno supradicto cepit unum quercum viridem in bosco de Budeston et quod filius Alani de Waley die Martis proxima ante festum Sancte Katerine anno supradicto cepit unum quercum viridem in bosco de Budeston et quod Henricus Broun die Lune proxima post festum Sancti Gregorii pape anno supradicto cepit unum quercum viridem in bosco de Tranemoll et quod Ricardus le Leder die Martis proxima post festum Sancti Gregorii anno predicto cepit unum quercum viridem in bosco de Netherbebynton et quod Willelmus de Neuton die Lune

and John de Brereton of 12d. by the pledge of John Domville; and Adam le Tynker of 12d. by the pledge of John de Launcelyn; and Henry Lytle of 6d. by the pledge of John Launcelyn.

1.36

It is also found that Robert Broun[1] on Tuesday after the feast of St Chad, bishop, in the twenty-seventh year of the present king (5 March 1353) took a green oak in Tranmere wood; and that Henry Broun on Monday after the feast of St Gregory, pope, in the above year (18 March 1353) took a green oak in Tranmere wood; and that Roger Pekok on Thursday after the feast of the Finding of the Holy Cross in the above year (9 May 1353) took a green oak in Lower Bebington wood and William de Neuton on Saturday after the feast of St Martin in the above year (16 November 1353) took a green oak in Lower Bebington without the view of the foresters against the assize of the forest. Therefore the sheriff is ordered to make them come. Afterwards they come and thereupon convicted they are handed over to prison.

Afterwards Robert Broun made fine of 12d. by the pledge of Henry de Hoton; and Henry Broun of 12d. by the pledge of Robert Broun and William Waleys; and Roger Pekok of 12d. by the pledge of Henry Bernard; and William de Neuton of 12d. by the pledge of Roger Pekok and William Waleys.

1.37

It is also established that Alan de Waley[2] on Monday after the feast of St Chad in the 28th year (3 March 1354) took a green oak in Bidston wood; and that John Launcelyn[3] on Tuesday after the feast [...] in the above year took a green oak in Bidston wood; and that Henry de Wylaston on Thursday after the feast of St Nicholas in the above year (11 December 1354) took a green oak in Bidston wood; and that the son of Alan de Waley on Tuesday before the feast of St Catherine in the above year (18 November 1354) took a green oak in Bidston wood and that Henry Broun on Monday after the feast of St Gregory, pope, in the above year (17 March 1354) took a green oak in Tranmere wood; and that Richard le Leder on Tuesday after the feast of St Gregory in the above year (18 March 1354) took a green oak in Lower Bebington wood; and that William de Neuton on Monday after the feast of the Purification of Blessed

1 1347 m. 4 Robert Broun took 3 oaks; fine 2s 0d.; pledge Richard de Pulton.
m. 1 Hugh Broun; 5 oaks & 2 *robora*; 40d.; William de Tranemoll.

2 1347 m. 1 Richard Waley; 4 oaks; 10s. 0d.; Roger Broun of Wimbolds Trafford.
m. 1 William Waley; 17 oaks & 12 *robora*; Tranmere wood; 40d.; Henry Bernard.

3 1347 m. 1d William Launcelyn; 26 oaks & 7 *robora*; 1½ marks; William de Tranemoll.
m. 2 Rosea Launcelyn; 4 oaks; 2s 0d.; Robert Launcelyn.
m. 2 Robert Launcelyn; 3 oaks; 2s 0d.; John de Ruyton.
m. 3 Richard Launcelyn; 41 oaks; 6s. 8d.; Robert Launcelyn.
m. 3 Catherine, wife of Richard Launcelyn; 10 oaks; Richard Launcelyn her son.
m. 6 Henry Launcelyn; 5 oaks.
m. 13d Richard Launcelyn; purprestures in Poulton Lancelyn and Spital.
m. 14 Richard Launcelyn; dug peat in Little Meols.

proxima post festum Purificationis Beate Marie anno predicto cepit unum quercum viridem in bosco predicto et quod Willelmus Clerkessone die Lune proxima post festum Sancti Cedde anno predicto cepit unum quercum viridem in bosco predicto sine visu forestariorum contra assisam foreste.

Ideo preceptum est vicecomiti quod venire faciat eos. Postea veniunt et super hoc convicti liberati prisone. Postea educti fecerunt finem videlicet predictus Alanus pro vj d. per plegium Johannis Launcelyn et predictus Johannes Launcelyn pro vj d. per plegium Johnannis Doune et Henricus de Wylaston pro vj d. per plegium Roberti Donvill et Willelmus Waleys et Johannes de Waleys pro vij d. per plegium Johannis Doune et Henricus Broun pro xij d. per plegium predictum et Ricardus le Leder pro xij d. per plegium Roberti Donvill et Willelmus de Neuton pro xij d. per plegium predictum et Willelmus Clerkessone pro xij d. per plegium Willelmi Waleys.

m. 2

1.38

Compertum est per rotulos predicti Willelmi de Stanlegh forestarii quod Ricardus de Thornton die Jovis proxima post festum Sancti Michelis anno regni domini regis nunc vicesimo nono cepit in bosco de Leghton ramalia et ramos et quod Johannes de Berneston die Lune proxima post festum Purificationis Beate Marie anno regni domini regis nunc supradicto cepit unum quercum viridem in bosco de Overbebynton et quod Johannes Starky die Martis proxima post festum Sancte Marie Magdalene anno supradicto in bosco de Tranemoll in quodem loco que vocatur le Lere que est in defensione sue [cepit] [...] anno unum quercum viridem sine visu forestariorum contra assisam foreste.

Ideo preceptum est vicecomiti quod venire faciat eos. Postea veniunt et super hoc convicti liberati prisone. Postea educti fecerunt finem videlicet Ricardus de Thornton pro *vj d.* per plegium ([Henrici]) de Hoton et Johannes de Berneston pro *xv d.* per plegium Henrici Bernard et Hugonis de Bebynton et Johannes Starky *ij s.* per plegium Willelmi Waleys.

1.39

Compertum est etiam quod Ricardus de Bechynton dum vixit die Martis proxima post festum Purificationis Beate Marie anno supradicto cepit unum quercum viridem

Mary (February 3 1354) in the above year took a green oak in the said wood; and that William Clerkessone on Monday after the feast of St Chad in the above year (March 3 1354) took a green oak in the said wood without the view of the foresters against the assize of the forest.

Therefore the sheriff is ordered to make them come. Afterwards they come and thereupon convicted they are handed over to prison. Afterwards having been brought out they made fine as follows: Alan of 6d. by the pledge of John Launcelyn; and John Launcelyn of 6d. by the pledge of John Doune; and Henry de Wylaston of 6d. by the pledge of Robert Donvill and William Waley; and John de Waleys of 7d. by the pledge of John Doune; and Henry Broun of 12d. by the previous pledge; and Richard le Leder of 12d. by the pledge of Robert Donvill; and William de Neuton of 12d. by the previous pledge; and William Clerkessone of 12d. by the pledge of William Waleys.

m. 2

1.38
It is found by the rolls of William de Stanlegh, forester, that Richard de Thornton[1] on Thursday after the feast of St Michael in the 29th year of the reign of the present lord king (2 October 1355) took branches and wood in Leighton wood; and that John de Berneston[2] on the Monday after the feast of the Purification of Blessed Mary in the above year (2 February 1355) took a green oak in Higher Bebington wood; and that John Starky[3] on the Tuesday after the feast of St Mary Magdalene in the same year (28 July 1355) took a green oak in a place called Le Lere in Tranmere wood in his own enclosure in the [...] year without the view of the foresters against the assize of the forest.

Therefore the sheriff is ordered to make them come. Afterwards they come and thereupon convicted they are handed over to prison. Afterwards they were brought out and made fine; that is Richard de Thornton for *6d.* by the pledge of Henry de Hoton; and John de Berneston for 15d. by the pledge of Henry Bernard and Hugh de Bebington; and John Starky *2s. 0d.* by the pledge of William Waleys.

1.39
It is found that Richard de Bechynton,[4] when he was alive, on Tuesday after the feast of the Purification of Blessed Mary in the above year (3 February 1355) took and

1 1347 m. 13d Peter de Thornton; purprestures in Stoke.
2 1347 m. 5d Robert de Berneston; 20 oaks; pledge John de Berneston.
3 See **1.27** note.
4 See **1.32** note.

et quatuor carectatas de ramail in bosco de Greves et abduxit sine visu etc[a]. Ideo respondet quidam Willelmus de Becheton consanguineus eius et heres qui venit et fecit finem pro *xij d.* per plegium Johannis Lascels et Johannis Donvill.

1.40

Compertum est etiam quod prior de *Birkeheved* qui nunc est die Lune proxima post festum Purificationis Beate Marie anno predicto cepit et habuit unum quercum viridem in bosco de Birkeheved et quod idem prior die Mercurii post festum Sancti Andree anno vicesimo quinto cepit unum quercum viridem in bosco de Birkeved et quod idem prior die Mercurii proxima post festum Sancti Andree apostoli anno vicesimo sexto cepit unum quercum viridem in bosco de Birkeved sine visu forestariorum contra assisam foreste.

Ideo preceptum est[b] vicecomiti quod venire faciat eum. Postea venit predictus prior et dicit quod ipse et omnes predecessores sui priores loci predicti semper a tempore quo non extat memoria hi et ipse similiter habuerunt et habuit in bosco predicto quercus et alias arbores in bosco de Birkeved qui est boscus suus proprius quercus et omnes alias arbores pro voluntate sua sine visu forestariorum absque interruptione et hoc paratus est verificare prout curia etc.

Et Willelmus de Wakebrugge qui sequitur pro domino comite dicit quod in ultimo itinere justiciariorum istius foreste scilicet Thome de Ferrar et sociorum suorum justiciariorum huiusmodi consimilis presentatio facta fuit per quemdam predecessorem ipsius prioris qui nunc est de qua quidem presentatione convictus fecit finem et de hoc vocat recordum; et similiter dicit quod ipse et predecessores sui non usi sunt habere quercus et alia necessaria in bosco predicto unde petit recordum etc. Et super hoc datus est dies predictis Willelmo qui sequitur etc. et predicto priori usque diem Lune in secunda septimana Quadragesime apud Cestr' etc. Ad quem diem apud Cestr' coram prefatis justiciariis etc. venit predictus prior et ulterius datus est ei dies usque diem Lune proximam post festum Assumptionis Beate Marie apud Cestr' coram eisdem justiciariis de audiendo inde judicium etc.

1.41

Compertum est etiam quod Henricus *dux* Lanc' per suos die Jovis proxima post festum Sancti Michelis anno vicesimo quarto cepit tres quercus in bosco de Budeston et idem dux die Mercurii proxima post festum Sancti Cedde anno predicto cepit unum quercum in bosco de Wolveton et idem dux[c] anno vicesimo sexto cepit per suos

a *sine visu etc.* interlined
b *preceptum est* interlined
c *die* struck through

carried away a green oak and four cartloads of branches in Greves wood without the view etc.

Therefore a certain William de Becheton, cousin and heir, answers, who came and made fine for *12d.* by the pledge of John Lascels and John Donvill.

1.40

It is also found that the present prior of *Birkenhead*[1] on Monday after the feast of the Purification of Blessed Mary in the above year (9 February 1355) took and kept a green oak in Birkenhead wood; and that the same prior on Wednesday after the feast of St Andrew in the 25th year (7 December 1351) took a green oak in Birkenhead wood; and that the same prior on Wednesday after the feast of St Andrew, apostle, in the 26th year (5 December 1352) took a green oak in Birkenhead wood without the view of the foresters against the assize of the forest.

Therefore the sheriff is ordered to make him come. Afterwards the prior comes and says that he himself and all his predecessors, priors of that place, always from time immemorial, they and he himself likewise, have had oaks and other trees in Birkenhead wood, which is his own wood, and oaks and all other trees at will without the view of the foresters and without interruption and this he is ready to prove, just as the court etc.

And William de Wakebrugge, who sues for the lord earl, says that in the last eyre of the justices of this forest, that is of Thomas de Ferrers and his fellow justices, a similar presentment of this kind had been made by a predecessor of the present prior himself, concerning which presentment, being convicted, he made fine; and accordingly he vouches the record; and likewise he says that he (the prior) and his predecessors were not accustomed to have oaks and other necessities in that wood, for which he asks for the record etc. Whereupon a day is given for William who sues etc. and for the prior, for Monday in the second week of Lent at Chester etc. (26 February 1358). On which day at Chester before the justices etc. the prior comes and a further day is given to him for Monday after the Assumption of Blessed Mary (20 August 1358) at Chester before the same justices to hear their judgement etc.[2]

1.41

It is also found that Henry, *duke* of Lancaster, through his men, on Thursday after the feast of St Michael in the 24th year (30 September 1350) took three oaks in Bidston wood; and the same duke on Wednesday after the feast of St Chad in the same year (3 March 1350) took an oak in Wooton wood; and the same duke in the 26th year

1 1347 m. 3d prior of Birkenhead: 124 oaks in Birkenhead, Wolverton; fine 13s. 4d.; Roger de Shribbok.

2 See claim **2.33**.

ballivos sex quercus virides in bosco de Budeston et tres in bosco de Wolveton[a] et unum quercum in bosco de Birkeheved ad edificandum quoddam molendinum apud Budeston in le Thwayt sine visu forestariorum et quod maererium antiqui molendini venditum fuit Ricardo del Hogh et quod idem dux per ballivos die Martis proxima ante festum Sancti Cedde anno vicesimo octavo cepit unum quercum viridem in bosco de Budeston et etiam vendidit diversis hominibus sex quercus virides sine visu forestariorum et contra assisam foreste etc.

1.42 <Bebynton>
Compertum est etiam quod Johanna domina de Overbebynton die Lune proxima ante festum Sancti Michelis anno xxiiij[to] cepit unum viridem quercum in bosco de Overbebynton et quod eadem Johanna die Mercurii proxima post festum Sancti Cedde episcopi anno xxviij[o] cepit unum quercum viridem in bosco de Overbebynton sine visu forestariorum contra assisam foreste.

Ideo preceptum est vicecomiti quod venire faciat eam etc. Postea venit predicta Johanna et dicit quod ipsa et alii domini eiusdem manerii quorum statum etc. ipsa habet habuerunt et succiderunt quercus et alias arbores pro voluntate sua ad housbote et haybote et aliis necessariis suis propriis etc. in bosco suo proprio sine visu etc.[b] et hoc petit quod inquiratur prout curia.

Et super hoc datus est ei dies usque diem Lune in secunda septimana Quadragesime etc. Ad quem diem apud Cestr' venit predicta Johanna et ulterius datus est ei dies usque diem Lune proximam post festum Assumptionis Beate Marie apud Cestr' coram eisdem justiciariis in eodem statu quo nunc.

1.43
Compertum est etiam quod Ricardus del *Hogh* die Lune proxima ante festum Inventionis Sancte Crucis anno xxiiij[to] cepit unum quercum viridem in bosco de Leghton et quod idem Ricardus die Martis proxima post festum Sancti Michelis anno vicesimo septimo cepit unum quercum viridem in bosco predicto et quod idem Ricardus die Martis proxima post festum Sancti Gregorii anno regni domini regis nunc vicesimo octavo cepit unum quercum viridem in eodem bosco et quod idem Ricardus die Martis proxima ante festum Sancti Cedde anno vicesimo nono cepit unum quercum viridem in eodem bosco sine visu forestariorum contra assisam foreste.

a *Wolveton* a lost township in Bidston, Wooton. See below, p. liv.
b *sine visu etc.* interlined

(1352–1353) through his bailiffs took six green oaks in Bidston wood and three in Wooton wood and an oak in Birkenhead wood for building a mill at Bidston in le Thwayt[1] without the view of the foresters; and that timber from the old mill was sold to Richard del Hogh; and that the duke through his bailiffs on Tuesday before the feast of St Chad in the 28th year (23 February 1354) took a green oak in Bidston wood and also sold six green oaks to various men without the view of the foresters and against the assize of the forest etc.[2]

1.42 <Bebington>
It is also found that Joan, lady of Higher Bebington,[3] on Monday before the feast of St Michael in the 24th year (27 September 1350) took a green oak in Higher Bebington wood; and that Joan on Wednesday after the feast of St Chad, bishop, in the 28th year (5 March 1354) took a green oak in Higher Bebington wood without the view of the foresters and against the assize of the forest etc.

Therefore the sheriff is ordered to make her come etc. Afterwards Joan comes and says that she and the other lords of the same manor, whose estate etc. she has, have had and felled oaks and other trees at their will for housebote and haybote and for their other personal necessities etc. in their own wood without the view etc., and she asks that this be enquired into, just as the court.

And whereupon a date is given her for Monday in the second week of Lent (26 February 1358) etc. On which day in Chester Joan comes and a further day is given her for Monday after the feast of the Assumption of Blessed Mary (20 August 1358) at Chester before the same justices, in the same state as now.[4]

1.43
It is also found that Richard del *Hogh*[5] on Monday before the feast of the finding of the Holy Cross in the 24th year (26 April 1350) took a green oak in Leighton wood; and that Richard on Tuesday after the feast of St Michael in the 27th year (21 October 1353) took a green oak in the same wood; and that Richard on Tuesday after the feast of St Gregory in the 28th year of the present lord king (18 March 1354) took a green oak in the same wood; and that Richard on Tuesday before the feast of St Chad in the 29th year (23 February 1355) took a green oak in the same wood without the view of the foresters against the assize of the forest.

1 Dodgson, *Place Names*, p. 312.
2 This is the only plea that is neither adjudged nor adjourned. See claim **2.45**.
3 1347 m. 3 Robert de Bebynton took 100 oaks in Bebington wood; fine 13s. 4d; pledges John Domvill, Henry de Hoton and Hamo de Massey of Puddington.
4 See claim **2.28**.
5 1347 m. 4d Richard del Hogh; 11 oaks; 14d.
m. 14 Richard del Hogh dug peat in Thornton Hough.

Ideo preceptum est vicecomiti quod venire faciat eum etc. Postea venit et super hoc allocutus dicit quod ipse et omnes antecessores sui tenentes manerii predicti quorum statum habet semper habuerunt in bosco predicto housbote et haybote sine visu forestariorum antiquo pretextu ad liberam consuetudinem suorum in Thornton absque interruptione et hoc petit verificare prout curia.

Et super hoc datus est ei dies usque diem Lune in secunda septimana Quadragesime etc. Ad quem diem apud Cestr' coram prefatis justiciariis etc. venit predictus Ricardus del Hogh in propria persona sua et ulterius datus est ei dies usque diem Lune proximam post festum Assumptionis Beate Marie apud Cestr' coram eisdem justiciariis etc.

1.44

Compertum est etiam quod Henricus de *Hoton* die Mercurii proxima ante festum Omnium Sanctorum anno regni domini regis nunc vicesimo secundo cepit unum quercum viridem in bosco de Hoton et quod idem Henricus die Mercurii proxima ante festum Omnium Sanctorum anno vicesimo septimo cepit unum quercum viridem in bosco de Hoton et quod idem Henricus die Mercurii Sabbatini proximi post festum Omnium Sanctorum anno vicesimo nono cepit unum quercum viridem in bosco de Hoton;

et quod Ranulphus de *Bruyn* die Lune proxima post festum Sancti Andree anno vicesimo octavo cepit unum quercum viridem in bosco de Netherbebynton;

et quod Robertus de *Pulle* die Mercurii proxima ante [festum][a] Sancti Marci evangeliste anno vicesimo nono cepit tres quercus in bosco de Netherpull;

et quod Johannes le *Whyte* die Martis proxima post festum Sancti Martini anno vicesimo nono cepit unum quercum viridem in bosco de Parva Neston;

et quod Stephanus de *Merton* die Veneris proxima post festum Sancti Andree apostoli anno xxix^mo[b] cepit unum quercum viridem in bosco de Gayton et quod idem Stephanus die Martis proxima post festum Sancti Gregorii anno vicesimo secundo cepit unum viridem quercum in bosco de Gayton;

a *festum* omitted in MS
b *anno xxix^mo* interlined

Therefore the sheriff is ordered to make him come etc. Afterwards he comes and, questioned on this, he says that he and all his ancestors, tenants of the aforesaid manor, whose estate he has, have always had housebote and haybote in the said wood without the view of the foresters by an ancient right in accordance with their own free custom in Thornton without interruption and this he seeks to prove, just as the court.

And whereupon a day is given to him for Monday in the second week of Lent etc. (26 February 1358). On which day at Chester before the aforesaid justices etc. Richard del Hogh comes in person and a further day is given him for Monday after the feast of the Assumption of Blessed Mary (20 August 1358) at Chester before the same justices etc.[1]

1.44

It is also found that Henry de *Hoton*[2] on Wednesday before the feast of All Saints in the 22nd year of the reign of the present lord king (29 October 1349) took a green oak in Hooton wood; and that Henry on Wednesday before the feast of All Saints in the 27th year (30th October 1353) took a green oak in Hooton wood; and that Henry on Wednesday in the week after the feast of All Saints in the 29th year (4 November 1355) took a green oak in Hooton wood;

and that Ranulf de *Bruyn* on Monday after the feast of St Andrew in the 28th year (1 December 1354) took a green oak in Lower Bebington wood;

and that Robert de *Pulle*[3] on Wednesday before the feast of St Mark, evangelist, in the 29th year (22 April 1355) took three oaks in Netherpool wood;

and that John le *Whyte*[4] on Tuesday after the feast of St Martin in the 29th year (17 November 1355) took a green oak in Little Neston wood;

and that Stephen de *Merton*[5] on Friday after the feast of St Andrew, apostle, in the 29th year (2 December 1356) took a green oak in Gayton wood; and that Stephen on Tuesday after the feast of St Gregory in the 22nd year (18 March 1348) took a green oak in Gayton wood;

1 See claim **2.19**.
2 1347 m. 4d Richard de Hoton took an oak.
m. 5 Joanna de Hoton; an oak; fine 2s. 0d.; pledge Wiliam de Stanlegh.
m. 5d Henry de Hoton; 20 oaks.
m. 13d Henry de Hoton; purprestures in Hooton.
3 See **1.29** note.
4 1347 m. 14 John le White dug peat in Hargreve and Little Neston.
5 1347 m. 5 Stephen de Merton; 180 oaks in Gayton wood.
m. 14 Stephen de Merton dug peat in Gayton.
m. 13d Richard de Merton dug peat in Bebington.

et quod idem Johannes le *Whyte* die Mercurii proxima ante festum Omnium Sanctorum anno xxij° (cepit) unum quercum viridem in bosco de Parva Neston;

et quod Hamo de Mascy die Veneris proxima ante festum Sancti Andree apostoli anno vicesimo secundo cepit unum quercum viridem in bosco de *Podynton* et quod idem Hamo die Martis ante festum Sancti Cedde anno vicesimo nono cepit unum quercum viridem in bosco de Podynton subboscum et ramayl sine visu forestariorum et contra assisam foreste.

Ideo preceptum est vicecomiti quod venire faciat eos et postea veniunt predicti Henricus de Hoton et alii in propriis personis suis et dicunt singillatim quod quidam Ranulphus comes Cestr' concessit baronibus suis Cestris' housbote et haybote in nemore suo de omni genere bosci sine visu forestariorum et confirmavit militibus et liberis tenentibus totius Cestris' et eorum heredibus suis predictas libertates per cartam ipsius Ranulphi quam hic profferunt que hoc testatur que alibi irrotulatur.

Et dicunt quod ipsi ut [milites et] liberi tenentes etc. semper a tempore confectionis predicte carte et similiter antecessores sui etc. sine interruptione [semper] a tempore quo non exstat memoria scilicet unus quisque pro se usi sunt et gavisi et hoc parati sunt verificare per patriam. Et super hoc datus est eis dies apud Cestr' die Lune in secunda septimana Quadragesime etc. Ad quem diem apud Cestr' coram prefatis justiciariis veniunt predicti Henricus de Hoton Ranulphus le Bruyn Robertus de Pulle Stephanus de Merton Johannes le Whyte Hamo de Mascy de Podynton in propriis personis suis.

Et ulterius datus est eis dies usque diem Lune proximam post festum Assumptionis Beate Marie apud Cestr' coram prefatis justiciariis etc.

ij 2

m. 2d

1.45

Compertum est etiam per rotulos eiusdem Willelmi quod Willelmus[a] abbas Cestr' die Martis proxima ante festum Sancti Michelis anno nunc vicesimo secundo cepit

a *Willelmus* interlined

and that the same John le *Whyte* on Wednesday before the feast of All Saints in the 22nd year (29 October 1348) took a green oak in Little Neston wood;

and that Hamo de Mascy[1] on Friday before the feast of St Andrew, apostle, in the 22nd year (28 November 1348) took a green oak in *Puddington* wood; and that the same Hamo on Tuesday before the feast of St Chad in the 29th year (24 February 1355) took a green oak in Puddington wood and underwood and branches without the view of the foresters and against the assize of the forest.

Therefore the sheriff is ordered to make them come and afterwards come Henry de Hoton and the others in person and they say separately that Ranulf, earl of Chester, granted to his barons of Cheshire housebote and haybote of all kinds of wood from their own woodlands without the view of the foresters; and he confirmed to his knights and free tenants of the whole of Cheshire and to their heirs the said liberties by the charter of Ranulf himself which they produce here, which bears witness to this, which is enrolled elsewhere.

And they say that they themselves, as knights and free tenants etc., always from the time the charter was made, and likewise their ancestors etc. without interruption always from time immemorial, that is each one for himself, have used and enjoyed them and this they are ready to prove before a jury of their countrymen.

Whereupon a day is given to them at Chester for Monday in the second week of Lent (26 February 1358) etc. On which day at Chester before the aforesaid justices Henry de Hoton, Ranulf le Bruyn, Robert de Pulle, Stephen de Merton, John le Whyte, Hamo de Mascy of Puddington come in person.

And a further day is given to them for Monday after the feast of the Assumption of Blessed Mary (20th August 1358) at Chester before the aforesaid justices etc.[2]

2 2

m. 2d

1.45

It is also found by the rolls of the same William that William, abbot of Chester,[3] on Tuesday before the feast of St Michael in the 22nd year (29 September 1349) had his

1 1347 m. 2d Thomas de Mascy of Puddington; 2 oaks. 'Mortuus est'.
m. 5 Hamo de Mascy; 100 oaks; Bidston wood, with others; 'They settled elswhere'; Robert de Salnyley, Robert de Berneston and his brother John.
m. 5 Thomas de Mascy of Puddington; 20 oaks.
m. 4d Cecilia, wife of Thomas de Mascy; 4 oaks.

2 See their claims **2.30, 2.26, 2.31, 2.1, 2.8,** nb John le Whyte no claim recorded, and **2.15**.

3 1347 m. 5d Abbot of Chester took 300 oaks in Wirral and 3 oaks in Lea.
mm. 13d and 14 Abbot of Chester; various purprestures in Wirral.

in bosco de Lee per servientes suos unum quercum viridem et idem abbas die et anno predictis cepit in bosco de Salghale duos quercus virides et in bosco de Grevesby unum quercum viridem et abbas qui nunc est anno[a] vicesimo quarto cepit duos quercus virides[b] in bosco de Grescow et idem abbas die Mercurii proxima post festum Sancti Nicholai anno vicesimo sexto cepit duos quercus in bosco de Lee et quod idem abbas die Jovis proxima ante festum Pentecostes anno vicesimo septimo cepit viginti querculos in grova de Brumburgh et idem abbas die Martis proxima ante festum Sancti Gregorii anno supradicto cepit in boscis de Grevesby Wodechirch et Knoctyrum quatuor quercus virides et quod idem abbas die Jovis proxima ante festum Sancti Marci evangeliste anno vicesimo nono cepit sex quercus in boscis de Estham et Brumburgh et ramayl ad faciendum molendinum suum de Ines et quod idem abbas die Martis proxima post festum Sancti Michelis anno supradicto cepit sex quercus in bosco de Salghale et de Lee sine visu forestariorum contra assisam foreste et [in][c] deteriorationem;

<[...] j D[...]>

et quod idem abbas a festo Pasche anno regis nunc tricesimo usque idem festum anno tricesimo primo prostravit centum et tres quercus virides et cepit de boscis de Estham Brumburgh Welondrys Fysswalhull Salghal et Lee et abduxit et quod idem abbas a festo Pasche anno xxx^{mo} usque idem festum anno xxxj^{mo} habuit coprones de xxix quercubus viridibus in boscis[d] de Salghale et Lee sine visu forestariorum in deteriorationem dicte [foreste];

<per xij juratores>

et quod idem abbas die Sabbati in Vigilia Sancte Trinitatis anno regni domini regis nunc tricesimo [cepit ... quercus][e] et dedit Roberto de Dukenfeld de bosco suo de Grescow et die Martis proxima post festum Sancti Hillarii anno vicesimo septimo idem abbas dedit Johanni de Lascels xj quercus de bosco predicto;

<[...]>

et quod idem abbas anno regni domini regis nunc tricesimo cepit xij quercus[f] virides in bosco de Salghale et quod idem abbas eodem anno cepit x coprones quercus de eodem bosco et eos cariavit extra forestam ad opus suum proprium et quod idem abbas cepit septem quercus in boscis de Estham et Brumburgh et quod idem abbas tenet[g] leporarios suos in foresta et est venator ad vulpes.

a *anno* interlined
b *virides* interlined
c *in* omitted in MS
d *bosco* MS
e *cepit ... quercus* perhaps omitted by scribe
f *quercus* repeated in MS
g *habet* struck through and *tenet* interlined

servants take a green oak in Lea wood; and the abbot on the same day and year took two green oaks in Saughall wood; and in Greasby wood a green oak; and the present abbot in the 24th year (1350–1351) took two green oaks in Grescowe wood; and the abbot on Wednesday after the feast of St Nicholas in the 26th year (12 December 1352) took two oaks in Lea wood; and that the abbot on Thursday before the feast of Pentecost in the 27th year (24 May 1353) took twenty young oaks in the grove of Bromborough; and the abbot on Tuesday before the feast of St Gregory in the above year (5 March 1353) took four green oaks in the woods of Greasby, Woodchurch and Noctorum; and that the abbot on the Thursday before the feast of St Mark, evangelist, in the 29th year (21 April 1355) took six oaks in Eastham wood and Bromborough wood and branches for making his mill at Ince; and that the abbot on Tuesday after the feast of St Michael in the above year (2 October 1355) took six oaks in Saughall wood and Lea wood without the view of the foresters against the assize of the forest and to its damage;

<[...] D[...]>

and that the same abbot from Easter in the 30th year of the present king (24 April 1356) to the same feast in the 31st year (9 April 1357) felled 103 green oaks and took them from the woods of Eastham, Bromborough, Welondrys, Fysswalhull,[1] Saughall and Lea and carried them off; and that the abbot from Easter in the 30th year (24 April 1356) to the same feast in the 31st year (9 April 1357) had the branches of 29 green oaks in the woods of Saughall and Lea without the view of the foresters to the damage of the said forest;

<by 12 jurors>

and that the same abbot on Saturday in the eve of the Holy Trinity in the 30th year of the reign of the present lord king (6 August 1356) [took … oaks] and gave them to Robert de Dukenfeld from his wood in Grescowe and on Tuesday after the feast of St Hilary in the 27th year (14 January 1354) he gave John de Lascels eleven oaks from the same wood;

<[...]>

and that the abbot in the 30th year of the reign of the present lord king (1356–1357) took twelve green oaks in Saughall wood; and that the same abbot in the same year took ten branches from an oak from the same wood and carried them outside the forest for his own use; and that the abbot took seven oaks in the woods of Eastham and Bromborough; and that the abbot keeps his greyhounds in the forest and hunts foxes.

1 Dodgson, *Place Names*, p. 244.

Ideo preceptum est vicecomiti quod venire faciat eum etc. Postea venit predictus abbas et super hiis allocutus dicit quod quo ad boscum habendum sine visu forestariorum ipse et omnes predecessores sui abbates loci predicti habuerunt boscum in omnibus locis predictis sine visu forestariorum ad cariandum quo volebant et quo ad habendos leporarios in foresta predicta ipse et omnes predecessores sui abbates loci predicti habuerunt leporarios in foresta predicta ad capiendos lepores. Et de hoc ponit se super patriam etc. Ideo fiat inde juria. Et super hoc datus est dies usque diem Lune in secunda septimana Quadragesime apud Cestr' coram prefatis justiciariis etc. Et idem dies datus est prefato abbati per attornatum suum predictum etc. et quia scrutatis rotulis Willelmi de Stanlegh forestarii de feodo foreste de Wyrhale non est compertum in eisdem quod idem Willelmus fecit aliquam presentationem de quercubus succisis in Estham Wode et Brumburgh nec de atachiamentis respondendis ut officio suo deceret set illud concelat, ideo ad judicium de eo et foresta predicta (sesiatur). Postea venit predictus et protulit breve domini comitis sub privato sigillo prefatis justiciariis hic in hec verba:

Edward eisnez filz du noble roi Dengleterre et de Fraunce prince de Gales ducs de Cornwaill **[...]]...]** counte de Cestr' a noz chers et bien amez monsire Richard de Wyllughby et ses compaignons justices de eire de noz forestes de Cestrs' saluz. Porceqe noz chers en dieu labbe et covent de Cestr' nous ount fait fin de cent livres pour touz les trespas de vert et de veneson presentees sur eux ou nul de eux devant vous ore a voz darreines sessions de eire de noz dites forestes et vous mandons qe vous proclames sessions de eire des ditez forestes faces entrer la dicte fyn a paier deinz trois auns proscheines avenirs a les termes de Pasqe et de Seynt Michel par oweles porcions et descharger les dites abbe et covent de touz les trespas susditez par force de la dite fyn et ceste letre vous ent serra garrant et donne souz nostre prive seal a Londres le tierz iour de Decembre lan du regne notre tres [cher] seignour et pierre le roi Dengleterre trentism primer et de Fraunce disoctism.

Pretextu cuius brevis idem abbas admissus est ad finem predictam *C librarum pro transgressione* viridis et venacionis ut in breve continetur solvendam eidem domino ad terminos prescriptos videlicet ad quemlibet terminum xxv marcas termino primo solutionis ad festum Pasche proximum futurum et sic de termino in terminum quousque etc.

1.46

Compertum est etiam per presentationes forestariorum quod Willelmus capellanus de Brumburgh die Martis proxima post festum Sancti Cedde anno regis nunc tricesimo primo cepit unum quercum viridem in bosco de Brumburgh et quod Willelmus Corset

Therefore the sheriff is ordered to make him come etc. Afterwards the abbot comes and, questioned on these matters, says that as for having wood without the view of the foresters, he himself and all his predecessors, the abbots of that place, had wood in the said places without the view of the foresters to carry away wherever they wanted; and as for keeping greyhounds in the forest, he himself and all his predecessors, the abbots of that place, kept greyhounds in the forest to catch hares. And concerning this he puts himself on the country etc. Therefore a jury is to be summoned. And accordingly a day is given for Monday in the second week of Lent (26 February 1358) at Chester before the above justices etc.; and the same day is given to the abbot through his attorney etc.; and because, after examining the rolls of William de Stanlegh, forester in fee of the forest of Wirral, it is not found in them that William made any presentment concerning oaks which had been cut down in Eastham Wood and Bromborough or concerning replying to attachments as his office decrees, but he is concealing it; therefore judgement is to be made about this and the said forest (is to be seized). Afterwards the abbot came and there put before the justices a writ of the lord earl under his privy seal in these words: Edward the eldest son of the noble king of England and of France, prince of Wales, duke of Cornwall, [...] [...], earl of Chester to our dear and well beloved Sir Richard de Wylughby and his fellow justices of eyre of our forests of Chester, greeting. Because our beloved in God the abbot and convent of Chester have made us a fine of £100 for all the trespasses of the vert and the venison presented against them or [nothing ....last session of the eyre of the said forests][1] and we command you to proclaim sessions of eyre of our forests, and that you have the fine entered, to be paid within the next three years in equal portions at the terms of Easter and of St Michael, and to discharge the abbot and convent of all the above trespasses by means of this fine; and this letter will be your warrant. Given under our privy seal in London, on the third day of December in the 31st year of the reign of our dearest lord and father, the king of England, the eighteenth of France (3rd December 1357).

On the authority of this writ the abbot was admitted to the said fine of *£100 for trespass* of vert and venison as is contained in the writ, to be paid to the lord at the terms as written above, that is at each term 25 marks, the first term to be paid the next Easter; and so from term to term until etc.

1.46

It is also found by the presentments of the foresters that William, chaplain of Bromborough, on Tuesday after the feast of St Chad in the 31st year of the present king (7 March 1357) took a green oak in Bromborough wood; and that William

1 Meaning unclear.

die et anno predictis cepit unum quercum viridem in bosco predicto et quod Henricus de Chorleton die Lune proxima post festum Sancti Barnabe apostoli anno tricesimo cepit duos quercus videlicet unum in bosco de Berneston et alterum in bosco de Gayton et Adam de Tranemoll die Martis proxima post festum Sancti Barnabas anno predicto cepit unum quercum viridem in bosco de Tranemoll et quod Willelmus le Reve de Landekan in vigilia Epiphanie anno tricesimo cepit duos quercus virides in Landekangreve et Willelmus Boydel de Tranemoll pro mortuo bosco in eodem bosco de Tranemoll capto die Sabbati proxima ante festum Purificationis Beate Marie anno xxiij° et Johannes de Bebyton die Martis proxima ante festum Sancti Luce evangeliste anno supradicto cepit unum quercum in bosco de Bebynton et quod Thomas Emmessone de Brumburgh die Veneris proxima post festum Translationis Sancti Thome anno tricesimo cepit unum quercum viridem in bosco de[a] Brumburgh et quod Ricardus de Moston die Veneris proxima post festum Sancti Hillarii anno xxx^mo^ cepit duos quercus in bosco de Estham et quod Johannes de Moston die Veneris proxima ante festum Sancti Johannis ante Portam Latinam cepit unum quercum viridem in bosco de Grescowe et quod Johannes Cort de Salghale in vigilia Epiphanie anno tricesimo prostravit duos quercus virides in Arwegreve et quod Johannes Broun de Upton die Veneris proxima ante festum Sancti Augustini anno supradicto cepit conprones unius quercus viridis in bosco de Wodechirch et quod Hugo de Fornby die Martis proxima ante festum Sancti Andree anno xxx^mo^ cepit unum quercum in bosco de Budeston et quod Willelmus le Harper die Lune proxima post festum Sancti Luce anno predicto cepit conprones unius quercus viridis in bosco de Wodechirch et quod Willelmus de Coventr' de Bebynton die Lune proxima ante festum Sancti Johannis ante Portam Latinam anno xxx^mo^ cepit unum quercum in bosco de Bebynton sine visu forestariorum contra assisam foreste.

Ideo preceptum est vicecomiti quod venire faciat eos. Postea veniunt et super hoc convicti liberati prisone. Postea educti redempti sunt videlicet:

Willelmus Capellanus pro xij d. per plegium Thome de Capenhurst et

Willelmus Corset pro xij d. per plegium Ade de Tranemoll et

Henricus de Chorleton pro ij s. per plegium Henrici de Hoton et

Adam de Tranemoll pro xij d. per plegium (Ranulphi) le Bruyn et

Willelmus le Reve pro ij s. per plegium Willelmi de Stanlegh et Henrici de Chorleton et

Willelmus Boydel pro vj d. per plegium Johannis Donvill et

a *Tranemoll* struck through

Corset on the same day and year took a green oak in the same wood; and that Henry de Chorleton on Monday after the feast of St Barnabas, apostle, in the 30th year (13 June 1356) took two oaks, that is, one in Barnston wood and the other in Gayton wood; and Adam de Tranemoll[1] on Tuesday after the feast of St Barnabas in the same year took a green oak in Tranmere wood; and that William le Reve of Landican on the eve of the Epiphany in the 30th year (5 January 1356) took two green oaks in Landecangreve[2]; and William Boydell[3] of Tranmere for dead wood taken on Saturday before the feast of the Purification of Blessed Mary in the 23rd year (31 January 1349) in Tranmere wood; and John de Bebynton[4] on Tuesday before the feast of St Luke, evangelist, in the above year (13 October 1349) took an oak in Bebington wood; and that Thomas Emmessone of Bromborough on Friday after the Translation of St Thomas in the 30th year (8 July 1356) took a green oak in Bromborough wood; and that Richard de Moston on Friday after the feast of St Hilary in the 30th year (15 January 1356) took two oaks in Eastham wood; and that John de Moston on Friday before the feast of St John before the Latin Gate took a green oak in Grescowe wood; and that John Cort of Saughall on the eve of the Epiphany in the 30th year (5 January 1356) cut down two green oaks in Arrowgreve; and that John Broun[5] of Upton on Friday before the feast of St Augustine in that year (26 May 1356) took branches from a green oak in Woodchurch wood; and that Hugh de Fornby on Tuesday before the feast of St Andrew in the 30th year (29 November 1356) took an oak in Bidston wood; and that William le Harper on Monday after the feast of St Luke in the same year (24 October 1356) took branches of a green oak in Woodchurch wood; and that William de Coventry of Bebington on Monday before the feast of St John before the Latin gate in the 30th year (2 May 1356) took an oak from Bebington wood without the view of the foresters against the assize of the forest.

Therefore the sheriff is ordered to make them come. Afterwards they come and thereupon convicted they are handed over to prison. Afterwards they are brought out and redeemed, namely:

William Chaplain for a fine of 12d. by the pledge of Thomas de Capenhurst and

William Corset of 12d. by the pledge of Adam de Tranemoll and

Henry de Chorleton of 2s. 0d. by the pledge of Henry de Hoton and

Adam de Tranemoll of 12d. by the pledge of Ranulf le Bruyn and

William le Reve of 2s. 0d. by the pledge of William de Stanlegh and

Henry de Chorleton and William Boydell of 6d. by the pledge of John Donvill and

1 1347 See **1.28** note.
2 Dodgson, *Place Names*, p. 268.
3 1347 See **1.32** note.
4 1347 See **1.42** note.
5 1347 See **1.36** note.

Johannes de Bebynton pro xij d. per plegium Thome de Capenhurst et

Thomas Emmessone pro xij d. per plegium Ranulphi le Bruyn et

Ricardus de Moston pro ij [s.] per plegium Henrici de Hoton et

Johannes de Moston pro xij d. per plegium Roberti de Berneston et

Johannes Cort pro ij s. per plegium Willelmi Waleys et

Johannes Broun pro xij d. per plegium Henrici [Ocllessone] et

Hugo de Fornby pro vj d. per plegium Thome de Capenhurst et

Willelmus Harper pro vj d. per plegium Hamonis de Mascy et

Willelmus de Coventr' pro xij d. per plegium Johannis Donvill.

1.47

Compertum est etiam per presentationes eorundem forestariorum quod Rogerus Hullessone de Wodechirch die Lune in Crastino Pasche anno xxx^{mo} cepit in bosco de Wodechirch tres querculos et quod Ricardus de Pulle de Irreby die Jovis proxima post festum Pasche anno xxx^{mo} cepit unum quercum viridem in bosco de Grescow et quod Johannes de Moston die Jovis proxima post festum Sancte Trinitatis anno xxx^{mo} cepit unum quercum mortuum in bosco de Knogburton et quod Robertus de Dukenfeld die Sabbati proxima ante festum Sancti Jacobi anno xxx^{mo} cepit unum quercum viridem in bosco de Grescowe et Hugo le Walker de Wodechirch die Jovis proxima ante festum Exaltationis Sancte Crucis anno xxx^{mo} cepit unum quercum viridem in bosco de Wodechirch et quod Ricardus le reve de Irreby die Veneris proxima post festum Purificationis Beate Marie anno xxxj^{mo} cepit duos quercus virides in bosco de Grescowe et quod Jacobus Spendelove per tres dies anno xxxj^{mo} cepit tres quercus virides de bosco de Tranemoll. Et quod Robertus [...] die Sabbati proxima ante festum Sancti Valentini anno xxx^{mo} cepit unum quercum viridem in bosco de Wolveton sine visu forestariorum et contra assisam foreste in deteriorationem eorundem boscorum. Ideo preceptum est vicecomiti quod venire faciat eos. Postea veniunt et super hoc convicti[a] liberati prisone. Postea educti redempti sunt videlicet:

Rogerus Hullessone pro vj d. per plegium Johannis de Leghton et Ricardus de Pulle pro xij d. per plegium Henrici de Chorleton et Johannes de Moston pro vj [d.] per plegium Roberti de Berneston et, Robertus de Dukenfeld pro xij d. per plegium Michaeli [Savage] et Hugo Walker pro xij d. per plegium Johannis Donvill et Ricardus le Reve pro ij s. per plegium Ricardi de Pulle et

Jacobus Spendelove pro [vj] s. et Robertus [...] pro [...]d. per plegium predictum etc.

a *convicti* interlined

John de Bebynton of 12d. by the pledge of Thomas de Capenhurst and

Thomas Emmessone of 12d. by the pledge of Ranulf le Bruyn and

Richard de Moston of 2s. 0d. by the pledge of Henry de Hoton and

John de Moston of 12d. by the pledge of Robert de Berneston and

John Cort of 2s. 0d. by the pledge of William Waleys and

John Broun of 12d. by the pledge of Henry [Ocllessone] and

Hugh de Fornby of 6d. by the pledge of Thomas de Capenhurst and

William Harper of 6d. by the pledge of Hamo de Mascy and

William de Coventr' of 12d. by the pledge of John Donvill.

1.47

It is also found by the presentments of the same foresters that Roger de Hullessone of Woodchurch on Monday the day after Easter in the 30th year (25 April 1356) took three oak saplings in Woodchurch wood; and that Richard de Pulle[1] of Irby on Thursday after Easter in the 30 th year (28 April 1356) took a green oak in Grescowe wood; and that John de Moston on Thursday after the feast of the Holy Trinity in the 30th year (23 June 1356) took a dead oak in Noctorum wood; and that Robert de Dukenfeld on Saturday before the feast of St James in the 30th year (23 July 1356) took a green oak in Grescowe wood; and Hugh le Walker of Woodchurch on Thursday before the feast of the Exaltation of the Holy Cross in the 30th year (8 September 1356) took a green oak in Woodchurch wood; and that Richard le Reve of Irby on Friday after the feast of the Purification of Blessed Mary in the 31st year (3 February 1357) took two green oaks in Grescowe wood; and that James Spendelove over three days in the 31st year (1357–1358) took three green oaks in Tranmere wood; and that Robert [...] on Saturday before the feast of St Valentine in the 30th year (13 February 1356) took a green oak in Wolveton wood without the view of the foresters and against the assize of the forest to the damage of the same woods. Therefore the sheriff is ordered to make them come. Afterwards they come and convicted of this they are handed over to prison. Afterwards they are brought out and redeemed, as follows: Roger Hullessone for a fine of 6d. by the pledge of John de Leghton; and Richard de Pulle for a fine of 12d. by the pledge of Henry Chorleton; and John de Moston 6d. by the pledge of Robert de Berneston; and Robert de Dukenfeld of 12d. by the pledge of Michael Savage; and Hugh Walker of 12d. on the pledge of John Donvill; and Richard le Reve of 2s. 0d. by the pledge of Richard de Pulle; and James Spendelove of 6s. 0d. and Robert [...] of [12]d by the said pledge etc.

1 1347 See **1.29** note.

m. 3

1.48

Compertum est etiam per rotulos dictorum forestariorum quod Thomas prior de Birkeheved Ricardus de Wolveton Willelmus filius Dawe Willelmus filius Willelmi de Claghton Ricardus filius Willelmi de eadem villa Johannes Faber de eadem Radulphus le Mayre de Secum Willelmus de Shroulakes Johannes de le Rake Ricardus del Halle Johannes le Barker Willelmus Coyde Rogerus Nerford Adam de Acton Johannes Faber de Lyscark Thomas Tasy Adam le Gose Thomas filius Willelmi de Pulton Johannes rector ecclesie de Kirkebywaley Huwet de Byram Henricus le Walker Willelmus de Stanay de Waleys Thomas de Neubolt Johannes Doune Thomas rector ecclesie de Thurstaneston et Johannes de Moston consueti sunt fodere turbas in vasto de Budeston extra coopertum scilicet Budeston Keer et eas asportare sine visu forestariorum et facere puteos profundos et largos et turbas asportare pro voluntate sua ad nocumentum ferarum.

Ideo preceptum est vicecomiti quod venire faciat eos et postea veniunt et super hoc convicti liberati prisone et postea educti redempti sunt videlicet:

predictus prior pro xij d. per plegium Ricardi de Wolveton et Willelmi filii Dawe et

Ricardus de Wolveton pro *vj d.* per plegium Willelmi filii Dawe et

Willelmus filius Dawe pro vj d. per plegium Willelmi filii Willelmi de Claghton et

Willelmus filius Willelmi pro vj d. per plegium Ricardi filii Willelmi de eadem et

Ricardus filius Willelmi pro vj d. per plegium Johannis Faber de eadem et

Johannes filius Fabri pro vj d. per plegium Radulphi le Mayre de Secum et

Radulphus le Mayre pro vj d. per plegium Willelmi de Shroulakes et

Willelmus de Shroulakes pro vj d. per plegium Johannis del Rake et

Johannes del Rake pro vj d. per plegium Ricardi del Halle et

Ricardus del Halle pro vj d. per plegium Johannis le Barker et

m. 3

1.48 <6d.>
It is also found by the rolls of the foresters that Thomas, prior of Birkenhead,[1] Richard de Wolveton, William son of Dawe, William son of William de Claghton, Richard son of William of the same town, John Faber[2] of the same, Ralph le Mayre of Seacombe, William de Shroulakes, John de le Rake, Richard del Halle, John le Barker, William Coyde, Roger Nerford, Adam de Acton, John Faber of Liscard, Thomas Tasy, Adam le Gose, Thomas son of William de Pulton,[3] John, rector of the church of Wallasey, Huwet de Byram, Henry le Walker, William de Stanay[4] of Wallasey, Thomas de Neubolt, John Doune, Thomas, rector of Thurstaston church and John de Moston were accustomed to dig peat in Bidston waste outside the covert, that is Bidston Car, and remove it without the view of the foresters, and to dig deep and large pits and to take away peat at their will to the harm of the beasts.

Therefore the sheriff is ordered to make them come and afterwards they come and convicted of this they are handed over to prison and afterwards they are brought out and redeemed, as follows:

the prior for a fine of 12d. by the pledge of Richard de Wolveton and William son of Dawe; and Richard de Wolveton of 6d. by the pledge of William son of Dawe; and

William son of Dawe of 6d. by the pledge of William son of William de Claghton; and

William son of William for a fine of 6d. by the pledge of Richard son of William of the same; and Richard son of William of 6d. by the pledge of John the smith of the same; and

John son of the smith of 6d. by the pledge of Ralph le Mayre of Seacombe; and

Ralph le Mayre for 6d. by the pledge of William de Shroulakes; and

William de Shroulakes of 6d. by the pledge of John del Rake; and

John del Rake for 6d. by the pledge of Richard del Halle; and

Richard del Halle of 6d. by the pledge of John le Barker; and

1 1347 See **1.40** note.

2 1347 m. 2 Thomas Faber took 1 *robur*; fine 2s. 0d.; pledge Richard le Weston.
m. 4d William Faber, 1 oak.
m. 6 Richard Faber, 3 oaks.

3 1347 m. 4 Richard de Pulton, 3 oaks; 2s. 0d.; Thomas Blonk.
m. 6 Catherine, lady of Pulton, 1 oak.

4 1347 m. 4 David de Staney, 60 oaks; his son David, 26 oaks; fine 13s. 4d; William son of Hugh de Staney.
m. 13d David de Staney, various purprestures.

Johannis le Barker pro vi d. per plegium Willelmi Coyde et

Willelmus Coyde pro vj d. per plegium Rogeri Nerford et

Rogerus Nerford pro vj d. per plegium Ade de Acton et

Adam de Acton pro vj d. per plegium Johannis Faber de Lyscark et

Johannes Faber pro vj d. per plegium Thome Tasy et

Thomas Tasy pro vj d. per plegium Ade le Gose et

Adam le Gose pro vj d. per plegium Thome filij Willelmi de Pulton et

Thomas filius Willelmi pro vj d. per plegium Johannis rectoris de Kirkebywaley et

Johannes rector pro vj d. per plegium Huweti de Byram et

Huwet pro vj d. per plegium Henrici le Walker et

Henricus le Walker pro vj d. per plegium Willelmi de Stanay de Walay et

Willelmus de Stanay pro vj d. per plegium Thome de Neubold et

Thomas de Neubold pro vj d. per plegium Johannis Doune et

Johannes Doune pro vj d. per plegium Thome rectoris ecclesie de Thurstanston et

Thomas rector pro vj d. per plegium Johannis de Moston et

Johannes de Moston pro vj d. per plegium Thome rectoris ecclesie de Thurstanston.

1.49

xij juratores ad articulos presentant quod Hamo de Mascy die Mercurii proxima ante festum Sancti Barnabe anno vicesimo septimo dedit Johanni de Lascels unum quercum viridem in bosco de Podynton qui quidem Johannes illum habuit sine visu forestariorum.

Ideo preceptum est vicecomiti quod venire faciat eum et postea venit et super hoc convictus liberatus prisone et eductus fecit finem pro *xij d.* per plegium Thome de Capenhurst.

1.50

Item presentant quod Ricardus de Becheton die Lune proxima ante festum Sancti Augustini anno vicesimo quarto vendidit Rogero Coventr' et Lych' episcopo unum quercum in bosco de Greves et quod Johannes de Leghton die Sabbati in vigilia

John le Barker[1] of 6d. by the pledge of William Coyde; and

William Coyde of 6d. by the pledge of Roger Nerford; and

Roger Nerford of 6d. by the pledge of Adam de Acton; and

Adam de Acton of 6d. by the pledge of John Faber of Liscard; and

John Faber of 6d. by the pledge of Thomas Tasy; and

Thomas Tasy of 6d. by the pledge of Adam le Gose; and

Adam le Gose[2] of 6d. by the pledge of Thomas son of William de Pulton; and

Thomas son of William for a fine of 6d. by the pledge of John, the rector of Wallasey; and

John, the rector of 6d. by the pledge of Huwet de Byram; and

Huwet of 6d. by the pledge of Henry le Walker; and

Henry le Walker of 6d. by the pledge of William de Stanay of Wallasey; and

William de Stanay of 6d. by the pledge of Thomas de Neubold; and

Thomas de Neubold of 6d. by the pledge of John Doune; and

John Doune of 6d. by the pledge of Thomas, rector of the church of Thurstaston; and

Thomas, the rector of 6d. by the pledge of John de Moston; and

John de Moston of 6d. by the pledge of Thomas, rector of the church of Thurstaston.

1.49
Twelve jurors present to the articles that Hamo de Mascy[3] on Wednesday before the feast of St Barnabas in the 27th year (5 June 1353) gave John de Lascels a green oak in Puddington wood and John had it without the view of the foresters.

Therefore the sheriff is ordered to make him come; and afterwards he comes; and convicted of this, he is handed over to prison and having been brought out he made fine of *12d.* by the pledge of Thomas de Capenhurst.

1.50
Item they present that Richard de Becheton[4] on Monday before the feast of St Augustine in the 24th year (24 May 1350) sold to Roger, bishop of Coventry and Lichfield, an oak in Greves wood; and that John de Leghton on Saturday the eve of

1 1347 m. 4d John Barker, 10 oaks.
2 1347 m. 2d Adam Goos, 1 oak; 2s. 0d.; Richard Launcelyn.
3 See **1.44** note.
4 See **1.39** note.

Sancte Trinitatis anno tricesimo dedit Johanni Doune unum quercum de bosco de Leghton;

eodem die et anno dedit Ranulpho le Bruyn unum quercum viridem in[a] eodem bosco, et idem Johannes vendidit die Lune in septimana Pasche anno xxxj^{mo} unum quercum parochianis de Neston pro *xiij s. iiij d.* in vastum et deteriorationem eiusdem bosci.

Ideo preceptum est vicecomiti quod venire faciat eos etc. et postea venit Willelmus de Becheton consanguineus et heres predicti Ricardi et fecit finem pro quercubus predictis pro *xx s.* per plegium Johannis Lassels et Roberti Bamville et Johannes de Leghton similiter venit et super hoc convictus liberatus prisone et eductus redemptus est pro xiij s. iiij d. per plegium Ranulfi le Bruyn. Et[b]

1.51
Item presentant quod Robertus de Dokenfeld nuper ballivus de Budeston anno regni domini regis nunc vicesimo tercio dedit maeremium tenentibus de Budeston videlicet rok' et rest' sine visu forestariorum.

<dimidia marca>

Ideo preceptum est vicecomiti quod venire faciat eum et postea venit et super hoc convictus liberatus prisone eductus redemptus est pro vj s. viij d. per plegium Ricardi de Whitelegh et Johannis de Leghton.

1.52
Item presentant quod boscus de Leghton destructus est et deterioratus per dominos de Leghton et variatos eiusdem ab anno domini regis nunc vicesimo usque annum vicesimum nonum ad dampnum *L s.* Ideo boscus predictus capiatur.

1.53
Item presentant quod prior de Birkeheved die dominica proxima ante festum Sancti Barnabe apostoli anno xxxj^{mo} dedit sex querculos Johanni Domvill de bosco suo[c] de Birkeheved et die Lune proxima post festum Sancti Luce anno vicesimo sexto dedit Willelmo de Stanlegh duos querculos et Johanni de Lascels duos querculos die et anno predictis sine visu forestariorum contra assisam.

<dimidia marca>

Ideo preceptum est vicecomiti quod venire faciat eum et postea venit et convictus liberatus prisone, et eductus redemptus est pro vj s. viij d. per plegium Willelmi de Stanlegh et Johannis de Lascels.

a *in* interlined
b Nothing follows this in the MS.
c *suo* interlined

the Holy Trinity in the 30th year (18 June 1356) gave John Doune an oak in Leighton wood;

on the same day and in the same year he gave Ranulf le Bruyn a green oak in the same wood; and John on Monday in Easter week in the 31st year (10 April 1357) sold an oak to the parishioners of Neston for 13s. 4d. to the waste and damage of the wood. Therefore the sheriff is ordered to make them come etc.; and afterwards William de Becheton, Richard's cousin and heir, comes and makes fine of *20s. 0d.* for the oaks by the pledge of John Lassels and Robert Bamville; and John de Leighton likewise comes; and thereupon convicted he is handed over to prison and having been brought out he is redeemed for *13s. 4d.* by the pledge of Ranulf le Bruyn. And

1.51
Item they present that Robert de Dokenfeld, former bailiff of Bidston, in the 23rd year of the reign of the present lord king (1349–1350) gave timber to the tenants of Bidston namely rok' and rest' without the view of the foresters.

<half a mark>

Therefore the sheriff is ordered to make him come. Afterwards he comes and thereupon convicted, he is handed over to prison, and having been brought out he is redeemed for 6s. 8d. by the pledge of Richard de Whitelegh and John de Leghton.

1.52
Item they present that Leighton wood was destroyed and damaged by the lords of Leighton[1] and various men of the same place from the 20th year of the present lord king (1346) to the 29th year (1355) to the damage of *50s. 0d.* Therefore the wood is to be taken.

1.53
Item they present that the prior of Birkenhead[2] on Sunday before the feast of St Barnabas, apostle, in the 31st year (3 June 1357) gave six oak saplings to John Domvill from his wood in Birkenhead; and on Monday after the feast of St Luke in the 26th year (17 December 1352) gave two oak saplings to William de Stanlegh and to John de Lascels two oak saplings on the same day and year without the view of the foresters against the assize.

<half a mark>

Therefore the sheriff is ordered to make him come; and afterwards he comes; having been convicted he is handed over to prison and having been brought out he is redeemed for 6s. 8d. by the pledge of William de Stanlegh and John de Lascels.

1 1347 m. 6 Magota de Leighton took 34 oaks.
m. 14 John de Leighton dug peat.

2 See **1.48** note.

1.54
Item presentant quod boscus de Tranemoll vastatus et deterioratus ab anno regis nunc vicesimo usque annum eiusdem vicesimum nonum per Ricardum Starkey Willelmum de Tranemoll et Willelmum filium eius dominos eiusdem ville et per Willelmum de Stanlegh et Johannem Lascels et subforestarios suos et Robertum Banville et Henricum Broun ad dampnum *C s.*

Ideo boscus *capiatur.*

1.55
Item presentant quod Johanna de Hoton, domina de Bebynton, die Lune proxima ante festum Sancti Andree anno xxvj dedit Willelmo de Stanlegh duos quercus in bosco de Bebynton, et quod idem Willelmus die Mercurii proxima post festum Sancti Dunstani anno vicesimo quarto cepit de bosco de Bebynton sex quercus sine licencia eiusdem Johanne et sex querculos. Ideo preceptum est vicecomiti quod venire faciat eos. Postea venit predicta Johanna et super hoc convicta liberata prisone educta fecit finem pro ij s. per plegios Johannis Doune et Willelmi de Stanlegh.

Et Willelmus de Stanlegh quo ad presens versus ipsam Johannam predictam dicit quod ipse habuit quercus illos ex dono predicte Johanne et non sine licencia sua et hoc petit quod inquiratur per patriam et predicta Johanna presens in curia et tam pro dicto comite quam pro se ipsa dicit quod ipse non habuit quercus illos ex dono suo et hoc petit similiter quod inquiratur per patriam.

Ideo capiatur inde inter eos juria. Set ponitur in respectum usque diem Lune in secunda septimana Quadragesime apud Cestr'. Ad quem diem apud Cestr' coram prefatis justiciariis etc. veniunt tam predicta Johanna quam predictus Willelmus et super hoc datus est eis dies apud Cestr' coram eisdem justiciariis die Lune proxima post festum Assumptionis Beate Marie.

1.56
Item presentant quod boscus de Netherbebynton est destructus per homines eiusdem ville ad dampnum *dimidie marce.*

1.57
Item presentant quod Henricus de Molyneux et Ricardus Haydok forestarii Willelmi de Stanlegh, die Lune proxima post festum Sancti Michelis anno vicesimo tertio habuerunt tres quercus in bosco de Netherbebynton de dono David de Morton et parcenariorum suorum sine licencia alicuius.

Ideo preceptum est vicecomiti quod venire *faciat* eos.

1.54

Item they present that Tranmere wood was wasted and damaged from the 20th year of the present king to the 29th year of the same (1346–1355) by Richard Starkey,[1] William de Tranemoll[2] and William, his son, lords of the same township, and by William de Stanlegh and John Lascels and their underforesters, and Robert Banville and Henry Broun[3] to the damage of *100s. 0d.*

Therefore the wood *is to be taken.*

1.55

They present that Joan de Hoton,[4] lady of Bebington, on Monday before the feast of St Andrew in the 26th year (26 November 1352) gave William de Stanlegh two oaks in Bebington wood and that William on Wednesday after the feast of St Dunstan in the 24th year (24 May 1350) took six oaks in Bebington wood without Joan's permission and six oak saplings.

Therefore the sheriff is ordered to make them come. Afterwards Joan comes and convicted of this she is handed over to prison. Having been brought out she made fine of 2s. 0d. on the pledges of John Doune and William de Stanlegh.

And William de Stanlegh, in this matter being present against Joan, says that he had those oaks as a gift from Joan and not without her permission and he asks for this, that an inquiry by jury should be held; and Joan is present in court and for the earl as well as for herself, she says that he did not have the oaks as a gift from her and likewise she asks that an inquiry by jury should be held.

Therefore a jury is to be summoned between them. But it is respited until Monday in the second week of Lent at Chester (26 February 1358). On which day at Chester before the justices etc. Joan and William come and thereupon they are given a day at Chester before the same justices for Monday after the feast of the Assumption of Blessed Mary (20 August 1358).

1.56

Item they present that Lower Bebington wood was destroyed by men of the same township to the damage of *half a mark.*

1.57

Item they present that Henry de Molyneux and Richard Haydok, foresters of William de Stanlegh, on Monday after the feast of St Michael in the 23rd year (5 October 1349) had three oaks in Lower Bebington wood as a gift from David de Morton and his parceners without permission from anyone. Therefore the sheriff is ordered *to make* them come.

1 See **1.27** note.
2 See **1.46** note.
3 See **1.36** note.
4 See **1.44** note.

1.58
Item presentant quod Willelmus de Stanlegh eodem die et anno habuit unum quercum ibidem et quod idem Willelmus habuit unum quercum in bosco de Stanay die Lune in festo Sancti Benedicti anno vicesimo septimo sine visu forestariorum et [ad][a] deteriorationem bosci et quod idem Willelmus de Stanlegh per servos suos et Johannes de Lascels equitator foreste per famulos suos ceperunt pro carucis suis maeremium [et][c] virgas in bosco de Prenton in deteriorationem bosci.

Ideo preceptum est vicecomiti quod venire faciat eos et postea veniunt predicti Willelmus et Johannes et super hoc allocuti dicunt quod ipsi in nullo sunt culpabiles, et de hoc ponunt se super patriam etc.

Ideo fiat inde juria et Robertus Banville fecit finem pro *ij s.* per plegium Ricardi le Bruyn et veniunt partes apud Cestr' die Lune in secunda septimana Quadragesime. Ad quem diem apud Cestr' coram justiciariis venit predicti Willelmus et deinde datus est ei dies apud Cestr' coram justiciariis die Lune proxima post festum Assumptionis Beate Marie.

Rotulus iij Wyrhale

m. 3d

1.59
Item presentant quod Willelmus de *Stanlegh* magister forestarius de Wyrhale per quinque annos iam continue elapsos [...] [...] hominibus de Netherbebynton quolibet anno xij[es] ad permittendum eos habere animalia sua depascentia in foresta [...] [...] ad nocumentum ferarum et destructionem.

Ideo preceptum est vicecomiti quod venire faciat eum et postea venit predictus Willemus [de] [Stanlegh] [...] [...] [...] dicit quod ipse in nullo est inde culpabilis et de hoc ponit se super patriam etc. Ideo fiat inde juria et preceptum est [vicecomiti quod] venire faciat xviij probos etc. die Lune in secunda septimana Quadragesime per quos etc. Ad quem diem venit predictus [Willelmus] et deinde datus est ei dies apud Cestr' die Lune proxima post festum Assumptionis Beate Marie.

a *ad* omitted in MS
b *et* omitted in MS

1.58
Item they present that William de Stanlegh on the same day and in the same year had an oak in the same place; and that William had an oak in Stanney wood on Monday the feast of St Benedict in the 27th year (21 March 1353)[1] without the view of the foresters and to the damage of the wood; and that William de Stanlegh through his servants and John de Lascels rider of the forest, through his household servants, took for their plough-teams timber and withies in Prenton wood to the damage of the wood.

Therefore the sheriff is ordered to make them come; and afterwards William and John come, and questioned concerning this say that they are in no way guilty; and about this they put themselves on the country etc. Therefore a jury is to be summoned; and Robert Banville made fine for *2s. 0d.* by the pledge of Richard le Bruyn; and the parties come to Chester on Monday in the second week of Lent (26 February 1358). On which day at Chester before the justices William come. He is then given a day at Chester before the justices for Monday after the feast of the Assumption of Blessed Mary. (20 August 1358)[2]

Roll 3 Wirral

m. 3d

1.59
Item they present that William de *Stanlegh*, master forester of Wirral, continuously for the last five years, twelve times in each year [...] the men of Lower Bebington so as to permit them to have their animals feeding in the forest [...] [...] to the harm of the beasts and the destruction of the forest.

Therefore the sheriff is ordered to make him come and afterwards William de Stanlegh comes and says that he is in no way guilty of it; and concerning this he puts himself on the country etc. Therefore a jury is to be summoned and the sheriff is ordered to make eighteen good men come etc. on Monday in the second week of Lent, (26 February 1358) by whom etc. On which day [William] comes and he is then given a day at Chester on Monday after the feast of the Assumption of Blessed Mary (20 August 1358)[3].

1 In 1353 the feast of St Benedict, and of his translation, both fell on Thursday.
2 See claims **2.11**, **2.29** and **2.51**.
3 See claim **2.11**.

1.60
Item presentant quod Willelmus tunc[a] abbas Cestr' proximus predecessor abbatis qui nunc est fecit quoddam clausum apud Halesutton cum quodam profundo fossato et una haya alta inclusum[b] ita quod fere non possunt intrare nec exire ad nocumentum ferarum [domini]. Abbas qui nunc est tenet clausum illum sic inclusum contra assisam foreste. Nesciunt qui [...] [...]. Ideo [preceptum] est vicecomiti quod venire faciat eum. Postea venit predictus abbas et inde allocutus nichil dicit.

Ideo clausum predictum prosternatur [...].

Et [...] [...] predictus abbas in *misericordia* pro contumacione. Nichil de misericordia ipsius abbatis quia alibi fecit finem etc.

1.61
Item presentant quod abbas de Basyngwerk qui nunc est anno regni domini regis tricesimo primo tenuit apud Caldaygraunge unam leporariam cum qua Rogerus le Wodeword subballivus ipsius abbatis cepit lepores in foresta et contra assisam eiusdem.

Ideo preceptum est vicecomiti quod venire faciat eum et postea venit idem abbas et non potest dedicere et petit se admitti ad finem faciendam cum domino in hac parte et admittitur pro *dimidia marca* per plegium Johannis de Lascels et Philippi de Raby.

1.62 <vj s. viij d.>
Item presentant quod Radulphus Patriksone de Haselwall Rogerus de Becheton Ricardus de Knouselegh et Henricus de Clynache subforestarii sub Willelmo de Stanlegh et Henricus Coly sub Henrico de Hoton equitatore anno regni domini regis nunc tricesimo primo mendicarunt blada a diversis hominibus infra forestam quam diu fuerunt in balliva sua ad nocumentum (prius) et contra assisam foreste.

Ideo preceptum est vicecomiti quod venire faciat eos et postea veniunt et convicti liberati prisone; postea educti redempti sunt quilibet eorum pro xl s. per plegios Willelmi de Bechynton Thome de Hoton Henrici de Hoton et Roberti de Berneston.

a *tunc* interlined
b *inclusum* interlined

1.60
Item they present that William, then abbot of Chester,[1] the immediate predecessor of the present abbot, made a close at Little Sutton, enclosed with a deep ditch and a high hedge, so that the beasts are not able to enter nor leave the close, to the harm of the beasts of the lord. The present abbot holds the close so enclosed against the assize of the forest. They do not know who [...] ...]. Therefore the sheriff is ordered to make him come. Afterwards the abbot comes and questioned about it says nothing. Therefore the close is to be levelled [...].

And [...] [...] the abbot is to be *in mercy* for contempt. Nothing of the amercement of the abbot because he made fine elsewhere etc.[2]

1.61
Item they present that the present abbot of Basingwerk[3] in the 31st year of the reign of the lord king (1357–1358) kept a greyhound bitch at Calday Grange with which Roger le Wodeword, under-bailiff of the abbot, took hares in the forest and against the assize of the same.

Therefore the sheriff is ordered to make him come; and afterwards the abbot comes and he cannot deny it; and he asks to be permitted to make fine with the lord in this matter and is admitted for *half a mark* by the pledge of John de Lascels and Philip de Raby.

1.62 <6s. 8d.>
Item they present that Ralph Patriksone of Heswall,[4] Roger de Becheton,[5] Richard de Knouselegh and Henry de Clynache, under-foresters under William de Stanlegh, and Henry Coly, deputy of Henry de Hoton,[6] rider, in the 31st year of the reign of the present lord king (1357–1358) begged corn from various men within the forest for as long as they were within their bailiwick to the harm (previously) and against the assize of the forest.

Therefore the sheriff is ordered to make them come; and afterwards they come and having been convicted, handed over to prison and afterwards brought out, each of them is redeemed for 40s. 0d. by the pledge of William de Bechynton, Thomas de Hoton, Henry de Hoton and Robert de Berneston.

1 See **1.45** note.
2 See **1.45** note.
3 1347 m. 14 The abbot dug peat in West Kirby.
4 1347 m. 5 Lord of Heswall 13 saplings in le Withies.
5 See **1.50** note.
6 See **1.55** note.

1.63

Item presentant quod Johannes Deneys cepit unum quercum in bosco de Leghton et branchiavit unam aliam quercum in mense [...] et quod Ricardus de Bechynton die Lune in vigilia Sancti Michelis anno vicesimo septimo cepit Henrico de Hoton unum quercum in bosco de Greves contra assisam foreste.

Ideo preceptum est vicecomiti quod venire faciat eos etc. et postea venit Johannes Deneys convictus liberatus prisone et eductus fecit finem pro *xiij s. iiij d.* per plegium Hamonis de Mascy et Thome de Capenhurst [...] [E...];

Et Willelmus de Bechynton consanguineus et heres Ricardi de Bechynton similiter fecit finem pro *xij d.* per plegium Johannis de Lassels et Roberti Danyell.

1.64

Compertum est per rotulos Johannis Doune nuper[a] capitalis forestarii foreste de Wyrhale quod Johannes Donvill die Jovis proxima post festum Pasche anno regni regis nunc tricesimo prostravit tres quercus in bosco de Netherbebynton et quod idem Johannes die Lune proxima post festum Sancti Thome apostoli anno regni domini regis nunc tricesimo cepit tres quercus in eodem bosco sine visu forestariorum.

Ideo preceptum est vicecomiti quod venire faciat eum. Postea venit. Convictus liberatus prisone[b] eductus redemptus est pro *vj s.* per plegium Hamonis de Mascy.

1.65

Compertum est etiam quod Rogerus de Ledesham Willelmus Wyllessone de Claghton Johannes filius Willelmi Russel eiusdem ville die[c] Mercurii proxima post festum Annunciationis Beate Marie anno xxxj^{mo} in quodam loco vocato Whistonclyf combusserunt jaunum filicem brueram et gorsteram circa grangiam de Wolveton ad nocumentum ferarum. Ideo preceptum est vicecomiti quod venire faciat eos et postea veniunt et convicti liberati prisone et educti fecerunt finem pro *iij s.* quilibet xij d.[d] per plegium Johannis de Domvill.

a *nuper* interlined
b *convictus liberatus prisone* interlined
c *Lune* struck through
d *quilibet xij d* interlined

1.63

Item they present that John Deneys took an oak in Leighton wood and lopped another oak in the month [...]; and that Richard de Bechynton[1] on Monday the eve of St Michael in the 27th year (28 September 1355)[2] took an oak in Greves wood for Henry de Hoton against the assize of the forest.

Therefore the sheriff is ordered to make them come etc; and afterwards John Deneys came and having been convicted, handed over to prison and brought out, made fine of *13s. 4d.* by the pledge of Hamo de Mascy and Thomas de Capenhurst [...] [E..];

and William de Bechynton, cousin and heir of Richard de Bechynton, likewise made fine of *12d.* by the pledge of John de Lassels and Robert Danyell.

1.64

It is found by the rolls of John Doune, the former chief forester of the forest of Wirral,[3] that John Donvill[4] on Thursday after the feast of Easter in the 30th year of the reign of the present king (28 April 1356) felled three oaks in Lower Bebington wood, and that the same John on Monday after the feast of St Thomas, apostle, in the 30th year of the reign of the present lord king (26 December 1356) took three oaks in the same wood without the view of the foresters.

Therefore the sheriff is ordered to make him come; and afterwards he comes and having been convicted, handed over to prison and brought out, he is redeemed for *6s. 0d.* by the pledge of Hamo de Mascy.

1.65

It is also found that Roger de Ledesham, William Wyllessone de Claughton, John son of William Russell of the same township on Wednesday after the feast of the Annunciation of Blessed Mary in the 31st year (29 March 1357) in a place called Whistoncliff[5] burned the furze, bracken, heath and gorse around the grange of Wolveton to the harm of the beasts. Therefore the sheriff is ordered to make them come; and afterwards they came and having been convicted, handed over to prison and brought out, they made fine of *3s. 0d.*, 12d. each, by the pledge of John de Domvill.

1 See **1.62** note.
2 Possibly the 29th year when the eve of St Michael fell on a Monday.
3 William Stanley forfeited his master-forestership in 1355, after his implication in the homicide of Richard Bechinton. John Done took over the office until 1357 (*ChAcc2*, pp. 176–77).
4 1347 m. 3 John Domvill 524 oaks 59 *robora* in Bebington wood; fine 20s. 0d.; pledge John de Capenhurst.
m. 14 John Domvill dug peat in Brimstage and Oxton.
5 Dodgson, *Place-names,* p. 168.

1.66

Compertum est etiam quod Stephanus de Merton die Veneris proxima post festum Annunciationis Beate Marie anno regni domini regis nunc tricesimo primo cepit et prostravit quemdam quercum in bosco de Gayton qui quidem Stephanus nuper manuopere eiusdem arestatus fuit per predictum forestarium et nec vadium ei liberare nec plegium invenire voluit set fecit ei resistentiam in contemptum domini per quod idem forestarius levavit hutesium.

<Merton>

Ideo preceptum est vicecomiti quod venire faciat eum et postea venit idem Stephanus et inde allocutus dicit quod ipse non est inde culpabilis et de hoc ponit se super patriam etc.

Ideo fiat inde juria.

Et super hoc datus est *dies* ei usque[a] diem Lune in secunda septimana Quadragesime.

1.67 <De hominibus leporariis in foresta>

Compertum est etiam quod Warinus Trussell chivaler Rogerus le Wodeward manens apud Caldaygraunge Johannes Domvill senior Willelmus de Stanlegh Ricardus de Hogh Henricus de Hoton et Henricus de Chorleton consueti sunt indies habere leporarios [...][b] ad lepores et vulpes in eadem foresta ad nocumentum ferarum et contra assisam foreste.

Ideo preceptum est vicecomiti quod venire faciat eos; et postea venit Henricus de Chorleton et non potest dedicere et petit se admitti ad finem cum domino faciendam et admittitur pro *xl d.* per plegium Johannis de Leghton et per plegium Johannis Blound et Roberti de Berneston quod ammodo se bene geret erga forestam et non forisfaciet in eadem et Willelmus de Stanlegh venit et dicit quod ipse non est culpabilis.

Et de hoc ponit se super patriam etc. Ideo fiat inde juria et super hoc *dies* datus est ei usque diem Lune in secunda septimana Quadragesime etc.

a *proximum* struck through
b [...] interlined

1.66
It is also found that Stephen de Merton on Friday after the feast of the Annunciation of Blessed Mary in the 31st year of the present lord king (31 March 1357) took and felled an oak in Gayton wood. Stephen was recently caught in the same act by the forester and refused to hand over a gage to him or find a pledge, but he resisted him in contempt of the lord wherefore the forester raised the hue.

<Merton>

Therefore the sheriff is ordered to make him come; and afterwards Stephen comes and questioned about it says that he is not guilty and concerning this puts himself on the country etc.

Therefore a jury is to be summoned.

Whereupon *a day* is given to him for Monday in the second week of Lent (26 February 1358).[1]

1.67 <Concerning men and hares in the forest>
It is also found that Warin Trussell,[2] knight, Roger le Wodeward, living at Calday Grange, John Domvill, the elder, William de Stanlegh, Richard de Hogh,[3] Henry de Hoton[4] and Henry de Chorleton were daily accustomed to keep their greyhounds for [hunting] hares and foxes in the same forest to the harm of the beasts and against the assize of the forest.

Therefore the sheriff is ordered to make them come and afterwards Henry de Chorleton comes and cannot deny it and asks to be admitted to making fine with the lord and is admitted for *40d.* by the pledge of John de Leghton; and by the pledge of John Blound and Robert de Berneston that from now on he will behave well towards the forest and do no wrong there and William de Stanlegh comes and says that he is not guilty.

And concerning this he puts himself on the country etc. Therefore a jury is to be summoned and accordingly a *day* is given to him for Monday in the second week of Lent etc. (26 February 1358).

1 See claim **2.11**.
2 1347 m. 3d Sir Warin Trussell 14 oaks; ½ mark; John Howet.
m. 14 Sir Warin Trussell dug peat in Willaston.
3 See **1.43** note.
4 See **1.55** note.

1.68 <iij s>
Compertum est etiam quod Robertus de Bamville[a] anno regni domini regis nunc tricesimo prostravit tres quercus in bosco de Tranemoll etc;

<xij d.>

et Henricus de Clynache dum fuit forestarius cepit unum quercum in eodem bosco et Johannes le Mercer anno predicto cepit unum quercum in eodem bosco;

<ij s.>

et Henricus Bernard eodem anno cepit duos quercus in eodem bosco et Willelmus del Wode eodem anno cepit quatuor quercus in eodem bosco et Henricus Brome cepit[b] duos quercus eodem anno in eodem bosco;

<j s.>

et Johannes le Cook de Birkheved eodem anno cepit unum quercum in eodem bosco sine visu forestariorum et contra assisam foreste.

Ideo preceptum est vicecomiti quod venire faciat eos. Postea veniunt predicti Robertus Johannes Henricus et Henricus et convicti liberati prisone et educti fecerunt finem videlicet

Robertus Bamville pro *iij s.* per plegium Henrici Coly et Willelmi de Bechynton et

Johannes le Mercer pro *xij d.* per plegium Henrici Bernard et Henrici [Clynache] et

Henricus Barnard pro *ij s.* per plegium Willelmi Waleys et

Johannes Launcelyn et Henricus Brom pro ij s. per plegium Roberti Barker et Willelmi Waleys.

Et Willelmus del Wode et Johannes Cok non veniunt.

1.69 <v s.>
Compertum est etiam per rotulos Henrici de Hoton equitatoris quod Willelmus Hullessone de W[odechurche] Willelmus Stanford de eadem Adam filius Thome de eadem Rogerus filius Willelmi de eadem Johannes filius Johannis de eadem anno regni domini regis nunc tricesimo foderunt turbas infra forestam apud le Lee et foderunt turbas et eas abduxerunt extra forestam ad usum suum proprium extra forestam ad nocumentum ferarum et contra assisam foreste.

Ideo preceptum est vicecomiti quod venire faciat eos. Postea veniunt et super hoc [allocuti dicunt quod non] possunt dedicere ac petunt se admitti ad finem cum domino faciendam et admittuntur videlicet qui[libet] eorum pro xij d. per plegium cujuslibet alterius etc.

a *ad* struck through
b *cepit* interlined

1.68 <3s. 0d.>
It is also found that Robert de Bamville in the 30th year of the reign of the present lord king (1356–1357) felled three oaks in Tranmere wood etc.;

<12d.>

and Henry de Clynache while he was forester took an oak in the same wood; and John le Mercer in the aforesaid year took an oak in the same wood;

<2s. 0d.>

and Henry Bernard[1] in the same year took two oaks in the same wood; and William del Wode in the same year took four oaks in the same wood; and Henry Brome took two oaks in the same year in the same wood;

<1s. 0d.>

and John le Cook of Birkenhead in the same year took an oak in the same wood without the view of the foresters and against the assize of the forest. Therefore the sheriff is ordered to make them come; afterwards came Robert, John, Henry and Henry and having been convicted, handed over to prison and brought out, they made fine; that is:

Robert Bamvill made fine of *3s 0d.* by the pledge of Henry Coly and William de Bechynton; and

John le Mercer of *12d.* by the pledge of Henry Bernard and Henry [de Clynache]; and

Henry Bernard of *2s. 0d.* by the pledge of William Waleys and

John Launcelyn; and Henry Brom of *2s. 0d.* by the pledge of Robert Barker and William Waleys.

And William del Wode and John le Cook do not come.

1.69 <5s. 0d.>
It is also found by the rolls of Henry Hoton, rider, that William Hullessone of W[oodchurch], William Stanford of the same, Adam son of Thomas of the same, Roger son of William of the same, John son of John of the same in the 30th year of the reign of the present lord king (1356–1357) dug peat within the forest at le Lee, and they dug peat and carried it away outside the forest for their own use outside the forest to the harm of the beasts and against the assize of the forest.

Therefore the sheriff is ordered to make them come. Afterwards they come and having been questioned about this, they say they cannot deny it and ask to be admitted to making fine with the lord and they are admitted, namely, each of them for 12d. by the pledge of one of the others etc.

1 1347 m. 1 Henry Bernard took 14 oaks and 3 *robora*; fine 40d.; pledge William Waley.

1.70 <comes Sar'>
Item presentant quod parcus Willelmi de Monte Acuto comitis Sar' apud Magnam Neston infra forestam non est clausus sufficienter ut decet per assisam foreste quin fere domini possint intrare et[a] exire ad destructionem ferarum et contra assisam.

<dies>

Ideo preceptum est vicecomiti quod venire faciat eum coram justiciariis apud Cestr' die Lune in secunda septimana Quadragesime etc. [...] venit [...] die Lune proxima post festum Assumptionis Beate Marie apud Cestr' etc.

m. 4

1.71
Iidem juratores presentant de defaltis eorum liberorum tenentium qui non veniunt coram justiciariis primo die itineris, videlicet:

1.72 <[b]>
Adam de Houghton Robertus Mayonessone, Willelmus filius Ade Hugo filius Johannis de Byton Willelmus de Wroghtinton Willelmus de Porter non veniunt primo die itineris. Ideo ipsi in misericordia etc.

1.73
Compertum est etiam per rotulos Johannis Doune nuper forestarii quod Robertus le clerk de Cestr' Willelmus Wastell et Thomas Birlewhitet die Martis proxima post festum Sancti Marci evangeliste anno regni domini regis nunc tricesimo primo fugaverunt cum duobus leporariis infra forestam iuxta boscum de Salghale pro leporibus capiendis quos attachiatos recenter super facto et alios misit ad castrum Cestr' qui modo veniunt et ponunt se inde in gratiam domini.

Et admittuntur videlicet Robertus pro *xx s.* per plegium Rogeri de Moldeworth et Johannis de Hockenhull; Willelmi Waley et Johannis Launcelyn qui etiam manucapti pro eo quod ammodo se bene gerent erga forestam et non forisfacient in eadem super periculum quod incumbit;

et Willelmus Wastell pro *x s.* per plegium Johannis Blound qui etiam *manucaptus* pro eo in forma predicta;

et Thomas Birlewhitet pro *x s.* per plegium Thome de Capenhurst et Johannis de Whytemur etc.

a *non* deleted and *et* interlined
b *misericordia* in margin struck through

1.70
Item they present that the park of William de Monte Acuto, *earl of Salisbury*, at Great Neston within the forest has not been enclosed adequately, as is fitting by the assize of the forest, so that the lord's beasts may not go in and out, to the harm of the beasts and against the assize.

<day>

Therefore the sheriff is ordered to make him come before the justices at Chester on Monday in the second week of Lent etc. (26 February 1358) [...] he comes to answer on Monday after the feast of the Assumption of Blessed Mary etc. (20 August 1358)[1]

m. 4

1.71
The same jurors present concerning the defaults of those free tenants who do not come before the justices on the first day of the eyre, that is:

1.72 <[2]>
Adam de Houghton, Robert Mayonessone, William son of Adam, Hugh son of John de Byton, William de Wroghtinton, William de Porter do not come on the first day of the eyre. Therefore they are to be in mercy etc.

1.73
It is also found by the rolls of John Doune, the former forester, that Robert the clerk of Chester, William Wastell and Thomas Birlewhitet on Tuesday after the feast of St Mark, evangelist, in the 31st year of the reign of the present lord king (2 May 1357), hunted with two greyhounds in the forest next to Saughall wood. They were recently attached in the act of taking hares and he sent them and others to Chester Castle, and they now come and put themselves therefore on the grace of the lord.

And they are admitted, that is Robert for *20s. 0d.*, by the pledge of Roger de Moldeworth and John de Hockenhull, William Waley and John Launcelyn, who are also mainperned for it to see that from now on they will behave well towards the forest and will do no wrong there, upon the peril which applies;

and William Wastell for *10s. 0d.,* by the pledge of John Blound, who is also *mainperned* for it in the above form;

and Thomas Birlewhitet for *10s. 0d.* by the pledge of Thomas de Capenhurst and John de Whytemur etc.

1 See claim **2.55**.
2 'mercy' in margin struck through.

Captiones averiorum in foreste locis vetitis

1.74

Compertum est per rotulos predicti Willelmi de Stanlegh quod xij porci Thome[a] villate de Budeston inventi fuerunt mense defenso in bosco de Budeston precii *iij s.*;

et quod Johannes de Pennesby capellanus habuit ibidem et in bosco de Upton vj porcos precii *xviij d.*;

et villata de Morton xx porcos in boscis de Budeston et Morton precii *v s.*;

et Johannes de Warrewyk habuit ibidem et in bosco de Upton xvj porcos precii *iiij s.*;

et prior de Birkeheved habuit in boscis de Birkeheved et Tranemoll xx porcos precii *v s.*;

et homines villate de Tranemoll habuerunt ibidem xij porcos precii iij s.;

et homines villate de Overbebynton habuerunt in bosco de Overbebynton tunc temporis xvj porcos precii iiij s.;

et homines villate de Netherbebynton habuerunt in bosco de Netherbebynton tunc temporis xx porcos precii v s.;

et homines villate de Hoton habuerunt viginti porcos tunc temporis in bosco de Hoton precii v s.;

et homines villate de Netherpulle habuerunt in bosco de Pulle tunc [pro] tempore xx porcos precii v s.;

et homines villate de Stanay habuerunt in bosco de Stanay tunc temporis pro[b] xij porcos precii iij s.;

et homines villate de Molynton Torald habuerunt tempore in bosco de Molynton xviij porcos precii *iiij s. vj ([d.);.]*;

et homines villate de Podynton habuerunt in bosco de Podynton tunc[c] tempore xx porcos precii v s.;

et homines villate de Parva Neston habuerunt in bosco de Parva Neston tunc tempore xij porcos precii iij s.;

et homines villate de Magna Neston habuerunt tunc temporis in boscis de Neston xij porcos precii iij s.;

a *Thome* interlined
b *pro* inserted in error?
c *tunc* interlined

Seizures of livestock in prohibited places in the forest

1.74
It is found by the rolls of William de Stanlegh that twelve pigs of Thomas of the township of Bidston were found in Bidston wood in fence month, price *3s. 0d.*;

and that John de Pennesby[1] chaplain had in the same place and in Upton wood six pigs, price *18d.*;

and the township of Moreton had twenty pigs in the woods of Bidston and Moreton, price *5s. 0d.*;

and John de Warrewyk had in the same place and in Upton wood sixteen pigs, price *4s. 0d.*;

and the prior of Birkenhead had twenty pigs in the woods of Birkenhead and Tranmere, price *5s. 0d.*;

and the men of the township of Tranmere had in the same place twelve pigs, price *3s. 0d.*;

and the men of the township of Higher Bebington had at that time sixteen pigs in Higher Bebington wood, price *4s. 0d.*;

and the men of the township of Lower Bebington had at that time twenty pigs in Lower Bebington wood, price *5s. 0d.*;

and the men of the township of Hooton had then at that time twenty pigs in Hooton wood, price *5s. 0d.*;

and the men of the township of Netherpool had then [for] the time twenty pigs in Pull wood, price *5s. 0d.*;

and the men of the township of Stanney had then at that time twelve pigs in Stanney wood, price *3s. 0d.*;

and the men of the township of Mollington Torald had at that time eighteen pigs in Mollington wood, price *4s. 6d.;*

and the men of the township of Puddington had then at that time twenty pigs in Puddington wood, price *5s. 0d.*;

and the men of the township of Little Neston had then at that time twelve pigs in Little Neston wood, price *3s. 0d.*;

1 1347 m. 1d Eleanor de Pennesby took 2 oaks; fine 40d.; pledge Roger Wayte.

et homines villate de Leghton habuerunt in bosco de Leghton tunc temporis xij porcos precii iij s.;

et homines villate de Gayton habuerunt in illo bosco tunc temporis vj porcos precii xviij d.;

et homines villate de Haselwall habuerunt in bosco de Haselwall tunc temporis xij porcos precii iij s.;

et homines villate de Berneston habuerunt in bosco de Berneston tunc temporis vj porcos precii xviij d.;

et homines villate de Wodchirche habuerunt in illo bosco tunc temporis xij porcos precii iij s.;

et homines villate de Shotewyk habuerunt in bosco de Shotewyk tunc temporis xij porcos precii iij s.;

et homines villate de Grevesby habuerunt tunc temporis in bosco de Gresby xx porcos precii v s.

Et ideo forisfiant domino sub preciis predictis etc.

Summa lxxix s.

Sequitur de Venatione

1.75 <misericordia>
Compertum est per rotulos eiusdem Willelmi quod anno regni domini regis nunc vicesimo quinto quidam damus inventus fuit mortuus et vulneratus in bosco de Prenton quo viso per villatos de Oxton Prenton Landekan et Tranemoll et per dictum forestarium et Johannem de Lascels equitatorem predicte villate tunc nichil dixerunt nec iam dicunt.

<misericordia>

Ideo ipsi onerentur etc. Tamen damus predictus portatus fuit usque castrum Cestr' prout [moris][a] est; qui respondeant de carne.

1.76
Item compertum est quod ad unum damum inventum mortuum in medio aque de Mersee anno supradicto inter tres villatas super visu corporis coram equitatore loco viridarii et predicto forestario villani de Oxton non veniunt.

Ideo ipsi in *misericordia.*

a *mors* MS here and in **1.79–1.81**. Perhaps the scribe miscontrued the Latin.

and the men of the township of Great Neston had then at that time twelve pigs in Neston woods, price *3s. 0d.*;

and the men of the township of Leighton had then at that time twelve pigs in Leighton wood, price *3s. 0d.*;

and the men of the township of Gayton had then at that time six pigs in that wood, price *18d.*;

and the men of the township of Heswall had then at that time twelve pigs in Heswall wood, price *3s. 0d.*;

and the men of the township of Barnston had then at that time six pigs in Barnston wood, price *18d.*;

and the men of the township of Woodchurch had then at that time twelve pigs in that wood, price *3s. 0d.*;

and the men of the township of Shotwick had then at that time twelve pigs in Shotwick wood, price *3s. 0d.*;

and the men of the township of Greasby had then at that time twenty pigs in Greasby wood, price *5s. 0d.* And therefore they are to be forfeited to the lord under the above prices etc.

Sum 79s. 0d.

Continuation: concerning Venison

1.75 <mercy>
It is found by the rolls of the same William that in the 25th year of the reign of the present lord king (1351–1352) a buck was found dead and wounded in Prenton wood. It was seen by the men of Oxton, Prenton, Landican and Tranmere and by the said forester and John de Lascels, rider of the township. They then said nothing nor do they say anything now.

<mercy>

Therefore they are to be charged etc. Nevertheless the buck was carried to Chester Castle as is the custom; they are to answer for the meat.

1.76
Item it is found that, regarding a buck found dead in the middle of the river Mersey between three townships in the said year, and the body having been viewed in the presence of the rider, acting as a verderer, and the said forester, the men of Oxton do not come. Therefore they are to be in *mercy*.

1.77
Item presentant quod ad unum damum inventum mortuum sine blaga coram equitatore loco viridarij et predicto forestario villa de Thyngwell non veniunt. Ideo ipsa in *misericordia* etc.

1.78
Compertum est etiam quod una bissa vulnerata[a] anno xxvj[to] inventa fuit mortua in bosco de Grevesby qua visa per villanos de Grevesby Upton Arwe et Thyngwell qui modo veniunt et dicunt quod Johannes Adam[b] de Arbygelot interfecit predictam bissam qui modo non venit nec prius attachiatus fuit nec scitur quo devenit et vicecomes testatur quod retraxit se actione predicta.

<et x>

Ideo exigitur et utlagatur etc. et quia hoc devenit in die et ceperunt malefactorem in illa villata, in *misericordia* etc.

1.79
Item presentant quod una dama inventa fuit mortua in campis de Claghton qua visa per villatos de Tranemoll Overbebynton Netherbebynton et Pulton anno regni domini regis nunc vicesimo sexto qui modo venerunt et nichil tunc dixerunt et modo predicti in curia nichil dicunt.

Ideo ipsi in *misericordia.* Et nichilominus predicta dama portata fuit ad castrum Cestr' prout [moris][c] est etc.

1.80
Compertum est etiam quod quidam damus inventus fuit mortuus in bosco de Grevesby quo viso per villatos de Upton Arwe Thyngwell in presencia ipsius forestarii qui de morte onerati nichil dixerunt nec iam dicunt. Ideo in *misericordia.* Et nichilominus corpus predicti dami portatum fuit

ad castrum Cestr' prout [moris][d] est etc.

1.81
Compertum est etiam quod quedam dama inventa fuit mortua suffocata per canes villanorum de Netherbebynton qua visa per villatas de Pulton, Overbebynton, Netherbebynton et Tranemoll anno xxviij[o] qui modo venerunt et nichil tunc dixerunt set nunc dicunt quod predicta dama suffocabatur per canes Ade de Tranemoll Rogeris de Bebynton et unum canem [...] ipsius Rogeris et unum canem Johannis de

a *vulnerata* interlined
b *Adam* interlined
c See note at **1.75**.
d See note at **1.75**.

1.77
Item they present that, regarding a buck found dead without a wound in the presence of the rider, acting as a verderer, and the said forester, the township of Thingwall does not come. Therefore it is to be in *mercy* etc.

1.78
It is also found that in the 26th year (1352–1353) a wounded hind was found dead in Greasby wood. It was seen by the men of Greasby, Upton, Arrowe and Thingwall, and they now come and say that John Adam of Arbygelot killed the hind; he does not now come, nor was he attached before, nor is it known what has become of him; and the sheriff bears witness that he has withdrawn himself from the said action.

<And ten>

Therefore he is exacted and outlawed etc.; and because he arrived on that day and they took the offender in that township, they are to be in *mercy.*

1.79
Item they present that in the 26th year (1352–1353) of the reign of the present lord king, a doe was found dead in the fields of Claughton. It was seen by the men of Tranmere, Higher Bebington, Lower Bebington and Poulton, and they first came and then said nothing and later they say nothing in the court.

Therefore they are to be in *mercy.* And nonetheless the doe was carried to Chester Castle as is customary.

1.80
It is also found that a buck was found dead in Greasby wood. It was seen by the men of Upton, Arrowe, Thingwall in the presence of the forester himself and, being guilty of the death, they said nothing nor do they say anything now.

Therefore they are to be in *mercy.* And nonetheless the body of the buck was carried to Chester Castle as is customary.

1.81
It is also found that in the 28th year (1354–1355) a doe was found dead, throttled by the dogs of the villagers of Lower Bebington. It was seen by the men of Poulton, Higher Bebington, Lower Bebington and Tranmere. They came previously and then said nothing, but now they say that the doe was throttled by the dogs of Adam de Tranemoll[1] and Roger de Bebynton[2] and a [...] dog of Roger himself and a dog of John

1 See **1.46** note.
2 See **1.46** note.

Bukestones et unum canem Alani de Lydeyate et unum canem Ricardi le Swynger corpus cuius portatum fuit ad castrum Cestr' prout [moris][a] est.

<[vicecomes] faciat>

Ideo preceptum est vicecomiti quod venire faciat eos etc.

1.82
Compertum est etiam quod anno vicesimo nono quedam bissa inventa fuit mortua in uno puteo turbarie largo et profundo in villa de Budeston que visa per villatas de Upton Budeston Morton et Kirkeby in Waley in presencia predicti forestarii qui nunc veniunt et dicunt quod sicut bissa predicta pertransire deberet noctanter iuxta puteum predictum pro victu querendo labentibus pedibus cecidit in [eundem][b]; et quesiti ad quam villatam pertinet puteus ille et quis illum fecit dicunt quod Henricus de Arwe illum fecit qui superstes est.

Ideo preceptum est vicecomiti quod venire faciat eum et postea venit predictus Henricus et inde allocutus non potest dedicere set petit se admitti ad finem cum domino ea actione facta.

Et admittitur videlicet pro *xx s.* per plegium Hamonis de Mascy et Henrici de Chorleton etc.

1.83
Compertum est per rotulos Henrici de Hoton, equitatoris quod die Jovis proxima ante festum Sancte Margarete virginis anno xxxj^{mo} quidam Robertus filius Thome de Grevesby hayward infra duos campos de Grevesby vidit duas bissas cum vitulis suis depascentes in campis eiusdem ville ita quod per excitationem predicti Roberti canis Philippi de Morton non expeditatus cepit unum vitulum. Qui super factum captus fuit et ductus ad castrum Cestr' et in modo venit coram justiciariis et super hoc convictus liberatus prisone.

<x s. in misericordia>

Postea redemptus est ad x s.per plegium Johannis Doun et Johannis Launcelyn qui etiam manucapti pro eo quod ammodo bene se geret et in foresta non forisfaciet.

1.84
Compertum est etiam per rotulos eiusdem Henrici quod unus damus submersus fuit in aqua de Dee et quod unus damus et una bissa submersi fuerunt in Budestonmos et unus stak inventus fuit in Waleypulle et una et unus stak inventi fuerunt mortui in boscis de Budeston et unus stak' inventus fuit mortuus in (Wallabres) et unus damus inventus fuit mortuus in bosco de Birkeheved et unus damus inventus fuit mortuus in

a See note at **1.75**.
b *eadem* MS

de Bukestones and a dog of Adam de Lydeyate and a dog of Richard le Swynger; the doe's body was carried to Chester Castle as is customary.

<sheriff to make them>

Therefore the sheriff is ordered to make them come etc.

1.82
It is also found that in the 29th year (1355–1356) a hind was found dead in a wide and deep turbary pit in the township of Bidston. It was seen by the inhabitants of Upton, Bidston, Moreton and Wallasey in the presence of the forester. They now come and say that, as the hind had to pass through next to that pit in the night when seeking food, its feet slipped and it fell in the same and, asked which township that pit belongs to and who made it, they say that Henry de Arwe made it and he is still alive.

Therefore the sheriff is ordered to make him come; and afterwards Henry comes and questioned about it he cannot deny it, but asks to be admitted to making fine with the lord for doing that action.

And he is admitted, that is for *20s. 0d.* by the pledge of Hamo de Mascy and Henry de Chorleton etc.

1.83
It is found by the rolls of Henry de Hoton, rider, that on Thursday before the feast of St Margaret, virgin, in the 31st year (20 July 1357) Robert, son of Thomas de Grevesby, hayward, in two fields of Greasby saw two hinds feeding with their calves in the fields of that township, so that an unlawed dog, belonging to Philip de Morton, urged on by Robert, took a calf. He was caught in the act and was taken to Chester castle and in that manner came before the justices and having been convicted of this is handed over to prison.

<10s. 0d. in mercy>

Afterwards he is redeemed for 10s. 0d. by the pledge of John Doun and John Launcelyn who were also mainperned so that he will from now on behave well and do no wrong in the forest.

1.84
It is also found by Henry's rolls that a buck was drowned in the river Dee; and that a buck and a hind were drowned in Bidston moss; and a stag was found in Wallasey Pool; and a hind and a stag were found dead in Bidston woods; and a stag was found dead in Wallabres; and a stag was found dead in Birkenhead wood; and a buck was found dead in Poulton wood; and a buck wounded by an arrow, dead, in

bosco de Pulton et unus damus vulneratus cum quadam sagitta [mortuus][a] in campo de Netherbebynton et quia usitatum est per ministros quod nichil aliud eis exigitur [...] nichil ulterius de eis etc.

4 iiij [Placita foreste itineris] [anno 31 Edwardi]

m. 4d

1.85

Responsio ad articulum de naviculis applicantibus infra forestam pro passagio. Juratores presentant quod Henricus le Brouster Willelmus filius Willelmi Alcok Willelmus filius Rogeri de Secum, et Willelmus filius Roberti de Secum batellarii de Secum usque Lyverpulle applicant [...]am infra forestam ducendo et reducendo homines ab anno vicesimo octavo usque nunc tam extraneos quam intrinsecos ad nocumentum ferarum istius foreste. Nesciunt quo waranto.

Postea veniunt predicti Henricus et alii et super premissis allocuti dicunt quod ipsi non sunt nisi servientes de Ricardi del Hogh nec Johannis de Lascels et super hoc predicti Ricardus del Hogh et Elena uxor eius et Johannes de Lascels pro se ipso ut domino manerii de Secum et dicunt quod ipsi[b] et alii quorum statum ipsi habent habuerunt batellagium [...] aquam de Mersee et ipsi similiter usque nunc habuerunt batellos suos cariantes homines venientes de comitatu Cestr' versus Lyverpulle per quamdam viam regiam vocatam le Blakestrete, ducentem per medium foreste usque Secum et deinde ultra aquam de Mersee et reducendo homines a Lyverpulle [...] [...] [...] usque Secum et capiendo stipendia rationabilia et hoc pretendunt verificare prout curia etc.

Et Willelmus de Wakebrugge qui sequitur pro domino comite dicit quod non est aliqua via regia vocata le Blakestrete nec esse potest de jure propter nocumentum ferarum; nec etiam iidem Ricardus Elena et Johannes sive ulli alii quorum statum ipsi habent unquam habuerunt aliquos batellos ducentes homines vel reducentes ultra aquam de Mersee prout supponunt et hoc paratus est verificare pro domino et Ricardus de Hogh et Elena et Johannes similiter.

Ideo fiat inde juria. Set ponitur in respectum usque diem Lune in secunda septimana Quadragesime etc. Ad quem diem apud Cestr' coram prefatis justiciariis etc. veniunt predicti Ricardus de Hogh et Johannes de Lascels et alii et ulterius datus est dies usque diem Lune[c] proximam post festum Assumptionis Beate Marie apud Cestr'.

a *mortua* MS
b *et dicunt quod ipsi* interlined
c *Lune* interlined

Lower Bebington field; and because it is a custom of the officials that nothing else is demanded of them nothing further from them etc.

4 iv
Pleas of the eyre of the forest
31st year of Edward's reign

m. 4d

1.85

Response to the article concerning boats plying for passage within the forest. The jurors present that Henry le Brouster, William son of William Alcock, William son of Roger de Secum and William son of Robert de Secum, boatmen of Seacombe, ply between Seacombe and Liverpool [...] within the forest, by taking and bringing back people, both residents and strangers, from the 28th year (1354–55) until now, to the harm of the beasts of this forest. They do not know by what warrant.

Afterwards Henry and the others come, and questioned on the above matters, say that they are only the servants of Roger del Hogh[1] and John de Lascels; and in reply to that, Richard del Hogh and Ellen his wife and John de Lascels for himself, as lord of the manor of Seacombe, say that they and others whose estate they have, have had the right to have boats [...] the Mersey water, and likewise up to now have had their boats carrying men coming from the county of Chester to Liverpool by the king's highway called le Blakestrete, going through the middle of the forest to Seacombe, and from there over the Mersey water, both by bringing men back from Liverpool [...] [...] to Seacombe and by taking reasonable payment; and this they claim to prove just as the court etc.

And William de Wakebrugge who sues for the lord earl says that there is no king's highway called le Blakestrete, nor is it lawfully possible because of harm to the beasts; also neither Richard, Ellen nor John nor any others whose estate they have, have ever had any boats taking or bringing back people across the Mersey water as they submit; and this he is ready to prove for the lord; and Richard de Hogh and Ellen and John likewise.

Therefore a jury is to be summoned. But it is adjourned until Monday in the second week of Lent etc. (26 February 1358). On that day Richard de Hogh and John de Lascels and the others come to Chester before the said justices etc. and a further date is given them for Monday after the feast of the Assumption of Blessed Mary at Chester (20 August 1358).

1 See **1.43** note.

Ad quem diem apud Cestr' venerunt partes predicte et ulterius datus est dies partibus usque diem Lune in crastino clausi Pasche eo quod juratores non veniunt. Ad quem diem apud Cestr' coram prefatis justiciariis veniunt partes predicte et ulterius datus est dies partibus usque diem Lune in crastino Sancte Trinitatis.

[a]Postea apud Cestr' eodem die coram prefatis justiciariis veniunt tam predictus Willelmus de Wakebrugge, qui sequitur pro domino quam prefati Ricardus de Hough et Elena uxor eius et Johannes Lassels in propriis personis et juratores similiter, qui de consensu partium electi triati et jurati dicunt super sacramentum suum quod a tempore quo non exstat memoria habebatur et ad huc habetur quedam via regia vocata le Blakestrete que se ducit a comitatu Cestr' usque Walaypulle versus Liverpulle et quod idem Ricardus Elena et Johannes et alii quorum statum ipsi habent quamdam partem batellagii [habent] cariando homines ultra aquam de Mersee usque Liverpulle in comitatu Lancastr' et reducendo homines usque in comitatum Cestr' prout iidem Ricardus, Elena, et Johannes in placitando supponunt.

Quesiti iidem juratores qualem partem batellagii predicti Ricardus Elena et Johannes habent in eodem batellagio dicunt quod predicti Ricardus et Elena de jure ipsius Elene habent quartam partem predicti batellagii et Johannes de Lassels de jure suo proprio habet quartam partem predicti batellagii; extra, sexta parte eiusdem, et ad terminum vite Aveline matris Ricardi Sampson ex demissione eiusdem Aveline quartam partem eiusdem batellagii; et Henricus del Lytherlond habet sex partes quarte partis predicti batellagii, set quis vel qui tenet vel tenent residuum batellagii predicti penitus ignorant. Quesiti etiam iidem juratores si predictum batellagium sit ad nocumentum ferarum dicunt precise quod non.

Et super hoc datus est dies tam predicto Willelmo qui sequitur quam predictis Ricardo Elene, et Johanni usque diem Lune proxima post festum Sancti Mathei apostoli ad audiendum inde iudicium suum. Postea continuato inde processu coram prefatis justiciariis apud Cestr' [ideo] dies datus est usque diem Veneris in secunda septimana Quadragesime. Ad quem diem apud Cestr' coram prefatis justiciariis venit tam predictus Willelmus de Wakebrugge qui sequitur etc. quam dictus Ricardus del Hogh nec Elena uxor eius non veniunt et testatum est per omnes ministros istius foreste quod obierunt. Et nichil ulterius de eis.[b]

[c]1.86

Pro passagio et batellagio de Burton in Wirhale episcopus Cestr' habet diem usque diem Lune in secunda septimana Quadragesime apud Cestr' et deinde habet diem usque diem Lune proximam post festum Assumptionis Beate Marie apud Cestr'.

a The following three paragraphs are written on a schedule stitched on here.
b The schedule ends here; nothing is written on the back of it.
c The next two paragraphs, written on the dorse of m. 4, continue as m. 4d.

On that day the parties come to Chester and a further day is given to the parties for Monday the day after the close of Easter (29 April 1359) because the jurors do not come. On that day the parties come to Chester before the justices and a further date is given to the parties for Monday the day after Holy Trinity (24 June 1359).

[1]Afterwards on the same day at Chester before the same justices come William de Wakebrugge who sues for the lord, Richard de Hough, Ellen his wife and John Lassels in person; and likewise the jurors, who with the consent of the parties having been chosen, tested and sworn, say on their oath that from time immemorial there was and there is still a king's highway called le Blakestrete, which goes from the county of Chester as far as Walaypull[2] opposite Liverpool, and that Richard, Ellen and John and others whose estate they have, have a part of the boat-hire for carrying men across the Mersey water to Liverpool in the county of Lancaster, and for bringing back men to the county of Chester, as Richard, Ellen and John submit in their plea.

Asked what portion of the boat-hire Richard, Ellen and John have in that boat-hire, the jurors say that Richard and Ellen have a quarter part of the boat-hire as of Ellen's right, and John de Lassels in his own right has a quarter part; in addition, by a sixth part[3] he holds a quarter part of the boat-hire for the term of the life of Aveline, mother of Richard Sampson, demised by Aveline; and Henry del Lytherlond holds six parts of a quarter part of the boat-hire but whoever holds or hold the remainder of the boat-hire they do not know at all. Also asked if hiring the boat is to the harm of the beasts the jurors decidedly say not.

And thereupon a date is given both to William who sues and to Richard, Ellen and John for Monday after the feast of St Matthew, apostle, for hearing their judgement (23 September 1359).

Afterwards the proceedings having been continued then before the same justices at Chester, [therefore] a day is given for Friday in the second week of Lent (6 March 1360). On that day at Chester before the justices comes William de Wakebrugge who sues etc.; and neither Richard del Hogh nor Ellen his wife come; and all the officials of this forest court bore witness that they have died. And nothing further about them.

1.86

For passage and boat-hire from Burton in Wirral, the bishop of Chester has a day for Monday in the second week of Lent (26 February 1358) at Chester, and he then has a day until Monday after the feast of the Assumption of Blessed Mary at Chester (20 August 1358).

1 What follows is written on a parchment schedule stitched on here.

2 Dodgson, *Place Names*, p. 333.

3 'by a sixth part' meaning uncertain.

1.87
Pro passagio et batellagio de Tranemoll Bebynton Brunburgh Estham Hoton Pulle Shotewyk et Calday datus est dies usque diem Lune in secunda septimana Quadragesime etc. apud Cestr', et deinde datus est dies usque diem Lune proximam post festum Assumptionis Beate Marie apud Cestr'.

Comitatus Cestr'

Comitatus Cestr'

Placita forestarum itineris
[anno 31mo Edwardi tercii]
Wyrhale

m. 5

1.88
Regardum foreste de Wyrhale factum et presentatum apud Cestr' coram Ricardo de Stafford et Ricardo de Wylughby militibus Johanne de Delves et magistro Johanne de Brunham juniore justiciariis domini principis ad itinerandum ad omnia placita foreste predicte assignatis die Veneris in crastino Sancti Mathei apostoli anno supradicto super sacramentum Willelmi de Stanlegh forestarii de feodo istius foreste et Johannis Donvylle Ricardi del Hough Henrici de Hoton Roberti de Berneston Thome de Hokenhull Henrici de Chorleton Willelmi Walays Roberti Baumvyll Adam del Lee Johannis Launcelyn Willelmi Gregory et Johannis de Lassels loco Johannis de Warrewyk qui infirmus est regardatorum eiusdem foreste et eiusdem Johannis de Lassels equitatoris eiusdem foreste ad hoc juratorum qui dicunt super sacramentum suum quod iam viginti annis elapsis edificate sunt in vasto ville de *Capenhurst* due domus[a] ad nocumentum ferarum per Johannem de Capenhurst qui obiit;

et Thomas de Capenhurst qui nunc est iam duodecim annis elapsis constructit ibidem septem alios domos in eodem vasto precii omnium domorum predictorum xl s.;

<viij li iiij s.>

et de valore earundem domorum per annum pro qualibet domo xij d. unde idem Thomas qui nunc tenens est respondebit domino.

Et domus predicte prosternantur et nichilominus idem Thomas in *misericordia*.

Summa

a *duas domos* MS

1.87
For passage and boat-hire from Tranmere, Bebington, Bromborough, Eastham, Hooton, Poole, Shotwick, and Caldy a day is given for Monday in the second week of Lent etc. (26 February 1358) at Chester, and a day is then given for Monday after the feast of the Assumption of Blessed Mary at Chester (20 August 1358).[1]

County of Chester

County of Chester

Pleas of the eyre of the forests
31st year Edward III
Wirral

m. 5

1.88
Regard of the forest of Wirral made and presented at Chester before Richard de Stafford and Richard de Wylughby knights, and John de Delves and master John de Brunham the younger, appointed justices in eyre of the lord prince for all pleas of the above forest on Friday the day after the feast of St Matthew, apostle, in the above year (22 September 1357), on the oath of William de Stanlegh, forester in fee of this forest, and of John Donvyll, Richard del Hough, Henry de Hoton, Robert de Berneston, Thomas de Hokenhull, Henry de Chorleton, William Walays, Robert Baumvyll, Adam del Lee, John Launcelyn, William Gregory and John de Lassels in the place of John Warreyk who is sick, regarders of the forest, and of the same John de Lassels, riding forester of the same forest, sworn for this, who say on their oath that: twenty years ago two buildings were erected in the waste of the township of *Capenhurst*, to the harm of the beasts, by John de Capenhurst[2] who has died;

and twelve years ago the present Thomas de Capenhurst erected there seven other buildings in the same waste, price of all the above buildings, 40s. 0d.;

<£8 4s. 0d.>

and concerning the value of the same buildings, it is 12d. a year for each building, for which Thomas the present tenant will answer to the lord.

And the buildings are to be pulled down and Thomas is nevertheless to be in *mercy.*

Sum [Blank]

1 This membrane has a flap stitched to the foot of the recto, which bears five lines of illegible writing with some Roman numerals.
2 1347 m. 1d John de Capenhurst took 12 oaks; fine 40d.; pledge Hamo de Mascy.

1.89 <xl li.>
Item presentant quod antecessores predicti Thome iam triginta annis elapsis assartaverunt xl acras terre in vasto eiusdem ville que vicesies inbladate sunt de yvernagio et tramesio precii acre per annum xij d. unde idem Thomas qui tenens est respondebit ac terra capiatur in manu domini.

1.90 <xxviij li.>
Item presentant quod iam xx annis elapsis assartate sunt ibidem per antecessores predicti Thome xl acre terre que xiiij^{ies} inbladate fuerunt de yvernagio et tramesio precii acre per annum xij d. unde idem Thomas qui tenens est respondebit et terra capiatur in manu domini.

1.91 <ix li.>
Item presentant quod iam xvj annis elapsis assartate sunt ibidem in vastis dicte ville xviij acre terre que x^{ies} inbladate sunt de yvernagio et tramesio precii acre per annum xij s.unde idem Thomas qui tenens est respondebit et terra capiatur in manu domini.

1.92 <ix li.>
Item presentant quod idem antecessores predicti Thome iam xxj annis elapsis construxerunt ibidem unum molendinum ventriticum quod est ad nocumentum ferarum.

Ideo forisfiat et deleatur precii molendini xl s. et de valore eiusdem per annum a tempore constructionis quolibet anno dimidie marce unde idem Thomas qui illud occupat respondebit.

1.93 <xj li. xvj s. viij d.>
Item presentant[a] quod iam xxx annis elapsis vij domus constructe fuerunt per eosdem antecessores[b] Roberti de Pulle[c] in vasto eiusdem ville ad nocumentum ferarum domini. Ideo forisfiant et deleantur precii omnium domorum xxvj s. viij d. unde idem Robertus qui tenens est respondebit et est valor dictorum domorum per annum [quemlibet][d] xij d. unde idem Robertus similiter respondebit.

1.94 <xx li.>
Item presentant quod idem Robertus tenet xx acras terre in eadem villa iam xxx annis elapsis per antecessores suos que xx^{ies} inbladate sunt de yvernagio et tramesio precii cujuslibet acre per annum xij d. unde idem Robertus qui tenens est respondebit et terra capiatur in manu domini.

a *quod Robertus de Pulle* struck through
b *predicti* struck through
c *de Pulle* interlined
d *quilibet* MS

1.89 <£40>
Item they present that the ancestors of Thomas 30 years ago assarted 40 acres of land in the waste of the same township which have yielded crops 20 times sown in winter and summer, price of an acre 12d. a year, for which Thomas who is the tenant will answer, and the land is to be taken into the lord's hands.

1.90 <£28>
Item they present that 20 years ago 40 acres of land were assarted in the same place by the ancestors of Thomas, which have yielded crops fourteen times sown in winter and summer, price of an acre 12d. a year, for which Thomas who is the tenant will answer, and the land is to be taken into the lord's hands.

1.91 <£9>
Item they present that sixteen years ago, eighteen acres of land were assarted there in the wastes of the said township, which have yielded crops ten times sown in winter and summer, price of an acre 12d. a year, for which Thomas who is the tenant will answer, and the land is to be taken into the lord's hands.

1.92 <£9>
Item they present that 21 years ago, the ancestors of Thomas constructed a windmill in the same place which is to the harm of the beasts. Therefore it is to be forfeited and destroyed, price of the mill 40s. 0d., and concerning the value of the same it is half a mark for each year from the time it was built, for which Thomas, who occupies it, will answer.

1.93 <£11 16s. 8d.>
Item they present that 30 years ago, seven buildings were erected in the waste of the same township by the same ancestors of Robert de Pulle,[1] to the harm of the lord's beasts. Therefore they are to be forfeited and destroyed, price of all the buildings 26s. 8d., for which Robert who is the tenant will answer; and the value of the buildings is 12d. for each year, for which Robert will answer similarly.

1.94 <£20>
Item they present that Robert holds 20 acres of land in the same township assarted 30 years ago by his ancestors, which have yielded crops 20 times in winter and summer, price of each acre 12d. a year, for which Robert who is the tenant will answer, and the land is to be taken into the hands of the lord.

1 See **1.47** note.

1.95 <xiiij li.>
Item presentant quod idem Robertus tenet xx acras terre in eadem villa iam xx annis elapsis assartatas per antecessores suos que xiiij[ies] inbladate sunt de yvernagio et tramesio precii cujuslibet acre per annum xij d. unde idem Robertus qui tenens est respondebit et terra capiatur in manu domini.

1.96 <vj li. xij s.>
Item presentant quod idem Robertus tenet xj acras terre in eadem villa iam xvj annis elapsis per ipsum assartatas que xj[ies] inbladate sunt de yvernagio et tramesio precii cujuslibet acre per annum xij d. unde idem Robertus qui tenens est respondebit et terra capiatur in manu domini.

1.97 <xxx li.>
Item presentant quod Ricardus del Hough iam lx annis elapsis assartavit xv acras terre in vasto ville de *Thornton Maheu* que xl[es] inbladate sunt de yvernagio et tramesio precii cujuslibet acre per annum xij d. unde idem Ricardus qui tenens est respondebit et terra capiatur in manu domini.

1.98 <xiiij li.>
Item presentant quod idem Ricardus iam xl annis elapsis assartavit x acras terre in vasto eiusdem ville que xxviij[ies] inbladate sunt de yvernagio et tramesio precii cujuslibet acre per annum xij d. unde idem Ricardus qui tenens est respondebit et terra capiatur in manu domini.

1.99 <iiij li. xviij s.>
Item presentant quod idem Ricardus iam xx annis elapsis assartavit vij acras terre in vasto eiusdem ville que xiiij[ies] inbladate sunt de yvernagio et tramesio precii acre per annum xij d. unde idem Ricardus qui tenens est respondebit et terra capiatur.

1.100 <iij li. xij s.>
Item presentant quod idem Ricardus iam xvij annis elapsis assartavit vj acras terre in vasto eiusdem ville que xij[es] inbladate sunt de yvernagio et tramesio precii cujuslibet acre per annum xij d. unde idem Ricardus qui tenens est respondebit et terra capiatur.

1.101 <iiij li.>
Item presentant quod idem Ricardus iam xiiij annis elapsis assartavit viij acras terre in vasto eiusdem ville que x[es] inbladate sunt de yvernagio et tramesio precii cujuslibet acre per annum xij d. unde idem Ricardus qui tenens est respondebit et terra capiatur.

1.95 <£14>
Item they present that Robert holds 20 acres of land in the same township, assarted 20 years ago by his ancestors, which have yielded crops fourteen times sown in winter and summer, price of each acre 12d. a year, for which Robert who is the tenant will answer, and the land is to be taken into the hands of the lord.

1.96 <£6 12s. 0d.>
Item they present that Robert holds eleven acres of land in the same township, assarted sixteen years ago by himself, which have yielded crops eleven times sown in winter and summer, price of each acre 12d. a year, for which Robert who is the tenant will answer, and the land is to be taken in to the hands of the lord.

1.97 <£30>
Item they present that Richard del Hough[1] 60 years ago assarted fifteen acres of land in the waste of the township of *Thornton Hough* which have yielded crops 40 times sown in winter and summer, price of each acre 12d. a year, for which Richard who is the tenant will answer, and the land is to be taken into the hands of the lord.

1.98 <£14>
Item they present that Richard 60 years ago assarted ten acres of land in the waste of the township the same township, which have yielded crops 28 times sown in winter and summer, price of each acre 12d. a year, for which Richard who is the tenant will answer, and the land is to be taken in to the hands of the lord

1.99 <£4 18s. 0d.>
Item they present that Richard 20 years ago assarted seven acres of land in the waste of the same township, which have yielded crops fourteen times sown in winter and summer, price of an acre 12d. a year, for which Richard who is the tenant will answer, and the land is to be taken.

1.100 <£3 12s. 0d.>
Item they present that Richard seventeen years ago assarted six acres of land in the waste of the same township, which have yielded crops twelve times sown in winter and summer, price of each acre 12d. a year, for which Richard who is the tenant will answer and the land is to be taken.

1.101 <£4>
Item they present that fourteen years ago Richard assarted eight acres of land in the waste of the same township, which have yielded crops ten times sown in winter and summer, price of each acre 12d. a year, for which Richard, who is the tenant will answer and the land is to be taken.

1 See **1.43** note.

1.102 <[cij s.]>
Item presentant quod idem Ricardus iam ix annis elapsis assartavit xvij acras et dimidiam in vasto dicte ville que vj^{es} inbladate sunt de yvernagio et tramesio precii cujuslibet acre per annum xij d. unde idem Ricardus qui tenens est respondebit et terra capiatur.

1.103 <[iiij li. vij s. vj d.]>
Item presentant quod idem Ricardus iam vij annis elapsis assartavit xvij acras et dimidiam in vasto dicte villa que v^{ies} inbladate sunt de yvernagio et tramesio precii cujuslibet acre per annum xij d. unde idem Ricardus qui tenens est respondebit et terra capiatur et pro iiij marleriis ibidem fossatis [ad nocumentum ferarum domini] unde idem Ricardus in misericordia ac impleantur ad custagia ipsius Ricardi.

1.104 <xv li. vj s. viij d.>
Item presentant quod idem Ricardus iam xl annis elapsis construxit ibidem in vasto predicto quoddam molendinum quod est ad nocumentum ferarum precii molendini xl s. et forisfiat domino [et deleatur].

Et est valor molendini per annum dimidie marce unde idem Ricardus respondebit.

Respice in tergo [presentationes] de [aliquibus] mal[...]

5

m. 5d

1.105 <vij li.>
Item presentant quod abbas de Basyngwerke iam xx annis elapsis assartavit x acras terre in vasto eiusdem ville de Thornton que xiiij^{ies} inbladate sunt de yvernagio et tramesio precii cujuslibet acre per annum xij d. unde abbas qui nunc est tenens respondebit et terra capiatur in manu domini.

1.106 <iij li. ij s. vj d.>
Item presentant quod idem abbas iam xij annis elapsis assartavit in vasto dicte ville vij acras terre iij rodas xj perticas que viij^{es} inbladate sunt de yvernagio et tramesio precii cujuslibet acre per annum xij d. unde abbas qui tenens est respondebit et terra capiatur.

Et idem abbas in misericordia pro ij marleris ibidem factis et preceptum est quod inpleantur ad custagia ipsius abbatis.

1.102 <[£5 2s. 0d].>
Item they present that nine years ago Richard assarted 17½ acres of land in the waste of the said township, which have yielded crops six times sown in winter and summer, price of each acre 12d. a year, for which Richard who is the tenant will answer and the land is to be taken.

1.103 <[£4 7s. 6d.]>
Item they present that seven years ago Richard assarted 17½ acres of land in the waste of the said township, which have yielded crops five times sown in winter and summer, price of each acre 12d. a year, for which Richard who is the tenant will answer and the land is to be taken and for four marl pits dug there to the harm of the lord's beasts. Therefore Richard is to be in mercy and they are to be filled in at Richard's own expense.

1.104 <£15 6s. 8d.>
Item they present that Richard 40 years ago constructed there a mill in the above waste which is to the harm of the beasts, price of the mill 40s. and it is to be forfeited to the lord [and pulled down].

And the value of the mill per year is half a mark for which the same Richard will answer.

Look overleaf for [presentments] concerning [some] [...]

5

m. 5d

1.105 <£7>
Item they present that the abbot of Basingwerk[1] 20 years ago assarted ten acres of land in the waste of the same township of Thornton, which have yielded crops fourteen times sown in winter and summer, price of each acre 12d. a year, for which the abbot, the present tenant, will answer and the land is to be taken into the lord's hands.

1.106 <£3 2s. 6d.>
Item they present that the same abbot twelve years ago assarted in the waste of that township 7 acres 3 roods 11 perches of land, which have yielded crops eight times sown in winter and summer, price of each acre 12d. a year, for which the abbot, the present tenant, will answer and the land is to be taken.

And the same abbot is to be in mercy for two marl pits made there and it is ordered that they are to be filled in at the abbot's own expense.

1 See **1.61** note.

1.107 <xx li.>
Item presentant quod Johannes Donvylle iam xxx annis elapsis assartavit in vasto de *Brunstath* xx acras terre que xx^es^ inbladate sunt de yvernagio et tramesio precii cujuslibet acre per annum xij d. unde idem Johannes qui tenens est respondebit et terra capiatur.

1.108 <xiiij li.>
Item presentant quod idem Johannes iam xx annis elapsis assartavit in vasto dicte ville xx acras terre que xiiij^ies^ inbladate sunt de yvernagio et tramesio precii cujuslibet acre per annum xij d. unde idem Johannes respondebit et terra capiatur in manu domini.

1.109 <viij li.>
Item presentant quod idem Johannes iam xij annis elapsis assartavit xx acras terre in vasto eiusdem ville que viij^es^ inbladate sunt de yvernagio et tramesio precii cujuslibet acre per annum xij d. unde idem Johannes respondebit et terra capiatur in manu.

Et idem Johannes pro vj marleris ibidem factis in *misericordia* et preceptum est quod inpleantur ad custagia ipsius Johannis.

1.110 <Storton> <iiij li. viij s.>
Item presentant quod Willelmus de Stanlegh iam xij annis elapsis assartavit in vasto ville de Storton xj acras terre que inbladate sunt viij^es^ de yvernagio et tramesio precii acre per annum xij d. unde idem Willelmus respondebit et terra capiatur ut supra.

Et idem Willelmus in misericordia pro una marlera ibidem facta et nichilominus inpleatur ad custagium ipsius Willelmi.

1.111 <iiij li. viij s.>
Item presentant quod Willelmus de Bechynton iam xvj annis elapsis assartavit viij acras terre in vasto eiusdem ville que xj^es^ inbladate de yvernagio et tramesio precii cujuslibet acre per annum xij d. unde idem Willelmus qui tenens est respondet et terra capiatur in manu domini.

Et idem Willelmus in *misericordia* pro j marlero ibidem facto et preceptum est quod inpleatur ad custagium ipsius.

1.107 <£20>
Item they present that John Donvylle[1] 30 years ago assarted in the waste of *Brimstage* 20 acres of land, which have yielded crops 20 times sown in winter and summer, price of each acre 12d. a year, for which John, the present tenant, will answer and the land is to be taken.

1.108 <£14>
Item they present that John 20 years ago assarted in the waste of that township 20 acres of land, which have yielded crops fourteen times sown in winter and summer, price of each acre 12d. a year, for which John will answer and the land is to be taken into the lord's hands.

1.109 <£8>
Item they present that John twelve years ago assarted 20 acres of land in the waste of the same township, which have yielded crops eight times sown in winter and summer, price of each acre 12d. a year, for which John will answer and the land is to be taken into the hands.

And the same John is to be in *mercy* for six marl pits made there and it is ordered that they are to be filled in at John's own expense.

1.110 <Storeton> <£4 8s.>
Item they present that William de Stanlegh twelve years ago assarted eleven acres of land in the waste of the township of Storeton, which have yielded crops eight times sown in winter and summer, price of an acre 12d. a year, for which William will answer and the land is to be taken as above.

And William is to be in mercy for a marl-pit made there and it is to be filled in nonetheless at William's own expense.

1.111 <£4 8s. 0d.>
Item they present that William de Bechynton[2] sixteen years ago assarted eight acres of land in the waste of the same township, which have yielded crops eleven times sown in winter and summer, price of each acre 12d. a year, for which William, the tenant, will answer and the land is to be taken into the hands of the lord.

And William is to be in *mercy* for a marl-pit made there and it is ordered that it is to be filled in at his own expense.

1 See **1.64** note.
2 See **1.62** note.

1.112 <lv s.>
Item presentant quod Willelmus de Stanlegh Ricardus de Bechynton et Willelmus de Laken iam xvj annis elapsis assartaverunt v acras terre in vasto ibidem que xj[es] inbladate sunt de yvernagio et tramesio precii acre per annum xij d. unde idem Willelmus Ricardus et Willelmus qui nunc sunt tenentes respondebunt videlicet quilibet eorum pro tercia parte et terra capiatur.

Et quilibet eorum fecit unam marleram ibidem. Ideo quilibet in *misericordia* et preceptum est quod inpleantur ad custagia ipsorum.

1.113 <lxvj s.>
Item presentant quod idem Willelmus Ricardus et Willelmus iam xvj annis elapsis assartaverunt vj acras terre in vasto ibidem que xj[es] inbladate sunt de yvernagio et tramesio precii cujuslibet acre per annum xij d. unde predicti qui sunt tenentes respondebunt videlicet quilibet etc. et terra capiatur.

Et illi in *misericordia* pro j marlero ibidem facto et preceptum est quod inpleatur ad custagia ipsorum.

1.114 <iiij li. viij s.>
Item presentant quod idem Willelmus Ricardus et Willelmus iam xvj annis elapsis assartaverunt in vasto ibidem viij acras terre que xj[es] inbladate sunt de yvernagio et tramesio precii acre per annum xij d. unde idem qui nunc sunt tenentes respondebunt videlicet quilibet eorum pro tercia parte et terra capiatur.

Et illi in *misericordia* pro j marlera ibidem facta et preceptum est quod inpleatur ut supra.

1.115 <iiij li. viij s. iiij d.>
Item presentant quod Willelmus de Bechynton iam xvj annis elapsis assartavit in vasto ibidem in uno loco ij acras terre et viij perticas et in alio loco ibidem assartavit v acras iij rodas xxxij perticas que xj[es] inbladate sunt de yvernagio et tramesio precii acre per annum xij d. unde idem Willelmus respondebit et terra capiatur.

Et in misericordia pro j marlero ibidem facto. Preceptum est quod inpleatur.

1.112 <55s. 0d.>
Item they present that William de Stanlegh, Richard de Bechynton and William de Laken[1] sixteen years ago assarted five acres of land in the waste there, which have yielded crops eleven times sown in winter and summer, price of an acre 12d. a year, for which William, Richard and William, the present tenants, will each answer for a third part and the land is to be taken.

And each of them made a marl-pit there. Therefore they are each to be in *mercy* and it is ordered that they are to be filled in at their own expense.

1.113 <66s. 0d.>
Item they present that William, Richard and William sixteen years ago assarted six acres of land in the waste there, which have yielded crops eleven times sown in winter and summer, price of each acre 12d. a year, for which they, the tenants, will each answer etc. and the land is to be taken.

And they are to be in *mercy* for a marl-pit made there and it is ordered that it is to be filled in at their own expense.

1.114 <£4 8s. 0d.>
Item they present that William, Richard and William sixteen years ago assarted eight acres of land in the waste there, which have yielded crops eleven times sown in winter and summer, price of an acre 12d. a year, for which they, the present tenants, will each answer for a third part and the land is to be taken.

And they are to be in *mercy* for a marl-pit made there and it is ordered that it is to be filled in as above.

1.115 <£4 8s. 4d.>
Item they present that William de Bechynton sixteen years ago assarted in the waste there 2 acres and 8 perches of land in one place and he assarted 5 acres 3 roods 32 perches in another place there, which have yielded crops eleven times sown in winter and summer, price of an acre 12d. a year, for which William will answer and the land is to be taken.

And he is to be in mercy for a marl-pit made there. It is ordered that it be filled in.

1 1347 m. 3d William de Laken took 2 oaks; fine 40d.; pledge William de Stanlegh.

1.116 <xxv s.>
Item presentant quod Alicia de Laken iam xvj annis elapsis assartavit ibidem in vasto ij acras terre j rodam iiij perticas que xj^{es} inbladate sunt de yvernagio et tramesio precii acre per annum xij d. unde eadem Alicia que tenens est respondebit et terra capiatur.

Et predicta Alicia in *misericordia* pro j marlero ibidem[a] facto et preceptum quod inpleatur etc.

1.117 <x li.>
Item presentant quod Willelmus de Prenton qui obiit iam xxx annis elapsis assartavit in vasto ville de *Prenton* x acras terre que xx^{es} inbladate sunt de yvernagio et tramesio precii acre per annum

xij d. unde Amicia filia et heres dicti Willelmi que nunc est tenens respondebit et terra capiatur.

1.118 <vij li.>
Item presentant quod idem Willelmus iam xx annis elapsis assartavit x acras terre in vasto ibidem que xiiij^{es} inbladate sunt de yvernagio et tramesio precii acre per annum xij d. unde Amicia filia et heres predicti Willelmi que tenens est respondebit et terra capiatur.

1.119 <Cx s.>
Item presentant quod idem Willelmus iam xvj annis elapsis assartavit ibidem x acras terre que xj^{es} inbladate sunt de yvernagio et tramesio precii acre per annum xij d. unde eadem Amicia que tenens est respondebit et terra capiatur.

1.120 <iiij li.>
Item presentant quod idem Willelmus iam xij annis elapsis assartavit ibidem x acras terre que viij^{es} inbladate sunt de yvernagio et tramesio precii acre per annum xij d. unde eadem Amicia que tenens est respondebit et terra capiatur. Et quia idem Willelmus fecit ibidem duo marlera ideo in *misericordia* et preceptum est quod inpleantur etc.

1.121 <iij s. iiij d.>
Item presentant quod idem Willelmus iam xij annis elapsis vastavit et destructit iij acres bosci in bosco de Prenton ad dampnum domini xl d. unde eadem Alicia que tenens respondebit et boscus capiatur etc.

a *ibidem* repeated in MS

1.116 <25s. 0d.>
Item they present that Amice de Laken sixteen years ago assarted 2 acres, 1 rood and 4 perches of land in the waste there, which have yielded crops eleven times sown in winter and summer, price of an acre 12d. a year, for which Amice, the tenant, will answer and the land is to be taken.

And Amice is to be in *mercy* for a marl-pit made there and it is ordered that it is to be filled in etc.

1.117 <£10>
Item they present that William de Prenton,[1] now dead, 30 years ago assarted ten acres in the waste of the township of *Prenton*, which have yielded crops 20 times sown in winter and summer, price of an acre 12d. a year, for which Amice, William's daughter and heiress, who is the present tenant, will answer and the land is to be taken.

1.118 <£7>
Item they present that William 20 years ago assarted ten acres of land in the waste there, which have yielded crops fourteen times sown in winter and summer, price of an acre 12d. a year, for which Amice, who is the tenant, daughter and heir of William, will answer and the land is to be taken.

1.119 <110s. 0s.>
Item they present that sixteen years ago William assarted ten acres of land in the waste there, which have yielded crops eleven times sown in winter and summer, price of an acre 12d. a year, for which Amice, who is the tenant, will answer and the land is to be taken.

1.120 <£4>
Item they present that twelve years ago William assarted ten acres of land there, which have yielded crops eight times sown in winter and summer, price of an acre 12d. a year, for which Amice, the tenant, will answer and the land is to be taken.

And because William made two marl pits there, therefore he is to be in *mercy* and it is ordered that they are to be filled in etc.

1.121 <3s. 4d.>
Item they present that twelve years ago William wasted and destroyed three acres of wood in Prenton wood to the loss of the lord 40d. for which Amice, who is the tenant, will answer and the wood is to be taken etc.

1 1347 m. 3 William de Prenton, 20 oaks; 6s. 4d; John de Middleton.

1.122 <xiiij li.>
Item presentant quod Jacobus de Pulle qui obiit iam xl annis elapsis assartavit x acras terre in vasto ville de *[Magna] Neston* que xxviij^{es} inbladate sunt de yvernagio et tramesio precii acre per annum xij d. unde Robertus filius suus qui [nunc] tenens est respondebit et terra capiatur.

1.123 <xxj li. [...]>
Item presentant quod idem Jacobus iam xx annis elapsis assartavit ibidem [in vasto] xxx [acras] terre que [...] inbladate sunt de yvernagio et tramesio precii acre per annum xij d. unde idem Robertus Pulle filius qui nunc est [tenens) respondebit. Idem Robertus in misericordia precii ij marcarum [dimidie] [...]. [Forisfaciant quod implicantur] [...] [...].

1.124
Item [presentant] quod idem Jacobus iam xx annis elapsis construxit ibidem in vasto quoddam [...] [...] [xx s.] et forisfiat [...] et prosternatur precii damni in eadem xx s. unde idem Robertus [...] [...] [xx] est valor [eiusdem] [...] [...][a] unde idem Robertus [respondebit].

m. 6

1.125 <xxvj li.>
Item presentant quod Rogerus de Leghton iam xxx annis elapsis assartavit in vasto ville de *Leghton* xxvj acras terre, que xx^{es} inbladate sunt de yvernagio et tramesio precii acre per annum xij d. unde Johannes de Leghton qui modo tenens est respondebit et terra capiatur in manu domini.

1.126
Item presentant quod boscus de Leghton vastatur de quercubus et deterioratur de subbosco per dominos de Leghton per communarios eiusdem ville ad dampnum domini *xl s.*, quiquidem boscus alias seisitus fuit in manu domini et nondum replegiatus unde Johannes de Leghton pro tribus partibus et comes Sar' pro quarta parte dampnorum predictorum respondebunt. Et boscus adhuc remanet in manu domini.

1.127
Item presentant quod Stephanus de Merton iam xij annis elapsis assartavit in vasto ville de *Gayton* extra coopertum iij acras et dimidiam et j rodam et x perticas et

a [...] interlined

1.122 <£14>
Item they present that James de Pulle,[1] who has died, 40 years ago assarted ten acres of land in the waste of the township of [*Great*] *Neston*, which have yielded crops 28 times sown in winter and summer, price of an acre 12d. a year, for which Robert, his son, who is now the tenant, will answer and the land is to be taken.

1.123 <£21 [...]>
Item they present that James 20 years ago assarted in the waste there 30 acres of land which have [...] [...] yielded crops in winter and summer, price per acre 12d. [...], for which Robert Pulle, the son, who is the present tenant, will answer. The same Robert is to be in mercy. Price 2½ marks [...]. They are to forfeit because they are implicated [...] [...]

1.124
Item they present that 20 years ago James built in the waste there a [...] [...] [...] [...] [20s. 0d.] and he is to be forfeit [. . .] and it is to be pulled down; price of the damage in the same 20s. 0d. for which Robert [...] [...] [20] value of the same [...] [...] 20s. 0d. and the value of the same [...] [...] [...] for which Robert [will answer].

m. 6

1.125 <£26>
Item they present that Roger de Leghton[2] 30 years ago assarted in the waste of the township of *Leighton* 26 acres of land which have yielded crops 20 times sown in winter and in summer, price of an acre 12d. a year, for which John de Leighton who is now the tenant will answer and the land is to be taken into the hands of the lord.

1.126
Item they present that Leighton wood was wasted of oaks and suffered loss of underwood, by the lords of Leighton through the commoners of the same township, to the harm of the lord of *40s. 0d.* This wood was seized into the hands of the lord elsewhere and is not yet repledged, for which John de Leighton will answer for three parts of the damages and the earl of Salisbury for the fourth part, and the wood still remains in the hands of the lord.

1.127
Item they present that Stephen de Merton[3] twelve years ago assarted in the waste of the township of *Gayton* outside the covert 3½ acres 1 rood and 10½ perches of land, which have yielded crops eight times sown in winter and in summer, price of

1 See **1.93** note.
2 See **1.50** note.
3 See **1.41** note.

dimidiam terre que viij[es] inbladate sunt de yvernagio et tramesio precii acre per annum xij d.,

<xxvi s. vi d.[a]>

unde idem Stephanus qui nunc tenens est respondebit et terra capiatur.

<xxx s. vj d.>

Et idem Stephanus in misericordia pro una marlera facta ibidem et preceptum est quod inpleatur etc.

1.128 <viij li. xiiij s. vj d.>
Item presentant quod parcenarii de Haselwell iam xxx annis elapsis assartaverunt in vasto ville de *Haselwell* viij acras et dimidiam et dimidiam rodam xvj perticas et dimidiam perticam et dimidiam quartam que inbladate sunt de yvernagio et tramesio xx[es] precii acre per annum xij d. unde parcenarii de Haselwell qui nunc sunt respondebunt et terra capiatur.

1.129 <vij li. ij s. [...] d.>
Item presentant quod idem parcenarii de Haselwall iam xx annis elapsis assartaverunt ibidem in vasto viij acras et dimidiam et dimidiam rodam xvj perticas et dimidiam et dimidiam quartam que xiiij[es] inbladate sunt de yvernagio et tramesio precii acre per annum xij d.unde idem parcenarii qui nunc sunt tenentes respondebunt et terra capiatur in manu domini.

Et quia quoddam marlerium factum est ibidem ideo predicti parcenarii in *misericordia* et preceptum est quod inpleatur ad custagia ipsorum parcenariorum.

1.130 <viiij li. xiij s. iiij d.>
Item presentant quod idem parcenarii iam xx annis elapsis constructerunt in vasto quoddam molendinum ventriticum quod est ad nocumentum ferarum precii xl s. unde idem parcenarii respondebunt et deleatur[b]. Et est valor illius per annum a tempore etc. dimidie marce unde idem parcenarii respondebunt.

1.131 <xiiij li. xvj s.>
Item presentant quod Robertus de Berneston iam xij annis elapsis assartavit in vasto ville de *Berneston* xxxvij acras et dimidiam ix perticas et dimidiam terre que viiij[es] inbladate sunt de yvernagio et tramesio precii acre per annum xij d. unde idem Robertus qui tenens est respondebit et terra capiatur.

Et idem Robertus in *misericordia* pro iij marleriis factis ibidem et preceptum quod inpleantur ad custagia ipsius Roberti.

a *xxvj s.vj d.* struck through
b *deliatur* MS

an acre 12d. a year, for which Stephen who is now the tenant will answer and the land is to be taken.

<30s. 6d.>

And Stephen is to be in mercy for a marl-pit there and it is ordered that it is to be filled in etc.

1.128 <£8 14s. 6d.>
Item they present that the parceners of Heswall 30 years ago assarted in the waste of the township of *Heswall* 8½ acres and half a rood and 16⅝ perches which have yielded crops 20 times sown in winter and in summer, price of an acre 12d. a year, for which the present parceners of Heswall will answer and the land is to be taken.

1.129 <£6 2s. [...]d.>
Item they present that the parceners of Heswall 20 years ago assarted in the waste there 8½ acres and half a rood and 16⅝ perches which have yielded crops fourteen times sown in winter and in summer, price of an acre 12d. a year, for which the parceners who are the present tenants will answer and the land is to be taken into the hands of the lord.

And because a marl-pit has been made there, the parceners are to be *in mercy* and it is ordered that it is to be filled in at the expense of the parceners.

1.130 <£8 13s. 4d.>
Item they present that the parceners 20 years ago built in the waste there a windmill which is to the harm of the beasts, price 40s. 0d., for which the parceners will answer and it is to be destroyed. And the value of the mill is half a mark a year from the time etc. for which the parceners will answer.

1.131 <£14 16s. 0d.>
Item they present that Robert de Berneston[1] twelve years ago assarted in the waste of the township of *Barnston* 37½ acres 9½ perches of land which have yielded crops eight times sown in winter and in summer, price of an acre 12d. a year, for which Robert who is the tenant will answer and the land is to be taken.

And Robert is to be in *mercy* for three marl pits made there and it is ordered that they are to filled in at Robert's expense.

1 See **1.38** note.

1.132 <vj li.>
Item presentant quod idem Robertus iam xij annis elapsis[a] constructit ibidem in vasto quoddam molendinum ventriticum quod est ad nocumentum ferarum precii xl s. unde idem Robertus respondebit et deleatur. Et est valor illius per annum dimidie marce a tempore ut supra.

1.133
Item presentant quod Willelmus de *Thyngwall* iam xij annis elapsis assartavit v acras terre et dimidiam et xiiij perticas in vasto de ville que viij[es] inbladate sunt de yvernagio et tramesio precii acre per annum xij d. unde idem Willelmus qui nunc tenens est [respondebit] et terre capiatur in manu domini.

Et idem Willelmus in *misericordia* pro j marleria facta ibidem et preceptum quod inpleatur etc.

1.134 <Arwe> <C s.>
Item presentant quod Petrus de Thornton et Thurstanus de Tyldeslegh iam xxx annis elapsis assartaverunt in vasto ville predicte v acras terre que xx[es] inbladate sunt de yvernagio et tramesio precii acre per annum xij d. unde heredes dicti Petri et predictus Thurstanus qui nunc sunt tenentes respondebunt et terra capiatur in manu domini.

1.135 <lxx s.>
Item presentant quod idem Petrus et Thurstanus de Tyldelegh assartaverunt in vasto eiusdem ville iam xx annis elapsis v acras terre, que xiiij[ies] inbladate sunt de yvernagio et tramesio precii acre per annum xij d. unde heredes predicti Petri et predictus Thurstanus de Tyldeslegh qui sunt tenentes respondebunt et terra capiatur etc.

1.136 <xlv s. vj d. ob.>
Item presentant quod predicti Petrus et Thurstanus iam xvj annis elapsis assartaverunt in vasto eiusdem ville [iv acras et] xxviij perticas et dimidiam terre que xj[es] inbladate sunt de yvernagio et tramesio precii acre per annum xij d. unde [Petri] heredes et Thurstanus respondebunt et terra capiatur etc. Et predicti heredes dicti Petri et Thurstanus in misericordia pro iij marleriis ibidem factis et preceptum quod inpleantur ad custagia ipsorum.

1.137 <Frankeby> <c xj s. j d.>
Johannes de Warrewyke qui obiit iam xxx annis elapsis assartaverunt in vasto ibidem v acras et dimidiam viij perticas terre, que xx[es] inbladate sunt de yvernagio

a *iam xij annis elapsis* interlined

1.132 <£6>
Item they present that Robert twelve years ago built in the waste there a windmill to the harm of the beasts, price 40s. 0d., for which Robert will answer and it is to be destroyed. And the value of the mill is half a mark a year from the time as above.

1.133
Item they present that William de *Thyngwall*[1] twelve years ago assarted 5½ acres and 14 perches of land in the waste of the township, which have yielded crops eight times sown in winter and in summer, price of an acre 12d. a year, for which William, who is the present tenant, will answer and the land is to be taken into the hands of the lord.

And William is to be in *mercy* for a marl-pit made there and it is ordered that it is to be filled in etc.

1.134 <Arrowe> <100s. 0d.>
Item they present that Peter de Thornton[2] and Thurstan de Tyldeslegh 30 years ago assarted in the waste of the said township 5 acres of land which have yielded crops 20 times sown in winter and in summer, price of an acre 12d. a year, for which the heirs of Peter, and Thurstan, the present tenants, will answer and the land is to be taken into the hands of the lord.

1.135 <70s 0d.>
Item they present that Peter and Thurstan de Tyldeslegh 20 years ago assarted in the waste of the same township five acres of land which have yielded crops fourteen times sown in winter and in summer, price of an acre 12d. a year, for which the heirs of Peter, and Thurstan de Tyldeslegh who are the tenants will answer, and the land is to be taken etc.

1.136 <45s. 6½d.>
Item they present that Peter and Thurstan sixteen years ago assarted in the waste of the same township 4 acres and 28½ perches of land which have yielded crops eleven times sown in winter and in summer, price of an acre 12d. a year, for which the heirs of Peter, and Thurstan will answer and the land is to be taken etc. And the heirs of Peter, and Thurstan are to be in mercy for three marl pits made there and it is ordered that they are to be filled in at their own expense

1.137 <Frankby> <111s. 1d.>
John de Warrewyke,[3] who has died, 30 years ago assarted 5½ acres 8 perches of land in that place which have yielded crops 20 times sown in winter and in summer, price

1 1347 m. 1d William de Thingwall took 6 oaks; fine 2s. 0d.; pledge Roger de Sybbrok.
2 See **1.38** note.
3 1347 m. 6 John de Warrwyk took an oak.

et tramesio precii acre per annum xij d. unde Johannes filius et heres qui nunc est tenens repondebit. Et terra capiatur ut supra.

Et idem Johannes in *misericordia* pro ij marleriis ibidem factis et preceptum est quod inpleantur.

1.138 <viij s.>
Item presentant quod Philippus de Egerton et Johannes de Lassels iam xij annis elapsis assartaverunt in vasto ville de *Neuton* extra coopertum j acram terre que viij[es] inbladate sunt de yvernagio et tramesio precii acre per annum [xij d.]. Predicti Philippus et Johannes qui nunc sunt tenentes respondebunt [et terra] capiatur.

1.139 <viij li. xiij s. iiij d.>
Item presentant quod abbas de Basyngwerk iam xx annis elapsis constructit ibidem in vasto quoddam molendinum ventriticum quod est ad nocumentum ferarum precii xl s. unde abbas qui nunc est respondebit.

Et est valor illius per annum a tempore constructionis dimidie marce unde predictus abbas similiter respondebit et deleatur.

1.140 <Calday grangea> <iij li. xvj s.>
Item presentant quod abbas de Basyngwerk iam xvj annis elapsis assartavit in vasto ibidem xij acras iij rodas [j perticam et] j quarterium terre que xj[es] inbladate sunt de yvernagio et tramesio precii acre per annum xij d. unde abbas qui nunc est [respondebit] et terra capiatur etc.

Et predictus abbas in misericordia quod unum marlerium ibidem est factum. Ideo preceptum est quod inpleatur. [...] quia includitur muro lapideo contra assisam [...] in misericordia et quod idem abbas constructit ibi [domus] [...] [...] ibidem que est nocumentiva feris domini precii dimidie marce [unde] idem abbas qui nunc est [...]. Et valor dicte domus per annum a tempore predicte[a] constructionis etc. xij d. unde idem abbas similiter respondebit.

C v li. xiij d.

a *predicte* interlined

of an acre 12d. a year for which John, the son and heir, who is the present tenant will answer. And the land is to be taken as above etc.

And John is to be in *mercy* for two marl pits made there and it is ordered that they are to be filled in.

1.138 <8s. 0d.>
Item they present that Philip de Egerton and John de Lassels[1] twelve years ago assarted in the waste of the township of *Newton* outside the covert one acre of land which has yielded crops eight times sown in winter and in summer, price of an acre 12d. a year. Philip and John the present tenants will answer and the land is to be taken etc.

1.139 <£8 13s. 4d.>
Item they present that 20 years ago the abbot of Basingwerk[2] built in the waste there a windmill which is to the harm of the beasts, price 40s. 0d., for which the present abbot will answer and the value of the mill is half a mark a year from the time it was built, for which the abbot [...] will answer and it is to be destroyed.

1.140 <Calday Grange> <£3 16s. 0d.>
Item they present that the abbot of Basingwerk sixteen years ago assarted in the waste there 12 acres 3 roods and 1¼ perches of land which have yielded crops eleven times sown in winter and in summer, price of an acre 12d. a year for which the present abbot will answer and the land is to be taken etc.

And the abbot is to be in mercy because a marl-pit was made there. It is therefore ordered that it is to be filled in. [...] because it is enclosed by a stone wall against the assize [...], [therefore he is to be] in mercy; and since the abbot erected a building there [...] [...] in the same place which is harmful to the lord's beasts, price of half a mark, for which the present abbot [...]. And the value of the building from the time it was built etc. is 12d. for which the abbot will likewise answer.

£105 13d.

1 1347 m. 2 Robert Lassels an oak; fine 2s. 0d.; pledge Roger de Coghull.
2 See **1.105** note.

De inbladationibus

6

m. 6d

1.141 <Thurstanston> <vj li. xv s. j d.>
Item presentant quod Johannes Doune iam xxx annis elapsis assartavit in vasto ibidem extra coopertum vj acras iij rodas j perticam et j quarterium terre que xx[es] inbladate sunt de yvernagio et tramesio precii acre per annum xij d. unde idem Johannes qui nunc tenens est respondebit et terra capiatur in manu domini.

1.142
Item presentant quod idem Johannes iam xxx annis elapsis construxit ibidem in vasto quoddam molendinum ventriticum quod est ad nocumentum ferarum precii xl s. unde idem Johannes respondebit et deleatur et est valor illius *[xl li.]*[a] per annum a tempore constructionis etc. unde idem Johannes similiter respondebit.

1.143 <Parva Moles> <v s. vj d.>
Item presentant quod Ranulphus le Bryn iam xvj annis elapsis assartavit in vasto ibidem medietatem j acre que xj[es] inbladate sunt de yvernagio et tramesio precii[b] per annum vj d.[c] unde idem Ranulphus respondebit et terra capiatur etc.

1.144 <xvij li. xix s. iiij d. ob.>
Item presentant quod abbas de Basyngwerk iam xxx annis elapsis assartavit in vasto ibidem iij acras prati et xvij acras iij rodas xxxv perticas pasture quod pratum quolibet anno falcatum fuit precii acre per annum xij d. et qualibet acra pasture valet singulis annis vj d. unde abbas qui nunc est respondebit et terra capiatur.

1.145 <xv s. x d.>
Item presentant quod idem abbas iam xxv annis elapsis[d] construxit ibidem quemdam domum bercarii in vasto ad nocumentum ferarum precii domus xl d. unde idem abbas respondebit et est valor dicte domus per annum vj d. unde idem abbas respondebit et deleatur[e] etc. Non includitur etc. Nichil in misericordia Abbas qui nunc est pro constructione domus predicte quia in tempore predecessoris sui constructa fuit.

a omitted in MS. Amount supplied from margination
b *acre* struck through
c *xij d.* struck through and *vj d.* interlined
d *iam xxv annis elapsis* interlined
e *deliatur* MS

Concerning corn sown

m. 6d

1.141 <Thurstaston> <£6 15s. 1d.>
Item they present that John Doune 30 years ago assarted in the waste there outside the covert 6 acres 3 roods 1¼ perches of land, which have yielded crops 20 times sown in winter and summer, price of an acre 12d. a year, for which John, who is the present tenant, will answer and the land is to be taken into the hands of the lord.

1.142
Item they present that John 30 years ago built in the waste there a windmill which is to the harm of the beasts, price 40s. 0d., for which John will answer and it is to be destroyed; and the value of it is [*£40*] a year from the time it was built, for which John will answer likewise.

1.143 <Little Meols> <5s. 6d.>
Item they present that Ranulf le Bryn[1] sixteen years ago assarted half an acre in the waste there which has yielded crops eleven times sown in winter and summer, price 6d. a year, for which Ranulf will answer and the land is to be taken etc.

1.144 <£17 19s. 4½d>
Item they present that the abbot of Basingwerk[2] 30 years ago assarted in the waste there three acres of meadow; and 17 acres, 3 roods and 35 perches of pasture, and that meadow was mown every year, price of an acre 12d. a year; and every acre of pasture is worth 6d. each year, for which the present abbot will answer and the land is to be taken.

1.145 <15s. 10d.>
Item they present that the abbot 25 years ago built in the waste there a sheepfold to the harm of the beasts, price of the fold 40d., for which the abbot will answer and it is valued at 6d. a year, for which the abbot will answer, and it is to be destroyed etc. It is not enclosed etc. The present abbot is not to be in mercy at all for the construction of the sheepfold, because it was built in the time of his predecessor.

1 See **1.36** note.
2 See **1.140** note.

1.146 <Magna Moeles> <xx li. xv s.>
Item presentant quod Henricus de Moeles iam xvj annis elapsis assartavit in vasto extra coopertum v acras terre que xj[es] inbladate sunt de yvernagio et tramesio precii acre per annum xij d. et assartavit ibidem in aliis locis duobus viij acras prati quod xvj[es] falcatum fuit precii acre per annum xij d. et similiter assartavit ibidem duobus locis xxix acras pasture precii cujuslibet acre per annum vj d. quolibet anno videlicet per xvj annos[a] unde idem Henricus respondebit et terra capiatur et non includitur.

1.147 <xvj s.>
Item presentant quod idem Henricus iam xvj annis elapsis vastavit ibidem extra coopertum dimidiam acram turbarie pro fossandis et vendendis turbariis que valet per annum quolibet anno xij d. unde idem Henricus respondebit et turbaria capiatur etc.

Et idem Henricus sit pro fossatione in *misericordia.*

1.148 <Kyrkeby Waley> <Cj s. j d.>
Item presentant quod Willelmus Gregorius et Hugo de Waley iam xx annis elapsis assartaverunt vij acras et dimidiam ij rodas j perticam et dimidiam quarterii terre que xiiij[es] inbladate fuerunt de yvernagio et tramesio precii acre terre per annum xij d. unde iidem Gregorius et Hugo respondebunt et terra capiatur ut supra.

1.149 <lxxij s. j d.>
Item presentant quod idem Willelmus et Hugo iam xx annis elapsis assartaverunt ibidem vij acras et dimidiam rodam xv perticas et quarterium pasture precii acre per annum vj d. unde idem Willelmus et Hugo respondebunt et terra capiatur etc.

1.150 <iiij li. xij s. iij d.>
Item presentant quod prior de Byrkeheved iam xxx annis elapsis assartavit ibidem in vasto iiij acras et dimidiam xviij perticas et dimidiam terre que xx[es] inbladate sunt de yvernagio et tramesio precii acre per annum xij d. unde prior qui nunc respondebit. Terra capiatur.

1.151 <iij li. ix s. iiij d.>
Item presentant quod idem prior iam xxx annis elapsis assartavit in vasto ibidem iiij acras et dimidiam xviij perticas et dimidiam pasture precii cujuslibet acre per annum vj d. unde idem prior qui tenens est respondebit et non includitur et terra capiatur ut supra.

a *videlicet per xvj annos* interlined

1.146 <Great Meols> <£20 15s. 0d.>
Item they present that Henry de Meoles[1] sixteen years ago assarted in the waste outside the covert five acres of land, which have yielded crops eleven times sown in winter and summer, price of an acre 12d. a year; and he assarted there in another two places eight acres of meadow, which was mown sixteen times, price of an acre 12d. a year; and likewise he assarted there in two places 29 acres of pasture, price for each acre 6d. a year, that is, for fifteen years, for which Henry will answer; and the land is to be taken and it is not enclosed.

1.147 <16s. 0d.>
Item they present that Henry sixteen years ago wasted in the same place outside the covert half an acre of turbary for digging and selling peat which is worth 12d. a year for each year, for which Henry will answer and the turbary is to be taken.

And Henry is to be in *mercy* for digging.

1.148 <Wallasey> <101s. 1d.>
Item they present that William Gregory and Hugh de Walay[2] 20 years ago assarted 7½ acres 2 roods and 1⅛ perches which have yielded crops fourteen times sown in winter and summer, price of an acre of land 12d. a year, for which Gregory and Hugh will answer and the land is to be taken as above.

1.149 <72s.1d.>
Item they present that William and Hugh 20 years ago in the same place assarted seven acres half a rood 15¼ perches of pasture, price for an acre 6d. a year, for which William and Hugh will answer and the land is to be taken etc.

1.150 <£4 12s. 3d.>
Item they present that the prior of Birkenhead[3] 30 years ago assarted in the waste there 4½ acres 18½ perches of land which have yielded crops 20 times sown in winter and summer, price of an acre 12d. a year, for which the present prior will answer. The land is to be taken.

1.151 <£3 9s. 4d.>
Item they present that the prior 30 years ago assarted in the waste there 4½ acres 18½ perches of pasture price of each acre 6d. a year, for which the prior who is the tenant will answer and it is not enclosed and the land is to be taken as above.

1 1347 m. 14 Radulphus de Meoles dug peat in Oldefield above Falles.
2 See **1.37** note.
3 See **1.48** note.

1.152 <xxxj li. xj s. iij d.>
Item presentant quod Ricardus Sampson et Willelmus filius Philippi de Becheton iam xxx annis elapsis assartaverunt ibidem in vasto xxxj acras ij rodas j quarterium in uno loco qui vocatur Kyppesnaypebutt que xx^{es} inbladate sunt de yvernagio et tramesio precii acre per annum xij d. unde idem Ricardus et Willelmus qui nunc sunt tenentes respondebunt et terra capiatur et non includitur.

1.153 <xvj s.>
Item presentant quod Hugo de Walay iam xxx annis elapsis assartavit ibidem in vasto iij rodas viij perticas terre que xx^{es} inbladate sunt de yvernagio et tramesio precii annum ix d. ob. unde idem Hugo qui nunc tenens est respondebit.

1.154 <Claghton> <xxix li xj s. iij d.>
Item presentant quod prior de Byrkeheved qui obiit iam xxx annis elapsis fecit quoddam assartum terre inter vicum le Blakestrete et le Pulle qui[a] ducit ad Cestr' quod[b] continet xxix acras dimidiam x perticas terre que xx^{es} inbladate[c] de yvernagio et tramesio precii acre per annum xij d. unde abbas [*sic*] qui nunc est respondebit et terra capiatur etc.

1.155 <iiij li. viij s. [iij d.]>
Item presentant quod idem prior iam xx annis elapsis assartavit ibidem in vasto quoddam assartum inter idem vicum qui ducit versus Cestr' et boscum quod vocatur Lassellesfeld continentem vj acras j rode x perticas j quarterium terre que xiiij^{es} inbladate sunt de yvernagio et tramesio precii acre per annum xij d. unde abbas [*sic*] qui nunc est respondebit et terra capiatur ut supra.

1.156 <[...] x s. ij d.>
Item presentant quod idem prior iam xvj annis elapsis assartavit ibidem in vasto v acras j rode xxxiiij perticas terre et dimidiam et quarterium que xij^{es} inbladate sunt de yvernagio et tramesio precii acre per annum xij d. unde prior qui nunc est respondebit et terra capiatur etc.

1.157 <xx li. v s.> <[...]>
Item presentant quod idem prior iam xvj annis elapsis assartavit ibidem quamdam placiam terre que vocatur *Carkelowegreve* et le Lassellesfeld iuxta vicum Cestr' continentem xxviij acras et ix perticas terre que xj^{es} inbladate sunt de yvernagio et tramesio precii acre per annum xij d. unde abbas [*sic*] qui nunc est respondebit et terra capiatur etc.

a *que* MS
b *que* MS
c *inbladate* struck through and then repeated

1.152 <£31 11s. 3d.>
Item they present that Richard Sampson and William son of Philip de Becheton[1] 30 years ago assarted in the waste there 31 acres 2¼ roods in a place called 'Kyppesnaypebutt' which have yielded crops 20 times sown in winter and summer, price of an acre 12d. a year, for which Richard and William, who are the present tenants, will answer and the land is to be taken and it is not enclosed.

1.153 <16s. 0d.>
Item they present that Hugh de Walay 30 years ago assarted in the waste there 3 roods 8 perches of land which have yielded crops 20 times sown in winter and summer, price 9½d. a year, for which Hugh who is the present tenant will answer.

1.154 <Claughton> <£29 11s. 3d.>
Item they present that a prior of Birkenhead, who is dead, 30 years ago made an assart of land, between the road 'le Blakestrete'[2] which leads to Chester and le Pulle[3]. This contains 29½ acres 10 perches of land which have yielded crops 20 times sown in winter and summer, price of an acre 12d. a year, for which the present abbot will answer and the land is to be taken etc.

1.155 <£4 8s. [3]d.>
Item they present that the same prior 20 years ago assarted in the waste there an assart between the same road which leads towards Chester and a wood which is called 'Lassellesfeld',[4] containing 6 acres 1 rood 10¼ perches which have yielded crops fourteen times in winter and summer, price of an acre 12d. a year for which the present abbot will answer and the land is to be taken as above.

1.156 <£[...] 10s. 2d.>
Item they present that the prior sixteen years ago assarted in the waste there five acres 1 rood 34¾ perches of land which have yielded crops thirteen times sown in winter and summer, price of an acre 12d. a year, for which the present prior will answer and the land is to be taken etc.

1.157 <£20 5s. 0d.>
Item they present that the prior sixteen years ago assarted there a piece of land which is called 'Carkelowegreve and Lassellesfeld' next to the Chester road, containing 28 acres and 9 perches, which has yielded crops eleven times sown in winter and summer, price of an acre 12d. a year, for which the present prior will answer and the land is to be taken etc.

1 See **1.112** note.
2 Dodgson, *Place Names*, p. 319.
3 Dodgson, *Place Names*, p. 333.
4 Dodgson, *Place Names*, p. 318.

1.158 <[...]>
Item presentant quod idem prior iam xvj annis elapsis assartavit in vasto ibidem quoddam assartum quod vocatur le Newfeld continentem vij acras iij rodas ix perticas et dimidiam terre que xj^{es} inbladantur precii acre per annum xij d. unde idem prior respondebit et capiatur ut [supra].

1.159
Item presentant quod idem prior qui obiit[a] iam xvj annis elapsis assartavit ibidem unam placiam terre vocatam le Birkhale continentem [...] acras et xxx rodas v perticas et dimidiam que xj inbladate sunt de yvernagio et tramesio precii acre per annum xij d. unde idem prior qui nunc est respondebit et terra capiatur [ut supra].

1.160
Item presentant quod quondam prior qui obiit iam xvj annis elapsis assartavit ibidem in vasto ex parte occidentali [...] unius [...] [...] Claghton [...] acras [...] xx perticas terre [...] [...] alia parte eiusdem [...] vij acras terre [j] [roda] [et] xxiij perticas [que] [xi^{es}] inbladate sunt de yvernagio et tramesio precii acre per annum xij d. unde prior [...][...] terra capiatur [...] [...] [...] [...] pro iij marleriis ibidem [factis] [...] [...] [...] [...] [...] [...] qui nunc est [...].

m. 7

1.161 <xvj li. v d.>
Item presentant quod dux Lancastr' iam xx annis elapsis assartavit in vastis de *Budestan* extra coopertum foreste xxij acras iij rodas xxj perticas et dimidiam terre vocate le Thwayt iuxta le Newemedewe que xiiij^{es} inbladate sunt precii acre per annum xij d. unde idem dux respondebit et terra capiatur ut supra.

1.162 <xxxiij li. ix s. iij d.>
Item presentant quod idem dux iam xx annis elapsis approviatum[b] tenet[c] quoddam pratum in separalitate de vasto predicto vocatum le Newemedewe continentem xxxiij acras j rodam xxxiiij perticas j quarteriam quod xx^{es} falcatum est precii acre xij d. per annum[d] unde idem dux respondebit et pratum capiatur etc. Includitur contra assisam.

1.163 <xxvij li. v s.>
Item presentant quod idem dux iam xx annis elapsis assartavit quamdam parcellam terre et prati vocatam Oldetwayt et Pykemedewe que continet xvj acras terre et xvj

a *qui obiit* interlined
b *approviatum* interlined in a later hand
c *tenet* interlined in a later hand
d *precii acre xij d. per annum* interlined

1.158 <[...]>
Item they present that the prior sixteen years ago asserted in the waste there an assart which is called 'le Newfeld' containing seven acres 3 roods 9½ perches, which have yielded crops eleven times, price of an acre 12d. a year, for which the same prior will answer and it is to be taken as above.

1.159
Item they present that the prior, who has died, sixteen years ago asserted there a piece of land called 'le Birkhale', containing [...] [...] acres and 30 roods 5½ perches of land, which have yielded crops eleven times sown in winter and summer, price of an acre 12d. a year, for which the present prior will answer and the land is to be taken as above.

1.160 <[...]>
Item they present that the previous prior, who has died, sixteen years ago asserted in the waste there in the western part [...] of a [...] [...] Claughton [...] acres [...] 20 perches of land [...] [...] in another part of the same [...] 7 acres of land 1 rood and 23 perches, which have yielded crops eleven times, sown in winter and in summer, price of an acre 12d. a year, for which the prior [...] [...] and the land is to be taken. [...] [...] [...] [...] for three marl pits made there [...] [...] [...] [...] [...] [...] the present [...].

m. 7

1.161 <£16 0s. 5d.>
Item they present that the duke of Lancaster 20 years ago asserted in the waste of *Bidston* outside the covert of the forest 22 acres 3 roods 21½ perches of land called 'le Thwayt' next to the Newemedowe[1] which have yielded crops fourteen times, price of an acre 12d. a year, for which the duke will answer, and the land is to be taken as above.

1.162 <£33 9s. 3d.>
Item they present that the duke for the last 20 years has held a meadow (approved) in severalty from the waste called 'the Newemedowe' containing 33 acres 1 rood 34¼ perches which have been mown 20 times, price of an acre 12d. a year, for which the duke will answer and the meadow is to be taken etc. It is enclosed against the assize.

1.163 <£27 5s. 0d.>
Item they present that the duke 20 years ago asserted a parcel of land and meadow called 'Oldetwayt'[2] and 'Pykemedewe'[3] which contains 16 acres of land and 16 acres of meadow and 8½ perches, which land has yielded crops fourteen times price of

1 Dodgson, *Place Names*, p. 312.
2 Dodgson, *Place Names*, p. 312.
3 Dodgson, *Place Names*, p. 312.

acras prati et viij perticas et dimidiam que terra xiiij[es] inbladata fuit precii acre per annum xij d. et pratum predictum quolibet anno falcatum fuit precii acre terre et prati xij d. per annum unde idem dux qui tenens est respondebit et terra capiatur.

1.164 <xxxvj li. vij s. iiij d.>
Item presentant quod idem dux assartavit iam xx annis elapsis in vasto ibidem alteram parcellam terre inter supradictam et le mare continentem lj acras iij rodas xxxij perticas et j quarteriam que quidem terra xiiij[es] inbladata fuit etc. precii acre per annum xij d. unde idem dux respondebit et terra capiatur etc.

1.165 <iij li. ij s. iij d.>
Item presentant quod idem dux tenet quoddam pratum approviatum xx annis elapsis[a] in separalitate iuxta pontem ex parte occidentali quod vocatur le Chestergre(n)e-medewe quod continet iij acras et xx perticas quod quidem pratum xx[es] falcatum fuit precii per annum xij d. et pratum capiatur etc.

1.166 <lj s. iij d.>
Item presentant quod idem dux iam xx annis elapsis tenet quoddam pratum approviatum[b] iuxta mossetum extendens versus Kyrkeby que continet ij acras et dimidiam et x perticas prati quod quidem pratum quolibet anno falcatum fuit precii acre per annum xij d. unde idem dux respondebit et pratum capiatur.

1.167 <C s. iij d.>
Item presentant quod idem dux tenet unam parcellam terre ex parte boriali predicti prati xx annis elapsis assartatam que continet vij acras xxv perticas et dimidiam que xiiij[es] inbladate sunt etc. precii acre per annum xij d. unde idem dux respondebit et terra capiatur etc.

1.168 <iiij li. xvij d.>
Item presentant quod idem dux tenet quamdam parcellam terre vocatam le Holdefeld et aliam parcellam subtus boscum de Wolleton xx annis iam elapsis assartatam que continent [xj] acras et dimidiam xix perticas et dimidiam et j quarteriam que xiiij[es] inbladate sunt precii acre per annum vj d. et non plus quia debilis est unde idem dux qui tenens est respondebit et capiatur ut supra.

1.169 <CCx li. vj s.>
Item presentant quod idem dux tenet ibidem quoddam mossetum xl annis iam elapsis assartatum et approviatum[c] quod continet Cv acras xxiiij perticas inclusas cum quadam haya in separali mosseto precii per annum quolibet anno xij d. unde idem

a *approviatum xx annis elapsis* interlined in a later hand
b *approviatum* interlined in a later hand
c *et approviatum* interlined

an acre 12d. a year; and this meadow has been mown every year, price of an acre of land and meadow 12d. a year, for which the duke who is the tenant will answer, and the land is to be taken.

1.164 <£36 7s. 4d.>
Item they present that the duke 20 years ago assarted in the same waste another parcel of land between the above parcel of land and the sea containing 51 acres 3 roods and 32¼ perches, which land has yielded crops fourteen times etc., price of an acre 12d. a year, for which the duke will answer and the land is to be taken etc.

1.165 <£3 2s.3d.>
Item they present that for the last 20 years the duke has held a meadow (approved) in severalty, next to the bridge on the western side which is called 'le Chestergrenemedewe',[1] which contains 3 acres and 20 perches, which meadow has been mown 20 times, price of an acre 12d. a year, and the meadow is to be taken etc.

1.166 <51s. 3d.>
Item they present that for the last 20 years the duke has held a meadow (approved) next to the moss extending towards Wallasey which contains 2½ acres and 10 perches of meadow, which meadow has been mown each year, price of an acre 12d. a year, for which the duke will answer and the meadow is to be taken etc.

1.167 <100s. 3d.>
Item they present that the duke holds a parcel of land on the northern side of the meadow mentioned above, which was assarted 20 years ago, and which contains 7 acres 25½ perches which have yielded crops fourteen times etc., price of an acre 12d. a year, for which the duke will answer and the land is to be taken etc.

1.168 <£4 17d.>
Item they present that the duke holds a parcel of land called 'le Holdefeld'[2] and another parcel below Wolleton[3] wood which was assarted 20 years ago which contain 11½ acres 19¾ perches which have yielded crops fourteen times price 6d. an acre a year; and not more because it is poor, for which the duke who is the tenant will answer and it is to be taken as above.

1.169 <£ 210 6s. 0d.>
Item they present that the duke holds in the same place a moss which was assarted (and approved) 40 years ago which contains 105 acres 24 perches, enclosed with a hedge in a separate moss, price 12d. each year, for which the duke will answer and the moss is to be taken as above, because there is harm to the lord's beasts, since

1 Dodgson, *Place Names*, p. 312.
2 Dodgson, *Place Names*, p. 313.
3 Dodgson, *Place Names*, p. 310.

dux respondebit et mossetum capiatur ut supra, eo quod nocumentum feris domini quia multi in foviis eiusdem submersi sunt. De quibus decem acre non sunt fossate set tenentur in separalitate alique falcate et alique non precii acre per annum [...] [...].

1.170 <vij li. iiij s.>
Item presentant quod idem dux tenet ibidem quoddam aliud mossetum a parte orientali cuiusdam vie extendentis per medium mosseti iam xij annis assartatum quod continet xij acras precii per acre per annum xij d. unde idem dux respondebit et mossetum capiatur etc.

1.171 <xij li. xvj s.>
Item presentant quod idem dux tenet quamdam parcellam terre inter le Forde et Budestanoldewode inter tristeram et bundas xxx annis iam elapsis assartatam que continent xij acras et dimidiam et j [rodam][a] et viij perticas terre que xx[es] inbladate sunt etc. precii acre per annum xij d. unde idem dux respondebit et terra capiatur ut supra.

1.172 <viij li. xix s. ij d.>
Item presentant quod idem dux tenet quamdam parcellam terre inter predictas bundas xx annis elapsis assartatam que continet xij acras et dimidiam[b] j rodam viij perticas terre que xiiij[es] inbladate sunt de etc. precii acre per annum xij d. unde idem dux respondebit et terra capiatur ut supra.

1.173 <lvj s.>
Item presentant quod idem dux tenet ibidem iuxta bundas predictas tres domus constructas in vasto extra coopertum precii domorum xx s. unde idem dux respondebit et deleantur et est valor per annum domorum iij s. per xij annos et unde idem dux respondebit et quia quoddam fossatum factum est ibidem contra assisam ideo deleatur[c] et dux pro tali inclusione in misericordia.

1.174 <iiij li. v s. x d.>
Item presentant quod idem dux tenet quamdam placeam[d] terre sub campo qui vocatur Eskeby xx annis elapsis assartatam que continet vj acras xxj perticas et dimidiam que xiiij[es] inbladate sunt de yvernagio et tramesio precii acre per annum xij d. unde idem dux respondebit et terra capiatur in manu domini etc.

1.175 <iij li. ij s. j d.>
Item presentant quod idem dux tenet quamdam alteram parcellam terre apud le Forde

a *rode* MS
b *et dimidiam* repeated and struck through
c *deliatur* MS
d *placeam* interlined

many of them have drowned in the ditches of the same. Ten of these acres are not ditched but are held in severalty, some mown and some not, price [...] an acre a year.

1.170 <£7 4s. 0d.>
Item they present that the duke holds in the same place another moss from the eastern side of a road extending through the middle of the moss which was assarted twelve years ago and which contains twelve acres, price of an acre 12d. a year, for which the duke will answer and the moss is to be taken etc.

1.171 <£12 16s. 0d.>
Item they present that the duke holds a parcel of land between le Forde[1] and Budestanoldewolde[2] between a tryst and the bounds which was assarted 30 years ago and which contains 12½ acres 1 rood and 8 perches of land which have yielded crops 20 times etc., price of an acre 12d. a year, for which the duke will answer and the land is to be taken as above.

1.172 <£8 19s. 2d.>
Item they present that the duke holds a parcel of land between these bounds which was assarted 20 years ago and which contains 12½ acres 1 rood and 8 perches of land which have yielded crops fourteen times etc.; the price of an acre is 12d. an acre a year, for which the duke will answer and the land is to be taken as above.

1.173 <56s. 0d.>
Item they present that the duke holds in the same place next to the aforesaid bounds three buildings erected on the waste outside the covert; price of the buildings 20s. 0d., for which the duke will answer and they are to be destroyed. The value of the buildings is 3s. 0d. a year for twelve years and for which the duke will answer; and because a ditch was made there against the assize it is to be destroyed and the duke is to be in mercy for such an enclosure.

1.174 <£4 5s. 10d.>
Item they present that the duke holds a plot of land below the field called 'Eskeby'[3] which was assarted 20 years ago and which contains 6 acres 21½ perches, which have yielded crops fourteen times sown in winter and summer, price of an acre 12d. a year, for which the duke will answer and the land is to be taken into the hands of the lord etc.

1.175 <£3 2s.1d.>
They present that for the last 20 years the duke has held another parcel of land on the southern side at le Forde,[4] which contains 4 acres 1 rood 30 perches, which have

1 Dodgson, *Place Names*, p. 319.
2 Dodgson, *Place Names*, p. 312.
3 Dodgson, *Place Names*, p. 311.
4 Dodgson, *Place Names*, p. 319.

ex parte australi xx annis elapsis que continet iiij acras j rodam xxx perticas que xiiij^es inbladata fuit etc. precii acre per annum xij d. unde idem dux respondebit etc.

1.176 <xx s.>
Item presentant quod boscus ibidem vastatur de magnis quercubus ad dampnum domini xx s. unde idem dux respondebit et boscus capiatur.

1.177 <xviij s. viij d.>
Item presentant quod quedam domus constructa est ibidem ad nocumentum ferarum. Ideo forisfiat et deleatur[a] precii dimidie marce unde idem dux respondebit pro x annis et est valor dicte domus per annum [...] unde idem dux similiter respondebit.

Et idem dux in *misericordia* pro ij marleriis factis ibidem et preceptum est quod inpleantur etc.

1.178 <Salghale Massi> <xx s. vj d.>
Item presentant quod dux Lancastr' tenet ibidem j acram prati cum iiij perticis prati approviatum de vasto iam xx annis assartatum quod iam xx^es falcatum fuit precii acre per annum xij d. unde idem dux respondebit et pratum predictum capiatur.

[CCCiiij] [...]li. [...]s. iij [d.]

vii

m. 7d

1.179 <Upton> <xj li. viij s.>
Item presentant quod Robertus de Pulle iam xxiiij annis elapsis assartavit in vasto eiusdem ville quoddam pratum continens ix acras et dimidiam prati quod quidem pratum quolibet anno falcatum est precii acre per annum xij d. unde idem Robertus respondebit et pratum predictum capiatur in manu domini.

1.180 <x li. xvj s.>
Item presentant quod Johannes de Warrewyk iam xxiiij annis elapsis assartavit ibidem quoddam pratum continens[b] ix acras quodquidam pratum falcatum fuit quolibet anno precii acre per annum xij d. unde idem Johannes respondebit et pratum predictum capiatur ut supra.

a *deliatur* MS
b *continent'* MS

yielded crops fourteen times sown etc., price of an acre 12d. a year, for which the duke will answer etc.

1.176 <20s. 0d.>
They present that the wood in the same place is wasted of great oaks to the damage to the lord of 20s. 0d., for which the duke will answer and the wood is to be taken.

1.177 <18s. 8d.>
Item they present that a building was erected in the same place to the harm of the beasts. Therefore it is to be forfeit and destroyed, price half a mark for which the duke will answer for ten years; and the value of the building is [...] a year for which the duke will answer likewise; and the duke is to be in *mercy* for two marl pits made there, and it is ordered that they are to be filled in etc.

1.178 <Saughall Massie> <20s. 6d.>
Item they present that the duke of Lancaster holds there 1 acre of meadow with 4 perches of meadow which were approved from the waste and assarted 20 years ago which have now been mown 20 times, price of an acre 12d. a year, for which the duke will answer and the meadow is to be taken.

[£ 304 [...]s. 3 [d.]]

m. 7d

1.179 <Upton> <£11 8s. 0d.>
Item they present that Robert de Pulle[1] 24 years ago assarted in the waste of the same township a meadow containing 9½ acres of meadow, which meadow was mown each year, price of an acre 12d. a year, for which Robert will answer, and the meadow is to be taken into the hands of the lord.

1.180 <£10 16s. 0d.>
Item they present that John de Warrewyk[2] 24 years ago assarted there a meadow containing nine acres which was mown each year, price of an acre 12d. a year, for which John will answer, and the meadow is to be taken as above.

1 See **1.122** note.
2 See **1.180** note.

1.181 <xv li. iiij s. ix d.>
Item presentant quod idem Johannes iam xxiiij annis elapsis assartavit ibidem in vasto unam parcellam terre continentem xix acras xxxvij perticas terre que abuttat super dictum pratum que xvj^{es} inbladate sunt etc. precii acre per annum xij d. unde idem Johannes qui tenens est respondebit et terra capiatur ut supra.

1.182 <xxxij s. iiij d.>
Item presentant quod idem Johannes iam xxiiij annis elapsis assartavit ibidem unam aliam parcellam terre que vocatur le Regges que continet ij acras iiij perticas que xvj^{es} inbladate sunt etc. precii acre per annum xij d. unde idem Johannes respondebit et terra capiatur ut supra.

1.183 <xlvij s. iiij d. ob.>
Item presentant quod decanus Sancti Johannis Cestr' tenet ibidem in vasto unam parcellam terre buttentem super ecclesiam que continet ij acras iij rodas et xxxiiij perticas terre que xxiiij annis iam elapsis assartata fuit que xvj^{es} inbladata fuit[a] precii acre per annum xij d. et terra capiatur.

1.184 <Morton> <xxxvj s. vj d.>
Item presentant quod Johannes Launcelyn iam xvj annis elapsis assartavit ibidem in vasto iij acras j rodam et xj perticas terre que xj^{es} inbladate sunt etc. precii acre per annum xij d. unde idem Johannes respondebit et terra capiatur ut supra.

1.185 <xix s. j d.>
Item presentant quod prior de Byrkheved qui obiit iam xvj annis elapsis assartavit ibidem in vasto j acram xxxj perticas et dimidiam prati quod quolibet anno falcatum est precii acre per annum xij d. unde prior qui nunc respondebit et dictum pratum capiatur.

1.186 <xxxix s. ix d.>
Item presentant quod Willelmus filius Willelmi Trussell de *Blaken* chivaler iam xxx annis[b] elapsis assartavit ibidem in vasto j acram iij rodas et xxxvij perticas herbagii iuxta le Stonibruge que xx^{es} inbladate sunt precii acre xij d.[c] etc. unde idem Willelmus respondebit et terra capiatur ut supra.

1.187 <xxxiij s. vj d.>
Item presentant quod idem Willelmus tenet ibidem apud le Pullehoux versus pontem quoddam mesuagium cum gardino adiacenti j rode et xv perticis terre[d] que iam xx annis elapsis assartatum et edificatum fuit precii mesuagii dimidie marce unde idem

a *que xvj^{es} inbladata fuit* interlined
b *acris* struck through and *annis* interlined
c *precii acre xij s.* interlined
d *terre* interlined

1.181 <£15 4s. 9d.>
Item they present that John 24 years ago assarted there in the waste a parcel of land containing 19 acres 37 perches of land which abuts on the meadow, which have yielded crops sixteen times etc., price of an acre 12d. a year, for which John who is the tenant will answer and the land is to be taken as above.

1.182 <32s. 4d.>
Item they present that John 24 years ago assarted there another parcel of land which is called 'le Regges'[1] which contains 2 acres 4 perches which have yielded crops sixteen times etc., price of an acre 12d. a year, for which John will answer and the land is to be taken as above.

1.183 <47s. 4½d.>
Item they present that the dean of St John's of Chester holds in the waste there a parcel of land abutting on the church containing 2 acres 3 roods and 34 perches of land, which was assarted 24 years ago and yielded crops sixteen times, price of an acre 12d. a year, and the land is to be taken.

1.184 <Moreton> <36s. 6d.>
Item they present that John Launcelyn[2] sixteen years ago assarted there in the waste 3 acres 1 rood and 11 perches of land which yielded crops eleven times etc., price of an acre 12d. a year, for which John will answer and the land is to be taken as above.

1.185 <19s. 1d.>
Item they present that a prior of Birkenhead[3] who has died, sixteen years ago assarted there in the waste 1 acre 31½ perches of meadow which was mown each year, price of an acre 12d. a year, for which the present prior will answer and the meadow is to be taken.

1.186 <39s. 9d.>
Item they present that William son of William Trussell[4] of *Blacon*, knight, 30 years ago assarted there in the waste next to le Stonibruge 1 acre 3 roods and 37 perches of pasture, which have yielded crops 20 times, price of an acre 12d. etc., for which William will answer and the land is to be taken as above.

1.187 <33s 6d.>
Item they present that William holds there at le Pullehoux towards the bridge, a messuage with an adjacent garden, 1 rood and 15 perches of land which 20 years ago was assarted and the messuage was built, price of the messuage half a mark, for

1 Dodgson, *Place Names*, p. 307.
2 See **1.37** note.
3 See **1.150** note,
4 1347 m. 5 William Trussel took 12 oaks in Blacon.

Willelmus respondebit et deleatur[a] et est valor illius per annum xij d. unde idem similiter respondebit. Et includitur.

1.188 <xxxij s. viij d.>
Item presentant quod idem Willelmus tenet ibidem versus Blaken in vasto quoddam mesuagium et j croftum continentem j rodam et viij perticas terre et dimidiam iam xx annis elapsis edificatum et assartatum precii mesuagii dimidie marce, unde idem Willelmus respondebit et forisfiat et deleatur[b] quia est ad nocumentum ferarum domini et est valor illius quolibet anno xij d. unde idem respondebit similiter et includitur contra assisam foreste.

1.189 <x li. xviij s. v d.>
Item presentant quod idem Willelmus Trussell tenet ibidem situm manerii de Blaken quod continet iij rodas dimidiam xiij perticas quod xxx annis elapsis constructum fuit in vasto quod est ad nocumentum ferarum precii domorum manerii C s. unde idem Willelmus respondebit et forisfiat et deleatur[c] et est valor illius per annum iij s.unde idem Willelmus similiter respondebit. Et includitur et valet per annum acre xij d. unde idem Willelmus respondebit.

1.190
Item presentant quod idem Willelmus tenet ibidem unum boscum continentem viij acras et dimidiam xxviij perticas terre quiquidam boscus amputatur in superioribus ramis ad dampnum domini *lx s.* unde idem Willelmus respondebit et boscus capiatur etc. Et includitur.

1.191 <xxvij li. xix s. v d.>
Item presentant quod idem Willelmus iam xxx annis elapsis assartavit ibidem in vasto in uno campo iuxta manerium ex parte occidentali xxvij acras iij rodas xxxv perticas et dimidiam j quarteriam terre que xx[es] inbladate sunt etc. precii acre per annum xij d. unde idem Willelmus respondebit et terra capiatur etc.

1.192 <xlj li. xviij s. vj d.>
Item presentant quod idem Willelmus iam xx annis elapsis assartavit ibidem in vasto in eodem campo extendente versus boscum de Saghale lix acras iij rodas xxiij perticas et dimidiam quarteriam que xiiij[es] inbladate sunt de yvernagio et tramesio precii acre per annum xij d. unde idem Willelmus respondebit et terra capiatur etc.

1.193 <xxiiij li. xiij s. xj d.>
Item presentant quod idem Willelmus iam xxx annis elapsis assartavit ibidem in vasto iuxta molendinum ventriticum xxiiij acras et dimidiam xxxij perticas et dimidiam

a *deliatur* MS
b *deliatur* MS
c *deliatur* MS

which William will answer and it is to be destroyed; and its value is 12d. a year for which he will answer likewise. And it is enclosed.

1.188 <32s. 8d.>
Item they present that William holds there in the same waste towards Blacon a messuage and 1 croft containing 1 rood and 8½ perches of land built and assarted 20 years ago, price of the messuage half a mark for which William will answer; and it is to be forfeited and destroyed because it is to the harm of the lord's beasts; and its value is 12d. for each year, for which he will answer likewise. And it is enclosed against the assize of the forest.

1.189 <£10 18s. 5d.>
Item they present that the same William Trussell holds there the site of the manor-house of Blacon which contains 3½ roods 13 perches which 30 years ago was built in the waste, which is to the harm of the beasts; price of the buildings of the manor 100s. 0d. for which William will answer; and it is to be forfeited and destroyed; and its value is 3s. 0d. a year for which William will answer similarly; and it is enclosed; and it is worth 12d. an acre a year, for which William will answer.

1.190
Item they present that William holds there a wood containing 8½ acres 28 perches of land. This wood is pruned of its higher branches to the damage of the lord of *60s.*, for which William will answer and the wood is to be forfeited etc. And it is enclosed.

1.191 <£27 19s. 5d.>
Item they present that William 30 years ago assarted there in the waste in a field next to the manor-house on the west 27 acres 3 roods 35¾ perches of land, which yielded crops 20 times etc., price of an acre 12d. a year, for which William will answer and the land is to be taken etc.

1.192 <£41 18s. 6d.>
Item they present that William 20 years ago assarted there in the waste in the same field extending towards Saughall wood 59 acres 3 roods 23¾ perches which have yielded crops fourteen times sown in winter and in summer, price of an acre 12d. a year, for which William will answer and the land is to be taken etc.

1.193 <£24 13s. 11d.>
Item they present that the same William 30 years ago assarted there in the waste next to the windmill 24½ acres 32½ perches of land which have yielded crops 20 times

terre[a] que xx[es] inbladate sunt etc. precii acre per annum xij d. unde idem Willelmus respondebit et terra capiatur etc. Et idem Willelmus in misericordia pro xij marleris ibidem factis unde preceptum est quod inpleantur ad custagia ipsius.

1.194 <viij li. xiij s. iiij d.>
Item presentant quod idem Willelmus iam xx annis elapsis construxit ibidem in vasto quoddam molendinum ventriticum precii [xl s.] unde idem Willelmus respondebit et est valor dicti molendini per annum dimidie marce unde idem respondebit etc.

1.195 <Wodebonk> <xiiij s.>
Item presentant quod Henricus de Hoton iam xx annis elapsis assartavit ibidem in vasto unam acram terre, que xiiij[es] inbladata fuit de yvernagio etc. precii acre per annum xij d. unde idem Henricus respondebit et terra capiatur.

1.196 <[…] li. […] s. […] d.>
Item presentant quod Nicholaus filius Hamonis le Massi et Thomas de [Hok]enhull iam xxx annis elapsis assartaverunt quamdam placeam terre in *Chyrcheschotewyk* continentem ix acras terre [...] [...] et in altero loco vocato le Oldefeld super le Overdepedale continenti v acras terre[b] que xx[es] inbladate sunt precii acre per annum vj d. unde idem Nicholaus et Thomas respondebunt et terra capiatur et dicti Nicholaus et Thomas in misericordia pro ij marleriis ibidem factis. Preceptum est [quod] […] etc.

1.197 <x li. vj s.>
Item presentant quod idem Nicholaus et Thomas iam xx annis elapsis assartaverunt unam quamdam placeam terre continentem ix acras j rodam et xiij perticas terre et in altero loco in vasto de Oldefeld super le Overdepedale assartaverunt v acras que xiiij[es] inbladate sunt etc. precii acre per annum xij d. unde Nicholaus et Thomas respondebunt et terra capiatur. Et idem Nicholaus et Thomas in misericordia pro ij marleris factis ibidem.

Ciiij[xx] xiij li. xx d.

m. 8

1.198 <Greves> <lxxij s. vj d.>
Item presentant quod Johannes de Leghton iam xxx annis elapsis assartavit in vasto iij acras et dimidiam xx perticas terre apud le greve iuxta le bonk que xx[es] inbladate sunt etc. precii acre xij d. unde idem Johannes respondebit et terra capiatur etc.

a *terre* interlined
b *terre* interlined

etc., price of an acre 12d. a year for which William will answer and the land is to be taken etc. William is to be in mercy for twelve marl pits made there wherefore it is ordered that they are to be filled in at his own expense.

1.194 <£8 13s. 4d.>
Item they present that William 20 years ago built in the waste there a windmill, price 40s. 0d., for which William will answer; and the value of the mill is half a mark a year, for which he will answer etc.

1.195 <Woodbank> <14s. 0d.>
Item they present that Henry de Hoton[1] 20 years ago asserted there in the waste one acre of land which has yielded crops fourteen times sown in winter etc. price of an acre 12d. a year, for which Henry will answer and the land is to be taken.

1.196 <£[…] […]s. […]d.>
Item they present that Nicholas son of Hamo le Massy[2] and Thomas de Hokenhull[3] 30 years ago assarted a plot of land in *Church Shotwick* containing nine acres of land [...] [...] and in another place called le Oldefeld above le Overderdale containing five acres of land which have yielded crops 20 times price 6d. an acre a year, for which Nicholas and Thomas will answer and the land is to be taken. And Nicholas and Thomas are in mercy for two marl pits made in the same place. It is ordered that […] etc.

1.197 <£10 6s. 0d.>
Item they present that the same Nicholas and Thomas 20 years ago assarted a plot of land containing 9 acres 1 rood and 13 perches of land and in another place in Oldfeld waste above le Overderdale they assarted five acres which have yielded crops fourteen times etc. price of an acre 12d. a year, for which Nicholas and Thomas will answer and the land is to be taken. And Nicholas and Thomas are in mercy for two marl pits made there.

£193 20d.

m. 8

1.198 <Greves> <72s. 6d.>
Item they present that John de Leghton[4] 30 years ago assarted in the waste 3½ acres 20 perches of land at le Greve next to le bonk which have yielded crops 20 times etc., price of an acre 12d. for which John will answer and the land is to be taken etc.

1 See **1.55** note.
2 See **1.464** note.
3 1347 m. 1d Thomas de Hokenhull took 8 oaks 6 *robora*; fine 4d; pledge John de […].
m. 4d Richard de Hokenhull 14 oaks; 40d.; John de Ruyton.
4 See **1.125** note.

1.199 <iiij li. iiij s.>
Item presentant quod idem Johannes iam xx annis elapsis assartavit ibidem in vasto vj acras terre que xiiij[es] inbladate precii acre per annum xij d. unde etc. et terra capiatur ut supra;

et quia ij marleria facta ibidem ideo predictus in *misericordia* et preceptum est quod inpleantur.

1.200 <xij li.>
Item presentant quod ibidem iam xxx annis elapsis[a] constructum est quoddam molendinum ventriticum quod est ad nocumentum ferarum domini precii xl s. unde idem [predictus][b] Johannes respondebit et est valor eiusdem molendini per annum dimidie marce unde idem Johannes similiter respondebit.

1.201 <Podynton> <xlvij s. v d.>
Item presentant quod Hamo le Mascy iam xvj annis elapsis assartavit ibidem in vasto iuxta brueram iiij acras j rodam x perticas terre que xj[es] inbladate sunt de yvernagio et tramesio precii acre per annum xij d. unde idem Hamo que tenens est respondebit et terra capiatur ut supra.

1.202 <vj li. iij s. x d.>
Item presentant quod idem Hamo et Ricardus de Podynton tenent ibidem in vasto in campo qui vocatur le Westanesfeld viij acras iij rodas et xvj perticas terre iam xx annis elapsis assartatas que xiiij[es] inbladate sunt etc. precii acre per annum xij d. unde idem Hamo et Ricardus respondebunt et terra capiatur ut supra.

1.203 <xij li. xiij s.>
Item presentant quod idem Hamo et parcenarii sui tenent ibidem in campo versus molendinum xij acras et dimidiam et dimidiam rodam vj perticas et j quarterium terre iam xxx annis elapsis assartatas que xx[es] inbladate sunt etc. precii acre per annum xij d. unde idem Hamo et parcenarii sui respondebunt.

1.204 <viij li. xvij s. iij d.>
Item presentant quod idem Hamo et parcenarii sui tenent ibidem in campo versus molendinum xij acras et dimidiam et dimidiam rodam vj perticas j quarterium terre iam xx annis elapsis assartatas que xiiij[es] inbladate sunt etc. precii acre per annum xij d. unde idem Hamo et predicti parcenarii respondebunt et terra capiatur ut supra.[c]

a *iam xxx annis elapsis* interlined
b *predictum* MS
c There is nothing in these two almost identical pleas (**1.203** or **1.204**) to indicate which is the correct one, except that **1.204,** which refers to 20 years (30 years in **1.203**), contains the verdict and is most likely to be the correct version.

1.199 <£4 4s. 0d.>
Item they present that John 20 years ago assarted in the waste there six acres of land, which yielded crops 14 times, price of an acre 12d. a year, for which etc. and the land is to be taken as above.

And because two marl pits are made in the same place, therefore he is to be in *mercy* and it is ordered that they are to be filled in.

1.200 <£12>
Item they present that 30 years ago a windmill was built in the same place to the harm of the lord's beasts, price 40s 0d.. for which John will answer; and the value of the mill is half a mark a year, for which John will answer likewise.

1.201 <Puddington> <47s. 5d.>
Item they present that Hamo de Mascy[1] sixteen years ago assarted in the waste next to the heath 4 acres 1 rood 10 perches of land, which have yielded crops eleven times sown in winter and summer, price of an acre 12d. a year, for which Hamo, who is the tenant, will answer and the land is to be taken as above.

1.202 <£6 3s. 10d.>
Item they present that Hamo and Richard de Podynton[2] hold in the waste there in a field which is called 'le Westanesfeld'[3] 8 acres 3 roods 16 perches of land assarted 20 years ago, which have yielded crops fourteen times etc., price of an acre 12d. a year, for which Hamo and Richard will answer and the land is to be taken as above.

1.203 <£12 13s. 0d.>
Item they present that Hamo and his parceners hold in the same place in a field towards the mill 12½ acres and half a rood 6¼ perches of land assarted 30 years ago, which have yielded crops 20 times etc., price 12d. an acre, for which Hamo and his parceners will answer.

1.204 <£8 17s. 3d.>
Item they present that Hamo and his parceners hold in the same place in a field towards the mill 12½ acres and half a rood 6¼ perches of land assarted 20 years ago, which have yielded crops fourteen times etc., price of an acre 12d. a year, for which Hamo and the parceners will answer and the land is to be taken as above.

1 See **1.196** note.
2 1347 m. 4 Gilbert de Puddington took 7 oaks; fine 40d.; pledge Roger de Coghull.
3 Dodgson, *Place Names*, p. 216.

1.205 <ij s.>
Item presentant quod idem Hamo et parcenarii sui tenent ibidem quandam aliam parcellam terre continentem xxiiij perticas que iam xx annis elapsis assartatas que xiiij^{es} inbladate sunt etc. precii ut supra unde idem Hamo et parcenarii respondebunt et terra capiatur ut supra.

1.206 <xlv s. ix d.>
Item presentant quod idem Hamo[a] tenet ibidem inter dictum campum et brueram v acras et dimidiam xxxvj perticas terre iam xijd. annis elapsis assartatas que viij^{es} inbladate sunt etc. precii acre xij d. per annum unde idem Hamo respondebit et terra capiatur.

Et idem Hamo et parcenarii sui in *misericordia* pro iiij marleriis ibidem factis et preceptum est quod inpleantur ad custagia ipsorum etc.

1.207 <Burton> <Cvij s.>
Item presentant quod episcopus Cestr' tenet ibidem iuxta mare unam parcellam terre continentem j acram j rodam x perticas terre que xxx annis elapsis assartate fuerunt et aliam parcellam continentem iiij acras vj perticas terre eodem tempore assartatas que xx^{es} inbladate sunt etc. precii acre per annum xij d. unde idem episcopus respondebit et terra capiatur etc.

1.208 <Parva Neston> <Cj s. v d. ob.>
Item presentant quod Johannes Blound tenet ibidem quandam parcellam terre inter boscum suum et mare continentem iiij acras et dimidiam et xvj perticas terre et aliam parcellam terre in le Bruche continentem iiij acras terre et dimidiam xix perticas et dimidiam j quarteriam que iam xvj annis elapsis assartate fuerunt que xj^{es} inbladate sunt etc. precii acre per annum xij d. unde idem Johannes respondebit et terra capiatur ut supra;

et idem Johannes pro j marlerio ibidem facto in *misericordia* et preceptum est quod inpleatur[b] ad custagia ipsius etc.

1.209 <Oxton> <x li. x s.>
Item presentant quod Johannes Dounvylle iam xxx annis elapsis assartavit ibidem in vasto x acras j rodam xxxix perticas et dimidiam j quarteriam terre in loco qui vocatur Lewynesfeld que xx^{es} inbladate sunt etc. precii acre xij d. per annum unde idem Johannes respondebit et terra capiatur.

a *et parcenarii sui* struck through
b *in* struck through

1.205 <2s. 0d.>
Item they present that Hamo and his parceners hold in the same place another parcel of land containing 24 perches assarted 20 years ago, which have yielded crops fourteen times etc., price as above, for which Hamo and the parceners will answer and the land is to be taken as above.

1.206 <45s. 9d>
Item they present that Hamo holds in the same place between the said field and the heath, 5½ acres 36 perches of land assarted twelve years ago, which have yielded crops eight times etc., price of an acre 12d. a year, for which Hamo will answer and the land is to be taken.

And Hamo and the parceners are to be in *mercy* for four marl pits made there and it is ordered that they are to be filled in at their own expense.

1.207 <Burton> <107s. 0d>
Item they present that the bishop of Chester holds there a parcel of land next to the sea containing 1 acre one rood 10 perches of land which had been assarted 30 years ago; and he assarted at the same time another parcel containing 4 acres 6 perches of land, which have yielded crops 20 times etc., price of an acre 12d. a year, for which the bishop will answer and the land is to be taken etc.

1.208 <Little Neston> <101s. 5½d>
Item they present that John Blound[1] holds there a parcel of land between his wood and the sea, containing 4½ acres and 16 perches of land; and he holds another parcel of land in le Bruche containing 4½ acres 19¾ perches which had been assarted sixteen years ago, which have yielded crops eleven times etc., price of an acre 12d. a year; for which John will answer and the land is to be taken as above.

And John is to be in *mercy* for a marl-pit made there and it is ordered that it is to be filled in at his own expense etc.

1.209 <Oxton> <£10 10s. 0d.>
Item they present that John Donnvyll[2] 30 years ago assarted in the waste there 10 acres 1 rood 39¾ perches of land in a place which is called 'Lewynesfeld',[3] which have yielded crops 20 times etc., price of an acre 12d. a year, for which John will answer and the land is to be taken.

1 1347 m. 4 Thomas Blound took 2 oaks; fine 2s. 0d.; pledge Richard de Pulton.
m. 5 John Blound 14 oaks in Little Neston wood.

2 See **1.107** note.

3 Dodgson, *Place Names*, pp. 260 and 271.

1.210 <xxviij s. x d,>
Item presentant quod idem Johannes iam xvj annis elapsis assartavit ij acras et dimidiam xix perticas terre ibidem in loco vocato le Haygreve que xj[es] que inbladate sunt etc. precii acre per annum xij d. unde idem Johannes respondebit et terra capiatur ut supra.

1.211 <Cvj s. iij d.>
Item presentant quod idem Johannes iam xv annis elapsis assartavit ibidem in vasto v acras et dimidiam xx perticas terre in loco subtus Arnowe et alias v acras in eadem villa eodem tempore assartavit que x[es] inbladate sunt etc. precii acre per annum xij d. unde idem Johannes respondebit et terra capiatur etc. Et idem Johannes in misericordia pro ij marleriis ibidem factis et preceptum est quod inpleantur etc.

1.212 <vij li>
Item presentant quod idem Johannes iam xv annis elapsis construxit ibidem in vasto quoddam molendinum ventriticum quod est ad nocumentum ferarum domini precii xl s. unde idem Johannes respondebit et est valor dicti molendini per annum a tempore constructionis dimidie marce.

1.213 <viij li. iiij s. ix d.>
Item presentant quod Willelmus de *Tranemul* et parcenarii sui tenent ibidem iuxta le Rake[a] ex parte australi[b] parcellam terre vocatam le Hethfeld continentem xiiij acras ij rodas xxxvij perticas terre [que][c] iam xvj annis elapsis assartate xj[es] inbladate precii acre terre per annum xij d. unde idem Willelmus et parcenarii respondebunt et terra capiatur.

1.214 <vij li. viij s. j d.>
Item presentant quod idem parcenarii tenent ibidem ex altera parte del Rake unam parcellam terre vocatam le Newefeld continentem x acras et dimidiam xiij perticas j quarteriam iam xx annis elapsis assartatas que xiiij[es] inbladate sunt precii acre per annum xij d. unde ut supra.

1.215 <lxv s. ij d.>
Item presentant quod Willelmus Walays et Willelmus de Tranemull iam xxx annis elapsis assartaverunt in quadam placea vocata le Wodbuttes[d] iij acras j rodam j

a *iuxta le Rake* interlined
b *unam per unam* struck through
c *que* omitted in MS
d superfluous *que continet* in MS

1.210 <28s. 10d.>
Item they present that John sixteen years ago assarted 2½ acres 19 perches of land there in a place called 'le Haygreve', which have yielded crops eleven times etc., price of an acre 12d. a year, for which John will answer and the land is to be taken as above

1.211 <106s. 3d.>
Item they present that John fifteen years ago assarted in the waste there 5½ acres 20 perches in a place below Arnowe[1] and he assarted another five acres in the same township at the same time, which have yielded crops ten times etc., price of an acre 12d. a year, for which John will answer and the land is to be taken etc. And John is to be in mercy for two marl pits made there and it is ordered that they are to be filled in etc.

1.212 <£7>
Item they present that John fifteen years ago built in the waste there a windmill which is to the harm of the lord's beasts, price 40s. 0d., for which John will answer; and the value of the mill every year from the time it was built is half a mark.

1.213 <Tranmere> <£8 4s. 9d.>
Item they present that William de Tranemul[2] and his parceners hold in the same place next to le Rake[3] on the southern side, a parcel of land called 'le Hethfield'[4] containing 14 acres 3 roods 37 perches of land assarted 16 years ago, which have yielded crops eleven times, price of an acre 12d. a year, for which William and the parceners will answer and the land is to be taken.

1.214 <£7 8s. 1d.>
Item they present that the same parceners hold in the same place from from the other side of le Rake one parcel of land called 'le Newfeld'[5] containing 10½ acres 13¼ perches assarted 20 years ago, which have yielded crops fourteen times, price of an acre 12d. a year, for which as above.

1.215 <65s. 2d.>
Item they present that William Walays[6] and William de Tranemull 30 years ago assarted in a plot of land called 'le Wodbuttes'[7] which contains 3 acres 1 rood 1¾

1 Dodgson, *Place Names*, p. 270.
2 See **1.46** note.
3 Dodgson, *Place Names*, pp. 260 and 261.
4 Dodgson, *Place Names*, p. 260.
5 Dodgson, *Place Names*, p. 261.
6 See **1.148** note.
7 Dodgson, *Place Names*, p. 261.

perticam et dimidiam et j quarteriam que xx[es] inbladate sunt precii acre per annum xij d. unde ut supra.

1.216 <cxv s. vj d.>
Item presentant quod idem Willelmus et Willelmus et Hamo de Mascy iam xiij annis elapsis assartaverunt ibidem unam placeam terre vocatam Bokenhull et Netherridyng[a] continentem v acras iij rodas iiij perticas et dimidiam que xx[es] inbladate sunt etc. precii acre per annum xij d. unde predicti respondebunt et terra capiatur.

1.217 <xlix s. x d.>
Item presentant quod Willelmus de Tranemull et Robertus filius eiusdem xx annis elapsis assartaverunt ibidem in vasto iij acras et dimidiam ix perticas j quarteriam in loco vocato le Overrydynges que xiiij[es] inbladate sunt etc. precii acre per annum xij d. unde idem predicti respondebunt et terra capiatur etc. Et parcenarii predicti in misericordia pro iij marleriis factis [et preceptum] est quod inpleantur ut supra.

1.218
Item presentant quod boscus ibidem vastatur ad dampnum [precii] *xl s.* unde parcenarii respondebunt et capiatur in manu domini.

m. 8d

1.219 <Overbebynton> <vij li. xj s. v d.>
Item presentant quod Robertus de Bebynton iam xx annis elapsis assartavit ibidem in vasto iuxta Risewalleheth[b] x acras iij rodas xj perticas et j quarteriam terre que xiij[es] inbladate etc. precii acre per annum xij d. unde heredes predicti Roberti qui nunc sunt tenentes respondebunt et terra capiatur in manu domini.

1.220 <xv li. xvj s.>
Item presentant quod idem Robertus iam xx annis elapsis assartavit ibidem in vasto quamdam placeam terre vocatam le Morefeld continentem xxij acras dimidiam et xiij perticas terre que xiiij[es] inbladate sunt etc. precii acre per annum xij d. unde idem heredes respondebunt et terra capiatur ut supra.

a *et Netherrridyng* interlined
b *iuxta Risewallehyth* interlined

perches which have yielded crops 20 times, price of an acre 12d. a year, for which as above.

1.216 <115s. 6d.>
Item they present that William and William and Hamo de Mascy[1] thirteen years ago assarted there a plot of land called 'Bokenhull'[2] and 'Netherridyng'[3] containing 5 acres 3 roods 4½ perches, which have yielded crops 20 times etc., price of an acre 12d. a year, for which they will answer and the land is to be taken.

1.217 <49s. 10d.>
Item they present that William de Tranemull and Robert, his son, 20 years ago assarted in the waste there 3½ acres 9¼ perches in a place called 'le Overrydynges',[4] which have yielded crops fourteen times etc. price of an acre 12d. a year for which they will answer and the land is to be taken as above.

And the parceners are to be in mercy for three marl pits made and it is ordered that they be filled in as above.

1.218
Item they present that a wood in the same place is wasted to the loss of *40s. 0d.*, for which the parceners will answer and it is to be taken into the hands of the lord.

m. 8d

1.219 <Higher Bebington> <£7 11s. 5d.>
Item they present that Robert de Bebynton[5] 20 years ago assarted 10 acres 3 roods and 11¼ perches of land in the waste there next to Rosewalleheth[6] which have yielded crops fourteen times etc., price of an acre 12d. a year, for which the heirs of Robert, the present tenants, will answer and the land is to be taken into the hands of the lord.

1.220 <£15 16s. 0d.>
Item they present that Robert 20 years ago assarted in the waste there a plot of land called 'le Morefeld'[7] containing 22½ acres and 13 perches of land which have yielded crops fourteen times etc., price of an acre 12d. a year, for which the heirs will answer and the land is to be taken as above.

1 See **1.201** note.
2 Dodgson, *Place Names*, p. 261.
3 Dodgson, *Place Names*, p. 261.
4 Dodgson, *Place Names*, p. 261.
5 See **1.46** note.
6 Dodgson, *Place Names*, p. 248.
7 Dodgson, *Place Names*, p. 247.

Et idem heredes in *misericordia* pro iiij marleriis factis ibidem et preceptum est quod inpleantur etc.

1.221 <Netherbebynton> <Cxij s. ix d.>
Item presentant quod parcenarii et liberi tenentes ville predicte iam xx annis elapsis assartaverunt ibidem in vasto unam parcellam terre vocatam les Acres iuxta le Rake ex parte boriali que continet viij acras viij perticas et dimidiam j quateriam et dimidiam terre que xiiij^{es} inbladate sunt etc. precii acre per annum xij d. unde idem parcenarii respondebunt et terra capiatur ut supra.

1.222 <iiij li. viij s. vj d.>
Item presentant quod idem parcenarii iam xvj annis elapsis assartaverunt ibidem in vasto in loco predicto viij acras viij perticas et dimidiam j quarteriam et dimidiam que xj^{es} inbladate sunt etc. precii acre per annum xij d. unde idem parcenarii qui nunc sunt tenentes respondebunt et terra capiatur.

1.223 <xj li. xix s. xj d.>
Item presentant quod idem parcenarii iam xx annis elapsis assartaverunt ibidem in vasto unam parcellam terre iuxta le Rake extendentem versus ecclesiam continentem xvij acras xxij perticas j quarteriam terre que xiiij^{es} inbladate sunt etc. precii acre per annum xij d. unde idem parcenarii qui nunc sunt tenentes respondebunt et terra capiatur ut supra.

Et idem parcenarii pro ij marleriis ibidem factis in *misericordia* et preceptum est etc.

1.224 <xvj s. ix d.>
Item presentant quod Ricardus filius Roberti Launcelyn de Bebynton inferior iam xxij annis elapsis assartaverunt ibidem in vasto quamdam parcellam terre vocatam Oselclyth continentem j acram xx perticas que xv^{es} inbladate sunt etc. precii acre per annum xij d. unde idem Ricardus qui tenens est respondebit et terra capiatur ut supra.

1.225
Item presentant quod vastum bosci factum est ibidem ad dampnum domini *xl s.* unde parcenarii bossi respondebunt et boscus capiatur etc.

1.226 <Pulton> <xxiij s. vij d.>
Item presentant quod Ranulphus le Bryn tenet ibidem de vasto unam parcellam terre vocatam Thurngrevefeld continentem j acram et dimidiam et xxx perticas terre que

And the heirs are to be in *mercy* for four marl pits made there and it is ordered that they are to be filled in etc.

1.221 <Lower Bebington> <112s. 9d>
Item they present that the parceners and the free tenants of the township 20 years ago assarted in the waste there in the said place a parcel of land called 'les Acres'[1] next to le Rake on the northern side which contains 8 acres 8¾ perches of land which have yielded crops fourteen times etc., price of an acre 12d. a year, for which the parceners will answer and the land is to be taken as above.

1.222 <£4 8s. 6d.>
Item they present that the parceners sixteen years ago assarted there in the waste in the said place 8 acres 8¾ perches which have yielded crops eleven times etc., price of an acre 12d. a year, for which the parceners, the present tenants, will answer and the land is to be taken.

1.223 <£11 19s. 11d.>
Item they present that the parceners 20 years ago assarted in the waste there a parcel of land next to le Rake, extending towards the church containing 17 acres 22¼ perches of land, which have yielded crops fourteen times etc., price of an acre 12d. a year, for which the parceners, the present tenants, will answer and the land is to be taken as above.

And the parceners are to be in *mercy* for two marl pits made there and it is ordered etc.

1.224 <16s. 9d>
Item they present that Richard, son of Robert Launcelyn[2] of Lower Bebington 22 years ago assarted in the waste there a parcel of land called 'Oselclyth' containing 1 acre 20 perches which have yielded crops fifteen times etc., price of an acre 12d. a year, for which Richard, the tenant, will answer and the land is to be taken as above.

1.225
Item they present that a waste was made in the wood there at a loss of *40s. 0d.* to the lord, for which the parceners of the wood will answer and the wood is to be taken etc.

1.226 <Poulton> <23s. 7d.>
Item they present that Ranulf le Bryn[3] holds a parcel of land called 'Thurngrevefeld'[4] in the waste there, containing 1½ acres and 30 perches of land which was assarted 20

1 Dodgson, *Place Names*, p. 249.
2 See **1.184** note.
3 See **1.143** note.
4 Dodgson, *Place Names*, p. 253.

iam xx annis elapsis assartate fuit et xiiij^{es} inbladate precii acre per annum xij d. unde idem Ranulphus respondebit et terra capiatur ut supra.

1.227 <xxx s. viij d.>
Item presentant quod idem Ranulphus tenet aliam parcellam ibidem de vasto iuxta le Chyrcheway continentem ij acras xxxj perticas et dimidiam j quarteriam terre iam xx annis assartatam elapsis et xiiij^{es} inbladate fuerunt precii acre per annum xij d. unde idem Ranulphus respondebit et terra capiatur ut supra.

1.228 <iiij li. vj s. viij d.>
Item presentant quod iiij mesuagia constructa sunt ibidem ad nocumentum ferarum precii dimidie marce unde predictus Ranulphus respondebit et forisfiant et deleantur[a] et est valor illorum per annum iiij s. quolibet anno a tempore constructionis predictorum cotagiorum videlicet xx annis elapsis.

1.229 <xxiij s. iiij d.>
Item presentant quod idem Ranulphus et Ricardus de Pulton tenent ibidem unum cotagium constructum in vasto ad nocumentum ferarum precii xl d. unde predicti Ranulphus et Ricardus respondebunt et forisfiat et deleatur[b] et est valor illius per annum a tempore constructionis quolibet anno xij d. unde predicti similiter respondebunt quod constructum fuit xx annis iam elapsis.

1.230 <lxxvij s.>
Item presentant quod idem Ranulphus et Ricardus iam xx annis elapsis assartaverunt ibidem in vasto in le Crokede Feld v acras et dimidiam terre que xiiij^{es} inbladate sunt etc. precii acre per annum xij d. unde idem Ricardus et Ranulphus respondebunt et terra capiatur ut supra.

1.231 <ix li. xj s. viij d.>
Item presentant quod idem Ranulphus le Bryn et heredes Petri de Thornton tenent ibidem quamdam parcellam terre del Spitel versus Pulton que continet xiij acras et dimidiam xxx perticas et dimidiam iam xx annis elapsis assartatas ibidem et xiiij^{es} inbladate fuerunt etc. precii acre per annum xij d. unde idem Ranulphus et heredes predicti Petri respondebunt et terra capiatur ut supra.

1.232 <xvj s. vj d.>
Item presentant quod idem Ranulphus et heredes predicti Petri tenent[c] ibidem[d] unam parcellam quod vocatur le Hertesflore in tristera continentem j acram et dimidiam terre[e] iam xvj annis elapsis assartatam et xj^{es} inbladatam precii acre xij d. unde etc.

a *deliantur* MS
b *deliatur* MS
c *tenet* MS
d *tenet ibidem* struck through
e *terre* interlined

years ago; and they have yielded crops fourteen times price of an acre 12d. a year, for which Ranulf will answer and the land is to be taken as above.

1.227 <30s 8d.>
Item they present that Ranulf holds another parcel assarted 20 years ago in the waste there next to the Chyrcheway, containing 2 acres 31¾ perches; and they have yielded crops fourteen times, price of an acre 12d. a year, for which Ranulf will answer and the land is to be taken as above.

1.228 <£4 6s. 8d.>
Item they present that four messuages have been built there to the harm of the beasts, price half a mark, for which Ranulf will answer and they are to be forfeited and destroyed; and they are valued at 4s. 0d. for each year from the time the cottages were built, that is for the last 20 years.

1.229 <23s. 4d.>
Item they present that Ranulf and Richard de Pulton[1] hold in the same place a cottage built in the waste to the harm of the beasts, price 40d. for which Ranulf and Richard will answer; and it is to be forfeited and destroyed; and it is valued at 12d. a year for each year from the time it was built, for which they will answer likewise since it was built 20 years ago

1.230 <77s. 0d.>
Item they present that Ranulf and Richard 20 years ago assarted 5½ acres of land in the waste there in le Crokede Feld[2] which have yielded crops fourteen times etc., price of an acre 12d. a year, for which Ranulf and Richard will answer and the land is to be taken etc.

1.231 <£9 11s. 8d.>
Item they present that Ranulf le Bryn and the heirs of Peter de Thornton[3] hold in the same place a parcel of land of le Spital towards Poulton which contains 13½ acres 30½ perches, assarted there 20 years ago; and they have yielded crops fourteen times etc., price of an acre 12d. a year, for which Ranulf and Peter's heirs will answer and the land is to be taken as above.

1.232 <16s. 6d.>
Item they present that Ranulf and the heirs of Peter hold in the same place a parcel of land which is called 'le Hertesflore'[4] in a tryst, containing 1½ acres of land assarted sixteen years ago, having yielded crops eleven times, price 12d. an acre, for which etc.

1 See **1.48** note.
2 Dodgson, *Place Names*, p. 253.
3 See **1.38** note.
4 Dodgson, *Place Names*, p. 253.

1.233 <xxxviij s. viij d.>
Item presentant quod idem Ranulphus et heredes predicti Petri tenent ibidem ij cotagia que iam xvj annis elapsis constructa fuerunt ad nocumentum ferarum domini precii cujuslibet xl d. unde predicti Ranulphus et heredes predicti Petri respondebunt et forisfiant et deleantur et est valor dictorum cotagiorum per annum a tempore constructionis in quolibet xij d.

1.234 <xxiiij s. xj d.>
Item presentant quod Ricardus de Pulton tenet ibidem unam parcellam terre in le Spitel subtus villam juxta le Rake continentem j acram iij rodas v perticas et dimidiam terre iam xx annis elapsis assartatas et xiiij[es] inbladate precii acre per annum xij d. unde idem Ricardus respondebit et terra capiatur ut supra.

1.235 <viij li. ix s. vj d.>
Item presentant quod Henricus de Hoton et Ranulphus le Bryn tenent ibidem quamdam parcellam terre vocatam le Stoples continentem xij acras xvij perticas et j quarterium terre iam xx annis elapsis assartatas et inbladate xiiij[es] fuerunt precii acre per annum xij d. unde etc.

1.236 <xxix s. v d.>
Item presentant quod Willelmus le Schepeherd tenet ibidem unam parcellam terre vocatam Baldanteresfeld continentem ij acras xvj perticas terre iam xx annis elapsis assartatas et inbladatas xiiij[es] etc. precii acre per annum xij d. unde idem Willelmus respondebit et terra capiatur ut supra.

1.237 <xj li. xiij s. j d.>
Item presentant quod Ranulphus le Bryn tenet ibidem unam parcellam terre vocatam le Newefeld continentem x acras xxiiij perticas terre et aliam parcellam terre vocatam le Mulnefeld continentem iij acras iij rodas xxiiij perticas terre et aliam parcellam vocatam le Turfsefeld continentem ij acras et dimidiam xvj perticas et dimidiam que iam xx annis elapsis assartate fuerunt et inbladate fuerunt xiiij[es] etc. precii acre per annum xij d. unde idem Ranulphus respondebit et terra capiatur ut supra.

1.238 <vij li. v s.>
Item presentant quod Ricardus de Pulton tenet ibidem inter le Newfeld et molendinum quamdam parcellam terre vocatam le Throleghfeld continentem x acras j rodam et xvij perticas terre iam xx annis elapsis assartatas et inbladate

1.233 <38s. 8d.>
Item they present that Ranulf and the heirs of Peter hold in the same place two cottages which were built sixteen years ago to the harm of the lord's beasts, price of each 40d., for which Ranulf and Peter's heirs will answer, and they are to be forfeited and destroyed; and the cottages are each valued at 12d. a year from the time they were built.

1.234 <24s. 11d.>
Item they present that Richard de Pulton[1] holds there a parcel of land in le Spital below the township next to le Rake containing 1 acre 3 roods 5½ perches of land assarted 20 years ago; and they have yielded crops fourteen times, price of an acre 12d. a year, for which Richard will answer and the land is to be taken as above.

1.235 <£8 9s. 6d.>
Item they present that Henry de Hoton[2] and Ranulf le Bryn hold in the same place a parcel of land called 'le Stoples' containing twelve acres 17¼ perches of land assarted 20 years ago; and they have yielded crops fourteen times, price of an acre 12d. a year, for which etc.

1.236 <29s. 5d.>
Item they present that William le Schepeherd holds there a parcel of land called Baldanteresfeld[3] containing two acres 16 perches of land assarted 20 years ago, and they have yielded crops fourteen times etc., price of an acre 12d. a year, for which William will answer and the land is to be taken as above.

1.237 <£11 13s. 1d.>
Item they present that Ranulf le Bryn[4] holds there a parcel of land called 'le Newefeld' containing 10 acres 24 perches of land, and another parcel of land called 'le Mulnefeld'[5] containing 3 acres 3 roods and 24 perches of land and another parcel of land called 'le Turfesfeld'[6] containing 2½ acres 16½ perches which were assarted 20 years ago; and they have yielded crops fourteen times etc., price of an acre 12d. a year, for which Ranulf will answer and the land is to be taken as above.

1.238 <£7 5s. 0d.>
Item they present that Richard de Pulton holds there between le Newfeld and the mill, a parcel of land called 'le Throleghfeld'[7] containing 10 acres 1 rood and 17 perches of

1 See **1.229** note.
2 See **1.195** note.
3 Dodgson, *Place Names*, p. 253.
4 See **1.226** note.
5 Dodgson, *Place Names*, p. 253.
6 Dodgson, *Place Names*, p. 253.
7 Dodgson, *Place Names*, p. 253.

fuerunt xiiij^{es} precii acre per annum xij d. unde idem Ricardus respondebit et terra capiatur ut supra.

1.239 <iiij li. viij s. ij d.>
Item presentant quod idem Ricardus tenet unam aliam parcellam ex parte occidentali molendini continentem iij acres et dimidiam terre et Henricus de Hoton tenet unam parcellam terre juxta mossetum continentem [...] [...] [...] [...] perticas terre et Henricus Colys Willelmus Janyn et Nichola uxor eiusdem Willelmi tenent unam parcellam continentem j acram terre que[a] iam xx annis elapsis assartate et inbladate sunt xiiij^{es}[b] de yvernagio et tramesio precii vj d. unde parcenarii qui sunt tenentes respondebunt et terra capiatur; et parcenarii et liberi tenentes de [...] in misericordia pro xx marleriis factis ibidem in novis assartis et preceptum est quod inpleantur ad custagia [ipsorum].

m. 9

1.240 <liij s. x d.>
Item presentant quod Philippus de *Raby* iam xxiiij annis elapsis assartavit ibidem in vasto iuxta bundas de Thornton iij acras j rodam xviij perticas et j quarteriam terre que xvj^{es} inbladate fuerunt de yvernagio et tramesio precii acre per annum xij d. unde idem Philippus respondebit et terra capiatur.

1.241 <xxij s.>
Item presentant quod idem Philippus iam xx annis elapsis assartavit ibidem in vasto iuxta brueram ex parte orientali ville de Raby j acram dimidiam xj perticas dimidiam et j quarteriam que xiiij^{es} inbladate sunt etc. precii acre per annum xij d. unde idem Philippus respondebit et terra capiatur etc. Et idem Philippus in misericordia pro j marlerio ibidem facto et preceptum est quod inpleantur etc.

1.242 <adhuc Netherbebynton alibi> <lv s. ij d.>
Item presentant quod Ricardus de Pulton et Johannes capellanus tenent ibidem unam parcellam vocatam le Chyrchefeld continentem iij acras iij rodas xxx perticas et dimidiam terre iam xx annis elapsis assartatas et xiiij^{es} inbladatas etc. precii acre per annum xij d. unde idem Ricardus et Johannes respondebunt et terra capiatur ut supra.

1.243 <iij s. vj d.>
Item presentant quod idem Johannes tenet ibidem unam parcellam terre iuxta fossatum de Drakeloweleyes continentem xxxvij perticas terre iam xvj annis elapsis assartatas et xj^{es}[c] inbladatas etc. precii acre per annum xij d. unde ut supra.

a *que* omitted in MS
b *xiiij^{es}* interlined
c ^{es} omitted in MS

land assarted 20 years ago and they have yielded crops fourteen times etc., price of an acre 12d. a year, for which Richard will answer and the land is to be taken as above.

1.239 <£4 8s. 2d.>
They item they present that Richard holds another parcel on the western side of the mill containing 3½ acres of land; and Henry de Hoton holds a parcel of land next to the moss containing [...] [...] [. . .] [. . .] perches of land; and Henry Colys, William Janyn and Nichola, William's wife, hold a parcel containing one acre of land, assarted 20 years ago, and they have yielded crops sown in winter and summer fourteen times, price 6d., for which the parceners, who are the tenants, will answer and the land is to be taken; and the parceners and free tenants of [...] are to be in mercy for 20 marl pits made there in new assarts and it is ordered that they are to be filled in at their own expense.

m. 9

1.240 <53s. 10d.>
Item they present that Philip de *Raby*[1] 24 years ago assarted there in the waste next to the bounds of Thornton 3 acres 1 rood 18¼ perches of land which have yielded crops sixteen times sown in winter and summer price of an acre 12d. a year, for which Philip will answer and the land is to be taken.

1.241 <22s.>
Item they present that the same Philip 20 years ago assarted there in the waste next to the heath on the eastern side of the township of Raby 1½ acres 11¾ perches which have yielded crops fourteen times sown in winter and summer, price of an acre 12d. a year etc., for which Philip will answer and the land is to be taken, etc. And Philip is to be in mercy for one marl-pit made there and it is ordered that it is to be filled in, etc.

1.242 <Continuation of Lower Bebington; elsewhere> <55s. 2d.>
Item they present that Richard de Pulton[2] and John, chaplain, hold there a parcel of land called 'le Chyrchefeld' containing 3 acres 3 roods 30½ perches of land which was assarted 20 years ago and yielded crops fourteen times etc., price of an acre 12d. a year, for which Richard and John will answer and the land is to be taken as above.

1.243 <3s. 6d.>
Item they present that the same John holds there a parcel of land next to the ditch of Drakeloweleyes[3] containing 37 perches of land which were assarted sixteen years ago and yielded crops eleven times etc., price of an acre 12d. a year, for which as above.

1 1347 m. 6 Robert de Raby took 5 oaks.
m. 14 Robert de Raby dug peat.
2 See **1.234** note.
3 Dodgson, *Place Names*, p. 250.

1.244 <ix s. vij d. ob.>
Item presentant quod Ricardus filius Johannis filii Henrici tenet ibidem aliam parcellam continentem dimidiam acram xxx perticas iam xx annis elapsis assartatam et xiiij[es][a] inbladatam etc. precii acre per annum xij d. unde predictus Ricardus respondebit et terra capiatur ut supra.

1.245 <xiij li. xviij s. iiij d.>
Item presentant quod Ricardus de Bunbury dominus de *Stanay* iam xx annis elapsis assartavit ibidem in vasto quamdam parcellam terre vocatam les Acres[b] continentem xix acras iij rodas xxj perticas j quarteriam que xiiij[es] inbladate sunt etc. precii acre per annum xij d. unde idem Ricardus respondebit et terra capiatur.

1.246 <Ciiij s.>
Item presentant quod idem Ricardus iam xxiiij annis elapsis assartavit ibidem ex parte australi del Rake in diversis parcellis vj acras et dimidiam et dimidiam perticam et j quarteriam que xvj[es][c] inbladate sunt etc. precii acre per annum xij d. unde etc. ut supra.

1.247 <xxix s. v d.>
Item presentant quod idem Ricardus iam xvj annis elapsis assartavit ibidem iuxta le Rake ij acras dimidiam xxviij perticas terre que xj[es][d] inbladate sunt etc. precii acre per annum xij d. unde etc. ut supra.

1.248 <xlviij s.>
Item presentant quod idem Ricardus tenet ibidem quoddam pratum et unam hayam prope iacentem qui continent ij acras dimidiam xxviij perticas iam xviij annis elapsis assartatas quod pratum quolibet anno falcatum fuit et hayea fuit depasta precii acre per annum xij d. unde idem Ricardus respondebit et pratum et haya capiantur etc;

et quia ij marleria facta ibidem ideo Ricardus in *misericordia* et preceptum est etc.

1.249 <xiiij li. ij s.>
Item presentant quod idem Ricardus iam xvj annis elapsis construxit ibidem in vasto vij mesuagia et unum molendinum ventriticum que sunt ad nocumentum ferarum precii cujuslibet mesuagii xl d. et molendini xl s. unde idem Ricardus respondebit et foresfiant et deleantur[e] et est valor dicti molendini per annum a tempore constructionis dimidie marce et cujuslibet mesuagii xij d. unde idem Ricardus similiter respondebit.

a *es* omitted in MS
b *vocatam les Acres* interlined
c *es* omitted in MS
d *es* omitted in MS
e *deliantur* MS

1.244 <9s. 7½d.>
Item they present that Richard son of John son of Henry holds there another parcel of land containing half an acre 30 perches which was assarted 20 years ago and yielded crops fourteen times etc., price of an acre 12d. a year, for which Richard will answer and the land is to be taken as above.

1.245 <£13 18s. 4d.>
Item they present that Richard de Bunbury, lord of *Stanney*, 20 years ago assarted there in the waste a parcel of land called 'les Acres' containing 19 acres 3 roods 21¼ perches which have yielded crops fourteen times etc., price of an acre 12d. a year, for which Richard will answer and the land is to be taken.

1.246 <104s. 0d>
Item they present that Richard 24 years ago assarted there on the southern side of le Rake[1] two acres in different parcels, 6½ acres and ¾ of a perch which have yielded crops sixteen times etc., price of an acre 12d. a year, for which etc. as above.

1.247 <29s. 5d.>
Item they present that Richard sixteen years ago assarted there next to le Rake 2½ acres 28 perches of land which have yielded crops eleven times etc., price of an acre 12d. a year, for which, etc., as above.

1.248 <48s. 0d.>
Item they present that Richard holds there a meadow and a hey lying near, which contain 2½ acres 28 perches assarted eighteen years ago; the meadow has been mown each year and the hey grazed, price of an acre 12d. a year for which Richard will answer and the meadow and the hey are to be taken, etc.;

and because two marl pits were made there, therefore Richard is to be in *mercy* and it is ordered, etc.

1.249 <£14 2s.>
Item they present that Richard sixteen years ago erected there in the waste seven messuages and a windmill which are to the harm of the of the beasts; the price of each messuage is 40d. and that of the mill is 40s 0d.. for which Richard will answer and they are to be forfeit and destroyed; and the value of the mill is half a mark a year from the time it was built, and of each messuage 12d., for which Richard will answer likewise.

1 Dodgson, *Place Names*, p. 250.

1.250 <Stoke> <xij li. vj s. vj d.>
Item presentant quod Petrus de Thornton iam xx annis elapsis assartavit ibidem in vasto quoddam pratum ex parte orientali ville continentem j acram et dimidiam per estimationem quod quolibet anno falcatum fuit precii acre per annum xij d. unde idem heredes ipsius Petri respondebunt et pratum capiatur; et idem Petrus iam xx annis elapsis assartavit ibidem in vasto xiij acras iij rodas viij perticas terre[a] que xiiij[es] inbladate sunt precii acre per annum xij d. unde idem heredes respondebunt et terra ut supra; et quia ij marleria facta[b] sunt ibidem ideo heredes predicti in misericordia et idem Petrus construxit ibidem quoddam cotagium super vastum quod est ad nocumentum ferarum precii xl d. et est valor illius per annum xij d. unde idem heredes respondebunt etc.

1.251 <Netherpulle>
Item presentant quod Robertus de Pulle iam xxiiij annis elapsis assartavit ibidem in vasto in loco qui vocatur le Oldefeld ix acras et dimidiam x perticas terre;

<viij li. vj s. ij d.>

et in alio loco iuxta le Rake iij rodas xij perticas j quarteriam terre[c] que xvj[es] inbladate sunt etc. precii acre per annum xij d. unde idem Robertus respondebit et terra capiatur.

1.252 <Ledesham>
Item presentant quod Hugo de Venables David de Egerton et Willelmus Gerard iam xvj annis elapsis assartaverunt in vasto ibidem vj[xx] acras xiij perticas iij quarterias terre que xj[es] inbladate sunt etc. precii acre per annum xij d. unde idem Hugo David et Willelmus respondebunt et terra capiatur etc;

<lxvj li. xj d.>

et quia vj marleria facta[d] sunt ibidem ideo predicti in *misericordia* et preceptum est quod inpleantur etc.

<xxxviij s. viij d.>

Item presentant quod idem David de Eggerton iam xvj annis elapsis construxit ibidem in vasto ij mesuagia que constructa fuerunt ad nocumentum ferarum domini precii cujuslibet mesuagii xl d. unde idem David respondebit et prosternantur et deleantur et est valor cujuslibet mesuagii per annum a tempore constructionis xij d. unde idem David respondebit etc.

a *terre* interlined
b *facti* MS
c *terre* interlined
d *facti* MS

1.250 <Stoak> <£12 6s. 6d.>
Item they present that Peter de Thornton[1] 20 years ago assarted there in the waste a meadow on the eastern side of the township containing 1½ acres by estimation which was mown every year, price of an acre 12d. a year, for which Peter's heirs will answer and the meadow is to be taken; and Peter 20 years ago assarted there in the waste 13 acres 3 roods and 8 perches of land which have yielded crops fourteen times, price of an acre 12d. a year, for which the heirs will answer etc., and the land as above;

and because two marl pits were made there, therefore the heirs are to be in mercy; and Peter built a cottage above the waste there which is to the harm of the beasts price 40d., and its value is 12d. a year for which the heirs will answer, etc.

1.251 <Netherpool>
Item they present that Robert de Pulle 24 years ago assarted in the waste there, in a place which is called 'le Oldefeld', 9½ acres 10 perches of land;

<£8 6s. 2d.>

and in another place next to le Rake 3 roods 12¼ perches of land which have yielded crops sixteen times etc., price of an acre 12d. a year, for which Robert will answer and the land is to be taken.

1.252 <Ledsham>
Item they present that Hugh de Venables,[2] David de Egerton and William Gerard[3] sixteen years ago assarted in the waste there 120 acres 13¾ perches of land which have yielded crops eleven times etc., price of an acre 12d. a year, for which Hugh, David and William will answer and the land is to be taken, etc.;

<£66 11d.>

and because six marl pits were made there, therefore these men are to be in *mercy* and it is ordered that the marl pits are to be filled in etc.

<£38 8d.>

Item they present that David de Eggerton sixteen years ago built in the waste there two messuages which were built to the harm of the lord's beasts, each messuage worth 40d., for which David will answer and they are to be pulled down and destroyed etc. and the value of each messuage is 12d. a year from the time it was built, for which David will answer etc.

1 See **1.231** note.
2 1347 m. 14 William Venables dug peat.
3 1347 m. 5 John Gerrard took 30 oaks.

1.253 <Hooton> <ix li. viij s. iiij d.>
Item presentant quod Henricus de Hoton tenet unam parcellam vocatam Rastyn continentem xv acras xxiij perticas et dimidiam terre et aliam parcellam vocatam Esthamfeld que continet j acram j rodam xxxv perticas terre et aliam parcellam vocatam Longeforlong continentem dimidiam acram iam xvj annis elapsis assartatas et xj^{es} inbladate sunt etc. precii acre per annum xij d. unde idem Henricus respondebit et terra capiatur etc.

1.254 <xviij s. xj d.>
Item presentant quod idem Henricus iam xiiij annis elapsis assartavit ibidem in vasto unam placeam terre vocatam Thornage continentem j acram iij rodas xxiij perticas et dimidiam et j quarteriam terre que x^{es} inbladate sunt etc. precii acre per annum xij d. unde idem Henricus respondebit et terra capiatur.

1.255 <viij s. x d.>
Item presentant quod idem Henricus iam xviij annis elapsis assartavit ibidem in vasto unam parcellam terre vocatam le Brom continentem dimidiam acram xxxviij perticas et j quarteriam terre que xij^{es} inbladate fuerunt etc. precii acre per annum xij d. unde idem Henricus respondebit et terra capiatur.

1.256 <ix s. xj d.>
Item presentant quod idem Henricus iam x annis elapsis assartavit ibidem in vasto quamdam parcellam terre vocatam le Kyllorus continentem j acram dimidiam xxiij perticas terre que v^{es} inbladate sunt etc. precii acre per annum xij d. unde idem Henricus respondebit et terra capiatur etc.

1.257 <Cix s. vj d.>
Item presentant quod idem Henricus iam xx annis elapsis assartavit ibidem in vasto unam parcellam terre vocatam Chelsrode continentem vij acras iij rodas xij perticas terre que xiiij^{es} inbladate sunt etc. precii acre per annum xij d. unde idem Henricus respondebit et terra capiatur ut supra.

1.258 <Ciij s. x d.>
Item presentant quod idem Henricus assartavit ibidem in vasto iam xij annis elapsis unam parcellam terre vocatam Kokkelade continentem j acram j rodam xxxj perticas terre et aliam parcellam terre ut supra; anticum molendinum continentem v acras xv perticas; et aliam placeam terre ad finem del Rake continentem v acras iij rodas xxx perticas terre et viij^{es} inbladate sunt precii acre per annum xij d. unde idem Henricus

1.253 <Hooton> <£9 8s. 4d.>
Item they present that Henry de Hoton[1] holds there a parcel of land called 'Rastyn',[2] containing 15 acres 23½ perches of land, and another parcel of land called 'Esthamfeld'[3] which contains 1 acre 1 rood 35 perches of land and another parcel called 'Longforlong'[4] containing ½ an acre which were assarted sixteen years ago and have yielded crops eleven times etc., price of an acre 12d. a year, for which Henry will answer and the land is to be taken, etc.

1.254 <18s. 11d.>
Item they present that Henry fourteen years ago assarted in the waste there a plot of land called 'Thornage',[5] containing 1 acre 3 roods 3¾ perches of land which have yielded crops ten times etc., price of an acre 12d. a year, for which Henry will answer and the land is to be taken.

1.255 <8s. 10d.>
Item they present that Henry eighteen years ago assarted in the waste there a parcel of land called 'le Brom'[6] containing half an acre 38¼ perches of land which have yielded crops twelve times etc., price of an acre 12d. a year, for which Henry will answer and the land is to be taken.

1.256 <9s. 11d.>
Item they present that Henry ten years ago assarted in the waste there a parcel of land called 'le Kyllorus' containing 1½ acres and 23 perches of land which have yielded crops five times etc., price of an acre 12d. a year, for which Henry will answer and the land is to be taken.

1.257 <109s. 6d.>
Item they present that Henry 20 years ago assarted in the waste there a parcel of land called 'Chelsrode' containing 7 acres 3 roods 12 perches of land which have yielded crops fourteen times etc., price of an acre 12d. a year, for which Henry will answer and the land is to be taken as above.

1.258 <103s. 10d.>
Item they present that Henry twelve years ago assarted in the waste there a parcel of land called 'Kokkelade' containing 1 acre 1 rood 31 perches of land; and another parcel of land as above; an ancient mill containing 5 acres 15 perches; and another plot of land at the end of the Rake containing 5 acres 3 roods 30 perches of land; and they have yielded crops eight times, price of an acre 12d. a year, for which

1 See **1.235** note.
2 Dodgson, *Place Names*, p. 191.
3 Dodgson, *Place Names*, p. 191.
4 Dodgson, *Place Names*, p. 191.
5 Dodgson, *Place Names*, p. 191.
6 Dodgson, *Place Names*, p. 191.

respondebit et terra capiatur etc.; et idem Henricus in misericordia pro ij marleriis ibidem factis et preceptum est quod inpleantur ad custagium ipsius Henrici etc.

1.259 <vj li.>
Item presentant quod idem Henricus [...] [...] in vasto iam xij annis elapsis quoddam molendinum ventriticum quod est ad nocumentum ferarum [...] [...] idem Henricus respondebit et est valor dicti molendini per annum a tempore constructionis quolibet anno [...] [...] [...] Henricus similiter respondebit etc.

1.260 <Molynton Thorauld> <lxv s. vij d.>
Johannes et Laurentius de Ruyton [...] de Molynton tenent j acram iij rodas iiij perticas [super] le Over[...] et iiij acras xxx perticas [...] [...] [ex] parte australi iam xvj[a] annis elapsis assartatas et xj^{es} inbladate precii acre per annum [...] [...] [...] [...] [...].

<Cx s.>

[...] [...] [...] [...] vij acras iij rodas xvj perticas terre iuxta[b] terram abbatis de [...] [...] [...] [...] [...] idem respondebit [...] ut supra.

9 ix

m. 9d

1.261 <Molynton Torald>
Item presentant quod Johannes de Ruyton et Willelmus Toraud iam xx annis elapsis assartaverunt ibidem in vasto lxxvij acras iij rodas xvj perticas et dimidiam;

<liiij li.>

et xiiij^{es} inbladate sunt de yvernagio et tramesio precii acre per annum xij d. unde idem Johannes et Willelmus respondebunt.

a *xj* crossed out and *xvj* interlined
b *iuxta* interlined

Henry will answer and the land is to be taken; and Henry is to be in mercy for two marl pits made there and it is ordered that they are to be filled in at the expense of Henry himself, etc.

1.259 <£6>
Item they present that Henry twelve years ago [...] in the waste [...] a windmill which is to the harm of the beasts [...] [...] Henry will answer; and the mill is valued at [...] [...] each year from the time it was built [...] [...] Henry will answer likewise etc.

1.260 <Mollington Torauld 65s. 7d.>
John and Laurence de Ruyton[1] [...] of Mollington hold 1 acre 3 roods 4 perches of land above le Over[...]; and 4 acres 30 perches [...] [...] on the south side which were assarted sixteen years ago; and they have yielded crops eleven times, price [...] an acre a year [...] [...] [...] [...].

<110s. 0d.>

[...] [...] [...] [...] 7 acres 3 roods 16 perches of land next to the land of the abbot of [...] [...] [...] [...] [...] will answer [...] as above.

m. 9d

1.261 <Mollington Torald>
Item they present that John de Ruyton[2] and William Toraud[3] 20 years ago assarted in the waste there 77 acres 3 roods 16½ perches;

<£54>

and they have yielded crops fourteen times sown in winter and summer, price of an acre 12d. a year, for which John and William will answer.

1 1347 m. 2d Thomas de Ruyton took 24 oaks; fine ½ mark; pledge John de Ruyton.
2 See **1.261** note.
3 1347 m. 2d Henry Torald took 17 oaks; fine ½ mark; pledge Roger de Eaton.
m. 3 William Torald 240 oaks; 20s 0d.; John Torald, Robert Laselles, William son of Marcus, Hugh son of [...].
m. 3d John Torald 32 oaks; 40s. 0d.; Richard Launcelyn.
m. 6 Richard Torald an oak.

1.262 <ix s. x d.>
Item presentant quod idem Johannes et Willelmus tenent ibidem boscum quod vocatur le Grene et includitur contra assisam foreste. Ideo predicti Johannes et Willelmus in misericordia.

1.263 <viij li. xiij s. iiij d.>
Item presentant quod idem Johannes et Willelmus constructerunt ibidem in vasto quoddam molendinum ventriticum iam xx annis elapsis quod est ad nocumentum ferarum domini. Ideo prosternatur et deleatur[a] precii molendini xl s. unde idem Johannes et Willelmus respondebunt et est valor dicti molendini a tempore constructionis quolibet anno dimidie marce unde similiter idem respondebunt.

1.264 <Molynton Banastre>
Item presentant quod Adam de Houghton similiter tenet ibidem v acras iij rodas vj perticas terre iam xx annis elapsis ibidem assartatas de vasto;

<iiij li. xij d.>

et xiiij^{es} inbladate fuerunt ut supra precii acre per annum xij d. unde idem Adam respondebit et terra capiatur ut supra;

et idem Adam in *misericordia* pro ij marleriis factis ibidem et preceptum est quod inpleantur etc.

1.265 <Bacford>
Item presentant quod Henricus de Massy tenet ibidem in vasto unam parcellam terre iuxta le Rake continentem xj acras j rodam xiij perticas et idem Henricus tenet ibidem aliam parcellam in fine ville continentem j rodam xxviij perticas et j quarteriam terre;

<vij li. xij s. x d. ob.>

et aliam parcellam terre continentem iij rodas xxxvij perticas et dimidiam terre iam xvj annis elapsis assartatas et xij^{es} inbladatas precii acre per annum xij d. unde idem Henricus respondebit.

1.266 <xxxvj s. vij d.>
Item presentant quod Robertus de Pulle tenet ibidem in vasto unam parcellam iuxta le Demmyng continentem iij acras j rodam xiij perticas terre iam xvj annis elapsis assartatas et xij^{es} inbladatas precii acre per annum xij d. unde idem Robertus respondebit et terra capiatur ut supra.

a *deliatur* MS

1.262 <9s. 10d.>
Item they present that John and William hold there a wood which is called le Grene;[1] and it is enclosed against the assize of the forest. Therefore John and William are to be in mercy.

1.263 < £8 13s. 4d.>
Item they present that John and William 20 years ago built there in the waste a windmill which is to the harm of the lord's beasts. Therefore it is to be pulled down and destroyed, price of the windmill 40s. 0d, for which John and William will answer; and the value of the mill is half a mark for each year from the time it was built, for which the same will answer likewise.

1.264 <Mollington Banastre>
Item they present that Adam de Houghton likewise holds there 5 acres 3 roods 6 perches of land assarted from the waste there 20 years ago;

<£4 0s. 12d.>

and they have yielded crops fourteen times as above, price of an acre 12d. a year, for which Adam will answer and the land is to be taken as above;

and Adam is to be in *mercy* for two marl-pits made there and it is ordered that they are to be filled in etc.

1.265 <Backford>
Item they present that Henry de Massy[2] holds in the waste there a parcel of land next to le Rake containing eleven acres one rood thirteen perches; and the same Henry holds there another parcel within the boundary of the township containing one rood 28¼ perches of land;

<£7 12s. 10½d>

and he holds another parcel of land containing three roods and 37½ perches of land assarted sixteen years ago and which have yielded crops twelve times, price of an acre 12d. a year, for which Henry will answer.

1.266 <36s. 7d.>
Item they present that Robert de Pulle[3] holds there in the waste a parcel next to le Demmyng containing three acres one rood thirteen perches of land assarted sixteen years ago and which have twelve times yielded crops, price of an acre 12d. a year, for which Robert will answer and the land is to be taken as above.

1 Dodgson, *Place Names*, p. 179. No record in Dodgson of le Grene in 1357, but recorded thus in 1278.
2 See **1.216** note.
3 See **1.179** note.

1.267 <xviij s. vj d.>
Item presentant quod abbas de Walley tenet ibidem in vasto unam acram et dimidiam et xxx perticas[a] iam xvj annis elapsis assartatam que xij^{es} inbladate sunt etc. precii acre per annum xij d. unde idem abbas respondebit et terra capiatur ut supra.

1.268 <vij li. xix s. xj d.>
Item presentant quod Henricus de Massy tenet ibidem unam parcellam terre iuxta bundas ville del Lee vocate Capenhurstacre continentem xiiij acras dimidiam vij perticas et j quarteriam terre iam xvj annis elapsis assartatas et xj^{es}[b] inbladatas etc. precii acre per annum xij d. unde idem Henricus respondebit et terra capiatur etc.; et idem Henricus in *misericordia* pro iiij marleriis ibidem factis et preceptum est quod inpleantur etc.

1.269 <Landecan> <Cxij s. ij d.>
Item presentant quod Robertus de Fouleshurst tenet ibidem unam placeam terre iuxta cruces continentem viij acras ij perticas [et dimidiam] terre que iam xx annis elapsis assartate fuerunt et xiiij^{es} inbladate fuerunt precii acre per annum xij d. unde idem respondebit et terra capiatur ut supra.

1.270 <xj li. xviij s. vij d.>
Item presentant quod idem Robertus iam xvj annis elapsis assartavit ibidem iuxta le Botham xxj acras et dimidiam xxxj perticas j quateriam terre que xj^{es} inbladate sunt de yvernagio et tramesio precii acre per annum xij d. unde idem Robertus respondebit et terra capiatur ut supra.

1.271 <Wylaston>[c]

1.272
Postea venit tota communitas foreste predicte et protulit breve (**7.23**) domini comitis sub privato sigillo justiciariis hic directum, quod alibi irrotulatur inter transcripta cartarum ipsius itineris, testificans quod[d] idem dominus de avisamento consilii sui pro proficuo et transquillitate hominum foreste de Wyrhale [concordavit][e] de capiendo de eis finem mille librarum et faciendo eos perdonationem de diversis inbladitionibus[f] et transgressionibus forestam tangentibus, quod continetur in quadam indentura nuper

a *perticas* interlined
b ^{es} omitted in MS
c There follows a space of approximately 20 cm. before **1.272**.
d MS includes a superflous *'quia'*.
e *est concordatus* MS. It is likely that the scribe converted the Anglo-French of the prince's direct speech in his letter to Richard de Wilughby (**7.23**) ('*sumez assentuz*' – 'We are agreed') literally, but into incorrect Latin.
f *inbladitionibus et* interlined

1.267 <18s. 6d.>
Item they present that the abbot of Whalley[1] holds there in the waste 1½ acres and 30 perches assarted sixteen years ago which have yielded crops twelve times etc., price of an acre 12d. a year, for which the abbot will answer and the land is to be taken as above.

1.268 <£7 19s. 11d.>
Item they present that Henry de Massy[2] holds there a parcel of land next to the boundaries of the township of Lea called 'Capenhurstacre'[3] containing 14½ acres 7¼ perches of land assarted sixteen years ago; and they have yielded crops eleven times etc., price of an acre 12d. a year, for which Henry will answer and the land is to be taken, etc.; and the same Henry is to be in *mercy* for four marl-pits made there and it is ordered that they are to be filled in etc.

1.269 <Landican> <112s. 2d.>
Item they present that Robert de Fouleshurst holds there a plot of land next to the crosses containing 8 acres 2½ perches of land which were assarted twenty years ago; and they have yielded crops fourteen times, price of an acre 12d. a year, for which he will answer and the land is to be taken as above.

1.270 <£11 18s. 7d.>
Item they present that the same Robert sixteen years ago assarted there next to le Botham[4] 21½ acres 31¼ perches of land which have yielded crops eleven times sown in winter and summer, price of an acre 12d. a year, for which Robert will answer and the land is to be taken as above.

1.271 <Willaston>[5]

1.272
Afterwards the whole community of the forest came and produced a writ[6] of the lord earl, sent here to the justices under the privy seal, which is enrolled elsewhere among the transcripts of charters of this eyre, bearing witness that the same lord on the advice of his council, for the profit and relief of the men of the forest of Wirral, has come to an agreement to take from them a fine of a thousand pounds and to pardon them for growing crops and for various trespasses concerning the forest as is

1 1347 m. 13d Abbot of Whalley dug peat at Stanney Grange.
2 See **1.265** note.
3 Dodgson, *Place Names*, p. 202, where he writes Capenhurstat.
4 Dodgson, *Place Names*, p. 268.
5 There is a blank space here on the manuscript of about 20cms before 1.272.
6 See entry **7.23** in the Transcript of Charters.

inde facta tam in presencia justiciariorum predictorum quam hominum predictorum, mandans eisdem justiciariis quod finem predictam ab eisdem hominibus recipiant et perdonationem huius [...]re faciant qualis[a] in predicta indentura continetur et petunt quod possint admitti per finem predictam [p…] [huius] [d..] habendam juxta tenorem indenture inde facte. [Et admittuntur per finem predictam per plegium cujuslibet alterius alteri [ut habeant] perdonationem prout etc. de quibus eadem communitas solvet domino per annum ad [duos] [terminos] [anni] [scilicet ad festa Sancti Martini et] Nativitatis Sancti Johnnes Baptiste CC libras per equales portiones etc. [sic de anno in annum] quolibet anno CC libras [q...que] M li [predicte] plenarie persolventur [incipiente] ad festum Sancti Martini anno regni domini regis nunc xxxiij et nisi [fecerit etc.] [concedit] [quod] [vicecomes] [faciat etc.] [de terris et catallis suis etc.] ad quorumcumque manus etc.][b]

a *qualem* MS

b Much of this final paragraph, beginning *'Et admittuntur'*, is lost. The text is supplied from the similar paragraph in the Delamere eyre roll.

contained in an indenture, recently made in consequence, in the presence both of the justices and of the aforesaid men, ordering the same justices that they are to receive the fine from the same men and grant pardon for this [...] such as is contained in the indenture; and they ask that by reason of the said fine they may be able to be admitted [to have the pardon] according to the wording of the indenture then made.

[And by reason of the fine they are admitted by the pledge of each other to have pardon just as, etc., concerning which the same community will pay to the lord a year at two terms of the year, that is at the feasts of Saint Martin and of the Nativity of St John Baptist £200 by equal portions etc., so from year to year each year £200 until the said thousand pounds is fully paid, beginning at the feast of Saint Martin in the 33rd year of the present lord king and if the community does not do this etc. he grants that the sheriff should act etc. with regard to their lands and goods etc. to whosever hands etc.][1]

1 Much of this final paragraph, beginning 'And by reason of the fine...', is lost. The translation is supplied from the similar paragraph in the Delamere eyre roll.

PLACITA CLAMEORUM FORESTE DE WYRHALE CALENDAR OF THE PLEAS OF THE CLAIMS OF THE FOREST OF WIRRAL

The claims of the Wirral Forest (**2.1** to **2.60** membranes 10 to 21d)

The twelve membranes contain 60 separate records of Wirral claims. These consist of submissions by 34 different people or parties:

Abbot of Basingwerk **2.9, 2.25, 2.42**
Abbot of Chester **2.18, 2.50**
Bebington, Joan, lady of **2.28**
Bechinton, (Bechynton) William de **2.21, 2.23**
Bernard, Henry of Tranmere **2.60**
Berneston, Robert de **2.32**
Bishop of Coventry and Lichfield, Roger **2.38**
Blound, John **2.10, 2.17, 2.48**
Bryn, Ranulf le and Cecily his wife **2.26**
Bunbury, Richard, relative and heir of David Bunbury **2.41**
Capenhurst, Thomas de **2.7, 2.16**
Domville (Donvyll, Donville), the elder **2.5, 2.14, 2.36**
Egerton, David de **2.24**
Gregory, William **2.52**
Henry, duke of Lancaster **2.45**
Hogh (Hough), Richard del **2.6, 2.19**
Hogh (Hough), Richard del and Ellen, his wife **2.46**
Hokenhull, Thomas de **2.40**
Hoton, Henry de **2.30**
Lasselles, (Lassels), John **2.29, 2.44**
Launcelyn, John **2.58**
Launcelyn, John and Margery his wife and Andrew del Brom **2.59**
Mascy, Hamo de **2.8, 2.15**
Merton, Stephen de **2.1**
Monte Acuto, William de, earl of Salisbury **2.55, 2.56**
Morton, Thomas de, son of Richard de **2.51**
Prior of Birkenhead **2.3, 2.4, 2.33**
Pulle, Robert de **2.31**
Raby, Philip de **2.27, 2.37**

Seynesbury, William de, chaplain **2.2**, **2.47**
Stanley, William **2.11, 2.12, 2.35, 2.43, 2.49**
and Stanley, William, son of William **2.53, 2.54**
Starkey, Robert of Tranmere **2.39**
Trussell, William of Acton, knight, son of William, **2.22, 2.57**
Trussell, Warin, knight **2.20, 2.34**
Wetefeld, John de, parson of Bebington **2.13**

Since there is a considerable similarity between the content of the claims, they are presented in calendared translations which lose little of the full version. One complete example of a claim, that of John Domville, the elder (**2.14**), is set out here in full text and translation.

m. 12

2.14 Wyrhale Johannes Domvill senior[1]
Johannes Domvill senior dat domino dimidiam marcam pro iterum clameo per plegium Roberti de Pulle. Et clamat pro se et heredibus in omnibus terris et tenementis in foresta de Wyrhall libere assartare terras suas infra divisas agriculture sue ac etiam si landa aut terra ipsius Johannis infra divisas villarum suarum fuerit[2] que prius culta fuit ubi nemus non crescat liceat eis illam colere sine herbergatione. Item clamat pro se et heredibus suis capere houxbote et haybote in nemore suo proprio de omni genere bosci infra forestam predictam sine visu forestariorum et mortuum boscum suum dare aut vendere cui voluerit et quod homines ipsius Johannis non inplacitentur de foresta pro superdicto nisi cum manuopere inveniantur.

Item clamat pro se heredibus suis hominibus tenentibus et firmariis suis infra manerium suum de Brunstath quod est infra forestam de Wyrhall in solo ipsius Johannis manerii sui predicti turbas fodere et blestas blestare siccare et cariare jaunum et filicem et brueram capere ad ardendum sine visu forestariorum rationabiliter pro focali. Item clamat pro se heredibus suis hominibus tenentibus et firmariis suis infra manerium suum de Oxton quod est infra forestam predictam in solo suo proprio manerii sui de Oxton turbas fodere blestas blestare siccare et cariare jaunum et filicem et brueram capere ad ardendum sine visu forestariorum rationabiliter pro focali.

Et dicit quod quo ad clameum libere assartandi terras suas infra divisas etc. ac etiam si landa aut terra ipsius Johannis etc. et similiter ad capere houxbote et haybote in nemoribus suis etc. et quod homines sui non inplacitentur pro superdicto etc. dicit quod quidam Ranulphus quondam comes Cestr' concessit baronibus suis comitatus predicti et heredibus suis libertatem assartandi terras suas infra divisas agriculture

1 *dimidiam marcam* struck through in margin
2 *fuerit* om MS The corrections indicated are based on the content of the original charter, see **7.9**

sue in foresta et si landa aut terra infra divisas ville sue fuerit que prius culta fuit ubi nemus non crescat liceat eis illam colere sine herbergatione et liceat eis houxbote et haybote in nemore suo capere etc. sine visu forestariorum et mortuum boscum suum dare etc. et quod homines eorum non inplacitentur pro superdicto de foresta nisi etc. Concessit etiam de se et heredibus communibus militibus omnibus et libere tenentibus totius comitatus predicti et eorum heredibus omnes libertates predictas per cartam ipsius Ranulphi quam hic profert et que hoc testatur quasquidem libertates dominus Edwardus quondam rex Anglie avus domini regis nunc eas recitando et ratificando concessit et confirmavit per cartam ipsius Edwardi quam hic profert et que hoc testatur cuius dat' est apud Westmonasterium xxx die Martii anno regni regis sui xxviij.

Dicit etiam quod dominus Edwardus nunc princeps Wallie et comes Cestr' concessit communitati Cestris' de qua ipse unus est quod haberent omnes libertates eidem communitati per Ranulphum dudum comitem Cestr' concessas[3] et per Edwardum nuper regem Anglie proavum suum confirmatas et[4] eisdem gauderent[5] pacifice quiete per cartam suam quam hic profert et que hoc testatur cuius dat' est apud Cestr' x die Septembris anno regni regis nunc Anglie xxvij[6] et Francie xiiij.

Et dicit quod tempore concessionis ipsius Ranulphi quidam Robertus Donvill miles antecessor ipsius Johannis fuit seisitus de maneriis predictis et ipse et omnes antecessores sui a tempore confectionis carte predicte fuerunt seisiti de libertatibus predictis sine inpedimento et hoc paratus est verificare etc.

Et quo ad turbas fodere blestas blestare[7] siccare et cariare et jaunum et filicem et brueram capere rationabiliter pro focali in maneriis suis predictis dicit quod ipse et omnes antecessores sui a tempore quo non exstat memoria perceperunt et habuerunt proficua predicta sibi et heredibus suis hominibus firmariis suis scilicet bondis et tenentibus ad terminum [annorum] et hoc paratus est verificare et petit libertates proficua predicta sibi allocari.

Et Willelmus de Wakebruge qui etc. dicit quod declaret curie cuiusmodi libertates clamat habere per ista vocabila housebote et haybote et Johannes dicit quod clamat pro se et heredibus suis in nemore suo proprio de omni genere bosci claudere et edificare et ardere sine visu forestariorum.

Et Willelmus de Wakebruge qui sequitur etc. dicit quod quo ad turbas fodere clameum suum predictum eidem Johanni in hac parte allocari non debet quia dicit quod, exquo turbas fodere est puteos facere in quibus in instanti itinere quam sepissime per forestarios et alios ministros istius foreste presentatum est quod diverse fere domini istius foreste in huiusmodi puteis exsistentibus submerse sunt quod manifeste cedit

3 *concessis* MS
4 *et* om. MS
5 *gaudeat* MS
6 *xx* MS. See also p. xxii 'The enrolment of Charters'
7 *blestas blestare* om. MS

in destructionem ferarum et contra assisam foreste, petit iudicium si ad huiusmodi proficuum habendum quod est contra assisam foreste et destructio ferarum admitti debeat per prescriptionem.

Et quia idem Johannes illud non potest dedicere, ideo consideratum quod quo ad turbas fodere nihil capiat per clameum suum set sit in misericordia.

Et idem Willelmus qui sequitur etc. quo ad ceteras libertates et proficua que clamat dicit quod idem Johannes nec antecessores sui a tempore concessionis predicti Ranulphi sive a tempore quo non exstat memoria non usi sunt libertatibus predictis absque divadiatione et inpedimento per forestarios et ministros prout clamat et hoc petit verificare pro domino.

Johannes similiter. Ideo fiat inde iuratio. Ad quem diem apud Cestr' coram prefatis justiciariis venit tam predictus Willelmus qui sequitur etc. quam predictus Johannes in propria persona sua et juratores similiter qui de consensu partium electi triati et jurati dicunt super sacramentum suum[8] quod idem Johannes et omnes antecessores sui a tempore quo non exstat memoria habuerunt et perceperunt libertates proficua predicta a tempore confectionis cartarum predictarum sine interruptione vel inpedimento qualicumque. Ideo consideratum est quod idem Johannes eas habeat et gaudeat sibi et heredibus suis, iure domini principis Wallie comitis Cestr' in omnibus semper salvo etc.

m. 12

2.14 Wirral John Domville, the elder[9] (See also **2.5**)

John Domville gives the lord half a mark for claiming a second time by the pledge of Robert de Pulle. And he claims for himself and his heirs, in all his lands and tenements in the forest of Wirral, the liberty to assart his lands within the bounds of his arable land and also if there is a glade or piece of arable land of John's within the bounds of his township, which used to be cultivated where wood does not grow, he is to be allowed to cultivate it as long as nothing is built there.

Item he claims for himself and his heirs to take housebote and haybote from every kind of wood in his own woodland within the forest without the view of the foresters, and to give or sell his dead wood to whoever he wishes, and that John's men are not to be impleaded for the above in matters concerning the forest, unless they are caught red-handed.

Item he claims for himself his heirs, his men, tenants and lease-holders, within his manor of Brimstage which is within the forest of Wirral, in the ground of the manor of John himself, to dig peat, to cut, dry and carry away turves and to take gorse,

8 *super sacramentum suum* interlined
9 Domville made this same claim at the 1347 eyre, m. 21.

fern and heather for burning, a reasonable amount for fuel, without the view of the foresters.

Item he claims for himself, his heirs, his men, tenants and lease-holders, within his manor of Oxton which is within the forest, in his own ground of his manor of Oxton, to dig peat and to cut, dry and carry away turves and to take gorse, fern and heather for burning, a reasonable amount for fuel, without the view of the foresters.

And he says that as for claiming the liberty of assarting his lands within the bounds of his arable land etc., and also if there is a glade or piece of arable land of John's etc. and likewise as for taking housebote and haybote in his woodlands etc. and that his men are not to be impleaded for the above etc. he says that Ranulf, former earl of Chester, granted to his barons of the said county and to their heirs the liberty of assarting their lands within the bounds of their arable land in the forest and, if there is a glade or piece of arable land within the bounds of their townships which used to be cultivated where wood does not grow, they are to be allowed to cultivate it as long as nothing is built there and that they are to be allowed to take housebote and haybote in their woodland etc. without the view of the foresters, and to give their dead wood etc. and that their men are not to be impleaded for the above in matters concerning the forest, unless etc.

He also granted from himself and his heirs to all commons, knights and free tenants of the whole county and to their heirs all the said liberties by the charter (**7.9**) of Ranulf himself which he produces here and which bears witness to this; which liberties by repeating and ratifying (**7.5**) them the lord Edward, former king of England, grandfather of the present lord king, granted and confirmed by the charter (**7.35**) of Edward himself, which he produces here and which bears witness to this, which is dated at Westminster 30 March in the 28th year of his reign (1300).

He says also that lord Edward, the present prince of Wales and earl of Chester, granted to the community of Cheshire, of which he is one, that they should have all the liberties granted to the same community by Ranulf, former earl of Chester, and confirmed to them by Edward, former king of England his great-grandfather, and that they should enjoy them peacefully and quietly by his charter (**7.14**) which he produces here and which bears witness to this, which was dated at Chester 10 September in the 27th[10] year of the reign of the present king of England, and of France the 14th (1353).

And he says that at the time of Ranulf's grant Robert Domville, knight, John's predecessor, was seised of the said manors and he and all his predecessors from the time the charter was made were seised of the above liberties without hindrance and this he is ready to prove etc.

And as for digging peat, cutting, drying and carrying away turves, and taking gorse, fern and heather, a reasonable amount for fuel, in his manors, he says that he and all

10 20th MS

his predecessors have from time immemorial taken and had the profits for himself and his heirs, his men and his lease-holders, that is bondsmen and tenants for a term of years, and this he is ready to prove, and he asks for the above liberties and profits to be allowed to him.

And William de Wakebrugge, who etc. says that he should show the court what kind of liberties he claims to have by these words housebote and haybote, and John says that he claims for himself and his heirs in his own woodlands from every kind of wood to fence, build and burn, without the view of the foresters.

And William de Wakebrugge who sues etc. says that as for digging peat, John's claim in this matter ought not to be allowed, because he says that, since digging peat makes pits, in which it has very often been presented in the present eyre by the foresters and other officials of this forest, that various beasts of the lord in this forest have been drowned in holes of this kind, which obviously results in the destruction of the beasts and is against the assize of the forest, he asks for judgement as to whether he ought to be admitted by prescription to having this kind of profit, which is against the assize of the forest and causes the destruction of the beasts.

And because John cannot deny this, therefore it is the judgement of the court that as for digging peat, he is to take nothing by his claim, but he is to be *in mercy.*

And William who sues etc. says that as for the other liberties and profits which he claims, neither John nor his predecessors, from the time of Ranulf's grant or from time immemorial, have enjoyed the said liberties without attachment and hindrance by the foresters and officials as he claims, and this he seeks to verify for the lord, and John likewise.

Therefore a jury is to be summoned. On which day at Chester before the same justices come both the said William who sues etc. and John in person and the jurors likewise, who having been chosen, tested and sworn with the consent of the parties, say on their oath that John and all his predecessors have, from time immemorial, had and taken the said liberties and profits from the time the charters were made, without interruption or any hindrance whatsoever.

Therefore it is the judgement of the court that John should have and enjoy them for himself and his heirs, saving always the right of the lord prince of Wales, earl of Chester in all things etc.

Summary of the contents of the claims

1. The sixty separate records of Wirral claims, membranes 10 to 21d, consist of submissions by 34 different people or parties, six of whom submitted two claims, so there are 40 claims altogether. 27 of the claimants listed above, most of whom are substantial landholders of Wirral, quoted Ranulf III's charter, made about 1215, as justifying their entitlement to assart their lands and to use their wood as they wish.

All gave the name of their predecessor who was living at the time of the charter. The relevant paragraph from Ranulf III's charter (**7.9** para 6) is as follows:

I also grant them the liberty of assarting their lands within the bounds of their arable land in the forest; and if there is a glade or piece of arable land within the bounds of any township belonging to them, which used to be cultivated and where wood does not grow, they are to be be allowed to cultivate it, as long as nothing is built there. And they may be allowed to take housebote and haybote in their woodland, of every kind of wood, without the view of the foresters, and give or sell their dead wood to whoever they wish; and their men are not to be impleaded in the forest court for any of the things mentioned above unless they are caught red-handed.

2. Seven of the claimants relied on other specific charters or inheritance rights, namely William Stanley, Stephen Merton, the abbot of Chester, Warin Trussell, William Trussell, the prior of Birkenhead and the bishop of Coventry and Lichfield.

3. Claims to all other rights, mainly digging peat, taking estovers and having unlawed dogs, were based on prescription and continuous user, since they had been enjoyed from time immemorial by the claimants' predecessors. Five claims for estovers were started, but not pursued.

4. The claims were generally presented to the court by the defendants' attorneys, although occasionally the defendant appeared in person. The case on behalf of the earl of Chester was put by his serjeant of pleas, William Wakebridge. After the claims had been stated and their justification submitted, William Wakebridge challenged each claim. He sometimes asked for definitions of terms, e.g. housebote and haybote or dimensions of ditches. He alleged the danger to the game of ditches caused by digging peat and in some cases called for the record of previous eyres to be examined. He finally stated that entitlement had not been proved. Three Wirral claims were rejected after William Wakebridge quoted the forest courts that had been held under Reginald de Grey in 1269–70 and the abbot of Vale Royal in 1285–86, or the eyre of Thomas de Ferrers in 1347. The prior of Birkenhead's claim (**1.40**) had been rejected by Reginald de Grey, and William Stanley's (**2.54**) by Thomas de Ferrers; John Domville's claim (**2.5**) had been considered and rejected by all three previous courts. Decisions of the earlier courts were quoted in thirteen other claims in the Delamere and Macclesfield sections of the record; in one case, in the claim of the abbot of Vale Royal (**4.1**), it was the claimant who quoted the decision of 1347 to prove his entitlement.

5. In most cases the issue was sent to a jury, but some judgements were made by the court; for example, in some claims for peat as the claimants 'cannot deny' that their ditches had caused harm to the beasts, the decision was taken summarily to refuse that part of the claim.

6. The jury decided and its verdict was recorded.

7. The record of the 27 standard claims goes as follows:

(i) the claim was stated by the claimant or the claimant's attorney;
(ii) the claim was then restated (but recorded in an abbreviated form), and
(iii) the supporting charters were quoted and produced;
(iv) the claimant named the predecessor living at the time of Ranulf III's charter (**7.9**),
(v) immemorial rights (rights of prescription and continuous user) were put forward for claims not specifically supported by charters.

8. William Wakebridge responded for the earl and asked for:

(i) definitions of terms (e.g. housebote and haybote) or dimensions (e.g. of the depth of ditches);
(ii) the claim to be rejected for a specific reason (e.g. because 'digging peat makes holes into which the lord's beasts have fallen');
(iii) the record to be produced of similar cases in previous hearings which had been unsuccessful.

9. About half of all the claims were made for rights in named manors. However, in the case of two manors, Moreton and Liscard, two or more people were recorded as claiming rights as lords in the same manor (Moreton: five: **2.23, 2.45, 2.51, 2.58, 2.59**; Liscard: two: **2.29, 2.31**). Tranmere was held by two lords, one of two-thirds and the other of a third, but the Moreton case is probably a clerical error. In Liscard there is no other evidence that John Lasselles had any manorial rights there, and so it is possible that he made a false claim.

2.1

Claimant: Stephen de Merton.
Property: Land in his manors of Gayton and Lach (Dennis).
Claims: (**i**) the rights expressed in Ranulf III's charter, when the property was in the hands of his predecessor, Ranulf de Merton;
(**ii**) the right to dig peat;
(**iii**) the right to cut turves, gorse, fern and heather, for fuel, without view of the foresters;
(**iv**) the right to have unlawed dogs;

Ranulf de Merton, Stephen's predecessor, at the lord Edward's request, in 1305 had exchanged his manor of Marton for the manors of Gayton and Lach (Dennis) with the abbot of Vale Royal so that the abbey could have its lands more conveniently situated. The condition of the exchange was that Ranulf would enjoy the same rights in Wirral as he had enjoyed in Marton. Stephen quoted three royal charters, **7.1, 7.2** and **7.3**, to substantiate his claims.

Challenge: William Wakebridge stated that his claim was unfounded, because Stephen had failed to establish that either he or his predecessors had received 'any gift made by the lord king or by his predecessors or subsequently by the present lord earl'.

Outcome: The court found that 'Stephen cannot deny this'.
Verdict: The verdict of the court was that 'Stephen should take nothing for his claim'.
(26 February 1358).

2.2 and **2.47**
Claimant: William de Seynesbury.
Property: Land in his manors of Upton and Frankby.
Claims: (**i**) the rights expressed in Ranulf III's charter, when the property was in the hands of his predecessor, W [...][...][...] of William [...][...];

The foot of membrane 10 is badly damaged and the rest of this part of William de Seynesbury's case and the verdict are illegible. The case was adjourned to 20 August 1358 (**2.47**) when William's other claims were presented, viz:

(**ii**) the right to cut turves, gorse, fern and heather, for fuel, without view of the foresters;
(**iii**) the right to keep unlawed dogs;
Challenge: William Wakebridge challenged all the claims.
Outcome: Issue sent to jury.
Verdict: Jury found in William's favour with regard to all the claims presented in **2.47**.
(20 August, 1358).

2.3 and **2.4** (See also **2.33** for the prior's claim to ferry rights)
Claimant: Prior of Birkenhead. The prior failed to appear at the first adjournment (probably on 26 February 1358) and paid half a mark to be allowed to claim a second time (in **2.4**). He also paid half a mark for his claim to be repledged, by the pledge of John de Lassels, so that he could expand on his claim for digging peat.
Property: All his land in Wirral
Claims: (**i**) the rights expressed in Ranulf III's charter, when the property was in the hands of Oliver, his predecessor as prior;
(**ii**) the right to dig peat;
(**iii**) the right to cut turves, gorse, fern and heather, for fuel, without view of the foresters;
(**iv**) the right to keep unlawed dogs;
(**v**) the right to have free mast for his pigs from 29 September to 11 November and pasture for all his pigs at all times of the year except for the fence month.
Challenge: William Wakebridge stated that none of the prior's claims was well founded.
Outcome: Issue sent to jury.
Verdict: Jury found in the prior's favour with regard to all his claims.
(20 August 1358).

2.5 and **2.14**

Claimant: John Domville, the elder, pledge of Robert de Pulle.
Property: Land in his manors of Brimstage and Oxton.
Claims: (**i**) the rights expressed in Ranulf III's charter, when the property was in the hands of his predecessor, Robert Domville, knight;
(**ii**) the right to dig peat;
(**iii**) the right to cut turves, gorse, fern and heather, for fuel, without view of the foresters;
(**iv**) the right to have greyhounds for hunting hares.
Challenge: William Wakebridge referred to the forest pleas of 1286 when Domville was fined £20 for keeping greyhounds. The verdict is illegible because of damage to membrane 10d, but, since all the other claims are repeated in **2.14**, it is likely that the claim to keep greyhounds was refused at the earlier hearing. William Wakebridge required him to define housebote and haybote and denied the claim to the right dig peat. Domville could not counter this, so this claim fell. William Wakebridge also asserted that Domville's other claims were not well founded.
Outcome: Issue sent to jury.
Verdict: Jury found in Domville's favour with regard to all the other claims in **2.14**.
(20 August, 1358).

2.6 and **2.19**

Claimant: Richard del Hough, the elder.
Property: A messuage and three bovates of land in Thornton Hough.
Claims: (**i**) the rights expressed in Ranulf III's charter when the property was in the hands of Matthew de Thornton, his predecessor;
(**ii**) the right to dig peat;
(**iii**) the right to cut turves, gorse, fern and heather, for fuel, without view of the foresters;
(**iv**) the right to keep unlawed dogs.

(Hough and his wife, Ellen, made a separate claim in almost identical terms in **2.46**, but specifically including 'Ellen's heirs' in the claim for rights in the township of Thornton Hough.)

Challenge: William Wakebridge required him to define housebote and haybote, which Richard did. He also denied Richard's claim to the right to dig peat. Richard could not counter this, so this claim fell. William Wakebridge also denied that the rest of Richard's claims were well founded.
Outcome: Issue sent to jury.
Verdict: Jury found in Richard's favour with regard to all his other claims.
(20 August, 1358)

2.7 and **2.16**

Claimant: Thomas de Capenhurst. (He paid half a mark, on the pledge of Hamo de Mascy, for inserting his claim for digging peat into **2.16.**)

Property: Land in the forest of Wirral.

Claims: **(i)** the rights expressed in Ranulf III's charter, when the property was in the hands of his predecessor, William de Capenhurst;
(ii) the right to dig peat;
(iii) the right to cut turves, gorse, fern and heather, for fuel, without view of the foresters;
(iv) the right to keep unlawed dogs.

Challenge: William Wakebridge required him to define housebote and haybote, which Thomas did. He denied the claim to the right to dig peat. Thomas could not counter this, so this claim fell. William Wakebridge also asserted that Thomas's claims were not well founded.

Outcome: Issue sent to jury.

Verdict: Jury found in Thomas's favour with regard to all his other claims. (20 August, 1358).

2.8 and **2.15**

Claimant: Hamo de Mascy. (He failed to appear at the adjourned hearing on 26 February 1358 and repledged his claim, on the pledge of [Thomas de] Capenhurst.)

Property: Land in the forest of Wirral.

Claims: **(i)** the rights expressed in Ranulf III's charter when the property was in the hands of his predecessor, Hamo de Mascy;
(ii) the right to dig peat;
(iii) the right to cut turves, gorse, fern and heather, for fuel, without view of the foresters;
(iv) the right to keep unlawed dogs.

Challenge: William Wakebridge required him to define housebote and haybote, which Hamo did. He denied Hamo's claim to the right to dig peat. Hamo could not counter this, so this claim fell. William Wakebridge also denied that Hamo's other claims were well founded.

Outcome: Issue sent to jury.

Verdict: Jury found in Hamo's favour with regard to all his other claims. (20 August, 1358)

2.9, 2.25 and **2.42**

Claimant: The abbot of Basingwerk. He appeared on the first day of the eyre when consideration of his claim was adjourned until 26 February 1358. He paid half a mark for his claim to be repledged, by the pledge of Philip de Raby. (**2.42** seems to belong chronologically after **2.9** but before **2.25**. It repeats the content of **2.9**, except that 'blestas blestare', 'to cut turves' is omitted; the phrase is interlined in **2.9.**)

Property: Land in his manor of Caldy and in the township of Thornton Hough;
Claims: (**i**) the right to dig peat;
(**ii**) the right to cut turves, gorse, fern and heather, for fuel, without view of the foresters;
(**iii**) the right to have unlawed dogs in Caldy.
Challenge: William Wakebridge asserted that all the abbot's claims were unfounded.
Outcome: Issue sent to jury
Verdict: Jury found in the abbot's favour with regard to all his claims, except for digging peat in Thornton Hough.
(20 August 1358).

2.10. 2.17 and **2.48**
Claimant: John Blound. (He failed to appear at the adjourned hearing, **2.10**, on 26 February 1358 and repledged and extended his claim on the pledge of William Braas.)
Property: Land in his manor of Little Neston (**2.10** and **2.48**) and in the township of Little Neston (**2.17**)
Claims: (**i**) the rights expressed in Ranulf III's charter, when the property was in the hands of his predessor, Hugh de Coroune;
(**ii**) the right to dig peat;
(**iii**) the right to cut turves, gorse, fern and heather, for fuel, without view of the foresters;
(**iv**) the right to have mast without pannage and common of pasture;
(**v**) the right to keep unlawed dogs.
Challenge: William Wakebridge required him to define housebote and haybote, which Blound did. In **2.17** William Wakebridge denied the claim to the right dig peat in the township of Little Neston. Blound could not counter this, so this claim fell. William Wakebridge also asserted that Blound's other claims were not well founded.
Outcome: Issue sent to jury.
Verdict: In **2.17** membrane 12d, which records this case, is damaged. The record shows that Blound was granted the rights which he claimed under the charters. The incomplete record presumably shows that he was refused his claim to dig peat and to take estovers (by prescription and continuous user). However in **2.48**, when he repledged his claim for half a mark on the pledge of William Braas, the jury found in Blound's favour with regard to these other claims, including the right to dig peat in his manor of Little Neston.
(20 August, 1358).

2.11, 2.12, 2.35, 2.43, 2.49, 2.53, and **2.54**

Claimant: William Stanley[11]

Property: The bailiwick of the forest of Wirral

Claim: Stanley's claims (apart from **2.34** where he claimed estovers for all his free tenements within the forest, but failed to appear) were all attempts to establish his right to the forestership of the Wirral forest and the profits attaching to it.

In **2.11** he claimed all the appurtenances of the bailiwick of the forest, together with a specific sum of money or food and lodgings in puture from each of the townships; escapes, dead venison and pelf. The case was adjourned to 26 February 1358. He failed to appear and he repledged the claim on the pledge of John de Lasselles.

The claims were repeated in **2.12** changing only the puture claim from 'the township of ...' to the 'resident or tenant of lodgings in...'; and substituting, for the sum of money, 'puture of food and lodgings'. The case was adjourned to 20 August 1358, but again he failed to appear. **2.43** records a further non-appearance. In **2.49** he repeated his other claims, but also restated the puture claims as either money or food and lodgings. He went on to prove his inheritance rights from Philip de Baumville, his wife's ancestor and a previous forester. After a further adjournment to 29 April, on 17 June 1360 he was allowed to change the amount of escape money to be charged from '4d.' to 'reasonable compensation...', on payment of a fine half a mark on the pledge of William Gregory. There were five more adjournments, on 23 September and 18 October 1359 and 10 January, 10 April and 29 May 1360. The further hearing on 16 October 1360 was told that William was dead. His son, William, then repeated the claim in **2.53**, amending it further in **2.54** to limit responsibility for paying puture to 'each tenant who holds three selions of hide land.'.

Challenge: William Wakebridge put up different objections each time Stanley appeared. In **2.49** he questioned Stanley's claim that he should be the one who 'by his will alone' assessed the fine to be paid for escapes, instead of relying on the 'prudence of twelve good and law-worthy men'. After the death of the elder William, William Wakebridge responded to the claim in **2.53** by objecting that the claim did not specify the exact amount of money to be paid in puture by the tenants of the townships. The younger Stanley's final presentation of his claim (in **2.54**) was countered by William Wakebridge when he reminded the court that Stanley's father made no mention of puture in the 1347 eyre, although his other claims included appointing six under-foresters and hunting with greyhounds.

Outcome: 'William cannot deny this.'

Verdict: The judgment of the court is that the claim is denied.

11 A full translation of the text of the judgments concerning Stanley in the 1347 eyre and a summary of the judgments reached in the 1357 eyre can be found in the *Black Prince's Register* volume iii, pp. 429–33. This concludes with the restitution of Stanley's forestership.

2.13

Claimant: John de Wetefeld, parson of Bebington.

Property: Township of Bebington, as pertained to his rectory and as enjoyed by all his predecessors.

Claims: (**i**) the right to dig peat;
(**ii**) the right to cut turves, gorse, fern and heather, for fuel, without view of the foresters;
(**iii**) the right to have mast;
(**iv**) the right to keep unlawed dogs;
(**v**) the right to housebote and haybote.

Challenge: William Wakebridge challenged all the claims.

Outcome: Issue sent to jury.

Verdict: Jury found in John's favour with regard to all his claims.
(20 August, 1358).

2.18 and **2.50**

Claimant: Abbot of Chester, represented by his attorney Richard de Manlegh. **2.50** is the same claim as **2.18**, but the outcome in **2.50** is that 'He did not appear'. Presumably the record in **2.18** refers to a hearing later than **2.50**.

Property: Land in all his manors in Wirral.

Claims: (**i**) the rights expressed in Ranulf III's charter, when the property was in the hands of his predecessor, Hugh;
(**ii**) the right to dig peat;
(**iii**) the right to cut turves, gorse, fern and heather, for fuel, without view of the foresters;
(**iv**) the right to hunt the fox and hare with greyhounds, in accordance with the grant of the lord Edward in 1285 (Charter **7.22**);
(**v**) the right to have mast in the forest at the time of mast and pasture for his demesne pigs all year in accordance with the grant of Ranulf III *c*.1208–1211 (Charter **7.24**)
(**vi**) the right to keep unlawed dogs;
(**vii**) the right to take 'outedracht' (meaning uncertain) in the forest;
(**ix**) the right to bring wastes and heaths into cultivation, to build houses and to make marl pits;

Challenge: William Wakebridge referred to previous decisions of this court not to allow the digging of marl pits 'in which the beasts have often drowned' and stated that erecting buildings and cultivating the waste were contrary to the assize of the forest. 'The abbot cannot deny this' and the court dismisses this claim.

Outcome: The other claims were referred to a jury.

Verdict: All the rest of the abbot's claims, except for the digging of peat, were awarded by the jury.
(20 August 1358)

2.20 and **2.34**

Claimant: Warin Trussell.

Property: His land in Willaston.

Claim: The right to assart, enclose and cultivate his land, in accordance with a charter granted to his mother, Maud, and his stepfather, Oliver de Bordeaux, by the prince of Wales (at the request of his father, Edward II) on 20 January, 1318 and confirmed by the Black Prince's letters patent on 8 April 1340 (**7.16**). The claim was refused in **2.20** (where a reference was made to an earlier judgement of the court, 'in prima sessione,' when 'Warin was not to take anything from his claim'.) He repledged and extended his claim, for 10s. 0d. In **2.34** he again produced the 1318 charter and the Black Prince's confirmation of it in 1340, in which the BP also granted Warin the rights he now claimed.

Challenge: William Wakebridge asked for the claim to be rejected 'because the prince of Wales was under age' when he sealed the charter and the document could therefore have 'no legal validity'.

Outcome: The issue was sent to a jury, but Warin did not appear.

Verdict: The claim was denied.
(20 August, 1358)

2.21, 2.35, 2.36, 2.37 and 2.44

Claimants: William de Bechinton,William Stanley, John Domville, senior, Philip de Raby and John Lassels.

Property: Land in Wirral, (Bechinton, Stanley, Raby and Lassels) and in Brimstage (Domville).

Claims: Estovers for their free tenements.

Outcome: All failed to appear.

2.22 and **2.57**

Claimant: William Trussell of Acton.

Property: His manor of Blacon.

Claims: The right to enclose, assart and cultivate all the wastes in his manor of Blacon.

He did not appear at **2.22** and was repledged for half a mark to **2.57**, by the pledge of John Hughcop. He also paid the half mark to amend his claim to include 'to himself and the heirs of his body'. He quoted the charter made in Chester on 20 January 1318, (confirmed by the Black Prince at Byfleet on 8 April 1340) (**7.16**) in favour of his mother, Maud, and his stepfather, Oliver de Bordeaux, by the then prince of Wales (at the request of his father, Edward II), which he confirmed, as Edward III, on 12 January 1329 (**7.31**). He also claimed that there was an agreement in the county court in Chester between Maud and another, recognising that the manor belonged to Maud. However, the record has been left blank; the name of the deforciant was not inserted.

Challenge: William Wakebridge's case is a little obscure. He referred to **2.22** and the present extension to include 'to have to himself and the heirs of his body' and 'seeks judgement concerning the variation'. Trussell lost the case 'because he cannot deny this'.

Outcome: The court decided, without reference to a jury, that the claim was to be refused.

Verdict: The claim was refused.

2.23

Claimant: William de Bechynton. He failed to appear at the first hearing on 25 September 1357 and repledged and extended his claim (half a mark), on the pledge of Thomas de Hokenhull.

Property: Land in his manors of Wallasey and Storeton.

Claims: (**i**) the rights expressed in Ranulf III's charter when the property was in the hands of his predecessor, Simon de Bechynton;
(**ii**) the right to dig peat;
(**iii**) the right to cut turves, gorse, fern and heather, for fuel, without view of the foresters;
(**iv**) the right to keep unlawed dogs;

Challenge: William Wakebridge stated that none of the claims was well founded.

Outcome: Issue sent to jury.

Verdict: Jury found in William's favour with regard to all his claims.
(20 August, 1358*)*.

2.24

Claimant: David de Egerton. He repledged and extended his claim, on the pledge of Thomas de Capenhurst.

Property: Land in his manor of Ledsham.

Claims: (**i**) the rights expressed in Ranulf III's charter when the property was in the hands of his predecessor, Peter de Wynfeld;
(**ii**) the right to cut turves, gorse, fern and heather, for fuel, without view of the foresters;
(**iii**) the right to keep unlawed dogs.

Challenge: William Wakebridge denied that the claims were well founded.

Outcome: Issue sent to jury.

Verdict: Jury found in David's favour with regard to all his claims.
(20 August, 1358*)*.

2.26

Claimant: Ranulf le Bruyn and Cecily, his wife.

Property: Lands in their manors of Poulton Lancelyn, Lower Bebington and Little Meols.

Claims: (**i**) the rights expressed in Ranulf III's charter when the property was in the hands of their predecessor, William Lancelyn;
(**ii**) the right to dig peat;

(**iii**) the right to cut turves, gorse, fern and heather, for fuel, without view of the foresters;
(**iv**) the right to keep unlawed dogs;

Challenge: William Wakebridge challenged all the claims and the claim to dig peat in Lower Bebington and Poulton was rejected.
Outcome: Issue sent to jury.
Verdict: Jury found in their favour with regard to all their other claims. (20 August, 1358).

2.27
Claimant: Philip de Raby.
Property: Lands in his manor of Raby.
Claims: (**i**) the rights expressed in Ranulf III's charter when the property was in the hands of his predecessor, Hugh de Raby;
(**ii**) the right to dig peat;
(**iii**) the right to cut turves, gorse, fern and heather, for fuel, without view of the foresters;
(**iv**) the right to keep unlawed dogs;
Challenge: William Wakebridge challenged all the claims.
Outcome: Issue sent to jury.
Verdict: Jury found in Philip's favour with regard to all his claims. (20 August, 1358).

2.28
Claimant: Joan, lady of Bebington. She paid half a mark, on the pledge of Henry de Hoton, for her claim to be repledged and extended.
Property: Land in her manor of Bebington.
Claims: (**i**) the rights expressed in Ranulf III's charter, when the property was in the hands of her predecessor, Robert de Bebington;
(**ii**) the right to dig peat;
(**iii**) the right to cut turves, gorse, fern and heather for fuel, without view of the foresters;
(**iv**) the right to keep unlawed dogs.
Challenge: William Wakebridge asserted that Joan's claims were not well founded.
Outcome: Issue sent to jury.
Verdict: Jury found in Joan's favour with regard to all her claims. (20 August, 1358).

2.29
Claimant: John Lasseles. He paid half a mark, on the pledge of Henry de Hoton, for his claim to be repledged and extended.
Property: Land in his manors of Poulton cum Seacombe, Liscard and Newton.
Claims: (**i**) the rights expressed in Ranulf III's charter, when the property was in the hands of his predecessor, Hugh de Coroune;

(**ii**) the right to dig peat;
(**iii**) the right to cut turves, gorse, fern and heather, for fuel, without view of the foresters;
(**iv**) the right to keep unlawed dogs.

Challenge: William Wakebridge asserted that John's claims were not well founded.
Outcome: Issue sent to jury.
Verdict: Jury found in John's favour with regard to all his claims.
(20 August, 1358).

2.30

Claimant: Henry de Hoton. He paid half a mark, on the pledge of Robert de Berneston, for his claim to be repledged and extended.
Property: Land in his manors of Hooton, Tranmere and Roweshotwyk (Woodbank)
Claims: (**i**) the rights expressed in Ranulf III's charter, when the property was in the hands of his predecessor, Robert de Hoton;
(**ii**) the right to dig peat;
(**iii**) the right to cut turves, gorse, fern and heather, for fuel, without view of the foresters
(**iv**) the right to keep unlawed dogs;
(**v**) the right to have mast in Hooton.
Challenge: William Wakebridge asserted that Henry's claims were not well founded.
Outcome: Issue sent to jury.
Verdict: The verdict has been lost on the damaged membrane.
(20 August, 1358).

2.31

Claimant: Robert de Poole. He paid half a mark for his claim to be repledged and extended.
Property: Land in his manors of Pool, Ashfield, Liscard and Capenhurst.
Claims: (**i**) the rights expressed in Ranulf III's charter, when the property was in the hands of his predecessor, Reginald de Pulle;
(**ii**) the right to dig peat;
(**iii**) the right to cut turves, gorse, fern and heather, for fuel, without view of the foresters;
(**iv**) the right to keep unlawed dogs.
Challenge: William Wakebridge asserted that Robert's claims were not well founded.
Outcome: Issue sent to jury.
Verdict: All claims were granted except for Robert's claim to dig peat.
(20 August, 1358).

2.32

Claimant: Robert de Berneston. He paid half a mark for his claim to be repledged and extended, by the pledge of Henry de Hoton.

Property: Land in his manor of Barnston.

Claims: (**i**) the rights expressed in Ranulf III's charter, when the property was in the hands of his predecessor, Hugh de Berneston;
(**ii**) the right to dig peat;
(**iii**) the right to cut turves, gorse, fern and heather, for fuel, without view of the foresters;
(**iv**) the right to keep unlawed dogs;
(**v**) the right to have pannage for all his pigs.

Challenge: William Wakebridge asserted that Robert's claims were not well founded.

Outcome: Issue sent to jury.

Verdict: All claims were granted except for Robert's claim to dig peat.
(20 August, 1358).

2.33 (See also **2.3** and **2.4**)

Claimant: The prior of Birkenhead.

Property: His manors of Birkenhead, Claughton, Wooton and Moreton.

Claims: (**i**) the right to operate a ferry across the Mersey to Liverpool and to provide lodgings for passengers, based on the charter of Edward II, 1318 (**7.25** and **7.26**);
(**ii**) the right to have his dogs unlawed in his manors in Wirral.

Challenge: William Wakebridge asked the prior to set out the tariffs for ferry passengers, and said they were unreasonable. He also said that the ferry caused harm to the beasts and was contrary to the assize of the forest.

Outcome: The issue was sent to a jury on 30 August 1358, but the sheriff 'did not return a panel.' He was therefore ordered to 'make 24 men come on 29 April 1359', when the case was adjourned until 17 June 1359.

Verdict: Both claims were granted.
(17 June 1359)

2.38

Claimant: Bishop of Coventry and Lichfield, represented by Simon Gentyl, his attorney. He claimed complete freedom from all forest obligations on all his holdings.

Property: His manor of Burton in Wirral.

Claim: The right to be 'free and quit of all matters concernng the forest, of pleas of the forest, of wastes which have been assarted and of regards of the forest and of all pleas and suits', based on Edward I's inspeximus in 1318 of three undated charters of Henry II and two of Richard I, both of 1189. (**7.34**)

Challenge: William Wakebridge denied that the bishop and his predecessors had held the rights continuously as the bishop claimed.
Outcome: The issue was sent to a jury.
Verdict: The claim was granted.
(20 August, 1358)

2.39
Claimant: Robert Starkey of Tranmere. He paid 3s. 4d. for his claim to be repledged, by the pledge of Thomas de Capenhurst.
Property: Land in his manor of Tranmere.
Claims: (**i**) the rights expressed in Ranulf III's charter, when the property was in the hands of his predecessor, Ranulf Starkey;
(**ii**) the right to dig peat;
(**iii**) the right to cut turves, gorse, fern and heather, for fuel, without view of the foresters;
(**iv**) the right to keep unlawed dogs;
(**v**) the right to have pannage for all his pigs.
Challenge: William Wakebridge asserted that Robert's claims were not well founded.
Outcome: Issue sent to jury.
Verdict: All claims were granted, except for Robert's claim to dig peat.
(20 August, 1358).

2.40
Claimant: Thomas de Hokenhull. He paid half a mark for his claim to be repledged, by the pledge of William de Bechynton.
Property: All his land in the forest of Wirral.
Claims: (**i**) the rights expressed in Ranulf III's charter, when the property was in the hands of his predecessor, Stephen de Hokenhull;
(**ii**) the right to cut turves, gorse, fern and heather, for fuel, without view of the foresters;
(**iii**) the right to keep unlawed dogs.
Challenge: William Wakebridge asserted that Thomas's claims were not well founded.
Outcome: Issue sent to jury.
Verdict: All Thomas's claims were granted.
(20 August, 1358).

2.41
Claimant: Richard, cousin and heir of David de Bunbury. He paid half a mark for his claim to be repledged, by the pledge of William de Spurstowe.
Property: Land in Little Stanney.
Claims: (**i**) the rights expressed in Ranulf III's charter, when the property was in the hands of his predecessor, Gilbert de Bunbury;

(**ii**) the right to dig peat;
(**iii**) the right to cut turves, gorse, fern and heather, for fuel, without view of the foresters;
(**iv**) the right to keep unlawed dogs.

Challenge: William Wakebridge asserted that John's claims were not well founded.
Outcome: Issue sent to jury.
Verdict: Richard was clearly under age and incapable of maintaining his claim. He must therefore await the age of his majority.
(20 August, 1358).

2.45
Claimant: Duke of Lancaster, represented by his attorney, William Criour.
Property: Land in his manors of Bidston, Saughall Massie and Moreton, which he held for the term of his life, demised by Roger Lestraunge of Knockin and Master Richard de Longmorle, parson of Ness.
Claims: (**i**) the rights expressed in Ranulf III's charter, when the property was in the hands of Hamo de Mascy, whose estate the duke and Roger and Richard now have;
(**ii**) the right to dig peat in Bidston, Saughall Massie and Moreton;
(**iii**) the right to cut turves, gorse, fern and heather, for fuel, without view of the foresters;
(**iv**) the right to keep unlawed dogs;
(**v**) the right to have pasture for all his livestock except goats, each year and at all times of the year, except for pigs in the fence month.

(Roger and Richard were summoned to testify on 6 September 1358, but did not appear; the duke's attorney was allowed to proceed without their evidence.)

Challenge: William Wakebridge asserted that the duke's claims were not well founded.
Outcome: Issue sent to jury.
Verdict: All claims were granted except for the duke's claims to dig peat (for which there was fine of ten marks).
(10 June 1359, after an adjournment from 29 April 1359)

2.46
Claimant: Richard del Hogh of Thornton and Ellen, his wife. The record also refers to part of their claim thus: 'And for increasing their claim for having dogs unlawed they give the lord 3s. 4d. by the pledge of John de Lassels.' (Richard made a separate claim in **2.19** in his own name for 'a messuage and three bovates of land in Thornton'. It was granted in full except for the digging of peat.)
Property: Lands in their manor of Thornton Hough.

Claims: (**i**) the rights expressed in Ranulf III's charter when the property was in the hands of their predecessor, Matthew de Thornton;
(**ii**) the right to dig peat;
(**iii**) the right to cut turves, gorse, fern and heather, for fuel, without view of the foresters;
(**iv**) the right to keep unlawed dogs.

Challenge: William Wakebridge required him to define housebote and haybote, which he did. William Wakebridge challenged all the claims.

Outcome: Issue sent to jury.

Verdict: Jury found in their favour with regard to all their claims.
(20 August, 1358).

2.51

Claimant: Thomas, son of Richard de Morton. He paid half a mark for his claim to be repledged, by the pledge of William Gregory.

Property: Land in his manor of Moreton.

Claims: (**i**) the rights expressed in Ranulf III's charter, when the property was in the hands of his predecessor, Richard de Morton;
(**ii**) the right to dig peat;
(**iii**) the right to cut turves, gorse, fern and heather, for fuel, without view of the foresters;
(**iv**) the right to have unlawed dogs.

Challenge: William Wakebridge asserted that Thomas's claims were not well founded.

Outcome: Issue sent to jury.

Verdict: Jury found in Thomas's favour with regard to all his claims after an adjourned hearing (on 23 September 1359).
(26 February 1361).

2.52

Claimant: William Gregory. He paid half a mark for his claim to be repledged, by the pledge of Thomas, son of Richard de Morton.

Property: Land in his manor of Moreton.

Claims: (**i**) the rights expressed in Ranulf III's charter, when the property was in the hands of his predecessor, Alan de Morton;
(**ii**) the right to dig peat;
(**iii**) the right to cut turves, gorse, fern and heather, for fuel, without view of the foresters;
(**iv**) the right to have unlawed dogs.

Challenge: William Wakebridge asserted that William's claims were not well founded.

Outcome: Issue sent to jury.

Verdict: Jury found in William's favour with regard to all his claims.
(26 February 1361).

2.55 and **2.56**

Claimant: William de Monte Acuto, earl of Salisbury. He paid half a mark for his claim to be repledged, by the pledge of Henry de Chorleton.

Property: Land in his manor of Great Neston and in Leighton.

Claims: (**i**) the rights expressed in Ranulf III's charter, when the property was in the hands of his predecessor, Robert de Monte Alto;
(**ii**) the right to cut turves, gorse, fern and heather, for fuel, without view of the foresters;
(**iii**) the right to have unlawed dogs.

Challenge: William Wakebridge referred to the 1347 eyre under Thomas de Ferrers, stating that neither then nor in other times in the past had the earl or his predecessors produced such claims in court.

Outcome: The court decided without reference to a jury.

Verdict: The court found that none of William's claims were valid.
The claim was reintroduced in **2.56**. when after seven further adjournments a jury found in the earl's favour on all counts.
(26 February 1361).

2.58

Claimant: John Launcelyn. He paid half a mark for his claim to be repledged, by the pledge of William Gregory, to include Margery, his wife, and Andrew del Brom

Property: Land in his manor of Moreton.

Claims: (**i**) the rights expressed in Ranulf III's charter, when the property was in the hands of his predecessoror, Hugh del Brom;
(**ii**) the right to dig peat;
(**iii**) the right to cut turves, gorse, fern and heather, for fuel, without view of the foresters;
(**iv**) the right to have unlawed dogs.

Outcome: John was given a day (23 September 1359), but he failed to appear. (He joined his wife, Margery, and Andrew del Brom in with his claim as appears in **2.59**, when all these claims were granted.)
(26 September 1359).

2.59

Claimant: John Launcelyn, his wife, Margery, and Andrew del Brom. They paid half a mark for their claim to be repledged, by the pledge of William Gregory.

Property: Land in their manor of Moreton.

Claims: (**i**) the rights expressed in Ranulf III's charter, when the property was in the hands of Margery's predecessor, Hugh del Brom;
(**ii**) the right to dig peat;
(**iii**) the right to cut turves, gorse, fern and heather, for fuel, without view of the foresters;

(**iv**) the right to have unlawed dogs.

Challenge: William Wakebridge asserted that all their claims were unfounded.

Outcome: Issue sent to jury.

Verdict: Jury found in their favour with regard to all their claims. (26 February 1361).

2.60

Claimant: Henry Barnard of Tranmere. He paid half a mark for his claim to be repledged, by the pledge of Philip de Raby.

Property: His free holding in the township of Tranmere (two messuages and 23 acres of land in the township).

Claims: estovers, housebote and haybote from the heaths and wastes of Tranmere.

Challenge: William Wakebridge asserted that his claim was unfounded.

Outcome: Issue sent to jury.

Verdict: Jury found in favour of Henry. (26 February 1361).

ENROLLED CHARTERS

The charters (**7.1–7.34/7.35**) membranes 47 to 52

34 documents are copied into membranes 47 to 52. They are designated as 'charters' in the heading at the beginning of m. 47, 'Transcripta cartarum', but they include also licences, letters patent, a final concord, inspeximuses and confirmations of charters.

Seven of the 34 charters have been transcribed in *Barraclough*; fourteen are fully calendared in the Calendars of Chancery or Cheshire Recognizance Rolls at the references given; thirteen are not known to have been transcribed or translated elsewhere and they are therefore set out in full text and translation.[1] Where other versions of the charters are known to exist their locations are noted.

22 of the 34 relate to Wirral claims, but most of these also have relevance to either Delamere or Macclesfield forests or both. Edward I's confirmation in 1300 of Ranulf III's charter (**7.9**) is referred to 27 times, but is not in fact enrolled. Enrolled are the confirmation he issued on 27 August 1265 before he became king (**7.5**) and another confirmation by the Black Prince as earl of Chester on 10 September 1353 (**7.14**). Although not inscribed in the roll of charters in CHES 33/6, the confirmation issued on 30 March 1300 by Edward I is included for reference at the end of the list as **7.35**.

m. 47

Charter **7.1** Edward I to Ranulf de Merton, dated at Caernarfon 22 October 1284
Calendared at *C.P.R.*, *1281–1292* p. 137

The king grants to Ranulf de Merton housebote and haybote in the forest of Delamere (Mara) in exchange for similar in Bradeford wood, which Edward transfers to the abbot of Vale Royal.

C 66/103 m. 2	Chancery copy
CHES 33/4 m. 32	1347 Chester copy
DL 39/1/19	1347 Earl of Lancaster's copy

1 Texts and translations of all the documents will be posted on the websites of the Ranulf Higden Society and the Record Society of Lancashire and Cheshire.

Charter **7.2** Ranulf de Merton to Walter, abbot of Vale Royal, no date, but see **7.3**. (The abbot's reciprocal charter to Ranulf is transcribed in *Ormerod* ii p. 97)

Ranulf, by a licence granted by the earl of Chester, exchanges his manor of Marton for the manors of Gayton and Lach Dennis with the abbot and convent of Vale Royal.

<Carta Abbatis de Valle Regali>
Sciant presentes et futuri quod ego Ranulphus de Merton dedi concessi et hac presenti carta mea confirmavi fratri Waltero abbati de Valle Regali et eiusdem loci conventui manerium meum de Merton cum pertinenciis ut in dominicis terris edificiis redditibus pratis pascuis pasturis boscis cum rationabilibus estoveriis ad predictum manerium de Merton spectantibus vastis aquis stagnis molendinis piscariis consuetudinibus villanis et eorum sequelorum homagiis releviis wardis escaetis cum reversione tenementorum que tenentur in dotem vel aliter ad terminum vite vel per feodum talliatum infra manerium predictum herietis gersumiis merchetis tallagiis et omnibus aliis ad predictum manerium quoquomodo spectantibus sine ullo retenemento; in escambium pro maneriis de Gayton in Wyrhale et de Lach super Ruddeheth cum pertinenciis ex licentia et voluntate domini Edwardi illustris regis Angl' primogeniti principis Wall' et comitis Cestr' per eosdem abbatem et conventum collatum et michi et heredibus meis inperpetuum possidendis prout in carta ipsorum abbatis et conventus michi inde confecta plenius continetur habendum et tenendum predictum manerium de Merton ex licencia et voluntate dicti domini Edwardi comitis Cestr' deafforestatum cum omnibus pertinenciis et iuribus suis ut predictum est predictis abbati et conventui et eorum successoribus et ecclesie sue Beate Marie de Valle Regali in liberam puram et perpetuam elemosinam ex concessione et voluntate predicti domini Edwardi principis Wall' et comitis Cestr' de eodem domino Edwardo capitali domini feodi illius et heredibus suis regibus Angl' inperpetuum adeo libere et quiete et pacifice cum omnibus libertatibus et liberis consuetudinibus sicut idem abbas et conventus et predecessores sui predicta maneria de Gayton et Lach per cartam domini regis Edwardi filii regis Henrici ante istud escambium factum tenuerunt.

Et ego prefatus Ranulphus et heredes mei predictum manerium de Merton cum pertinenciis suis quibuscumque ut predictum est prefatis abbati et conventui et eorum successoribus et ecclesie sue Beate Marie predicte contra omnes gentes warantizabimus et defendemus inperpetuum. In cuius rei testimonium huic carte sigillum meum apposui. Hiis testibus dominis Willelmo Trussell, tunc justiciario Cestr', Hamone de Mascy, Radulpho de Vernun, Hugone de Venables, Ricardo de Mascy, Johanne de Orreby, Petro de Dutton milite, Roberto de Brescy, tunc vicecomite Cestris', Johanne de Wetenhale, Johanne de Legh, Roberto de Wynynton et aliis.

<Charter of the abbot of Vale Royal>
Let all men present and future know that I, Ranulf de Merton, have given, granted and by this my present charter confirmed to brother Walter, abbot of Vale Royal, and to the convent in the same place, my manor of Marton with its appurtenances as in demesne lands, buildings, rents, meadows, pasture, pasturage, woods with reasonable

estovers belonging to the aforesaid manor of Marton, with the wastes, waters, ponds, mills, fisheries, customary service of our villeins and their families, homages, reliefs, wards, escheats with reversion of tenures, which are held by dowry or otherwise, for the term of life or by fee tail within the aforesaid manor, with heriots, fines, merchets, tallage and all other things belonging to the aforesaid manor in any way without any reservation, in exchange which is made by the same abbot and convent (by the licence and will of the lord Edward the prince of Wales and earl of Chester, first-born son of the illustrious king of England) for the manors of Gayton in Wirral and of Lach Dennis with appurtenances to be held both to me and to my heirs for ever just as is more fully contained in the charter of the abbot and convent now granted to me, to have and to hold to the said abbey and convent and their successors and their church of the Blessed Mary of Vale Royal the aforesaid manor of Marton, which has been disafforested by the licence and will of the said lord Edward earl of Chester, with all its appurtenances and rights as is aforesaid, in free, pure and perpetual alms by the grant and will of the aforesaid lord Edward prince of Wales and earl of Chester from the same lord Edward the chief lord of that fee and from his heirs, the kings of England for ever, thus to hold freely quietly and peacefully with all liberties and free customs just as the same abbot and convent and their predecessors held the aforesaid manors of Gayton and Lach Dennis by the charter of the lord king Edward son of king Henry before this exchange was made.

And I, Ranulf, and my heirs will warrant and defend for ever against all men the said manor of Marton with whatsoever appurtenances as is aforesaid to the abbot and convent and their successors and their said church of the Blessed Mary. In witness whereof I have affixed my seal to this charter. These being witnesses: the lords William Trussell, then justiciar of Chester, Hamo de Mascy, Ralph de Vernon, Hugh de Venables, Richard de Mascy, John de Orreby, Peter de Dutton knight, Robert de Brescy, then sheriff of Cheshire, John de Wetenhale, John de Legh, Robert de Wynynton and others.

Charter **7.3** The prince of Wales to Ranulf de Merton, dated at Winchester 24 March 1305

The prince gives Ranulf de Merton a licence, as required by the statute of mortmain, to exchange his manor of Marton with the manors of Gayton and Lach Dennis held by the abbot and convent of Vale Royal.
C 53/99 m. 16 (33) 6 Ed II 1 Nov 1312 Winton Inspeximus

<Carta abbatis de Valle Regali>
Edwardus illustris regis Angl' filius princeps Wall' comes Cestr' Pontivi et Montistrollu omnibus ad quos presentes littere pervenerint salutem.

Cum in statuto de terris et tenementis ad manum mortuam non ponendis edito contineatur quod non licet viris religiosis seu aliis ingredi feodum alicuius ita quod ad manum mortuam deveniat sine licencia domini nostri regis et capitalis domini de quo res illa inmediate tenetur et ad [nos] [licenciam huiusmodi] de terris et tenementis ad manum mortuam ponendis per totum comitatum Cestr' dare pertineat cum voluerimus sicut ad ipsum dominum regem dare pertinet alibi in regno suo et in inquisitione quam per dilectum et fidelem Willelmum Trussell justiciarium comitatus predicti nuper fieri fecimus compertum sit quod non [est] ad dampnum vel preiudicium nostrum aut aliorum si concedamus Ranulpho de Mertone quod manerium suum de Mertone cum pertinenciis in comitatu predicto quod [est] in foresta nostra de la Mare quod quidem tenetur de nobis in capite dare possit et assignare dilectis nobis in Christo abbati et conventui de Valle Regali habendum et tenendum eisdem abbati et conventui et eorum successoribus in liberam puram et perpetuam elemosinam ac etiam deafforestatum inperpetuum in escambium pro manerio de Gayton cum pertinenciis in foresta de Wyrhale in eodem comitatu quod iidem abbas et conventus tenent deafforestatum et pro manerio de Lach Dennise in Ruddeheth cum pertinenciis in eodem comitatu que quidem maneria iidem abbas et conventus tenent de nobis in capite in puram et perpetuam elemosinam de quibus quidem maneriis prefatum Ranulphum de nostra licencia feoffare intendunt ut accepimus habendum et tenendum eidem Ranulpho et heredibus suis de nobis et heredibus nostris predicta maneria de Gaytone et de Lach Dennise cum pertinenciis per eadem servicia per que idem Ranulphus predictum manerium de Merton de nobis tenuit

nos eisdem abbati et conventui et Ranulpho volentes gratiam in hac parte facere specialem concessimus eidem Ranulpho et licenciam dedimus pro nobis et heredibus nostris quantum in nobis est quod ipse predictum manerium de Mertone cum pertinenciis dare possit et assignare predictis abbati et conventui habendum et tenendum eisdem abbati et conventui et eorum successoribus in perpetuum in liberam puram et perpetuam elemosinam ac etiam deafforestatum de nobis et heredibus nostris regibus Angl' et cum omnibus aliis libertatibus et liberis consuetudinibus que in predictis maneriis de Gayton et Lach Dennise habere consuerunt et secundum quod melius et liberius in carta domini Edwardi regis patris nostri eisdem facta continetur in escambium pro eisdem maneriis de Gayton et Lach Dennise

et similiter quod ipsi abbas et conventus feoffare possint prefatum Ranulphum de predictis maneriis de Gayton et Lach Dennise habendum et tenendum sibi et heredibus suis de nobis et heredibus nostris regibus Angl' in capite per omnia illa servicia et consuetudines per que predictum manerium de Mertone tenere debuit et consuevit ita quod loco manerii de Mertone extunc deafforestati predictum manerium de Gayton inperpetuum remaneat afforestatum et oneratum erga nos et alios quoscumque de omnimodis condicionibus de quibus predictum manerium de Mertone prius fuit oneratum

et eisdem abbati et conventui quod ipsi predictum manerium de Merton cum pertinenciis a prefato Ranulpho recipere possint et tenere sibi et successoribus suis sicut dictum est tenore presentium similiter licenciam dedimus specialem nolentes quod predictus Ranulphus et heredes sui seu prefati abbas et conventus vel successores sui ratione statuti predicti seu escambii predicti per nos vel heredes nostros justiciarios escaetores vicecomites vel alios ballivos seu ministros quoscumque occasionentur molestentur in aliquo seu graventur. In cuius rei testimonium sigillum nostrum presentibus est appensum.

Dat' apud Kenintone xxiiij die Martii anno regni domni regis patris nostri tricesimo tercio.

<Charter of the abbot of Vale Royal>
Edward, son of the illustrious king of England, prince of Wales, earl of Chester, count of Ponthieu and Montreuil, to all to whom these present letters will come, greeting.

Since it is included in the published statute, concerning lands and holdings not being placed in mortmain, that men of religion or others are not allowed to enter anyone's fee in such a way that it might become mortmain, without the permission of our lord the king and of the chief lord of whom it is held immediately, and since it belongs to us to give a licence of this kind throughout the whole county of Cheshire concerning lands and holdings being placed in mortmain whenever we wish, just as it belongs to the lord king himself elsewhere in his kingdom; and since, in the inquisition which we recently caused to be held by our beloved and faithful William Trussell, justiciar of the said county, it was found that it would not be harmful or prejudicial to us or to others if we were to grant to Ranulf de Merton that he himself should be able to give and assign his manor of Marton with appurtenances in the said county, which is in our forest of Delamere, which is held of us in chief, to our beloved in Christ, the abbot and convent of Vale Royal, to have and to hold to the abbot and convent and their successors in free, pure and perpetual alms, and also disafforested for ever, in exchange for the manor of Gayton with appurtenances in the forest of Wirral in the same county which the same abbot and convent hold disafforested; and in exchange for the manor of Lach Dennis with appurtenances in the same county, which manors the abbot and convent hold of us in chief in pure and perpetual alms, with which manors they intend to enfeoff Ranulf in accordance with our permission as we have accepted, to have and to hold to the same Ranulf and his heirs, of us and our heirs, the manors of Gayton and Lach Dennis with appurtenances by the same services by which the same Ranulf held the manor of Marton of us, we, being willing to grant a special favour in this matter to the same abbot and convent, and to Ranulf, have granted and given permission to the same Ranulf, on behalf of ourselves and our heirs, as far as we have the power, that he himself should be able to give and assign the manor of Marton with appurtenances to the abbot and convent, to have and to hold to the same abbot and convent and their successors, in free, pure and perpetual alms, and also disafforested, of us and our heirs the kings of England, and with all liberties and free customs which they were accustomed to have in the manors of Lach Dennis and Gayton, and according to that which is better or more freely contained in the charter of Edward the king our father, made for the same, in exchange for the same manors of Gayton and Lach Dennis and likewise that the abbot and convent themselves should be able to enfeoff Ranulf with the manors of Gayton and Lach

Dennis to have and to hold to himself and his heirs, of us and our heirs the kings of England in chief, in return for all those services and customs in return for which he was obliged and accustomed to hold the manor of Marton so that in place of the manor of Marton, henceforth disafforested, the manor of Gayton should remain afforested for ever and burdened towards us and whoever else with the conditions of every kind with which the manor of Marton was previously burdened. And we have likewise given the present special permission to the same abbot and convent that they themselves should be able to receive the manor of Marton with appurtenances from Ranulf and to hold it to themselves and to hold it to their successors, as has been said by the tenor of the presents, being unwilling that Ranulf and his heirs or the abbot and convent or their successors, by reason of the aforesaid title or exchange, should be interfered with, molested or oppressed by us or our heirs, justices, escheators, or any other bailiffs or ministers whatsoever. In testimony of which our seal has been appended to these present letters.

Given at Kennington 24 March in the 33rd year of the reign of the lord king our father. (24 March 1305)

Charter **7.4** Edward I to his justiciar of Chester and the forest officers in the county, dated at Woodstock 7 February 1277.
Calendared at *C.P.R.*, *1272–1281* pp. 193–194.

The king instructs them not to disturb the abbey since its lands have been disafforested in Darnhall, Weaverham and Conwardesley. (The abbey moved to Vale Royal in 1281.)

C 66/96 m. 22	Chancery copy
CHES 33/4 m. 32d	1347 Chester copy
DL 39/1/19	1347 Earl of Lancaster's copy

Charter **7.5** The Lord Edward to the community of Cheshire, dated at Chester 27 August 1265
Calendared at *C.P.R.*, *1258–1266* pp. 499–501. See also Charter **7.35**.
J.R. Studd, ed. 'A catalogue of the acts of the Lord Edward, 1254–72, number 904' (University of Leeds Ph.D. thesis, 1971).

He confirms Ranulf III's liberties (see **7.9**) to the people of Cheshire and gives them some additional legal rights.

C 66/120 mm. 22–30	30 March 1300 Westminster Inspeximus
C 53/162 m. 11	14 November 1389 Inspeximus

These two inspeximuses confirm both Ranulf III's Great Charter (**7.9**) and this charter made by Edward before he became king.

Charter **7.6** Ranulf II to the abbey of Basingwerk, dated at Chester 1135–1140
Barraclough number 37.

He grants the manor of (Great) Caldy to the abbey of Basingwerk, with some small reservations.

Charter **7.7** Ranulf III to William de Vernon, dated 1221–1223
Barraclough number 408.

He grants the wood of Marple and Wybersley to William de Vernon for the service of finding a forester.

m. 47d

Charter **7.8** Edward III to Roger de Swynerton, dated at Nottingham 16 July 1334
Reference at *C.C.R., 1327–1341* p. 445 to Edward III's inspeximus, dated 25 May 1338, of this charter dated 16 July 1334.

The king grants to Roger de Swynerton and his heirs the manor of Great Barrow in Cheshire and of Rushton, Cornford, Alstonfield and Cauldon in Staffordshire with land and property to the value of £300 a year, forfeited by Hugh le Despenser, former earl of Winchester, which Roger had hitherto held for the term of his life. The grant is for good service and also to enable him to discharge his new duties as a banneret.

C 66/183 m. 1	Chancery copy
C 53/125 m. 18 25 May 1338	Inspeximus
CHES 33/4 m. 31d	(recorded here as *Carta Roberti de S'*) 1347 Chester copy
DL 39/1/19 m. 27	1347 Earl of Lancaster's copy

Cheshire Record Office DCH/G, 1 Dec 1356 Inspeximus

<Carta Rogeri de Swynerton>
Edwardus dei gratia rex Anglie dominus Hibernie et dux Aquit' omnibus ad quos presentes littere pervenerint salutem. Sciatis quod cum nos nuper pro bono servicio quod dilectus et fidelis noster Rogerus de Swynerton nobis inpenderat et extunc impenderet et ut ipse in statu baneretti de quo per preceptum nostrum oneratus extitit se posset melius continere concessissemus de assensu consilii nostri providere eidem de trescentis libratis terre et redditus per annum infra regnum nostrum ad vitam suam habendum et postmodum inter alia terras et tenementa que prefato Rogero eo pretextu concessimus ad vitam suam habendum concesserimus eidem Rogero omnia maneria terras et tenementa cum pertinentibus que fuerunt Hugonis le Despenser nuper comitis Wynton in comitatibus Staff' et Cestr' et que ratione forisfacture eiusdem Hugonis in manu nostra extiterunt habendum ad terminum

vite sue in partem satisfactionis trescentarum libratarum terre et redditus predictarum ac iam prefatus Rogerus nobis supplicaverit ut ei concedere velimus quod ipse habere possit et tenere sibi et heredibus suis manerium de Magna Barwe cum pertinentibus in dicto[2] comitatu Cestr' ac omnia terras tenementa et redditus cum pertinentibus in Ruscheton Corneford Austanfeld et Caldon in dicto comitatu Staff' que fuerunt prefati Hugonis et que ad sexaginta et quatuordecim libras extendebantur per annum una cum feodis advocationibus et libertatibus ac omnibus aliis pertinentibus suis in recompensatione trescentarum libratarum terre et redditus earundem nos premissorum consideratione ac optentu laudabilis obsequii quod idem Rogerus nobis indies impendit ipsumque credimus impensurum volentes eius supplicationem gratiose animare in hac parte volumus et concedimus pro nobis et heredibus nostris prefato Rogero quod ipse habeat et teneat sibi et heredibus suis dictum manerium de Barwe cum pertinentibus ac omnia terras et tenementa et redditus cum pertinentibus in dictis villis de Rushton Corneford Austansfold et Caldon que sic fuerunt prefati Hugonis et que predictus Rogerus modo tenet virtute concessionis nostre supradicte una cum feodis militum advocationibus ecclesiarum et capellarum libertatibus et omnibus aliis ad eadem manerium terras tenementa et redditus quoquo modo spectantibus de nobis et heredibus nostris ac aliis capitalibus dominis feodorum illorum per eadem servicia per que eadem manerium terre tenementa et redditus cum pertinentibus tenebantur antequam ad manus nostras per forisfacturam predictam sic devenerunt imperpetuum in plenam satisfactionem trescentarum libratarum terre et redditus predictarum.

In cuius rei testimonium has litteras nostras fieri fecimus patentes.

Teste me ipso apud Notyngham sextodecimo die Julii anno regni nostri octavo. (1334)

<Margin Charter of Roger de Swynerton>
Edward by the grace of God, king of England, lord of Ireland and duke of Aquitaine, to all to whom the present letters will come, greeting.

Know that since, for the good service which our beloved and faithful Roger de Swynnerton had devoted to us, and thereafter was going to devote to us, and in order that he might be better able to maintain himself in the status of banneret with which he has been charged by our command, we had already agreed, with the assent of our council, to provide the same Roger with three hundred librates of land and rent a year within our kingdom to hold for life and we subsequently, among the other lands and tenements which we have granted to the said Roger for that reason, have granted to the same Roger to hold for life all the manors, lands and tenements with appurtenances which belonged to Hugh le Despenser, formerly earl of Winchester, in the counties of Stafford and Chester and which were in our hand by reason of Hugh's forfeiture, to hold for the term of his life in part satisfaction of the said three hundred librates of land and rents, and the said Roger has now beseeched us that we agree to

2 *dicto* interlined

grant to him that he himself might be able to have and hold to himself and his heirs the manor of Great Barrow with appurtenances in the said county of Chester, and all the lands, tenements and rents with appurtenances in Rushton, Cornford, Alstanfield and Cauldon in the said county of Stafford, which belonged to the said Hugh and which are valued at seventy-four pounds a year, together with fees, advowsons and liberties and all their other appurtenances, in final satisfaction for the three hundred librates of land and their rents, we in consideration of the foregoing and on account of the praiseworthy service which the same Roger devotes to us every day, and which we believe he himself will continue to devote, we, being willing graciously to support his entreaty in this matter, will and grant, for ourself and our heirs, to the said Roger that he himself should have and hold to himself and his heirs the said manor of Barrow with appurtenances and all the lands and tenements and rents with appurtenances in the said townships of Rushton, Cornford, Alstanfield and Cauldon which belonged to Hugh and which the said Roger now holds by virtue of our grant mentioned above, together with fees of knights, advowsons of churches and chapels, liberties and all other things in any way belonging to the same manor, lands, tenements and rents of us and of our heirs and of other chief lords of those fees, in return for the same services in return for which the same manor, lands and rents with appurtenances were held, before they thus came into our hands for ever by the aforesaid forfeiture, in full satisfaction of the three hundred librates of land and rent.

In testimony of which I have caused these our letters to be made patent.

Witness myself at Nottingham on the 16th day of July in the eighth year of our reign. (1334)

Charter **7.9** The Common Charter of Cheshire: Ranulf III's charter to the people of Cheshire dated June–Sept 1215
Barraclough number 394

He grants to the people of Cheshire comprehensive rights, including those in the forests, in parallel with those granted by King John in Magna Carta.

Charter **7.10** Letters patent of the Black Prince, pardoning the abbey and convent of St Werburgh, Chester, dated at Chester 10 September 1353.
Calendared at *Ch.R.R.* p. 514

The prince pardons the abbey for making without licence new-ploughings, marl pits and buildings on their land in various parts of the forests.
CHES 2/36 m. 4d (1) Chester Chester copy

<Margin Carta abbatis Cestr'>
Edwardus illustris regis Anglie et Francie primogenitus princeps Wallie dux Cornubie et comes Cestr' omnibus ad quos presentes littere pervenerint salutem. Sciatis quod

nos de gratia nostra speciali perdonavimus pro nobis et heredibus nostris dilectis nobis in Christo abbati et conventui Sancte Werburge Cestr' transgressiones quas ipsi et predecessores eorum nobis fecerunt faciendo frussuras marleras et edificia in solo eorundem abbatis et conventus alicubi infra metas aut bundas quarumcumque forestarum nostrarum in comitatu nostro Cestr', licentia nostra aut progenitorum nostrorum super hoc non obtenta, nolentes quod predicti abbas et conventus aut eorum successores per nos vel heredes nostros, justiciarios nostros foreste vel heredum nostrorum, vicecomites ballivos forestarios viridarios regardatores vel alios quoscumque ministros nostros vel heredum nostrorum forestarum predictarum sive alios occasione frussurarum marlerarum aut edificiorum predictorum hactenus ut permittitur facere[3] calumpnentur molestentur in aliquo seu graventur.

In cuius rei testimonium has litteras nostras fieri fecimus patentes.

Dat' per manum nostram apud Cestr' decimo die Septembris anno regni carissimi domini nostri patris et regis Anglie vicesimo septimo et Francie quartodecimo. (1353)

<Margin Charter of the abbot of Chester>
Edward, first-born son of the illustrious king of England and France, prince of Wales, duke of Cornwall and earl of Chester, to all to whom the present letters will come, greeting. Know that of our special grace we have pardoned for ourself and our heirs our beloved in Christ, the abbot and convent of Saint Werburgh of Chester, the trespasses which they and their predecessors have done to us by making new ploughings, marl pits and buildings in the land of the abbot and convent in various places within the boundaries or limits of any of our forests in our county of Chester, without obtaining a licence from us or from our progenitors to do this, being unwilling that the abbot and convent or their successors through us or our heirs, through our justices of the forest or those of our heirs, namely, sheriffs, bailiffs, foresters, verderers, regarders, or through any other at all of our ministers of the forests or those of our heirs, or through others, should be accused, troubled in anything or oppressed by reason of the said new ploughings, marlpits and buildings as they have been permitted to do hitherto.

In testimony of which we have caused these our letters to be made patent.

Given by our hand at Chester on the 10th day of September in the 27th year of the reign of our most dear father and king of England, and of France the 14th.

3 superfluous *non* in MS?

m. 48

Charter **7.11** The Lord Edward to John de Grey, dated at Southwark 21 February 1259

He grants the manor of Rushton to John de Grey in return for the service of one knight.

<Carta Rogeri de Gray>
Edwardus illustris regis Anglie primogenitus archiepiscopis episcopis abbatibus prioribus comitibus baronibus justiciariis vicecomitibus prepositis ministris et omnibus ballivis et fidelibus suis salutem.

Sciatis nos dedisse concessisse et hac carta nostra confirmasse dilecto et fideli nostro Johanni de Grey pro homagio et servicio suo totum manerium nostrum de Ruston in comitatu Cestr' cum omnibus pertinentibus suis absque ullo retinemento, habendum et tenendum eidem Johanni et heredibus suis vel assignatis de nobis et heredibus nostris imperpetuum libere quiete bene integre cum omnibus libertatibus et liberis consuetudinibus ad idem manerium pertinentibus cum boscis planis pratis pascuis aquis molendinis et omnibus asiamentis adiacentibus faciendo inde nobis et heredibus nostris ipse et heredes et assignati sui servicium feodi unius militis pro omni servicio consuetudine exactione secta curia et demanda. Quare volumus et firmiter precipimus pro nobis et heredibus nostris quod prefatus Johannes et heredes vel assignati sui imperpetuum habeant et teneant de nobis et heredibus nostris predictum manerium de Ruston cum omnibus pertinentibus suis libere quiete bene et integre cum omnibus libertatibus et liberis consuetudinibus ad idem manerium pertinentibus cum boscis planis pascuis aquis molendinis et omnibus asiamentis adiacentibus et cum omnibus que in dicto manerio habuimus et faciendo inde nobis et heredibus nostris ipse et heredes vel assignati sui servicium feodi unius militis pro omni servicio consuetudine exactione secta curie et demanda sicut predictum est.

Hiis testibus Stephano Longespee tunc justiciario nostro Hibernie Johanne de Baillol Rogero de Monte Alto tunc justiciario nostro Cestr' Alano la Zouche Rogero de Clyfford Willelmo la Zouch Hamone extraneo Ada de Gesemuth Gudone la Zouch et aliis.

Dat' per manum nostram apud Sutwerk vicesimo primo die Februarii anno regni domini regis patris nostri quadragesimo tercio. (1259)

<Charter of Roger de Gray>
Edward, first-born son of the illustrious king of England, to the archbishops, bishops, abbots, priors, earls, barons, justices, sheriffs, reeves, ministers and all his bailiffs and faithful subjects, greetings. Know that we have given, granted and by this our charter have confirmed to our beloved and faithful John de Grey, in return for his homage and service, the whole of our manor of Rushton in the county of Chester

with all its appurtenances without any reservation to have and to hold to the same John and his heirs or assigns of us and our heirs for ever freely, quietly, well, wholly with all the liberties and free customs belonging to the same manor, with woods, open lands, meadows, pastures, waters, mills and all easements appertaining thereto, by doing, himself and his heirs and assigns, from these, the service of one knight's fee to us and our heirs, in return for all service, custom, exaction, suit of court and demand. Wherefore, we wish and firmly command for ourselves and our heirs that the said John and his heirs or assigns should have and hold for ever of us and our heirs the said manor of Rushton with all its appurtenances freely, quietly, well and wholly with all the liberties and free customs belonging to the same manor with woods, open lands, pastures, waters, mills and all easements appertaining thereto and with all that we had in the said manor and, by doing, himself and his heirs or assigns, from these, the service of one knight's fee to us and our heirs, in return for all service, custom, exaction, suit of court and demand, as stated above.

These being witnesses: Stephen Longspee, then our justiciar of Ireland, John de Baillol, Roger de Monte Alto, then our justiciar of Chester, Alan la Zouch, Roger de Clyfford, William la Zouch, Hamo Lestrange, Adam de Gesemuth, Guy la Zouch and others.

Given by our hand at Southwark on the 21st day of February in the 43rd year of the reign of our father, the lord king. (1259)

Charter **7.12** Henry III to John de Grey, dated at Windsor 15 December 1263
Calendared at *C.C.R., 1257–1300* p. 47

The king confirms the grant by his son, the Lord Edward, of the manor of Rushton to John de Grey for the service of one knight.
C 53/53 m. 4 (97) Chancery copy

Charter **7.13** Edward I to Ranulf of Little Over, dated at Bristol 2 January 1285
Calendared at *C.C.R., 1257–1300* p. 283
C 53/73 m. 31 Chancery copy

The king exchanges land in Little Over etc. with Ranulf of Little Over for land in Marlston cum Lache, plus grants relating to pannage, multure at the Dee Mills and tolls, (part of the arrangements for the transfer to Vale Royal).

Charter **7.14** The Black Prince's charter to the community of Cheshire, dated at Chester 10 September 1353.[4]
Translation of inspeximus by Richard II 14 November 1389 at *C.C.R., 1341–1417* pp. 313–14

The prince confirms the rights granted by Ranulf III (**7.9**) to the men of Cheshire, grants a cancellation of the general eyre of 1353 for a fine of 5,000 marks, appoints justices of trailbaston in place of the justices in eyre, abolishes the custom of *thwertnik* and confers some other rights in addition.

CHES 2/36 m. 4	Chester copy
	(Incomplete; only the first third legible)
C53/162 m. 11	14 Nov 1389 Inspeximus

m. 48d begins half way through **7.14**

Charter **7.15** Ranulf III to Combermere Abbey, dated 1190–1194
Barraclough number 240, where Barraclough gives his reason for judging this charter and the others to Combermere abbey to be largely forgeries.

Ranulf III grants to Combermere Abbey a carucate of land in Wincle in the forest of Macclesfield, with pasture for specified beasts, and liberties and privileges for the monks and their men.

Charter **7.16** Letters patent of the Black Prince to Oliver de Bordeaux and his wife, Maud, dated at Byfleet 8 April 1340.

The prince confirms his father's grant (20 January 1318) to Oliver de Bordeaux and his wife, Maud, (William Trussell's widow) of rights of assart in Willaston (Wirral), Blacon, Ashton and Rode and gives the same rights in Willaston to Warin Trussel, her son. Charter **7.31** includes an inspeximus of the 1318 charter only.

CHES 33/4 m. 33d	1347 Chester copy
DL 39/1/19 m. 33d	1347 Earl of Lancaster's copy

<[...] Wille[...] [...] Will[...] Trussell>[5]
Edwardus illustris regis Anglie primogenitus dux Cornubie et comes Cestr' omnibus

4 The inspeximus records the date of this charter as the 20th year of Edward's reign in England, and his 14th year as king of France. The 14th year of France is the 27th year of England. The mistake is repeated in the calendar. The damaged copy in the Cheshire Recognizance Roll is enrolled in the regnal year 27 Edward III, thus confirming that the correct year is 1353. See introduction, p. xxii.

5 In the record of the 1347 eyre this charter is designated in the margin as 'Charter of Warin Trussell'.

ad quos presentes littere pervenerint salutem. Inspeximus litteras patentes quas dictus dominus pater[6] noster dum[7] dominus comes Cestr' existebat dilectis nobis Oliverio de Burdeux et Matilde uxori eius fecit fieri in hec verba:

Edwardus illustris regis Anglie filius comes Cestr' omnibus ballivis et fidelibus suis ad quos presentes littere pervenerint salutem. Sciatis quod ad rogatum predicti domini nostri domini regis Anglie patris nostri carissimi concessimus et licenciam dedimus pro nobis et heredibus nostris dilectis nobis Olivero de Burdeux et Matilde uxori eius quod ipsi omnia vasta sua in maneriis suis de Wylaston Blaken Asscheton et Rode que sunt infra metas forestarum nostrarum in comitatu nostro Cestr' tam de hereditate quam de dote ipsius Matilde includere possint parvo fossato et bassa haya secundum assisam forestarum predictarum et ea inclusa assartare et in culturam redigere et ea sic redacta tenere possint sibi et heredibus predicte Matilde inperpetuum sine redemptione occasione vel inpedimento nostro vel heredum nostrorum justiciariorum forestariorum seu aliorum ministrorum nostrorum quorumcumque.

In cuius rei testimonium has litteras nostras fieri fecimus patentes.

Dat' sub sigillo scaccari nostri Cestr' apud Cestr' xx die Januarii anno regni predicti domini regis patris nostri carissimi xi. (1318)

Nos autem predictam concessionem acceptantes approbantes et confirmantes concessimus et licenter dedimus pro nobis et heredibus nostris dilecto nobis Warino Trussell militi nunc tenenti predictum manerium de Wylaston quod ipse omnia vasta eiusdem manerii que sunt infra metas forestarum nostrarum in predicto comitatu nostro Cestr' includere possit parvo fossato et bassa haya secundum assisam forestarum earundem et ea inclusa assartare et in culturam redigere et ea sic inclusa assartata et in culturam redacta tenere sibi et heredibus suis inperpetuum sine redemptione occasione vel impedimento nostri vel heredum nostrorum justiciariorum forestariorum seu aliorum ministrorum nostrorum quorumcumque sicut predictum est superius.

In cuius rei testimonium has litteras nostras fieri fecimus patentes.

Dat' apud Byflete viii die Aprilis anno regni predicti domini regis patris nostri carissimi quartodecimo. (1340)

<[...] William [...] [...] William Trussell>
Edward, first-born son of the illustrious king of England, duke of Cornwall and earl of Chester, to all to whom the present letters will come, greetings. We have inspected the letters patent which our lord father, while he was still earl of Chester, caused to be made in favour of our beloved Oliver de Bordeaux and his wife Maud in these words:

Edward son of the illustrious king of England, earl of Chester, to all his bailiffs and faithful subjects to whom the present letters will come, greetings. Know that at the

6 *pater* interlined
7 *olim* MS perhaps by scribal error in converting from the direct speech of the original?

request of our said lord, lord king of England our dearest father, we have granted and given licence for ourselves and our heirs, to our beloved Oliver de Bordeaux and Maud, his wife, that they themselves can enclose all their wastes in their manors of Willaston, Blacon and Ashton and Rode, which are within the boundaries of our forests in our county of Chester, both of inheritance and from Maud's dowry, with a small ditch and a low hedge, according to the assize of the said forests and having enclosed them can assart and bring them into cultivation, and having thus brought them into cultivation, can hold them to themselves and Maud's heirs for ever without payment of fine, interference or hindrance from ourselves or our heirs, from our justices, foresters or any other of our ministers at all.

In witness of this we have caused these our letters to be made patent.

Given under the the seal of our exchequer of Chester, at Chester on the 20th day of January in the eleventh year of the reign of the lord king our most beloved father etc. (1318)

Now we accepting, approving and confirming the said concession, have granted and given licence for ourselves and our heirs to our beloved Warin Trussell, knight, now the tenant of the manor of Willaston, that he himself can enclose all his wastes of the same manor, which are within the boundaries of our forests in our said county of Chester, with a small ditch and a low hedge, according to the assize of the same forests, and having enclosed them can assart and bring them into cultivation, and, having thus enclosed, asserted and brought them into cultivation, can hold the land to himself and his heirs for ever without payment of fine, interference or hindrance from ourselves or our heirs, from our justices, foresters or any other of our ministers at all just as is stated above.

In witness of this we have caused these our letters to be made patent.

Given at Byfleet on the 8th day of April in the 14th year of the reign of the said Edward lord king our most beloved father. (1340)

m. 49

Charter **7.17** John of Scotland, earl of Chester and Huntingdon, to Combermere Abbey, dated at Chester 4 April 1234
Barraclough number 463

He grants to Combermere Abbey pasture for specified beasts and liberties and privileges for the monks and their men in the forest of Macclesfield, saving only the earl's right of hunting.

Charter **7.18** Edward, earl of Chester, to John Trussell, dated at Chester 12 April 1317

He grants to John Trussell of Kibblestone assarts in Ashton in the forest of Delamere and North Rode in the forest of Macclesfield and pasture in Ashton.

CHES 33/4 m. 33d	1347 Chester copy
DL 39/1/19	1347 Earl of Lancaster's copy

<Carta Willelmi Trussell de Cublesdon>[8]
Edwardus illustris regis Anglie filius comes Cestr' justiciariis vicecomitibus forestariis et omnibus ballivis fidelibus et ministris suis in comitatu Cestr' salutem. Sciatis quod ad rogatum dicti domini regis patris nostri concessimus dilecto et fideli nostro Johanni Trussell de Cublesdon et heredibus suis ac tenentibus suis manerii sui de Ashton communiam pasture ad omnimoda animalia sua propria in foresta nostra[9] de Mare in comitatu predicto cum libero ingressu et egressu ad eandem. Concessimus etiam predicto Johanni et heredibus suis quod ipsi omnia vasta in maneriis suis de Ashton et Northrode que sunt infra metas forestarum nostrarum de Mara et Maclesfeld in comitatu predicto includere parvo fossato bassa haya secundum assisam forestarum predictarum et ea inclusa assartare et in culturam redigere et ea sic inclusa assartata et in culturam redacta tenere possint sibi et heredibus suis inperpetuum sine redemptione occasione vel inpedimento nostri vel heredum nostrorum justiciariorum forestariorum seu aliorum ministrorum nostrorum quorumcumque. Et nos vobis mandamus quod ipsum Johannem heredes et tenentes suos predictos communiam pasture ad omnimoda animalia sua propria in predicta foresta nostra[10] de Mara habere ac etiam omnia vasta sua in maneriis suis predictis includere assartare et in culturam redigere et ea sic inclusa assartata et in culturam redacta tenere[11] permittatis absque inpedimento vostri vel aliorum ministrorum nostrorum quorumcumque.

In cuius rei testimonium has litteras fieri fecimus patentes.

Dat' sub sigillo scaccarii nostri Cestr' apud Cestr' xij die Aprilis anno regni domini Edwardi patris mei decimo. (1317)

<Charter of William Trussell of Kibblestone>
Edward, son of the illustrious king of England, earl of Chester, to his justices, sheriffs, foresters and all his bailiffs, faithful men and ministers in the county of Chester, greetings. Know that at the request of our father the said lord king, we have granted to our beloved and faithful John Trussell of Kibblestone and his heirs and his tenants of his manor of Ashton common of pasture for their own animals of every kind in our forest of Mara in the said county with free entry and egress to the same forest. We

8 In the record of the 1347 eyre this charter is designated in the margin as 'Charter of John Trussell'.
9 *nostra* interlined
10 *nostra* interlined
11 *possint* struck through

have also granted to the said John and his heirs that they shall be able, in accordance with the assize of the said forests, to enclose with a small ditch and a low hedge all the wastes in his manors of Ashton and Northrode which are within the boundaries of our forests of Mara and Macclesfield in the said county; and to assart the land so enclosed and to bring it into cultivation; and to hold that land, so enclosed, assarted and brought into cultivation, to himself and his heirs for ever without fine, interference or hindrance from us or our heirs, justices, foresters or any other of our ministers whosoever. And we command that you permit John himself, his heirs and his said tenants to have common of pasture for their own animals of every kind in our forest of Mara and also to enclose all his wastes in his said manors, to assart them and to bring them into cultivation; and to hold that land so enclosed, assarted and brought into cultivation free from any hindrance from you or from any other of our ministers whosoever.

In testimony of which we have caused these letters to be made patent.

Given under the seal of our exchequer of Chester at Chester on the 12th day of April in the tenth year of the reign of our father, Edward. (1317)

Charter **7.19** Edward I to Walter de Langton bishop of Coventry and Lichfield, dated at Canterbury 15 September 1299
Calendared at *C.P.R., 1292–1301* p. 439 where the date is given as 18 September 1299 not 15 September

The king grants to the bishop the right to enclose his wood in Tarvin and to make a deer-leap there in the forest of Delamere.

C 66/119 m. 11	Chancery copy
CHES 33/4 m. 33d	1347 Chester copy
DL 39/1/19 m. 29	1347 Earl of Lancaster's copy

Charter **7.20** Richard I to Bishop Hugh of Coventry, dated at Canterbury 30 Nov 1189

The king grants to bishop Hugh of Coventry immunity from various fines in all his holdings in Coventry, Lichfield, Chester, Shrewsbury and Gnosall.

C 53/76/ m. 18 (70)	Chancery copy
CHES 33/4/ m. 33d	1347 Chester copy
DR/10/1406/c, pp. 28–29	(Shakespeare) Inspeximus

<Carta Episcopi>
Ricardus dei gratia rex Anglie dux Norm' Aquit' comes Andeg' archiepiscopis episcopis abbatibus prioribus comitibus baronibus justiciariis vicecomitibus et omnibus ballivis suis et fidelibus salutem. Sciatis nos concessisse et hac presenti carta confirmasse dilecto ac familiari nostro Hugoni Coventr' episcopo et successoribus suis episcopis Coventr' ut omnia maneria sua et omnes terre sue et omnes homines

sui et omnia maneria et omnes terre et omnes homines ecclesie sue de Coventr' et ecclesie sue de Lich' et de Cestr' et de Salop' et de Gnousale et omnium ecclesiarum suarum inperpetuum libera sint et quieta de murdro de latrocinio de schiris de hundredis et sectis schirarum et hundredorum de auxsiliis vicecomitis de foresta et placitis foreste de vastis et assartis et rewardis foreste et operibus castellorum et murorum et stagnorum et omnibus placitis et querelis. Quare volumus et firmiter precipimus ut omnia maneria et omnes terre et homines predicti episcopi et successorum eius et predictarum ecclesiarum inperpetuum libera sint et quieta.

Testibus Hugone Dunelm', Huberto Saresb' episcopis Roberto comiti Leicestr' Willelmo Marescall', Henrico de Longo Campo apud Cant' xxx die Novembris.

Dat' per manum Willelmi Elyensis electi cancellarii nostri regni nostri anno primo. (1189)

<Charter of the bishop>
Richard by the grace of God king of England, duke of Normandy and Aquitaine, count of Anjou, to the archbishops, bishops, abbots, priors, earls, barons, justices, sheriffs and all his bailiffs and faithful men greeting. Know that we have granted and by this present charter have confirmed to our beloved and familiar Hugh, bishop of Coventry, and to his successors, bishops of Coventry, that all his manors and all his lands and all his men and all the manors and all the land and all the men of his church of Coventry and of his church of Lichfield and of Chester and of Shrewsbury and of Gnosall and of all his churches be free and quit for ever of murder fines and of larceny fines, of shires, of hundreds and of suits of shires and hundreds, of sheriff's aid, of forest and pleas of the forest, of wastes and assarts and regards of the forest and of works of the castles and walls and ponds, and of all pleas and suits. Wherefore we wish and firmly command that all the manors and all lands and men of the said bishop and his successors and of the said churches may be free and quit for ever.

Witnessed by Hugh of Durham, Hubert of Salisbury, bishops, Robert, earl of Leicester, William Marshall, Henry de Longchamp at Canterbury on the 30th day of November.

Given under the hand of William the elect of Ely,[12] our chancellor, in the first year of our reign. (1189)

Charter **7.21** Hugh, earl of Chester, to Robert Grosvenor, dated at Chester *c.* 1162–1173
Barraclough number 163

He grants to Robert the township of (Little) Budworth and certain hunting rights in Delamere forest.

12 William Longchamp was elected bishop of Ely, 15th September 1189, and consecrated on 31st December following. (F.M. Powicke and E.B. Fryde, *Handbook of British Chronology*, Royal Historical Society Guides and Handbooks No. 2, 1961, p. 223).

m. 49d

Charter **7.22** Edward I to Simon, abbot of Chester, dated at Westminster 12 June 1285
Calendared at *C.C.R., 1257–1300* p. 292

The king grants to the abbot of Chester, certain hunting rights in Cheshire, in substitution for the more comprehensive rights granted in a previous charter, which the king has inspected, to abbot Ralph by Ranulf II, which rights Simon had surrendered to the king.

C 53/73/ m. 25(79)	Chancery copy
CHES 33/4/ m. 30d	1347 Chester copy
DL 39/1/19 m. 26	1347 Earl of Lancaster's copy

Charter **7.23** The Black Prince to Sir Richard Willoughby and other justices of the forest eyre in Cheshire, dated at London 28 February 1358
Calendared at *B.P.R.*, iii p. 298

Letter from the prince to Sir Richard instructing him to negotiate with the people of Delamere and Mondrum forest for a fine of £2,000 as well as a fine from Macclesfield. They are to discharge their obligations to him exactly as had already been agreed with the people of the forest of Wirral for £1,000 and to collect the fine from Wirral. (French)
E 36/279 (fo. 63v)

m. 50

Charter **7.24** Ranulf III to the abbey of St Werburgh, dated at Chester *c.*1208–1211
Barraclough number 232

He grants to the abbey of St Werburgh tithes of demesne fisheries of Rhuddlan and of mills at Englefield, plus other rights.

Charter **7.25** Edward II to the prior of Birkenhead, dated at Sheen 20 February 1318
Calendared at *C.P.R., 1327–1330* pp. 108–109.

The king gives the priory the right to build lodging-houses and sell provisions to people using the ferry to Liverpool.

C 66/149/ m. 34	Chancery copy
CHES 33/4/ m. 32	13 April 1330 Woodstock Inspeximus (See also **7.26**)

Charter **7.26** Edward III to the prior of Birkenhead, dated at Woodstock 13 April 1330.
Calendar of Edward III's inspeximus at *C.P.R., 1327–1330* p. 505

Edward III's charter confirming rights given to the prior of Birkenhead (in **7.25** above) to provide food and accommodation for travellers using the ferry and granting an additional right to run the ferry and charge passengers.

C 66/173/ m. 33	Inspeximus
CHES 33/4/ m. 32	1347 Chester copy

<Carta prioris de Byrkehed>
Edwardus dei gratia rex Anglie dominus Hibernie et dux Aquit' omnibus ad quos presentes littere pervenerint salutem. Inspeximus litteras patentes domini Edwardi nuper regis Anglie patris nostri in hec verba:

Edwardus dei gratia rex Anglie dominus Hibernie et dux Aquit' omnibus ad quos presentes littere pervenerint salutem. Sciatis quod cum a villa de Lyverpol in comitatu Lancastr' usque ad prioratum de Byrkeheved in comitatu Cestr' et ab eodem prioratu usque ad predictam villam ultra brachium maris ibidem commune passagium habeatur ac propter diversitatem temporum et varias tempestates homines de dicto comitatu Cestr' usque ad partes comitatus Lancastr' ibidem transire volentes in magna multitudine pluries impeditos ad dictum prioratum oportuit declinare pro eo quod in loco passagii predicti non sunt aliqui domus pro huiusmodi hominibus hospitandis nec victualia pro sustentatione dictorum hominum inveniuntur emenda quorum pretextu prioratus predictus ultra vires facultatum suarum de huiusmodi omnibus hactenus extitit oneratus et predicti homines fatigati multipliciter et gravati, nos volentes in hac parte remedium adhibere de nostra gratia speciali concessimus et licenciam dedimus pro nobis et heredibus nostris quantum in nobis est dilectis nobis in Christo priori et conventui prioratus predicti quod ipsi in solo suo proprio apud Byrkeheved in loco passagii predicti vel prope prout convenientius fieri poterint domos sufficientes pro huiusmodi hominibus hospitandis construere et eas constructas tenere possint sibi et successoribus suis inperpetuum, et quod homines in domibus illis mansuri victualia pro sustentatione hominum ibidem dictum brachium maris transiturorum emere possint et vendere sine occasione vel impedimento nostri vel heredum nostrorum justiciariorum escaetorum vicecomitum aut aliorum ballivorum seu ministrorum nostrorum quorumcumque.

In cuius rei testimonium has litteras nostras fieri fecimus patentes.

Teste me ipso apud Shene xx die Februarii anno regni nostri undecimo.

Nos autem concessionem predictam ratam habentes et gratam pro nobis et heredibus nostris quantum in nobis est, prefatis priori et conventui et eorum successoribus concedimus et confirmamus sicut littere predicte rationabiliter testantur. Volentes [...] eis pro utilitate per aquam ibidem transire volentium gratiam facere ampliorem, concessimus pro nobis et heredibus nostris prefatis priori et conventui quod ipsi et eorum successores inperpetuum habeant ibidem[13] passagium ultra dictum brachium maris tam pro hominibus quam pro equis et aliis rebus quibuscumque et pro passagio illo recipiant rationabiliter prout fuerit faciendum, sine occasione vel impedimento nostri vel heredum nostrorum aut ministrorum nostrorum quorumcumque salvo iure nostro et alterius cuiuscumque.

In cuius rei testimonium has litteras nostras fieri fecimus patentes.

Teste me ipso apud Woodstok[14] xiii die Aprilis anno regni nostri quarto. (1330)

<Charter of the prior of Birkenhead>
Edward by the grace of God king of England, lord of Ireland, duke of Aquitaine to all to whom the present letters will come, greetings. We have inspected the letters patent of the lord Edward lately king of England our father in these words:

Edward by the grace of God king of England, lord of Ireland and duke of Aquitaine to all to whom the present letters will come, greetings. Know that since from the town of Liverpool in the county of Lancaster to the priory of Birkenhead in the county of Chester and from the same priory to the aforesaid town a common passage is used across the arm of the sea there and on account of the changeability of the weather and frequent storms men who want to cross in great numbers from the county of Chester to the parts of the county of Lancaster are often held up and have to turn to the priory for this reason, and that in the place of the passage there are not any houses to accommodate such men nor are provisions found to be bought for sustenance of the said men; for which reasons the priory has hitherto been burdened beyond the capacity of its means by all the things of this kind and the aforesaid men are much vexed and burdened. Wishing to apply a remedy in this matter, of our special grace we have granted and given a licence, for ourselves and our heirs as far as we have the power, to our beloved in Christ the prior and the convent of the priory that they themselves in their own land in Birkenhead at the place of the aforesaid passage, or as near as it can be done most conveniently, can build sufficient houses to accommodate such men and can hold the houses when they have been built to themselves and their successors for ever; and that the men who will stay in those houses can buy and sell provisions for the sustenance of those who are going to cross the arm of the sea in the same place without interference or hindrance of us or our heirs, justices, escheaters, sheriffs or any bailiffs or ministers whatsoever. In witness whereof we have caused these our letters to be made patent. Witnessed by me myself at Sheen on the 20th day of February in the 11th year of our reign. (1318)

Moreover, having approved and ratified the aforesaid concession for ourselves and our heirs, as far as is in our power, we grant and confirm it to the said prior and convent and their successors, just as the aforesaid letters reasonably attest. Being willing [...] to make a greater concession to them for the convenience of those who

13 *dictum* struck through
14 *Westmonasterium* MS, but thus in CPR

want to cross the water in that place, for ourselves and our heirs, we have granted to the said prior and convent that they themselves and their successors should forever have a passage there across the arm of the sea, for both men and horses and any other things whatsoever, and that they should receive for that passage reasonable payment in proportion to what will have to be done without any obstruction or hindrance of us or our heirs or any of our ministers whatsoever, saving our rights and those of anyone else.

In witness whereof we have caused these our letters to be made patent. Witnessed by me myself at Woodstock on 13 April in the fourth year of our reign. (1330)

Charter **7.27** Edward III to his mother, queen Isabella, dated at Westminster 30 March 1345
Calendared at *C.P.R., 1343–1345* pp. 447–48

The king's charter to his mother, queen Isabella, confirming her lands throughout England (listed) which will give her an annual income of £3,000.
C 66/213/ m. 23 Chancery copy

m. 50d

Charter **7.28** Queen Isabella, Edward III's mother, to William de Monte Acuto, earl of Salisbury, dated at Walton 12 July 1338
Calendared at *C.P.R., 1338–1340* p. 114

Isabella grants for her life to William the castle and manor of Hawarden, the manors of Lea (Newbold), Bosley and Neston in Cheshire and the castle and town of Mold, plus the stewardship of Chester.
C 66/193/ m. 10 16 July 1338 Ipswich Inspeximus

Isabella dei gratia regina Anglie domina Hibernie et comitissa Pontivi universis hoc scriptum visuris vel audituris salutem in domino.

Noveritis nos dedisse concessisse et reddidisse nobili viro domino Willelmo de Monte Acuto comiti Sarum

*castrum et manerium de Hawardyn cum pertinentibus ac

*maneria de Lee Boselee et Neston cum pertinentibus in comitatu Cestr' et

*castrum et villam de Monte Alto cum pertinentibus necnon

*senescalciam Cestr' una cum omnibus ad eandem senescalciam in eodem comitatu Cestr' et comitatu de Flynt et in Wallia pertinentibus, feodis militum, advocationibus ecclesiarum, wardis, maritagiis et releviis ad dicta castra maneria et senescalciam pertinentibus dumtaxat exceptis, que quidem castra maneria et senescalcia quondam fuerunt Roberti de Monte Alto senescalli Cestr' et que tenebamus ad terminum vite nostre, quorum etiam reversionem, que ad excellentissimum principem dominum Edwardum regem Anglie illustrem filium nostrum carissimum et heredes suos post decessum nostrum spectabat, idem dominus rex prefato comiti dedit et concessit habendum post mortem nostram sibi et heredibus suis habendum et tenendum: predicta castra maneria et senescalciam cum pertinentibus predictis ad totam vitam nostram simul cum forestis chaceis parcis boscis molendinis et piscariis stagnis et aquis et warennis feriis mercatis libertatibus tam regalibus quam aliis liberis consuetudinibus wreccis maris et quibuscumque aliis ad eadem castra maneria et senescalciam spectantibus adeo plene et integre sicut habuimus et tenuimus sine ullo retinemento, feodis advocationibus wardis maritagiis et releviis ad ea pertinentibus ut predicitur ac maneriis membris terris et tenementis et omnibus aliis que ad dictam senescalciam in Anglia extra dictos comitatus et Walliam spectant tantum exceptis, de capitalibus dominis feodorum illorum per servicia inde debita et consueta in escambium pro sexcentis marcis nobis per prefatum comitem concessis percipiendis[15] singulis annis apud Turrim nostram de Servat London ad festa sancti Michelis et Pasche per equales partes

(i) de illis mille marcis quas dictus dominus rex de exitibus conagii stani in comitatu Cornubie per manus collectoris sive custodis eiusdem custagii qui pro tempore foret prefato comiti concessit percipiendis sub certa forma in litteris patentibus[16] ipsius domini regis inde confectis contenta ac etiam

(ii) de maneriis et aliis terris et tenementis prefati comitis tam in Anglie quam in Wallie ad totam vitam nostram prout in scripto eiusdem comitis nobis inde confecto plenius est expressum.

In cuius rei testimonium sigillum nostrum huic prefato scripto apposuimus. Hiis testibus dominis Nicholao de la Beche Johanni de Molyns Waltero de Chesthunt militibus Johanne Giffard Thoma de London clericis et aliis.

Dat' apud Waldon xij die Julii anno regni regis Edwardi terci post conquestum duodecimo. (1338)

Isabella, by the grace of God, queen of England, lady of Ireland and countess of Ponthieu, to all who will see or hear this writing, greetings in the Lord.

You will know that we have given, granted and restored to the noble man, lord William de Monte Acuto, earl of Salisbury,

*the castle and manor of Hawarden with their appurtenances, and

15 *percipiendis* interlined
16 *C.P.R., 1338–1340* p. 115

*the manors of Lea, Bosley and Neston with their appurtenances in the county of Cheshire and

*the castle and township of Mold with their appurtenances and also

*the stewardship of Chester together with all the rights appertaining to the same stewardship in the county of Cheshire and in the county of Flint and in Wales, excluding only the knights' fees, advowsons of churches, wardships dower rights, and the reliefs pertaining to the said castles, manors and (stewardship)

which castles, manors and stewardship were once those of Robert de Monte Alto, steward of Chester, and which we held for the term of our life.

The reversion of these, which belonged to the most excellent prince, lord Edward, illustrious king of England, our dearest son, and to his heirs after our death, the same lord king gave and granted to the said earl to hold after our death, to himself and his heirs to have and to hold the said castles, manors and stewardship with their appurtenances for the whole of our life together with the forests, chases, parks, woods, mills and fisheries, ponds and waters, warrens, enclosures, fairs, markets, liberties, both royal and other free customs, wreck of the sea and any other rights belonging to the same castles, manors and stewardship, as fully and wholly as we have had and held them without any retention, excepting only fees, advowsons, wardships, dower rights and reliefs pertaining to them as stated above, and the manors, members, lands and holdings and all other rights which belong to the said stewardship in England outside the said counties and in Wales of the chief lords of those fees in return for services owed for these and customary in exchange for six hundred marks granted to us by the said earl, to be received each year at our tower of Servat in London on the feast of St Michael and at Easter, in equal payments from:

(i) those thousand marks which the said Lord king has granted to the said earl out of the income from the coinage of tin in the county of Cornwall by the hands of the collector or from the custodian of the coinage, whoever he may be for the time being, to be received under the certified form contained in letters patent of the lord king himself made for this purpose and also

(ii) from the manors and other lands and holdings of the said earl both in England and in Wales for the whole of our life as has been set out more fully in the document of the same earl made for us for this purpose.

In testimony of which we have set our seal to the said document in the presence of these witnesses: lords Nicholas de la Beche, John de Molyns, Walter de Chesthunte, knights, John Gifford, Thomas de London, clerks and others.

Given at Walton on the 12th day of July in the twelfth year of the reign of King Edward III after the conquest. (1338)

m. 51

Charter **7.29** Edward III to William de Monte Acuto, earl of Salisbury, dated Westminster 1 October 1337
Calendared at *C.C.R., 1327–1341,* pp. 432–33 and at *Ch.R.R., 1341* p. 349

The king grants to William the reversion on the death of Queen Isabella of the castle and manor of Hawarden, the stewardship of Chester, the manors of Lea (Newbold), Bosley and Neston in Cheshire, and the castle and town of Mold and extensive holdings throughout England (listed) in return for military and financial services.
C 53/124/m. 4 (6) (nb. m. 4 is a correction of m. 5) Westminster Chancery copy
CHES 2/71/ m. 12 (1) 21–22 R II 1397–1399 Inspeximus

Charter **7.30** Robert de Monte Alto and his wife, Emma and Master Henry de Clyffe, dated at Chester 9 June 1327 (The acknowledgement in Chester is dated 26 April 1327.)

Final concord between Robert de Monte Alto and his wife, Emma, and Master Henry de Clyffe, who acknowledges their rights to the castle and manor of Hawarden, the manors of Lea and Bosley and the stewardship of Chester, with reversion in default of male heirs to Queen Isabella, for the life of Edward III, with remainder to John of Eltham.
CHES 31/2 (6) Chester copy

< [................]>
Hec est finalis concordia facta in pleno comitatu Cestr' die Martis proxima ante festum sancti Barnabe Apostoli anno regni regis Edwardi tercii post conquestum primo coram Ricardo Dammary tunc justiciario Cestr' Willelmo de Baggelegh Willelmo de Brerton militibus Willelmo de Mobberlegh Roberto de Prayers Willelmo de Prayers Johanne de Wetenhale Johanne de Wrennebury et aliis de regis fidelibus tunc ibidem presentibus inter Robertum de Monte Alto et Emmam uxorem eius querentes et magistrum Henricum de Clyffe clericum deforciantem de castro et manerio de Harwardyn senescalcia Cestr' et maneriis de Lee et Boselee cum pertinentibus in comitatu Cestr' ipso comitatu in manu ipsius domini regis existente: scilicet quod predictus Robertus recognovit castrum maneria et senescalciam predictam cum pertinentibus esse ius ipsius Henrici ut illa quidem Henricus habet ex dono predicti Roberti. Et pro hac recognitione fine et concordia idem Henricus concessit predicto Roberto et Emme castrum maneria et senescalciam predictam cum pertinentibus et illa eis reddidit in eodem comitatu habendum et tenendum eisdem Roberto et Emme et heredibus masculis de corpore ipsius Roberti exeuntibus de domino rege et heredibus suis ut de comitatu predicto per servicia que ad predicta castrum maneria et senescalciam pertinent imperpetuum; et si idem Robertus obierit sine herede masculo de corpore suo exeunte, tunc post mortem predictorum Roberti

et Emme castrum maneria et senescalcia predicta cum pertinentibus remaneant Isabelle regine Anglie matri ipsius domini regis habendum et tenendum eidem regine ad totam vitam suam de predicto domino rege et heredibus suis ut de comite predicto per servicia predicta, ita quod post mortem ipsius regine predicta castrum maneria et senescalcia cum pertinentibus remaneant Johanni de Eltham fratri ipsius domini regis habendum et tenendum eidem Johanni et heredibus de corpore suo exeuntibus de ipso domino rege et heredibus suis ut de comite predicto per servicia predicta imperpetuum.

Et si idem Johannes obierit sine herede corpore suo exeunte, tunc predicta castrum maneria et senescalcia cum pertinentibus remaneant regi et heredibus suis imperpetuum.

Recognitiones ipsius finis facte fuerunt coram ipso rege apud Stamford die Lune proxima post quindenam Pasche anno regni sui primo et misse Ricardo Dammary justiciario Cestr' sub pede magni sigilli ipsius regis per brevem suum ad finem inde in curia Cestr' levandum et ingrossandum que quidem recognitiones [...] cum dicto breve [...] [...bus] inde de attornato [pede] istius finis sunt confecte.

<[...]>
This is the final concord made in the full county court of Chester on Tuesday before the feast of St Barnabas, the apostle, in the first year of the reign of king Edward III after the conquest in the presence of Richard Dammary, then justiciar of Chester, William de Baggelegh, William de Brerton, knights, William de Mobberley, Robert de Prayers, William de Prayers, John de Wetenhall, John de Wrenbury, and others of the king's faithful subjects then present in the same place between Robert de Monte Alto and Emma, his wife, querents, and Master Henry de Clyf, clerk, deforciant concerning the castle and manor of Hawarden, the stewardship of Chester and the manors of Lea and Boseley with their appurtenances in the county of Chester when the earldom was in the hands of the lord king himself; namely that the said Robert has acknowledged the said castle, manors and stewardship with their appurtenances to be the right of Henry himself, as Henry holds them from the gift of the said Robert.

And in return for this acknowledgement, settlement and agreement Henry has granted to Robert and Emma the castle, manors and stewardship with their appurtenances and he has restored these to them in the same court to have and to hold to the same Robert and Emma and their heirs male issuing from the body of Robert himself, from the lord king and his heirs, as of the said earldom, in return for the services which belong to the castle, manors and stewardship forever. And if the same Robert dies without male heirs issuing from his own body, then after the death of Robert and Emma the castle, manor and stewardship with their appurtenances are to revert to Isabella, queen of England, mother of the lord king himself, to have and to hold to the same queen for the whole of her life of the lord king and his heirs, as of the said earl, in return for the said services, so that after the death of the queen herself the castle, manors and stewardship with their appurtenances are to revert to John de

Eltham, brother of the lord king himself, to have and to hold to the same John and to his heirs issuing from his body, of the lord king himself and his heirs, as of the said earl, in return for the said services forever.

And if the same John dies without a male heir issuing from his own body, then the castle, manors and stewardship with their appurtenances are to revert to the king and his heirs forever.

The acknowledgements of this fine were made in the presence of the king himself at Stamford on Monday after the quinzaine of Easter in the first year of his reign (26 April 1327) and were sent to Richard Dammary, justiciar of Chester, under the foot of the king's great seal, by his own writ, to levy and engross the fine from there in the court of Chester, which acknowledgements [...] with the said writ [...] [. . .] [. . .], were then made by the attorney [with the foot of that fine].

m. 51d

Charter **7.31** Edward III to Oliver and Maud de Bordeaux, dated at Leicester 10 January 1329
Calendared at *C.P.R., 1327–1330* pp. 346–47

Inspeximus by Edward III of two earlier charters, made when he was earl of Chester, of grants to Oliver and Maud of rights to enclose assarts in Willaston, Blacon, Ashton and (North) Rode (20 January 1318, confirmed in **7.16**), and of rights of pasture in Ashton (16 October, 1319).
C 66/170/ m 1 12 Jan 1329 2 Ed III Leicester Chancery copy

Charter **7.32** Black Prince to the abbot of Chester, dated at Chester 8 December 1357
Calendared at *Ch.R.R., 3 December, 1357*, p. 515

The prince pardons the abbot of Chester for building his watermill at Ince and for making an enclosure at Little Sutton in Wirral in return for a fine of £100.

CHES 2/40/ m. 3d (4)	8 Dec 1357	31 Ed III	Chester	Pardon
E 36/279 (f 157 & 156d)	3 Dec 1357	31 Ed III	London	Order

<Carta Abbatis Cestr' de fine pro transgressione molendini de Ynes>
Edwardus illustris regis Anglie filius princeps Wallie dux Cornubie et comes Cestr' omnibus ballivis ministris et fidelibus suis ad quos presentes littere pervenerint salutem. Quia de gratia nostra speciali et per finem centum librarum quem dilecti nobis abbas et conventus ecclesie Sancte Werburge Cestr' nobiscum fecerunt et quem finem fecimus intrari in rotulis sessionum itineris forestarum nostrarum

Cestris' perdonavimus eis transgressionem de hoc quod dictus abbas de novo levavit unum molendinum aquaticum super Inssemerssh in una tristera inter forestam de Mara et forestam de Wyrhale et de factura stagni dicti molendini ac etiam de hoc quod Willelmus abbas predecessor dicti abbatis qui nunc est fecit unum clausum apud Hallesutton inclusum per palitia et fossatum in dicta foresta de Wyrhale, concessimus etiam dictis abbati et conventui quod ipsi possent habere sibi et successoribus suis imperpetuum dictum molendinum cum stagno supradicto et etiam clausum apud Hallesutton inclusum per palitia et fossatum sufficientia melius quo sciverunt et potuerunt pro commodo suo sine impedimento nostri aut heredum nostrorum justiciariorum escaetorum vicecomitum aut aliorum ballivorum seu ministrorum nostrorum quorumcumque.

In cuius rei testimonium has litteras nostras fieri fecimus patentes.

Dat' apud Cestr' octavo die Decembris anno regni domini Edwardi regis patris nostri tricesimo primo. (1357)

<Charter of the Abbot of Chester concerning a fine for his trespass concerning a mill at Ince.>
Edward, son of the illustrious king of England, prince of Wales and duke of Cornwall and earl of Chester to all his bailiffs, ministers and faithful subjects to whom the present letters will come, greetings. Since of our special favour and in return for a fine of £100, which our beloved the abbot and convent of the Church of St Werburgh of Chester have paid to us, and which fine we have caused to be entered in the rolls of the sessions of the eyre of our forests of Cheshire, we have pardoned them their trespass in that the abbot erected a new water-mill in Ince Marsh in a tryst between the forest of Delamere and the forest of Wirral, and for creating a pond for the mill; and also for this, that abbot William, the predecessor of the present abbot, made a close at Little Sutton enclosed by a palisade and a ditch in the forest of Wirral, we have also granted to the abbot and convent that they may hold to themselves and their successors for ever the mill with the pond and also the close at Little Sutton enclosed by an adequate palisade and ditch (or better since they knew and were able for their own advantage) without hindrance from us or our heirs, justices, escheators, sheriffs or others of our bailiffs or ministers whosoever.

In testimony whereof we have caused these our letters to be made patent.

Dated at Chester on the 8th day of December in the 31st year of the reign of lord Edward, the king, our father. (1357)

Charter **7.33** Black Prince to John of Ardene, dated at Chester 20 September 1358
Calendared at *Ch.R.R., 20 September, 1358,* p. 515

Inspeximus and ratification by the prince of Sir John de Ardene's grant of permission to the abbot of Chester (on 13 September 1358. See *Ch.R.R.* p. 515.) to take 30 cartloads of turf a year from Elton Moss for his almonry in Ince.
CHES 2/40/ m. 4(1) Chester copy
CHES 2/84/ m. 4(5) 24 Aug 1412 12–13 H IV Chester Chester copy

<Margin Abbas Cestr' pro Eltonmos>
Edwardus illustris regis Anglie filius princeps Wallie dux Cornubie et comes Cestr' omnibus ballivis ministris et fidelibus suis ad quos presentes littere pervenerint salutem. Inspeximus cartam quam Johannes de Ardena miles fecit abbati Cestr' et eiusdem loci conventui eorumque successoribus in hec verba:

Universis Christi fidelibus presens scriptum visuris vel audituris Johannes de Ardena miles salutem in domino sempiternam. Noverit universitas vestra me pro me et heredibus meis concessisse abbati Cestr' et eiusdem loci conventui eorumque successoribus ad capiendum et fodiendum in bruera mea de Elton in illa placea que vocatur Eltonmos in quacumque parte illius placee sibi melius viderint expedire sine visu et liberatione ballivorum meorum triginta carectatas turbarum singulis annis et liberam chaceam cariandi predicta triginta carectatas turbarum per terras meas de Elton usque ad elemosinariam predicti abbatis in Ines cum carectis de predicta elemosinaria in predicta bruera de Elton et inde redeundo ad predictam elemosinariam in predicta villa de Ines quocumque tempore anni et quotienscumque singulis annis sibi et conventui suo eorumque successoribus viderit vel viderint expedire sine contradictione mei et heredum meorum et assignatorum vel aliquorum ex parte mea seu aliquorum ex parte heredum vel assignatorum meorum.

Et si contigit quod aliquo tempore vel aliquo anno predictus abbas et conventus et successores sui per superinundationem aquarum vel aliquo alio modo impeditus vel impediti fuerint quominus predictas triginta carectatas turbarum querere fodere cariare poterit vel poterint bene liceat predicto abbati et conventui eorumque successoribus sequenti anno et annis sequentibus predictas triginta carectatas turbarum querere fodere cariare illius manerii de quo supradictum est preter predictas triginta carectatas turbarum singulis annis capiendas.

Et ego predictus Johannes et heredes mei predictas triginta carectatas turbarum cum foditione chacia et cariatione de predicta bruera de Elton ad predictam elemosinariam in Ines singulis annis querendo et redeundo contra omnes homines imperpetuum warantizabimus et defendemus.

In cuius rei testimonium tam ego quam predicti abbas et conventus sigilla nostra apposuimus.

Hiis testibus Roberto de Brescy Ricardo de Kyngeslegh Jacobo de Pulle Willelmo de Hellesby Willelmo de Trofford Ricardo le marescallo de Elton et aliis.

Nos autem concessionem predictam ratam habentes et gratam eam pro nobis et heredibus nostris quantum in nobis est predictis abbati et conventui loci predicti eorumque successoribus ratificamus et confirmamus prout carta predicta rationabiliter testatur.

Hiis testibus domino[17] Henrico duce Lancastr' domino Ricardo comite Arundell domino Willelmo de Monte Acuto comite Sarum' domino Bartholomeo de Burghersh justiciario nostro Cestr' Johanne de Delves locum tenente predicti justiciarii Magistro Johanne de Brunham juniore camerario nostro Cestr' et aliis.

Dat' apud[18] Cestr' sub sigillo scaccarii nostri ibidem vicesimo die Septembris anno regni domini Edwardi regis patris nostri tricesimo secundo. (1358)

<Abbot of Chester for Elton Moss>
Edward, son of the illustrious king of England, prince of Wales, duke of Cornwall and earl of Chester, to all his bailiffs, ministers and faithful men to whom the present letters will come, greetings. We have inspected the charter which John de Ardene, knight, made to the abbot of Chester and the convent of the same place and their successors in these words:

John de Ardene to all of Christ's faithful who will see or hear this present writing, everlasting well-being in the Lord. Everyone of you will have known that I have granted on behalf of myself and my heirs to the abbot of Chester and the convent of the same place and their successors the right to dig and take away every year thirty cartloads of turves in my heath of Elton in that place which is called Eltonmos, in whatever part of that place they consider it to be most convenient, without the view and delivery of my bailiffs; and that I have granted free right for carrying the said thirty cartloads of turves through my lands from Elton as far as the almonry of the said abbot in Ince with carts, from the said almonry in the said heath of Elton, and from there returning to the said almonry in the said township from Ince at whatever time of the year and as often in each year as he or they consider to be convenient to himself and his convent and their successors without objection from me or my heirs and assigns or from anyone on my part or from anyone on the part of my heirs or assigns.

And if it happens that at any time or in any year the said abbot and convent and their successors will have been prevented by reason of flood or any other cause from being able to find dig and carry off the said thirty cartloads of turves, it is to be freely permitted to the abbot and convent and their successors in the following year and the following years to find dig and carry off the said cartloads of turves from that manor from which it has been said above in addition to the said thirty cartloads of turves that may be taken every year.

17 *domino* interlined
18 *apud* repeated in MS

And I the said John and my heirs will warrant and defend against all men the said thirty cartloads of turves forever with the right to dig and carry them off with free right of cartage every year, by getting and returning from the said heath of Elton to the said almonry at Ince.

In testimony of this both I and the said abbot and convent have set our seals before these witnesses: Robert de Brescy, Richard de Kyngeslegh, James de Pulle, William de Hellesby, William de Trofford, Richard Marshall of Elton and others.

We, having ratified and approved the said concession, ratify and confirm it on behalf of ourselves and our heirs, as far as we have the power, to the said abbot and convent of the said place and their successors, just as the said charter reasonably attests.

In the presence of these witnesses: lord Henry duke of Lancaster, lord Richard earl of Arundel, lord William de Monte Acuto earl of Salisbury, lord Bartholomew de Burghersh our justiciar of Chester, John de Delves lieutenant of the said justiciar, Master John de Brunham the younger our chamberlain of Chester, and others.

Dated at Chester under the seal of our exchequer in the same place on the twentieth day of September in the thirty second year of the reign of the Lord Edward our father. (1358)

m. 52

Charter **7.34** Edward I to the bishop of Coventry and Lichfield, dated at Westminster 1 June 1290
Transcribed at *C.C.R., 1257–1300*, pp. 346–48

Inspeximus and confirmation to the bishop, by Edward I of three undated charters of Henry II and two of Richard I (both of 1189) granting liberties in all the bishop's holdings in Chester and elsewhere.

C 53/76/ m. 18 (70)	Chancery Copy
CHES 33/2/m. 3d	4 July 1286 Inspeximus
DR/10/1406/c (pp. 28–29)	Shakespeare Inspeximus

(CHES 33/2/m. 3d and Shakespeare DR/10/1406/c, pp. 28–29 are copies only of Richard I's second charter of 30 November 1189, also found at **7.20**.)

Charter **7.35** Edward I to the men of Cheshire, dated at Westminster 30 March 1300
Calendared at *C.C.R., 1292–1301* pp. 499–501

The king confirms for the second time (see **7.5**) the liberties granted to the men of Cheshire by Ranulf III (see **7.9**). This charter is not in fact enrolled, although it is referred to 27 times.

C 66/120/m. 22 pp. 499–501	Inspeximus of Ranulf III's Great Charter

ROLLS OF THE ATTORNEYS

(**8.1–8.60**; mm. 53, 53d)

m. 53
Rotuli de attornatis in itinere forestarum de Mare Mondrem Wyrhale et Maclesfeld coram prefatis justiciariis.

Rolls of the attorneys in the eyre of the forests of Delamere, Mondrum, Wirral and Macclesfield before the said justices.

8.1 Johannes de Brerton persona ecclesie de Walay ponit loco suo Johannem Dounvyll seniorem in omnibus placitis et querelis per ipsum vel contra ipsum motis vel movendis coram justiciariis durante itinere foreste ac etiam propter apparentiam suam in itinere.

8.1 John de Brereton, parson of the church of Wallasey, appoints in his place John Domville, senior, in all pleas and suits moved or to be moved, by him or against him, before the justices during the eyre of the forest and also instead of his own appearance in the eyre.

The following defendants appointed their attorneys in the same or a very similar form of words:

8.2	Philip de Egerton	Michael Scot or William Criour
8.3	David de Calvylegh	Michael Scot or William Criour
8.4	William de Monte Acuto, earl of Salisbury	Henry de Chorleton or Thomas, the receiver of Hawarden
8.5	Roger, bishop of Lichfield	Simon Gentyll or Ranulf Rotour or Robert Horn
8.6	John de Stafford	William de Wetenhale of Alpraham
8.7	William de Monte Acuto, earl of Salisbury	John de Davenport of Welltrough or Henry de Chorleton (Wirral and Macclesfield).

8.8	Joan, wife of Michael Scot	Michael, her husband
8.9	William de Seynesbury, chaplain	Ranulf Rotour or William Trofford
8.10	John de Warrewyk, senior	William de Seynesbury, chaplain
8.11	Reginald de Gray, lord of Rushton	Robert de Everdon, parson of the church of Tarporley, or Ranulf Rotour
8.12	Robert de Fouleshurst	William Stanlegh
8.13	The abbot of Chester	Ranulf Rotour, Richard de Manlegh or William de Trofford
8.14	William, son of William Trussell, knight	Henry de Chorleton
8.15	Agnes, wife of Richard de Wynynton, knight	Hugh de Leghton
8.16	William, son of John Trussell, knight	Peter de Northlegh, clerk (Macclesfield)
8.17	John Domville, senior	John de Scolalgh or William Criour (Macclesfield).
8.18	The abbot of Chester	Ranulf Rotour or Adam le Clerk, Richard de Manlegh or William de Trofford (Macclesfield)
8.19	Maud, wife of Hamo de Massy, knight	Henry de Hoton
8.20	The abbot of Lilleshall	Ranulf Rotour or Richard de Manlegh
8.21	Thomas de Swynerton	Robert, son of Roger de Knytleye and Michael Scot, together and separately
8.22	Agnes, wife of John de Wetenhale	Ranulf de Wetenhale
8.23	Richard, earl of Arundel	Richard Gouth or William de Acton (Delamere)
8.24	John de Wetenhale of Minshull	Ranulf de Wetenhale
8.25	John, abbot of Whalley	Adam de Castelford, fellow monk, or Henry de Hoton
8.26	Richard le Vernon, knight	William Wolf or Roger de Schrygelegh (Macclesfield)

8.27	Isabelle, wife of John de Legh, knight	William de Wetenhale of Alpraham
8.28	The abbot of Combermere	Hugh de Chatterton or William Criour
8.29	The community, township of Macclesfield	William le Criour
8.30	Philip de Egerton	Ranulf Bryn, David de Calvylegh or William Criour
8.31	It is granted by the justices that Peter de Northlegh may sue for William, son of Matthew de Hulgreve, who is under age.	
8.32	The abbot of Saint Werburgh of Chester	Richard de Manlegh or William de Trofford
8.33	William de Monte Acuto, earl of Salisbury	Thomas Waryn, Thomas de Thressk or William Saladyn
8.34	William le Prayers de Badylegh	Richard Doune
8.35	Roger de Court	Peter de Northlegh
8.36	William Trussell of Kibblestone	John Huwet or Henry de Chorleton, and also for liberties.
8.37	Warin Trussell	John Lasselles and Thomas de Warrewyk

m. 53d

Attorneys, continued

8.38	Ellen, wife of Richard del Hough	Richard del Hough or Robert de Pulle
8.39	The abbot of Vale Royal	Peter de Northlegh, clerk
8.40	The abbot of Cumbermere	Peter de Northlegh, clerk
8.41	John de Hyde, knight	Peter de Northlegh and Adam de Mottrom

The following attorneys were admitted on 20 August 1358 for the second adjournment **(8.42–8.60)**

8.42	The abbot of Cumbermere	Robert de Dyton, clerk
8.43	William Trussell of Kibbleston, knight	John Huwet or Peter de Northlegh
8.44	Hamo de Mascy of Puddington (*de placito quo waranto)*	Thomas de Capenhurst or Robert Starky of Tranmere
8.45	Philip de Egerton	Michael Scott or William Criour
8.46	Cecilia, wife of Ranulf le Bryn	Ranulf le Bryn
8.47	John de Wetefeld, parson of Bebington	Peter de Northlegh, clerk
8.48	Joan, lady of Bebington	Peter de Northlegh, clerk
8.49	David de Egerton	Michael Scott or William Criour
8.50	Richard de Bunbury (under age, by permission of the justices)	Philip de Raby
8.51	Richard Doune, forester in fee	Peter de Northlegh, clerk
8.52	John Blound	Philip de Raby
8.53	William de Monte Acuto, earl of Salisbury	Thomas de Thressk or Peter de Northlegh, clerk
8.54	The abbot of the house of the Blessed Mary of Basingwerk *(in placito quo waranto)*	Robert de Dytton, clerk
8.55	Henry, duke of Lancaster	Thomas de Mascy, William de Hallum or William Criour
8.56	Richard Doune	Peter de Northlegh, clerk
8.57	Robert de Legh	Hugh de Chaterton or Adam de Kyngeslegh, clerk (Macclesfield)
8.58	Margaret, wife of John Launcelyn	John Launcelyn
8.59	Andrew del Bron, (under age, by permission)	John Launcelyn
8.60	The abbot of Whalley	Richard de Aston

REPLEVIN ROLL

(**9.1–9.86**; mm. 54, 54d and 55)

Roll of the replevin of lands and tenements within the forest of Mare and Mondrum, September 1353

m. 54

Rotulus replevine terrarum et tenementorum infra forestam de Mara et Mondrem seisitorum in manus domini comitis Cestr' per Ricardum de Stafford et Ricardum de Wylughby milites justiciarios foreste assignatos mense Septembri anno regni regis Edwardi tertii post conquestum vicesimo septimo.

Roll of the replevin of lands and tenements within the forest of Mare and Mondrem, seized into the hands of the lord earl of Chester by Richard de Stafford and Richard de Wylughby, knights, appointed justices of the forest, in the month of September in the 27th year of the reign of King Edward the third, after the conquest (September 1353).

9.1 William de Crue replegiat omnia terras et tenementa sua infra forestam de Mara et Mondrem seisita in manus domini comitis Cestr' per justiciarios predictos usque ad proximum iter justiciariorum foreste ad respondendum dicto domino comiti de exitibus medio tempore perceptis si dicto domino comiti adiudicentur et cetera per plegium David de Calvilegh Hugonis Browe et Johannis de Elton.

9.1 William de Crue repledges all his lands and tenements within the forest of Delamere and Mondrum, seized into the hands of the lord earl of Chester by the said justices, until the next eyre of the justices of the forest, to answer to the lord earl for the revenues taken in the meantime, if they are to be awarded to the lord earl etc., by the pledge of David de Calvilegh, Hugh Browe and John de Elton.

The following land-owners repledged their lands and revenues in the same form of words by the pledges as indicated:

9.2	David de Calvilegh	Richard de Hogh and John Donne
9.3	Thomas Danyers	William de Praers
9.4	William de Praers	Thomas Danyers

9.5	Thomas Donne of Cronton	Nicholas de Manlegh and John Donne
9.6	Roger, son of Hugh de Venables	Hugh de Venables and William de Venables of Bradwall
9.7	Thomas de Elton	Richard de Thornton of Elton and Robert le Boor
9.8	Richard de Thornton of Elton	Thomas de Elton and Robert le Boor
9.9	Catherine, daughter of Richard de Thornton	Thomas de Elton and Richard de Thornton of Elton
9.10	John de Hardeshull and Margaret, his wife	John de Wetenhale and William de Munshull
9.11	Lawrence, son of Thomas de Dutton, and Henry his brother	Thomas de Dutton and Michael Scot
9.12	William, son of Hugh de Crue	Robert de Ridelegh of Tarporley and Henry de Munshull of Cholmondeston
9.13	William, son of Thomas de Crue, living in Aston and Mondrum	Roger de Cholmondelegh and John, son of William
9.14	Roger, bishop of Coventry and Lichfield	Henry de Weston and Richard de Wevyr
9.15	Ellen, wife of Peter de Legh, lady of Betchton	Matthew Dounville and Thomas de Whelok
9.16	Robert, son of Ranulf de Pulle	Richard de Fouleshurst and Richard de Prestlond
9.17	John, son of Hugh de Merbur	John Starky of Stretton and Alan de Acton
9.18	William de Bolde and Margaret, his wife	John Starky of Stretton and John, son of Hugh de Merbur
9.19	William, son of John de Wevere	Robert, son of Ranulf de Pulle, and William, son of David de Crue
9.20	Robert de Acton	Richard de Acton and Adam de Moldesworth
9.21	William, son of Hugh de Acton	Adam de Acton and Richard de Acton
9.22	Ranulf, son of Gilbert de Acton	Robert de Acton and William de Acton

9.23 [.........] Acton	[.........] de Acton and John de Merbur
9.24 [.........] de Acton	Robert de Acton and William de Acton
9.25 Peter de Calvylegh	William de Bulkelegh de Alstanton and Hugh de Wordhull
9.26 William de Bulkelegh de Alstanton	Peter de Calvylegh and Hugh de Wordhull
9.27 [.........] de Wordhulle	Peter de Calvylegh and William de Bulkelegh de Alstanton

m. 54d

9.28 [.........] son of William de Crue	Richard (de Derynton) and [.........] de Wetenhale
9.29 [........] de Munshull	[Richard de Munshull] and William de Wetenhale

The following entry is crossed out.

9.30 [.........] de Cronton	John, son of John de Morbur, and Peter de Northlegh
9.31 Peter de Northlegh	[.........] Doune and John de Sorby
9.32 [..........] and Agnes his wife	John, son of David de Malpas and Ranulf de Lee
9.33 [.............................]	Henry de Se[...]greve and Alan de Acton
9.34 Robert de Bulkylegh of Alstanton	Hugh de Wordehull and Thomas de Morton
9.35 Roger, son of William de Happesford	Robert, son of Thomas, son of Roger de Onston, and John, son of Roger (Floegtis)
9.36 Richard Doune of Utkinton	Thomas de Slyne and Richard de Manlegh

9.37	Margery, wife of Richard de Stoke of Wardle	Hugh de Wordhull and Richard, son of Peter de Wetenhale
9.38	Robert del Brugge of Frodsham	Thomas, son of Thomas de Acton, and Alan de Acton
9.39	William, son of Matthew de Hulgreve junior, and Richard, son of Matthew de Hulgreve senior	William de Spurstowe and Peter del Cleyes
9.40	John Baretz and Isabella, his wife	Robert, son of Richard de Acton, and David de Clutton
9.41	Roger de Overton	Robert, son of Stephen del Mulne, and William de Cotegreve
9.42	Robert, son of Stephen del Mulne	Roger de Dutton and William de Cotegreve
9.43	Hugh, son of Hugh de Aldresey	William, son of Henry de Overton, and David de Overton
9.44	Thomas de Spurstowe	Ranulf, son of Radulf de Wetenhale, and Richard Harald
9.45	Thomas, son of Radulf de Wetenhale	Ranulf, son of Radulf de Wetenhale, and Richard Harald
9.46	Ranulf, son of Radulf de Wetenhale	Thomas de Spurstowe and Richard Harald
9.47	Joan, daughter of Henry de Munshull	William, son of William de Minshull, and Thomas de Spurstowe of Minshull
9.48	Richard Harald	Thomas de Spurstowe and Ranulf, son of Radulf de Wetenhale
9.49	Robert de Barwe, clerk, and Matilda, his wife	Nicholas de Manlegh and Richard de Manlegh
9.50	Margery, daughter of William Launcelyn of Frodsham	Richard de Manlegh and Robert de Barwe, clerk
9.51	Richard de Manlegh	Nicholas de Manlegh and William de Frodesham
9.52	Ranulf de Stoke, senior	William de Maynwaryng and Richard de Derynton

m. 55

Terre replegiate in ultimo regardo in foresta de Wyrhale equitate

Lands repledged having been ridden in the last regard in the forest of Wirral

The form of the first of these entries (**9.53**) is:

9.53 Johannes Domvill senior venit et replegiat terram suam in Brunstath et Oxton in ultimo regardo foreste de Wyrhale equitatam usque ad proximum iter justiciariorum foreste predicte et ad respondendum domino de exitibus si eidem domino adiudicantur per plegium Willelmi de Werberton junioris chivalier et Johannis Domvill junioris etc.

9.53 John Domvill, senior, comes and repledges his land in Brimstage and Oxton ridden in the last regard of the forest of Wirral in the period up to the last eyre of the justices of the said forest and to answer to the lord for the revenues if they are awarded to the lord, on the pledge of William de Werberton, junior, knight, and of John Domville, junior, etc.

The form of the second Wirral entry (**9.54**) is repeated without significant variation in all the rest of the Wirral replevins (**9.55–9.86**) and is:

9.54 Johannes Doune replegiat terram suam in Thurstaneston equitatam in forma predicta per plegium Ricardi del Hogh et Roberti de Pulle.

9.54 John Doune repledges his land in Thurstaston ridden in the said form by the pledge of Richard del Hogh and Robert de Pulle.

9.55	Richard del Hogh of Thornton, land in Thornton	Robert de Pulle
9.56	Thomas de Capenhurst, land in Capenhurst	Richard del Hogh and Robert de Pulle
9.57	Robert Starky, land in Tranmere	John Doune and John Batyn
9.58	John de Benyan, land in Capenhurst	Richard del Hogh and Thomas de Capenhurst
9.59	John son of John de Burton, land in Mollington Torold	Thomas de Capenhurst and Robert de Pulle
9.60	Robert de Pulle, land in Poole, Backford, Capenhurst, Upton and Ashfield	Richard del Hogh and Thomas de Capenhurst

9.61	Philip de Raby, land in Raby	Richard del Hogh and Thomas de Capenhurst
9.62	Thomas de Hokenhull, land in Church Shotwick	William Stanley and Stephen de Merton
9.63	Ameria, daughter of William de Prenton, land in Prenton	Thomas de Capenhurst and Robert Sanky
9.64	Nicholas, son of Hamo de Mascy, and Margery, Hamo's wife, land in Shotwick	the aforesaid pledge
9.65	John de Leghton, land in Leighton and in le Greves	Stephen de Merton, John de Batyn de Burton, Philip de Raby
9.66	Hamo de Mascy of Puddington, land in Puddington	Thomas de Capenhurst and Robert de [.........]
9.67	Henry, duke of Lancaster, land in Bidston, Moreton and Saughall Massie	Richard de Aston and Richard de [.........]
9.68	Thomas, prior of Birkenhead, land in Claughton and Wallasey	John Doune [.........] [.........],William Waleys of Tranmere
9.69	Richard, son of Philip de Pulton, land in Poulton Lancelyn and Bebington	Robert of Tranmere and John Launcelyn of Morton
9.70	John Batyn of Burton, land in Lower Bebington	Thomas de Starky and Thomas [.........] de [.........]
9.71	John Blound of Chester, land in Little Neston	Robert de Berneston and P[.......................]
9.72	William Stanley, senior, land in Storeton	Philip de Raby and Thomas de [..........]
9.73	Robert de Berneston, land in Barnston and elsewhere	Henry de Hoton and Thomas de Hokenhull
9.74	Henry de Hoton, land and his mill in Hooton	Robert de Berneston and Thomas [.........]
9.75	Stephen de Merton, land in Gayton	John Batyn, Henry de Chorleton, Thomas de Hokenhull
9.76	William de Tranemoll, land in Tranmere	Henry de Hoton and Robert de Ber[neston]

9.77	Maud, wife of Hamo de Mascy, and Henry, his son, his land in the same forest	Henry de Hoton and Robert de Berneston
9.78	Joan, wife of Robert de Bebyngton, land in Higher Bebington	John de Wetfeld, parson of the church of Bebington, and Ranulf le Bruyn
9.79	Richard, son of John, son of Henry of Lower Bebington, (under age), land in the same township	John de Wetfeld, parson of the church of Bebington, and John de Bebington, chaplain
9.80	Richard de Bunbury, land in Stanney	William de Spurstowe, the [….........] of [.........]
9.81	Richard, son of William de Tranemol, land in Tranmere	John de Wetefeld, parson of Bebington, and John de Bebington, chaplain
9.82	Robert de Bebington, chaplain, land in Lower Bebington	John de Wetefeld, parson of Bebington and Richard, son of William de Tranemoll
9.83	Ranulf le Bruyn, land in Poulton Lancelyn, Lower Bebington and Little Meols	Richard del Hogh and John de Leghton
9.84	Richard, son of Robert Launcelyn, (under age), land in Lower Bebington	Ranulf le Bryn and Robert Starky
9.85	William, son of John Torald, all his land in the same forest	Adam del Legh and Ranulf Raket
9.86	Henry de Waley, land in Wallasey	Henry de Chorleton and Richard de Pulton

GLOSSARY

advowson	the right to present a clergyman to a benefice.
agister	forest official who received payment for the pannage of commoners' pigs.
agistment	the practice of letting out land in summer to graze cattle at a fixed price per head.
almonry	a place where alms were distributed; the residence of an almoner.
amercement	a lighter fine, often for non-appearance.
approvement	any improvement or exploitation of resources in the forest, as e.g. buildings, marlpits, enclosures etc.
appurtenances	rights or privileges, belonging to another more important right or privilege, and passing in possession with it.
assart	to clear for cultivation by cutting down trees and grubbing out their roots.
assize of the forest	forest law.
avower	one who claims the authority of, or puts himself under the patronage of someone.
bailiff	the manorial lord's representative or estate manager, but subordinate to the steward.
bailiwick	an area under the jurisdiction of a bailiff or other official.
banneret	a knight able and entitled to bring a company of men at arms into the field under his own banner, and who ranked next to a baron and above other knights.
beadle	a parish officer with various duties which varied depending on locality.
bondsman	a man bound to a lord in various degrees of villeinage.
bovate	a measure of arable land of variable size.
cantred	a hundred; a district containing a hundred townships especially used in Wales.
carucate	theoretically the amount of land which could be ploughed in a year by using one plough with an eight-ox team. It comprised eight bovates.
close	an enclosure, often from the open fields.
commote	a territorial and administrative subdivision of a cantred.
constable	an officer appointed by the manor or parish with a wide range of duties which varied with place and time.
covert	a thicket hiding game.

customary services	services due from tenants and defined by the custom of the manor.
deer-leap	a construction around an enclosure allowing deer to leap in but hindering their departure.
deforciant	the defendant in the levying of a final concord.
demesne	the land retained by the lord of the manor for his own use.
demise	to let, to convey a property by lease.
easement	a right over another's property, a *jus in re aliena*.
enfeoff	to put a tenant legally in possession of a property.
escape	a perquisite allowed to the forester for animals straying in the forest.
escheat	the reversion of an estate to the lord or Crown which occurred when the tenant died without heirs, or where the heir had not yet attained his majority or where the tenant had committed an offence requiring the forfeiture of the estate.
essoin	a reason for non-attendance at court.
estovers	an allowance of wood etc. for fuel. See **2.5** '...estovers...that is digging peat and cutting turves, and cutting and carrying away gorse and fern and heather for burning.'
expeditation	see 'lawing'.
eyre	a court held by itinerant judges who rode on circuit to hold sessions in various places.
fence month	closed season for deer, the fortnight before 24th June and the fortnight after.
fine	payment agreed between the court and the guilty person to bring the matter to an end.
foggage	a type of pasturing of cattle.
forest	an area of land where wild beasts and game were protected for the use of the king or Black Prince.
forester	a forest officer.
forester in fee	hereditary forester
free tenant	one who holds or possesses lands or tenements by deed.
gage	offer as guarantee.
grange	land belonging to a monastery.
le grimstall	meaning uncertain, perhaps a reference to 'corn'.
hallmote	a manorial court.
hambling	see 'lawing'.
hauberk	a piece of defensive armour, usually of ring or chain mail, which adapted itself readily to the motions of the body.
haybote	the right to take 'all kinds of wood for burning, building and fencing.' (See **2.17**).
hayward	an official who supervised the repair of manor or parish fences, looked after the common stock of animals and impounded stray cattle.

heriot — an obligation of an heir of a deceased tenant to give to the lord the best beast of the deceased.

hey — an enclosed piece of land.

hide land — land divided into hides, also land subject to public obligations.

housebote — the right to take timber for building.

implead — to sue someone in a court of justice.

indenture — a deed between two or more parties with mutual covenants, executed in two or more copies, all having their tops or edges correspondingly indented or serrated for identification and security; hence, a deed or sealed agreement or contract between two or more parties, without special reference to its form.

infanganotheof — jurisdiction over a thief apprehended within the manor or territorial limits to which the privilege was attached; the right of the lord of a manor to try and hang a thief caught within its limits.

in mercy — the state of being liable to an amercement.

inspeximus — a charter in which the grantor has inspected an earlier charter which he recites and confirms.

justiciar — a royal justice, or in Cheshire's case the judge of the Chester county court who was also the supreme administrative official in the earldom.

knight's fee — a feudal tenure which obliged the holder to provide military service to the crown or a member of the nobility.

lawing — partial disabling of dogs, by removal of some of their claws or cutting into their footpads (also called 'expeditation' or 'hambling').

ley — grassland.

lorica — a cuirass or corslet of leather.

mainperners — persons standing surety (mainprise) for a defendant's appearance or good behaviour.

marl pit — pit used to obtain marl, decayed chalky soil, used as fertiliser.

mark — 160 pence, that is 13s. 4d.

mast — the fruit of beech, oak, chestnut, and other woodland trees, especially when fallen and used as food for pigs.

merchet — a payment from an unfree tenant on the occasion of the marriage of his daughter.

messuage — a house and the land immediately around it.

mete — boundary.

mortmain — When land was granted by laymen to ecclesiastical bodies it became free of escheats, reliefs etc. and this resulted in a loss of income to the manorial lord both at the time and for

	the foreseeable future. Edward I, by Statutes of Mortmain in 1279 and 1290, prohibited the transfer of land to an ecclesiastical body without the lord's permission. (*manus mortuus* – dead hand)
multure	a toll consisting of a proportion of the grain carried or of the flour made, paid to the proprietor or tenant of a mill, usually in return for grinding corn.
neif	a manorial tenant born in a state of bondage or serfdom.
outedracht	an abstract, extract; (meaning unclear. See **2.18**)
pannage	the right to put pigs in the forest between Michaelmas and Martinmas (29 Sept–11 Nov); the payment made to the owner of a woodland for this right.
parcener	one who has an equal share in the inheritance of an ancestor; a joint tenant.
parson	a holder of a parochial benefice in full possession of its rights and dues; a rector.
pelf	forfeited goods, the right to take goods as a forfeit.
pleas	cases or actions at law.
pledge	a guarantor who saw that the fine was paid.
purpresture	any approvement (q.v.) carried out without permission in the forest.
puture	food or fodder claimed by forester, an allowance of food. By this period it had been commuted to a monetary payment.
quitclaim	a formal renunciation or relinquishing of a claim.
reeve	strictly speaking, a deputy; in the case of a manor, usually a man of villein status elected by his fellow tenants to organise the daily business of the manor.
regard	a three-yearly official inspection of the forest, to inquire into assarts and purprestures.
regarders	persons who carried out the regard, in company with the foresters.
repledge	to pay a sum (i) to have one's case restated in a different form or (ii) to retrieve disputed land or rights from the lord, subject to later review.
replevin	the legal process by which a property in dispute is taken back into the hands of the ostensible owners after they have given a surety (on the pledge of a third party) to hand over the land and all its revenues to the lord if the judgement is eventually made against them.
riders	mounted foresters, appointed by the lord of the forest.
sak(e)	a contention at law; a suit, cause, action.
scot (sheriff's)	a customary tax laid on, or a contribution paid by subjects according to their ability; a custom paid for the use of a sheriff or bailiff .

seisin	a term meaning possession rather than ownership (A grant of land was valid only when the tenant had been given livery of seisin – a symbolic gift, such as a piece of turf from the land in question, by the outgoing tenant or by the lord of the manor.)
seised of	in possession of.
severalty	an estate in severalty is one which is is held by the tenant in his own right only.
sok(e)	a right of local jurisdiction.
tallage	a tax exacted by the manorial lord on his tenants.
t(h)eam	a family or brood of young animals.
tenement	a piece of land held of a lord by a tenant.
thwertnyk	defence against a charge by downright denial.
t(h)ol	that by which one makes things; tools, machinery.
tolcester	ale tax.
township	a division of a parish which formed a unit of local administration.
trist/tryst	a hunting station in a deer forest.
turbary	the right to dig peat (There is a difference between 'turbas fodere' and 'blestas blestare'. The former is translated throughout as 'to dig peat'; the latter as 'to cut turves'.)
under-forester	an officer of the forest, under the master or chief forester.
verderers	officials responsible for attending the swanimote courts.
vert	all that bears green leaves in the forest.
villein	a general term to describe an unfree tenant after the Norman conquest.
wayf	the right to impound property without an owner.
waste	land used commonly by tenants, usually on manor boundaries.
withies	tough flexible branches.

INDEX

Roman numerals (i–lix) – Introduction
Arabic numerals in **bold** – paragraphs in sections **1–2, 7–9**